STUDIES IN ARCHITECTURE

EDITED BY ANTHONY BLUNT, JOHN HARRIS AND
HOWARD HIBBARD

VOLUME XIV

THE LIFE AND WORK OF C. R. COCKERELL, R.A.

DAVID WATKIN

THE LIFE AND WORK

OF

C. R. COCKERELL

DAVID WATKIN

Fellow of Peterhouse, Cambridge
and
University Lecturer in History of Art

A. ZWEMMER LTD
LONDON

By the same Author

Thomas Hope (1769-1831) And The Neo-Classical Idea (John Murray, 1968).

Sale Catalogues of Libraries of Eminent Persons, Volume 4, Architects, Edited, with introductions, by D. J. Watkin (Mansell & Sotheby Parke-Bernet, 1972).

COPYRIGHT © 1974. A. ZWEMMER LTD.

PUBLISHED BY

A. ZWEMMER LTD. 76–80 CHARING CROSS ROAD, LONDON WC 2

ISBN: 0 302 02571 5

MADE AND PRINTED IN GREAT BRITAIN

BY ROBERT STOCKWELL LTD, LONDON SE1

To
A. N. G.

Contents

Abbreviations Used in the List of Plates

CC — Crichton Collection, Anglesey

CUL — Cambridge University Library

FMC — Fitzwilliam Museum, Cambridge

ID — Cockerell's *Ichnographica Domestica*, Crichton Collection, Anglesey

RIBA — Royal Institute of British Architects, Drawings Collection

V & A — Victoria and Albert Museum, London, Print Room

List of Plates

Text Illustration

Photographic Acknowledgements

Stewart Bale Ltd, Liverpool: 143, 145
Lionel Bell, London: 8, 11, 13, 20–5, 35, 42–44, 49, 55, 63, 68, 71, 73, 81, 93, 113, 119–20, 125, 148–51
Tony Bentley, Anglesey: 5, 10
Blinkhorn's, Banbury: 38
Hugh Brady, Dundalk: 58
Geremy Butler, London: 28–9, 32–3, 41, 86–9, 91, 94, 110, 127, 136, 138, 146–7
Cambridge University Library: 17, 83–5, 90, 98
Country Life: 46–8, 50–2, 54, 107–9, 111–2, 114–8, 156
Department of the Environment: 69
Fitzwilliam Museum, Cambridge: 153–4
R. B. Fleming & Co Ltd, London: 6–7
Great London Record Office: 128
The Green Studio Ltd, Dublin: 56–7
D. Griffiths, Manchester: 129
Guildhall Library, London: 121, 123–4
John Heesom, Cambridge: 3–4, 12, 14–15, 18, 26, 30–1, 59, 66, 92, 99, 104–5, 140, 157, 168–9
F. Jewell-Harrison, Bedford: 80, 134–5, 144, 166
Liverpool Corporation, City Engineers Department: 158–65
Liverpool School of Architecture: 133
E. J. McParland: 60
National Monuments Record, Edinburgh: 40, 167
National Monuments Record, London: 19, 27, 34, 36–7, 53, 62, 64–5, 67, 70, 72, 74–8, 101, 130–2, 137, 142
Royal Academy of Arts, London: 9, 16
Royal Commission on Historical Monuments: 95–6, 102–3, 152
Royal Institute of British Architects: 8, 20–5, 35, 42–3, 63, 71, 73, 81, 93, 113, 119–20, 125, 148–51, 170
Gavin Stamp: 2, 97
Timothy Summerson: 141
The author: 61, 155

Acknowledgements

My thanks should first of all go to Mrs B. J. Crichton, Cockerell's great-great-grand-daughter, for her hospitality and her permission to use the many papers of Cockerell—including his diaries—in her possession. Descendants of Cockerell's patrons who have helped me are the Earl and Countess of Plymouth, Sir Richard and Lady Acland and Captain Nigel Naper, M.C.

I am especially grateful to Sir John Summerson, C.B.E., and Mr Howard Colvin, C.B.E., who read through the whole book in typescript giving much valuable information and advice. Amongst the many others who have helped in different ways I would like to mention Mr Bruce Allsopp, Mr Giles Barber, Mr Nicholas Cooper, Mr John Cornforth, Mr John Harris, Mr Simon Houfe, Dr J. Quentin Hughes, the Reverend Chancellor J. R. Lloyd Thomas, Mr Ian Lowe, Mr L. A. Lucas, Mr Gregory Martin, Dr Adrian Mathias, Mr D. Pepys Whiteley, Professor Barry Supple and Mr Ben Weinreb. The staff of the following institutions have done much to make my research easier: the Bank of England, the National Westminster Bank, the Guardian Royal Exchange Assurance Group, and the Royal Insurance Group; Guildhall Library; the Church Commissioners; the Public Record Office; the Essex, Hertfordshire, Norfolk and Norwich, and Wiltshire Record Offices; Richmond Public Library and the National Library of Scotland; the National Monuments Record; the Royal Institute of British Architects; and the Victoria and Albert Museum.

A Note on the Principal Manuscript Sources

The huge quantity of unpublished material on Cockerell makes his biographer's role at once delightful and daunting. There is so much that without grotesquely overloading the pages of this book with footnotes, it would be impossible to cite the precise source each time it is quoted. The reader is therefore referred to the following guide to the principal sources used and to the principal chapters in which they occur.

1. *Diaries*. Chapters II to VII, and IX to X.

These recently came to light in the possession of Cockerell's great-great-granddaughter, Mrs B. J. Crichton. They begin in 1821 and cover his life and career in immense detail up to 1828, the year of his marriage. They are continued in an increasingly perfunctory form until 1832—although the volume for 1831 is missing. Since they amount to about three quarters of a million words in length, the decision as to how much of them should be published, and in what form, has been a difficult one. Clearly they could not be published in full, though an edition is certainly desirable. Nor could they be presented in the form of a diary as such, for they constitute in effect an architectural commonplace-book rather than a conventional diary. Thus they consist for the most part in comments on the progress of his own buildings and in judgements on the works of his contemporaries. Being extremely telegraphic in form they do not lend themselves to sustained quotation.

2. *Letters*. Chapters I and X.

Some of the letters Cockerell wrote and received on his Grand Tour of 1810-1817 are in the Department of Classical Antiquities at the British Museum; others —of more personal interest—are in the possession of Mrs B. J. Crichton. The journal which Cockerell kept on this tour was fortunately edited and published in 1903 by his son, S. P. Cockerell, as *Travels in Southern Europe and the Levant, the Journal of C. R. Cockerell, R.A.* The quotations from this journal in the first chapter of the present book have been considerably amplified by the numerous unpublished letters owned by Mrs Crichton.

Cockerell's letters from 1836-1841 to Sir Thomas Dyke Acland, Bart. are at the Devon County Record Office. These are quoted from *passim* but particularly in the account of Killerton chapel in Chapter X.

3. *Drawings*. Chapters IX to XIV.
The principal collections of Cockerell's architectural drawings[1] are at
(a) the Victoria and Albert Museum
(b) the R.I.B.A. Drawings Collection
(c) the Bank of England
(d) Oxford University Archives (for the Ashmolean Museum)
(e) University Library, Cambridge.

4. *Lecture Notes*. Chapter VIII.
(a) Library of the Royal Academy of Arts
(b) Library of Trinity College, Cambridge
(c) R.I.B.A. Drawings Collection

5. *Building Committee Minutes*. Chapters XII and XIII.
(a) Bank of England
(b) Oxford University Archives (for meetings of the Delegates of the Taylorian Institute and University Galleries)
(c) Liverpool and London and Globe Insurance Company
(d) London and Westminster Bank

6. *The Goodchild Album*. For all Cockerell's buildings from 1833 to 1859.
This is a MS. scrap-book compiled by J. E. Goodchild in 1889 and entitled, *Reminiscences of my Twenty-six years Association with Professor C. R. Cockerell, Esqr.* It was acquired by the late Sir Albert Richardson, and is still in the possession of his family.

NOTE
In the quotations from Cockerell's letters and diaries in this book Cockerell's spelling has been retained but some punctuation has been added.

1. Large collections of Cockerell's topographical and archaeological sketches and drawings are at the Department of Classical Antiquities, British Museum; the R.I.B.A. Drawings Collection; and the Gennadius Library, American School of Classical Studies, Athens.

B

Introduction

COCKERELL fits into no category. He is neither wholly Georgian nor wholly Victorian; neither wholly an archaeologist nor wholly an architect; neither gentleman of leisure nor professional man. He thus disapproves of the Greek Revival but also of the Gothic Revival; he makes revolutionary archaeological discoveries but fails to publish them;[1] he submits to the indignity of architectural competitions but fails to win them. As a result he is remembered only for an unrivalled knowledge of the classical language of architecture which has proved insufficient to endear him to an English audience.

Thus, he has become a 'headmaster' amongst English architects, revered but unapproachable.[2] Thus, too, he is one of the few major English architects who have never been the subject of an architectural biography, though from time to time bouquets have been respectfully handed to him: for example Fergusson in 1873 made the remarkable claim for the Ashmolean that 'there is perhaps no building in England on which the refined student of Architecture can dwell with so much pleasure',[3] and even Philip Webb observed of the same building that it 'expresses what I mean by imagination with graceful simplicity.'[4] But while in the nineteenth century books were written on Rickman, Pugin, Barry and Scott and, more recently, on Hawksmoor, Chambers, Adam, Wyatt, Nash, Soane, Holland and even Wyatville, Cockerell has been ignored.

The first signs of awakening interest in Cockerell came in the 1890's. For forty years after his death architecture followed a course so different from anything he had desired or conceived, so decked with borrowed plumes, so colourful and varied, that few people bothered to give much thought to his solitary quest for perfection. Yet by the 1890's, so fast does the tide of taste turn in Western civilization, he was already beginning to be regarded as a hero by a group of architects anxious to usher in a new phase of the Classical Revival. Professor Aitchison published a paper on him in 1890, in 1896 J. J. Joass published a drawing of his Sun Assurance Office, in 1897 Paul

---

1. His assistant, Goodchild, records that as late as 1851 Cockerell said to him, 'I must see if I can wipe off some of the disgrace in the delay in publishing my Aegina and Phigaleia work.'

2. His two assistants were called, appropriately, Goodchild and Noble.

3. J. Fergusson, *History of the Modern Styles of Architecture*, 2nd ed., 1873, p. 349. In the 1st edition of 1862 Cockerell is surprisingly not mentioned.

4. In a letter to Lethaby of 3 July 1904, quoted in W. R. Lethaby, *Philip Webb and his Work*, 1935, p. 138.

Waterhouse wrote an article lamenting the destruction of his Hanover Chapel, and in 1899 J. M. Brydon eulogized him in the pages of the *R.I.B.A. Journal*.[5] In the new century A. E. Richardson finally reinstated Cockerell's reputation as part of his programme of establishing a *beaux-arts* classicism in this country. Some of his own buildings, particularly the New Theatre at Manchester of 1912 (Pl. 169), are successfully Cockerellian in character.

The biographer of Cockerell cannot but feel that he is walking in the footsteps of Richardson. Richardson had intended writing a book on Cockerell but instead produced a brilliant study of *Monumental Classic Architecture in Great Britain and Ireland* (1914), one of the most important books of architectural history to appear in England in modern times. Its numerous splendid illustrations, many of buildings by Cockerell, argued cogently for the continuity of a living classical tradition from Inigo Jones to the present day. For the first time the Gothic Revival was put in its place as a provincial by-way which need not long detain the student of the mainstream of British architecture. Such an approach is what we expect from a French rather than from an English author. Thus, Hautecoeur's standard eight-volumed history of French post-mediaeval architecture is entitled simply, *L'Histoire de l'architecture classique en France*.

The architectural revolution which Richardson hoped to effect occurred not in England but in America. However, the flame of enthusiasm for Cockerell was kept alight by the brilliant and influential critic, H. S. Goodhart-Rendel, who owed much to Richardson and his francophile master, Verity. In what is still the best book on English nineteenth- and twentieth-century architecture, Goodhart-Rendel wrote of Cockerell: 'Never has there been a more accomplished English architect than he, nor one more originally creative.'[6] Today it is Sir John Summerson, himself a pupil of Richardson, who imparts to many of the younger generation something of his own enthusiasm for Cockerell's rich but fastidious classical language, although he has published virtually nothing on the subject. Professor Henry-Russell Hitchcock, on the other hand, has devoted a number of pages to Cockerell in his two-volumed history of *Early Victorian Architecture in Britain* (1954) – though the arrangement of the subject-matter by building types renders impossible any overall appreciation of the achievement of individual architects. Hitchcock, moreover, found it difficult to digest an architect like Cockerell, having been brought up on a diet

5. In 1891 the Royal Academy Silver Medal was won by F. E. Ward with measured drawings of the Hanover Chapel which were published in *The Architect*, vol. 47, 1892, pp. 29 & 45.

6. *English Architecture since the Regency*, 1953, p. 74.

composed of the 'organic' Frank Lloyd Wright, who despised what little he knew of the classical tradition, and of the 'utilitarianism' of the International Modern style.

Other reasons for the general lack of understanding of Cockerell are not hard to find. He was a European in an increasingly nationalist age. From the age of twenty-two to twenty-nine he had lived and worked in Turkey, Greece and Italy with young French, German, Italian and Danish scholars and artists, thereby acquiring an essentially European vision rare in this country since the Whig settlement of 1688: in 1823 he described himself as 'half a mediterranean'. Another reason for his relative obscurity is that it has been impossible to make historical generalizations which include him since he was so indifferent to the fashions and trends of his day. This indifference led him to ignore the rising tide of the Gothic Revival. The moral fervour with which that revival was preached has encouraged modern critics to regard it as forward-looking and praiseworthy, and the Classical Revival as backward-looking and reprehensible. It is consequently Pugin not Cockerell whom the modern age has canonized; Pugin, whose considered opinion of Cockerell's masterpiece, the Ashmolean Museum, was that it constituted 'another unsightly pile of pagan details . . . [which] if it pleases the admirers of gin-palace design . . . will draw down the indignation of every true disciple of Catholic and consistent architecture.'[7] Cockerell's view of Gothic, however, was a more mature and informed one than Pugin's of classical architecture. He realized that there was much to be dis-covered concerning the Gothic technique of the *coupe des pierres*, of the proportional systems used, and of the role of sculpture in Gothic architecture. The research he undertook and some of the discoveries he made in these fields are of outstanding importance. It is to be hoped, indeed, that the present book will help to establish Cockerell for the first time as a pioneer architectural historian.

However, he paid the penalty for not adapting himself to the spirit of the age or, even, to that of his profession. Like some of the English architects he most admired – Inigo Jones, Wren, Vanbrugh – he was not by his earliest inclinations drawn towards an architectural career. Though the son of a successful architect, he was extremely reluctant to adopt what he imagined would be a difficult and distasteful profession. In a revealing letter to his father written from Milan in 1816 he observes: 'I am an artist & nothing but an artist. I am a good painter spoilt. The more I have seen of Italy the more

7. *An Apology for the Revival of Christian Architecture in England*, 1843, p. 3, n. 3.

persuaded I am that I was born a painter. If I must adopt architecture I must appear in this and this only, as professor of the beautiful in architecture. I earnestly request you therefore my dear Father that you will not make me a common man of business. do not make interest for any intended buildings or speculations of any kind. If I have any merit I shall be invited to undertake them. if I have none I care not even to ask for them. I could never apply to be the architect of any building. I cannot submit to a job.'

This exaggerated delicacy, this dedication, ignorance of the arts of self-advertisement, aloofness and intense fastidiousness, this refusal to compromise and, ultimately, his preoccupation with the internal problems of design and structure of every task rather than with the wider human problems – in other words, his aristocratic view of art – made him singularly ill-adapted for achieving success in Victorian England, in an architectural profession dominated by the competition. Thus, though he was appointed architect to St. Paul's Cathedral and the Bank of England and received academic honours from learned societies throughout Europe, he lost one by one the major commissions which an easier and more adaptable man in his position might have gained. His competition designs were rejected for the New Palace of Westminster, the Reform Club, the Carlton Club, the Royal Exchange, the Duke of York's Column, the National Gallery and University College, London. In the 1820's he lost commissions for churches in London, Bristol and Yorkshire by his insistence on the classical as opposed to the Gothic style. An apparent change of heart in the following decade did not quite do the trick. Thus the only projects he initiated in the year 1838, at the height of his powers as an architect, were for a neo-Jacobean chapel at Harrow and a neo-Romanesque chapel in Devon.

His isolation from contemporary trends was neatly conveyed by John Philip in the narrative sculpture on the podium of the Albert Memorial (Pl. 2) where, shortly after his death in 1863, he was portrayed in unlikely conjunction with Barry and Pugin. Sir Charles Barry, the contemporary who won nearly all the competitions Cockerell ever entered, is a genial, portly, Pickwickian figure vainly attempting to engage in conversation a stern unyielding Cockerell. Pugin, swathed gracefully in some indeterminate ecclesiastical robe, serenely ignores both of them and gazes vapidly into the middle distance.

It will be appreciated, too, that his remoteness from contemporary practice meant that he exercised little influence. He had certainly given valuable advice to Elmes and Basevi, but these two brilliant architects died young. We know that Pennethorne admired him and that he, in turn, welcomed

Pennethorne as a 'representative of the school to which we both belong.'[8] Dobson and David Bryce had evidently learnt from him as had also his son, F. P. Cockerell, whose Freemasons Hall, Great Queen Street, London, of 1866, is a coarse pastiche of his father's style. Further examples of his architectural influence will be suggested in the Epilogue, but it is probably true to say that the artist closest to Cockerell in taste and attitude was the sculptor, Alfred Stevens, whose remarkable talents he had been quick to spot and encourage. Like Stevens, Cockerell made endless, rapid, pencil sketches in which details of both line and mass were continually being subtly re-modelled. This process continued long after contract drawings had been settled and work on construction begun. Indeed, his assistant Goodchild tells us how, 'he would frequently say when a design had been approved and the work ordered to be proceeded with, now then, hitherto we have been working only upon paper, now we are going to put it into durable brick, stone and iron to last for two or three hundred years to our credit or discredit; therefore let us overhall it and see if it is all right.'

Cockerell's private wealth enabled him to indulge this independent spirit. Goodchild regarded Robert Smirke with his enormous practice as a mere 'Architectural Manufacturer ... a mechanic with no feeling for *art* but working for money', and contrasted him with Cockerell, 'full of an intense love of his art, and ever anxious to do his best so that, in his words, "the work might be in some degree instructing and worthy of imitation", working less for money than for the glory of the art.'

If we look at the list of buildings which Cockerell did not execute his career may seem something of a failure, but Gervase Crouchback's dictum, 'quantitative judgments don't apply', is surely especially applicable to Cockerell. There can be no doubt that he will be remembered for his individual positive achievement, for a great sequence of personal master-pieces which are unique in English architecture: the branch Banks of England at Bristol, Manchester and Liverpool; the magnificent interiors of St. George's Hall, Liverpool; the Taylorian Institute and University Galleries at Oxford and the great gaunt wing which is all that was executed of his University Library at Cambridge. Here in these compelling buildings he combines the grandeur of Wren and the imagination of Hawksmoor with a classical scholarship that is all his own.

8. *Papers Read at the R.I.B.A. Session 1856–7*, 1857, Appendix, p. 6, where Pennethorne tells how: 'When I was a young man going abroad, the then young Robert Cockerell had just returned from foreign travel with a high reputation. I was recommended by Mr. Nash to go to him, and by his urgent advice I paid more attention to the palaces and modern architecture of Italy than to the works of ancient art.'

PART I

Traveller and Diarist

CHAPTER I

The Grand Tour, 1810-1817

Charles Robert Cockerell was born in London on 27 April 1788, the third of the eleven children of the eccentric architect but successful surveyor, Samuel Pepys Cockerell (1754-1827). S. P. Cockerell was a grandson of the diarist Samuel Pepys' nephew and heir, John Jackson, and a brother of Sir Charles Cockerell who, having acquired a large fortune in the East India Company, spent much of it on the celebrated mansion of Sezincote. This was designed for him in 1805 by S. P. Cockerell as the first and, indeed, the last Indian country house in Europe. A sister of S. P. Cockerell and Sir Charles married the wealthy John Belli (1740-1805), private secretary to Warren Hastings. Their daughter Mary Belli married William Howley (1766-1848), a future Archbishop of Canterbury. Thus, though the family into which C. R. Cockerell was born was *nouveau-riche*, its members had attained considerable position through a powerful combination of talents and will-power. S. P. Cockerell was clearly a man of singular ambition though not so much for himself as for his children. He approached architecture, or so it must have seemed to the young and sensitive C. R. Cockerell, as a matter of financial speculation. It was inevitable that anyone of C. R. Cockerell's character should have reacted against such an approach, and the austere though eclectic scholarship of his own work is in part the product of such a reaction.

S. P. Cockerell became Surveyor of the Parish of St George's, Hanover Square, in 1774, Clerk of the Works at the Tower of London in 1775, Surveyor of the Admiralty in 1786 and of the Foundling and Pulteney Estates in 1788. He was surveyor also of the sees of Canterbury and London, of the East India Company from 1806 to 1824, and of St Paul's Cathedral from 1811 to 1819. He drew sufficient income through these appointments to design a handsome house for himself at 29 North Side, Clapham Common, (later the home of Sir Charles Barry) and to move from Clapham in August 1800 to what was, effectively, a country house in London, Westbourne Lodge, Paddington (demolished in 1846). This had been built by the architect Isaac Ware in the 1740s for his own residence. In 1802 he acquired the lease of 8 Burlington Street which the young C. R. Cockerell later used both as a residence and an architectural office.

As an architect, S. P. Cockerell is memorable for originality rather than quality and he can hardly be said to have developed a consistent style. Like Tatham and Bonomi he was clearly dissatisfied with the dull good manners of late eighteenth-century architectural taste but lacked the large vision or the scholarship to establish an alternative within the framework of the classical tradition. His principal buildings, then, are not the dull Admiralty House, Whitehall, nor Gore Court, Kent, with its somewhat crude Ionic order, but bizarre follies such as the neo-Norman Tickencote church, or the neo-Indian Sezincote. However, he put his gifts as a speculator to good use in disposing middle-class housing on the Bloomsbury estates of the Governors of the Foundling Hospital. His report for the Governors written in 1790 has been described by Sir John Summerson as summarizing 'the cardinal principles of Georgian town-planning'.[1]

It will become clear how little this aspect of the architectural profession appealed to C. R. Cockerell. Nevertheless, the fruits of it bought for him not only the advantage of a gentleman's education at a public school – a privilege not shared by Soane, Nash, Wilkins or Smirke – but also the Grand Tour of seven and a half years without which his life's work would have been impossible.

Life at Westminster School when Cockerell arrived in 1802 was harsh and crude but it doubtless prepared him, as it was intended to do, for the deprivations and suffering of later life: in his case of extensive travels and illnesses in Greece and Turkey. It is, however, interesting to realize that he would have seen each year in the Latin Play the remarkable back-cloth depicting Athens, devised in 1758 by no less than James or 'Athenian' Stuart himself. Perhaps he may also have seen the superb domed staircase of Ashburnham House (though it was not yet part of the school), which, then attributed to Inigo Jones, may have influenced his staircases at the Travellers' Club and Oakly Park.

Some time after his sixteenth birthday Cockerell left Westminster and began his architectural training in his father's office. The principal work upon which his father was engaged at that moment was Sezincote which is hardly a building that can be said to have exercised a decisive influence on Charles' architectural development. In the summer of 1806 his father sent him on a tour of the West country and Wales in the company of the

---

1. *Georgian London*, 1st ed., 1945, p. 150.

Daniells, the brilliant topographical water-colourists who had done much to popularize Indian scenery and architecture. Thomas Daniell was at this time laying out the enchanting Indian gardens at Sezincote.

The nineteen-year-old Cockerell's *Memorandum* of this tour survives. We learn that 'Mr D.[aniell] says that many parts of the cathedral [Salisbury] are perfectly Indian' – a picturesque view of Gothic reminiscent of the younger Dance. At Plymouth he sketched a pleasing vignette: 'the mouth of the river Tamur . . . is at present entirely filled with French ships taken chiefly in this war, some of them serving as prison hulks for the French prisoners. I shall never forget the melancholy air a poor fellow played from a little grilled window as we passed under the ship. No Englishman who has seen Plymouth & all its wonders will ever be apprehensive of being disturbed by an invasion. It is indeed a most striking place.' At Ilfracombe, 'J. D.[aniell] was delighted & says the foliage approached nearest to India of any he ever saw.'

At Hafod, in Cardiganshire, seat of the remarkable connoisseur Thomas Johnes, he was fortunate enough to see Nash's little-known 'Moorish' library. He wrote of Hafod: 'some good pictures of Hodge's, a Vandyke & a few good pictures. House is not very good, chiefly by Nash; the library is a good room but affected as Nash's things generally are – 8 marble columns of slim Doric supporting a gallery. A[n] antique mosaic very fine. One of the sides of the octagon leads into a Conservatory: a good idea.'

In 1809 Cockerell was sent to work in the office of Robert Smirke, only seven years his senior. Smirke, a friend of S. P. Cockerell, had just gained the commission for the Royal Opera House, Covent Garden, on the drawings for which young Cockerell worked. With its large Doric portico the Opera House was one of the programmatic buildings of the Greek Revival and had the ungainly air of being so. The alleged lack of relationship of the portico and front block to the structure behind was particularly censured at a Royal Academy Lecture by Soane who went so far as to prepare a drawing to illustrate the point.

A year of these labours was thought enough for Cockerell. The arrival, at Covent Garden, of the first Greek Doric portico in London signalled the departure of Cockerell for Greece. In 1810 his father determined on a course of foreign travel to complete his son's architectural education. In Greece, his father believed, his son would be able to acquire the first-hand knowledge of ancient architecture which would enable him on his return to become the leader of what was clearly to be the fashion of the day, the Greek Revival. As it turned out, Cockerell was too complex a figure for the story to be as simple as that, and it was Smirke and Wilkins who remained the leaders of the Greek Revival.

In 1810 most of the Continent was, of course, closed to Englishmen. Turkey, which included Greece, was open and it was for Constantinople that Charles Cockerell set out on Saturday, 14 April 1810. Rather curiously he was travelling as a King's messenger with despatches for the fleet at Cadiz, Malta and Constantinople. This was an arrangement suggested by William Hamilton, then Under-Secretary of State for Foreign Affairs and a great friend of the Cockerell family. Cockerell was accompanied as far as Salisbury by his master Robert Smirke.

In Constantinople, Cockerell met the British Ambassador, Robert Adair, his successor Stratford Canning (1776–1880), Lord Byron and John Cam Hobhouse (1786–1869). His chief friends, however, were Sir William Ingilby Bart., of Ripley Castle, Yorkshire, and the talented Liverpool architect, John Foster (c. 1786–1846). He spent much time in preparing drawings of the principal buildings of the Porte but considered that: 'To architecture in the highest sense, viz. elegant construction in stone, the Turks have no pretension. The mosques are always copies of Santa Sophia with trifling variations, and have no claim to originality. The bazaars are large buildings, but hardly architectural. The imarets, or hospitals, are next in size ... but neither have they anything artistic about them. ... The dwelling-houses have the air of temporary habitations. ... But the most charming things are the kiosks. You can imagine nothing slighter than their architecture is. They are entirely of wood, and even the most extensive are finished in about two months. They display the customs of the Sultans, and they are such as you might imagine from reading the "Arabian Nights" – golden halls with cupolas, domes and cullices hanging over pools of water, with fountains and little falls of water, all in the genuine Turkish taste. ... The Turks seem to be the only people who properly appreciate broad sunshine and the pleasure of a fine view. Unfortunately, the Turkish, which is something like Persian style, only appears in the architecture. As to decoration, I was bitterly disappointed to find that they now have no manner peculiar to themselves of ornamenting these fanciful interiors. They are done in the old French crinkum-crankum [i.e. Rococo] style by rascally rene-gades, and very badly.'

Soon Cockerell began preparations for his departure with Ingilby and Foster for Greece. In his passport Stratford Canning described him, in that section of a British Passport still reserved for the enumeration of physical pecularities, as possessing 'occhi, negri e splendenti; naso fino ... fronte, di marmo ... in somma Apollo lui stesso.' It will be well to remember, as we follow Cockerell on his travels, that we are in the company of a man who achieved popularity and success not only by his extraordinary talents but by his singular physical beauty, his black and lustrous eyes, his delicate nose, his marble forehead, his resemblance, indeed, to Apollo himself. Doubtless Canning was exaggerating; nevertheless the sensitive fastidious face with its large and soulful almond eyes, which Ingres drew seven years later in Rome confirms the basis of truth in Canning's eulogy (Pl. 1).

Introspective Cockerell certainly was, yet he was given to bursts of high enthusiasm which clearly made him an entertaining companion. Such was his thrill on his first visit to a classical site that when, stopping at the Plain of Troy on his way to Athens with Ingilby and Foster, the tomb of Patroclus was pointed out to him he took off his clothes and ran round it naked three times in imitation of Achilles.

Some pleasing details of his stay and friends in Athens are given in an unpublished letter to his sisters written from Athens on 19 January 1811.

Athens Jany: 19. 1811.

My Dear Sisters,

... Know then my Dear Sisters that in better health I never was & more happy I never was & am convinced never shall be. These are the Elysinean days that I shall remember all my life with the utmost pleasure and gratitude to my father who allows me them. I have no care but ... the fear that I shall not answer the expectation that may be formed of me. You know I am never content with my labours ... I hinted in my letter of Dec[r] to John my having met here with a young man of very superior merit, architect to the King of Bavaria, the Baron de Haller.[2] he is 36 y[s] old, very scientific in his profession & as an artist more compleat than I can ever hope to be, he knows no pleasure but in the pursuit of his science, the love of which led him to give up his employment in Germany for the completion of his educa[n] & travel to Rome and Greece with a very poor allowance. He has studied at Rome nearly two years where with great application he had studied all the refinements of his art. he came here in Oc[tr] with 4 other Germans ... [We] have sworn eternal friendship ... & we have formed our plans for the Tour of Greece & if possible of Sicily. You will therefore in future always hear of me in *partner*ship. I have obtained him ample employment from Graham an Englishman here to make drawings &c.

2. Carl Haller von Hallerstein (1774–1817), German archaeologist and architect who submitted designs unsuccessfully for the Glyptothek at Munich and the Walhalla near Regensburg.

which will assist his means of travelling . . . as a True German he naturally borders on the phlegmat^c & in fits of melancholy which occur moralizes & sometimes worse is as dull as a Tombstone. his spirits never rise above the Tenor . . . Gropius introduced me on my arrival here to Haller & we have worked together ever since. I have found Gropius a most excellent & agreable man . . .

Foster . . . is an excellent tempered fellow & as our style of life is entirely different we never clash, we have a house looking over the plain of Athens on one side & the Acropolis on the other, we have a garden full of large orange trees in full fruit & a tall Palm Tree which is conspicuous from afar. – we have a complete English society here, Graham a friend of John's a very very excellent fellow, Haygarth another Camb^e man Ld. Byron & till lately some worthy Danes & Germans, they are now parted for Con^e – I have found Fauvel the French Consul a very polite man & very useful . . . & as an excellent artist he has collected many beautiful things in his house. Lusieri I have not found so agreable as Hamilton painted to me . . . I have not given him the sketches of the Elgin antiquities which as I hear they are sold to Gover^{mt} will be curious . . . the Society of Athens is in every respect hateful, the men even have nothing to do but pick to pieces their neighbours. . . .

In this varied cosmopolitan society of scholars and artists the twenty-two-year-old Cockerell found an immediate welcome. This helped establish those broad European sympathies which account in part for his subsequent detachment from the fashions and preoccupations of Victorian England.

In their quest for widening their understanding of the classical past, Cockerell and his friends were anxious to answer the questions left unanswered by Stuart and Revett in their pioneer survey of Greek architecture. The interest of Cockerell and his colleagues centred particularly, as Cockerell later observed, on the correspondence of the temples 'with the principles handed down to us by Vitruvius as derived from the old Hellenic race, – the arrangement and order of their interiors, – the mode of executing the masonry, the roof, and the tiles which covered them, – and the ornamental accessories of sculpture and painting, their acroteria and their pediments, which formed so large a proportion of the merit and interest of Grecian works of art.'

In April 1811, Cockerell, Foster, Haller and Linckh determined to make a tour in the Morea but before doing so wished to inspect the remains of the Late-Archaic Temple of Jupiter Panhellenius on the island of Aegina, a

three hours' sail from Athens. Of their experiences at Aegina we must let
Cockerell tell the tale:

'As we were sailing out of the port (of the Piraeus) in our open boat we
overtook the ship with Lord Byron on board (on his return to England).
Passing under her stern we sang a favourite song of his, on which he looked
out of the windows and invited us in. There we drank a glass of port with
him, Colonel Travers, and two of the English officers . . . We slept very well
in the boat, and next morning reached Aegina. The port is very picturesque.
We went on at once from the town to the Temple of Jupiter, which stands
at some distance above it; and having got together workmen to help us in
turning stones, &c., we pitched our tents for ourselves, and took possession
of a cave at the north-east angle of the platform on which the temple
stands – which had once been, perhaps, the cave of sacred oracle – as a
lodging for the servants and the janissary. The seas hereabouts are still
infested with pirates, as they always have been. One of the workmen pointed
me out the pirate boats off Sunium, which is one of their favourite haunts,
and which one can see from the temple platform. But they never molested
us during the twenty days and nights we camped out there, for our party,
with servants and janissary, was too strong to be meddled with. We got
our provisions and labourers from the town, our fuel was wild thyme, there
were abundance of partridges to eat, and we brought kids of the shepherds,
and when work was over for the day, there was a grand roasting of them
over a blazing fire with an accompaniment of native music, singing and
dancing. On the platform was growing a crop of barley, but on the actual
ruins and fallen fragments of the temple itself no great amount of vegetable
earth had collected, so that without very much labour we were able to find
and examine all the stones necessary for a complete architectural analysis and
restoration. At the end of a few days we had learnt all we could wish to
know of the construction, from the stylobate to the tiles, and had done all
we came to do.

'But meanwhile a startling incident had occurred which wrought us all to
the highest pitch of excitement. On the second day one of the excavators,
working in the interior portico, struck on a piece of Parian marble which, as
the building itself is of stone, arrested his attention. It turned out to be the
head of a helmeted warrior, perfect in every feature. It lay with the face
turned upwards, and as the features came out by degrees you can imagine
nothing like the state of rapture and excitement to which we were wrought.
Here was altogether a new interest, which set us to work with a will. Soon

another head was turned up, then a leg and a foot, and finally, to make a long story short, we found under the fallen portions of the tympanum and the cornice of the eastern and western pediments no less than sixteen statues and thirteen heads, legs, arms &c. all in the highest preservation, not 3 feet below the surface of the ground. It seems incredible, considering the number of travellers who have visited the temple, that they should have remained so long undisturbed.'

Foster and Linckh now removed the marbles to Athens leaving Cockerell and Haller to conclude negotiations for their purchase with the local inhabitants. 800 piastres, or about £40, was the small price finally fixed. In an unpublished letter to his brother John of 13 May, after his return to Athens, Cockerell explained how: 'we did not finish our great work until the 16th: day after our arrival when with our 16 statues &c we completed our researches drawings &c of the Temple of which we have made some important discoveries in the arche^e, & a restoration of the Hypethral & other circumstances a sketch of which I shall send to astonish Albany [i.e. Smirke] ... We are now hard at work joining the broken pieces, and have taken a large house for the purpose. Some of the figures are already restored, and have a magnificent effect. we have not yet discovered the subject of the Groups the figures are abo. 5 to 5.6 high in very powerful action evidently in combat, the Costumes are of the most antique kind I have ever seen, the Helmets are made to cover the nose & face as those you remember in Hope's book, Grieves to protect the skin & large bucklers. There are two in high preservation which draw a bow, the hands pulling the string & arrow are wonderfully beautiful, some are clad in a leathern coat & a costume something resembling the Roman, I have seen such at the Parthenon, in general how^r they are without drapery of any kind, & the anatomy & contour I assure you are equal to anything I have yet seen. Our council of artists here considers them as not inferior to the remains of the Parthenon & certainly in the second rank after the (Belvedere) Torso, Laocoon & other famous statues ... tell Smirke that I trust from my success in arch^l discoveries by digging hitherto, to bring a good collection home with me.'

The ultimate destiny of the marbles was a problem which naturally exercised the excavators a good deal. Cockerell and Foster were anxious for them to find a home in the British Museum, while Haller and Linckh were, understandably, equally anxious for them to go to Germany. In the meantime, in the interests of safety, it was necessary to remove the marbles as far as possible from the Turks. Thus they were carried on the backs of mules across Megaris to Porto Germano whence they were conveyed by ship to Zante and then, when that island seemed likely to be attacked by the French, to Malta. Cockerell conveyed his wishes for their future to the British Ambassador at the Porte and, through William Hamilton, to the British Government. Henry Gally Knight (1786–1846), the M.P. and architectural historian, now arrived in Athens with Fazakerley, another English traveller, and offered £2,000 to Linckh and Haller to relinquish their shares on the understanding that Cockerell and Foster would do likewise and that the whole collection would be presented to the British Museum. As Cockerell cannily wrote to his father on 1 July 1811: 'I hope you will approve of my intention to give my portion to the Museum sho^d anyone offer to purchase the other shares for the same purpose, surely the reputation of having *found* & given them will be of much more value than the sum I might otherwise receive.' However this happy arrangement was not to be. The two Germans were not content with receiving £1,000 each for marbles for which they had paid £10 each, so the four men decided that a public sale would be the only way of resolving their difficulties. Announcements of a sale to be held in Zante in November 1812 were accordingly inserted in the *Gazette* of every country in Europe and a merchant settled in Athens by name of Gropius was appointed as agent in the business.

Hamilton persuaded the Prince Regent to make a handsome offer of £6,000 to £8,000 for the sculpture and, somewhat prematurely, to send out H.M.S. *Paulina*, a Brig of War, for its transport home from Malta. To Malta also was dispatched Taylor Combe, Keeper of Antiquities at the British Museum, to make a bid on behalf of the British Government. However, despite the removal of the marbles for safe-keeping from Zante to Malta the sale took place as originally advertised at Zante, in the absence of Mr. Taylor Combe. Here, the sculpture was purchased on behalf of the Crown Prince Ludwig of Bavaria by Wagner who had been despatched from Rome for the purpose. The only other bid was made on behalf of the French government.

Hamilton attempted unsuccessfully to prove that the sale was illegal and Cockerell declared in a letter to his father that Gropius had not dared to show his face in Malta on account of certain pecuniary transactions in which he had been involved. In his recriminations, which included attacks on Taylor Combe as well as on Gropius, Cockerell never criticized Haller who, as architect to Prince Ludwig, can hardly have been unbiased. Indeed Haller together with Karl von Fischer subsequently prepared plans at Prince Ludwig's request for a museum in Munich to house the Aeginetan sculpture.

The superb Glyptothek erected in 1816 to designs by Leo von Klenze was, after the Townley Gallery at the British Museum, the first public sculpture gallery ever built. In its blending of the architecture, painting and sculpture of the ancient world with those of modern times it was one of the key monuments of European neo-classicism. Its execution in a country recently defeated in a major war was an astonishing gesture of confidence in the role of art in the process of national regeneration.

The marbles were assembled, restored and painted in Rome under the direction of Wagner and Thorvaldsen and in 1820 the entrance-hall of the museum was adorned with a fresco by the Nazarene painter, Cornelius, 'symbolizing the glory, tragedy and ultimate salvation of the creative artist.' However, Thorvaldsen's man-handling of classical sculpture was soon to appear over-confident and old-fashioned and Cockerell was sharply critical of it in his book of 1860. The sculpture was in fact of three different periods and its correct disposition poses problems today.

Having discovered and even owned for a short time the first major examples of Late-Archaic sculpture known to the modern world, Cockerell was fortunate enough to make a discovery of similar magnitude in the following year. On 18 August 1811 he and his three archaeologist companions set out from Zante on a tour of the Morea. Their particular object was the temple of Apollo Epicurius in Arcadia (Pls 3 & 4) which, though ascribed by Pausanias to the hand of Ictinus himself, was little-known on account of its remote site and the attendant dangers of malaria and bandits. Cockerell's son describes how they 'arrived in a fine afternoon at Andritzena, the nearest village to their appointed destination, where they had arranged to pass the night. On the side of a deep declivity, the houses rising one above another amidst gardens and woodland scenery, the oak, the platanus, and the cyprus; this romantic site presented picturesque attractions wholly irresistible to artists, and they remained to sketch while their attendants moved forward to obtain a lodging for them.' The following day they proceeded up the mountains to the temple for two and a half hours where they pitched their tents below the ruins. 'It is impossible to give an idea', wrote Cockerell, 'of the romantic beauty of the situation of the temple. It stands on a high ridge looking over lofty barren mountains and an extensive country below them. The ground is rocky, thinly patched with vegetation, and spotted with splendid ilexes. The view gives one Ithome, the stronghold and last defence of the Messenians against Sparta, to the south-west; Arcadia, with its many hills, to the east; and to the south the range of Taygetus with still beyond them the sea . . . We spent altogether ten days there, living on sheep and butter, the only good butter I have tasted since leaving England, sold to us by the few Albanian shepherds who lived near. Of an evening we used to sit and smoke by a fire, talking to the shepherds till we were ready for sleep.' One day when Cockerell and Haller were scrambling about amongst the fallen columns taking their measurements, 'a fox that had made its home deep down amongst the stones, disturbed by the unusual noise, got up and ran away . . . Cockerell ventured in, and on scraping away the accumulations where the fox had its lair, he saw by the light which came down a crack among the stones, a bas relief.' Stackelberg claims that the particular relief was that numbered 530 in the catalogue of the Phigaleian Marbles at the British Museum, adding naïvely that 'one may still trace on the marble the injuries done by the fox's claws.' Cockerell made a rough sketch of the slab and covered it up again. It seemed clear from the position in which it lay that the whole frieze would also be found near it. Rumours soon grew of the riches which had been uncovered and excavations were ordered to be stopped until the sanction of the Vizier at Tripolizza, the seat of government in the Morea had been obtained. Permission was given in 1812 on the condition that half the proceeds from the sale of anything discovered be made over to the Vizier. Unfortunately, Cockerell's absence in Sicily prevented him from participating in the full excavation of the temple undertaken in June to August 1812 in a party increased by the addition of Stackelberg, Brøndsted,[3] Gropius, the Austrian Consul at Athens, and the English traveller Leigh. However, Haller made over all his own notes to Cockerell and these formed the basis of his publication of the temple in 1860. The magnificent frieze, uncovered in its entirety, was conveyed to Zante where it was sold to the British Government in 1813. Cockerell incorporated casts of it in three of his buildings, whilst the highly independent Ionic order of the temple recurs with powerful effect in many of his works. The only remaining original fragment of one of the interior Ionic capitals is the volute presented to the British Museum by Cockerell who had carried it away with him on his first visit.

After his premature departure from Bassae, Cockrell completed his tour of the Morea, visiting briefly Sparta, Argos, Tiryns, Mycenae, Epidaurus and Corinth. Back in Athens he met the Hon. Frederick North (1766–1827), the colourful Chancellor of the University of Corfu and later Lord Guilford.

---

3. Peter Oluf Brøndsted (1780–1842), Danish archaeologist, of whom Cockerell saw much on his stay in London in 1826. He dedicated to Thorvaldsen and Cockerell vol. II of his *Voyages dans la Grèce* (Paris, 2 vols, 1826–30), describing them as: 'Dignes disciples et heureux imitateurs de Phidias et d'Ictinus'.

North intended making an expedition to Egypt up the Nile as far as Thebes and persuaded Cockerell and Foster to join him. They set off together with the Hon. Frederick Douglas towards the end of 1811 spending some time in Crete on the way. Here Mr. North, frightened by the violence of the winds gave up all idea of proceeding to Egypt – much to Cockerell's annoyance. Instead, he and Foster determined on 'a tour of the Seven Churches' to inspect the great Hellenistic sites in Asia Minor. Beginning at Smyrna, they visited Pergamum, Sardis, Ephesus, Priene, and Side. The combination of large scale with decorative delicacy of this still little-known phase of classical architecture was destined to have the profoundest effect on Cockerell's subsequent architectural development.

Cockerell and Foster arrived at Malta on 18 July 1812 where Cockerell was confined to bed for three weeks with a fever. But by 28 August he was in Sicily where he spent some months studying the principal Greek temples and in particular 'applying myself with close attention and infinite pleasure to attempting to reconstruct the Temple of Jupiter Olympius [at Girgenti]. The examination of the stones and the continual exercise of ingenuity kept me very busy, and at the end the successful restoration of the temple gave me a pleasure which was only to be surpassed by that of originally conceiving the design.'

From December 1812 to February 1813 Cockerell was in Syracuse, re-covering from his grave illness in Malta and preparing the drawings for the plates of the book on Aegina and Phigaleia which he intended to publish with Haller. After the disastrous sale of the Aegina marbles he left for Zante in the hope of repairing the damage done. Unable to achieve any success he left for Athens where he continued his labour of preparing the Aegina and Phigaleia plates. Alas, a recurrence of his old fever struck him down on 22 August. For a month his faithful friend Haller never left his bedside while the grim treatment of those days was carried on: leeches externally and calomel internally. 'When', as his son later wrote, 'the patient had been brought by this treatment so low that his heart was thought to have stopped, live pigeons were cut in half and the reeking portions applied to his breast to restore the vital heat . . . They even got so far as to speak of his burial, and it was settled it should be in the Theseum, where one Tweddle, an English-man, and other foreigners had been interred, and where Haller himself was laid not many years after.' In a letter to his sister Anne, written from Athens on 10 November 1813, he described how 'All the neighbouring Churches were lighted night and day for my relief & my nurse confidently assures me that it was Panagia Castriotissa (the Virgin of the Castle) who saved me.'

On his recovery Cockerell set out on his travels once more and in January 1814 we find him in Janina, the capital of Ali Pasha.[4] Here he had an audience with the great Ali Pasha in one of his eight palaces in the town and later 'occupied a wet three days in drawing an interior view of a kiosk of the vizier's at the Beshkey Gardens at the north end of the town.' He sent this enchanting water-colour home to his father who exhibited it at the Royal Academy in 1818 (Pl. 5). On 14 January 'We called in the evening to take leave of Ali Pasha. He was on that day in the Palace of the Fortress at the extremity of the rock over the lake. We passed through the long gallery described by Byron, and into a low anteroom, from which we entered a very handsome apartment, very warm with a large fire in it, and with crimson sofas trimmed with gold lace. There was Ali, today a truly Oriental figure. He had a velvet cap, a prodigious fine cloak; he was smoking a long Persian pipe . . . Hanging beside him was a small gun magnificently set with diamonds, a powder-horn; on his right hand also was a feather fan. To his left was a window looking into the courtyard, in which they were playing the djerid, and in which nine horses stood tethered in their saddles and bridles, as though ready for instant use. I am told this is a piece of form or etiquette.' Later Cockerell discusses the vizier's political and social impact: 'As for Ali Pasha's government, one has to remember what a chaotic state the country was in before he made himself master of it . . . No stranger could travel in it, nor could the inhabitants themselves get about. Every valley was at war with its neighbour, and all were professional brigands. All this Ali has reduced to order. There is law – for everyone admits his impartiality as compared with that of rulers in other parts of Turkey – and there is commerce. He has made roads, fortified the borders, put down brigandage, and raised Albania into power of some importance in Europe.'

Cockerell returned once more to Athens to his old quarters at Madame Masson's with Haller and Stackelberg. He intended to complete the Aegina and Phigaleia drawings and to be present at Zante during the sale in May 1814 of the Phigaleian Marbles. Back in Athens after a successful sale he was delighted to meet his 'friends and old schoolfellows, Spencer Stanhope and his brother. Conceive our pleasure in talking at Athens over Westminster stories and all out adventures since we left.' Between August and October he was enfeebled by a return of his old fever but was so far recovered as to be 'tempted by my friend Linckh to ride to Piraeus, to join in celebrating the anniversary of the victory of Salamis – on 25th October – by a fete on the

4. See W. Plomer, *Ali the Lion, Ali of Tebeleni, Pasha of Jannina, 1741–1822,* 1st ed., 1936.

island of Pystalia, where the thickest of the fight was waged ... We embarked from Piraeus in a large boat, accompanied by music – to wit, fiddles and tambourines – as is the Athenian fashion, and a great cargo of provisions ... All set out in the greatest glee. Beyond the port, in the open sea, some countenances began to change ... A small bay was found and all leapt ashore, crossing themselves and thanking their stars for their deliverance. A fire was lighted, the lamb roasted in no time, a cloth laid on the ground, and all set to ... Music's soft enchantment then arose, and the most active began a dance, truly bacchanalian, while the rest lingered over the joys of the table. Punch crowned the feast. All was rapture; moderation was no longer observed, and the day closed with a pelting of each other with the bones of the slain, amidst dancing, singing, and roars of laughter or applause. I venture to assert that not one thought was given to the scene before us, or the occasion, by any one member of the party except my friend Linckh who, having brought tools for the purpose, carved on the rock an inscription which will one day be interesting to those who may chance to light upon it a thousand years hence – "Invitation (or repast) in memory of the immortal Salamanian combat".'

Cockerell's son tells us the strange story of how at about this time his father became possessed of a portion of the Panathenaic frieze of the Parthenon. Hearing Cockerell was about to leave Athens for good, the commandant of the castle on the Acropolis, who was by now an old friend of his, said that 'he knew Cockerell was very fond of old sculptured stones, so if he liked to bring a cart to the base of the Acropolis at a certain hour at night (it could not be done in the daytime for fear of giving offence to the Greeks) he would give him something. Cockerell kept the appointment with the cart. As they drew near there was a shout from above to look out, and without further warning the block which now forms the right-hand portion of Slab I of the South Frieze now in the British Museum was bowled down the cliff. Such a treatment of it had not been anticipated, but it was too late for regrets. The block was put on the cart, taken down to the Piraeus, and shipped at once. Cockerell presented it to the British Museum, and its mutilated appearance bears eloquent testimony to its rough passage down the precipices of the Acropolis.'

Before he finally left Athens yet another piece of fifth-century sculpture was to come into Cockerell's possession. He had returned to Aegina in December 1814 for a fortnight to correct and check the drawings of the Temple of Aphaea and in the course of digging at the foot of the two remaining columns of the Temple of Minerva discovered, as he related to his father in a letter of 23 December, 'a very beautiful Parian marble foot (size of life), with a sandal, of precisely the same school & style with those of our Panhellenian discovery'. This foot was subsequently presented to the Glyptothek at Munich.

In the same letter he sent details of one of his most brilliant discoveries of his whole tour: the entasis of Greek columns. The letter encloses a note to Smirke, also dated 23 December 1814, written on a piece of paper twenty-one inches long by six wide and illustrated with a diagram of one of the columns of the Parthenon to show the curvature. The sketch shows with dotted lines how a rod or line stretched from the top of the column begins to depart from the shaft at the height of 17 ft. 7 in. and leaves 2 inches at the base of the column. Similarly, a line stretched from the under edge of the last fillet of the capital to the base touches at 11 foot and leaves 3/4 of an inch at the base. 'You will say', he explains to Smirke, 'I ought to have done it more accurately, with more precision; if you will send me a couple of English carpenters I shall be able to do it better, with the difficulties met with here I have found no other means of ascertaining this curious point. the Temples of M. Polias, Erectheum &c. are also swelled – I have just returned from a trip to Egina whither I took also my ladders. the anc^t T^e of Jup: Panhell^s has also the entasis in precisely the same proportion with Minerva, i.e. in a col 17.2. the swelling is half an inch at 6 ft. height from the base. in Theseus I have not been able to ascertain it from the ruined state of the cols: it is the case with the Corinthian Cols: of Hadrian, & I have no doubt that it was a general rule with the Greek architects.' He adds, in the account sent to his father, that 'it is a most curious fact which has hitherto escaped Stuart & our most accurate observers – indeed it is so delicate that unless one measures it, the eye alone cannot perceive it.'

What a man! What an eye! At the age of twenty-six his visual training was such that he noticed immediately what had escaped the attention of the most skilled archaeologists of his own and earlier days; yet, with all the fastidiousness of the true scholar he was at once modest enough to apologize for the clumsiness of his method of proof, and cautious enough not to invent a reason for the existence of what he had proved.

The abdication of Napoleon in April 1814 was to transform Cockerell's Grand Tour by the consequent opening of the kingdoms of Naples and Rome. On 15 January he left Greece for Rome in the company of Linckh. Three months later they arrived in Naples where Cockerell saw much of the antiquarian, William Gell, and made himself so familiar with Pompeii that Gell 'proposed to him to join him in writing an itinerary of that place.'

It was not until July that Cockerell reached Rome. Here he was greeted enthusiastically by an artistic society similar to but more brilliant than that which he had found so congenial in Athens four years earlier. Whereas then he had been scarcely more than a promising boy, now he was a man of fulfilled achievement. Indeed, for a young man of twenty-six his achievements seem hardly credible: the discovery and acquisition of the two major groups of Greek sculpture after the Parthenon frieze; the discovery of polychromy at Aegina; of a unique Ionic order at Bassae; and finally of the use of entasis on the columns of the Parthenon. Add to this the facts that he was an artist of considerable talent, well-off and extremely good-looking, and it is not difficult to realize how completely he took by storm the artistic society of Rome which then included Ingres, Canova, Thorvaldsen, Cornelius, Overbeck, Schadow, Hess, Vogel, the brothers Riepenhausen and Knoering. 'If I were a little more vain', he wrote to his father on 18 August 1815, 'I should be out of my wits at the attention paid me here. I have an audience daily of savants, artists & amateurs who come to see my drawings; envoys and ambassadors beg to know when it will be convenient for me to show them some sketches; Prince Poniatowski and Prince Saxe-Gotha beg to be permitted to see them. they are but slight, & in truth but poor things, but done & finished on the spot. [They say to me:] c'est la Grece enfin c'est la le veritable pays! Ah Monsieur que vous etes heureux d'avoir parcouru ce beaux pays. I explain them some constructions, some beauties which they dont understand, oh! que c'est merveilleux, ah! mais Monsᵣ ces sont des choses fort interressantes mais vous les publierez mais vous nous donnerez le bonheur de les posseder. mais ces sont des choses extremement interessantes, enfin c'est de la Grece. – & in truth the Publishers & readers are so reduced to read & publish the Roman antiquities which have been given a thousand times that the avidity for novelty is great beyond measure, & Greece is here as much as elsewhere in Fashion – on my arrival here I visited all the artists, architects &c to observe their manner of study & see what was to be done, & it is with satisfaction & gratitude that I reflect on my travels in Greece which have opened my eyes enlarged & elevated my ideas, which are also new & different from the trodden & repeated imitations I find here. Greece has its merits which I feel now most powerfully. I see without prejudice I am unconfined by the chains of school, I feel independent & free & have studied in a new & venerable field which has taught me the way to observe objects in this country, & reap the real advantages from them. thus at least I flatter myself.

'I arrived here on the 28 July with Mess: Linckh, Denison & Tupper very happily tho' there were reports of robbers everywhere on the road – I was exceedingly struck with Rome . . . in every poorest building is a style, a something superior to what I have hitherto seen . . .

'Greek is the Fashion & all noodles are ashamed of being out of the fashion – I am delighted at what you say on Italian architecture it is just what I would wish to have written myself, nothing can be more true, & tho' *out of fashion* it is most particularly necessary for all the purposes of practice in arch^e & by no means to be neglected in any point of view.'

The impact of Rome was evidently considerable – as indeed it must be on all visitors – but particularly on one of Cockerell's visual sensitivity who had spent so long in countries where the only buildings of quality were in ruins. The astonishing visual unity of Baroque Rome in which, as he perceptively observed, even the poorest building is marked by the touch of a common style, must have struck him as a novelty little short of miraculous.

His letter to his father continues:

'There are no English here except some few passengers & Lady Westmorland, a very cleaver (sic) well bred & agreable chatterer, who has been very civil to me & has made me lose several hours which might be better employed but she is fortunately going away. several letters to Roman nobles I have avoided giving as a means of keeping out of all scrapes & dangers from the celebrated Roman Fair, & the idle society of the people in general.

'I am surprised to find not a single English artist here. So Canova is gone to England, I hope not to execute the paltry monument of Lord Nelson he has published here which would be a disgrace to our glorious nation & his great fame. Canova has his merits but all agree that his reputation is greater & that he succeeds in nothing but tender subjects – Venus, Hebe, Psyche.'

This was a subject about which Cockerell felt surprisingly strongly and he enlarged on his feelings in a further letter to his father written in December 1815:

'I hope Canova will not be too much admired in England & that a man looked up to by the schools of the Continent as a great & extraordinary genius should be forgotten because he is a countryman. I mean Flaxman, as far superior as a poet in the comprehension & elevation of his art as "Hyperion to a Satyr". Canova by the very nice & laboured finish he gives to his works has deceived and captivated all the world, nobody ever *worked* the marble as he does. his is certainly art, but it is nothing but art – & Tasso says that is truly art where only art is not seen. One single idea of grace he certainly has & as you say he puts the soft & tender into everything, man woman & child. Napoleon said, il n'y a qu'un pas entre le sublime et le ridicule, and this is clearly exemplified in the works of Canova, for when he attempts the sublime he is perfectly absurd – even his grace is meritricious & one sees clearly that his Terpsichore was conceived in the Palais Royale or at some Ball in Rome, her head dress precisely that which the most perfect which the present school of Friseurs acknowledges. Canova is no poet, he has no severe & elevated idea of his art at least in comparison with Flaxman. may our sense & Taste defend us from his Monument to Lord Nelson, the four quarters of the globe with elephant's heads & american feathers, the hackneyed plan of a square upon a round, the bas reliefs representing a dead Roman born from a galley to Brittania in the dress of a theatrical Priestess. What is the English tar to say when he sees his beloved Nelson in a Roman petticoat, why will he say are British Sailors to imitate a Roman dress, are we not as original as great a people as ever ruled the waves & influenced the world! every age has had ingenuity enough to make its costume interesting in sculpture & none have had the sublimity or the poverty of idea as to despise that of their age but we.'

Much of his time in Rome was spent in preparing for publication his Grecian drawings. However, 'reflecting with pain on my ignorance of the deeper parts of arithmetic algebra &c I have determined to occupy myself zealously in this study 2 hours per day & have accordingly a master for the purpose. thus I have the hope of remedying this great defect in me & arming myself for future practice.'

The more the day drew near when he would have to adopt the architectural career his father had determined for him the more his doubts grew, reaching their climax just over a year later in November 1816. At the moment, however, they were tentatively expressed and were introduced in his letter to his father of August 1815 in the following devious way:

'. . . I cannot but be the more persuaded of what I have always ventured to recommend, that you should gradually relinquish all extraneous business. I mean all but those of office at the India Hoe St. Paul's &c. the necessity of it is evident first for yourself & then for me, you know that I am nothing but an artist & shall never be anything else, I never shall nor can pretend to understand the calculation of evaluations which you are so deeply informed on. I shall never wish to occupy myself in this study. I am artist & nothing else & this is the a (sic) path sufficiently large & respectable, & tho' I may be in circumstances but mediocre all my life yet you know also that it is just what suits my turn of mind – I can live with little & have no expensive desires. your kind motive for keeping up general business is on my acco^t my sincere prayer & desire is that you will abandon it . . .'

Extracts from a letter to his father of four months later give a few more details of his life in Rome and a sensitive description of the character of the Phigaleian marbles:

Rome. December 28. 1815

My dear Father,
The latest intelligence I have from home is by your excellent letter of the 12 Novr: in which you give me the joyful assurance of Anne's happy accouchment . . . I am continuing to make a collection of books . . . I have procured a beautiful edition of Fontana's Vatican & Feraboschi's account[5] of the defects in St. Peter which you mention, also a beautiful copy of Zabaglia.[6] I am much obliged for the list of your architectural library. – I hope you will have recd: the notice I sent you of the embarkation of my Vases from Naples with the Bill of Lading accompanying it which for safety's sake I send you the copy. I have also mentioned my fragment of the Frieze of the Parthenon several times & hope you may have recd: it from Corfu by this time . . . I will bear in mind the candelabras of Westbourne, but altho' this is a manufactory of such works there are so few in good taste or equal to those in England that there are but few temptations but I will be on the lookout. One of your former letters so quieted my apprehensions about the publication of the Girgenti Temple that I have thought little more about it. I have shown it to several travellers in Sicily who are equally astonished & interested about it & I am sure a publication in England of it may do me honour. It is exceedingly gratifying to me to find every day something in my portfoglio turning to account. I had the pleasure of showing to Col: Catinelli who fortified Genoa lately my fortifications of Syracuse & the studies I have made of that subject in Greece. He assures me that they are invaluable notices new in modern warfare & that they show that we who suppose ourselves so well informed on this subject know but little compared to the ancients. I have mentioned to you in a former letter that I have found upwards of 150 inscriptions amongst my papers & that most of these are unpublished. I have had them copied fair & they are now in the hands of a great savant Mr. Akerblad for his perusal & he promises to give me his

---

5. Martinus Feraboscas, *Architettura della Basilica di S. Pietro in Vaticano*, Rome, 1684.
6. *Descriptione translationis Obelisci Vaticani*, 1743.

notes on them. Indeed without vanity I may say that I have made not an ill-use of my travels & opportunities . . . I have invitations from Princes & Ambassadors & every person of distinction in Rome & every kindness possible from the English Travellers . . . I should not mention it if I were not sure that it would give you the greatest satisfaction. I am harassed to show my drawings & a day seldom passes in which I have not visits on their account . . . I have now a portfoglio of some 15 in a state to show of the most interesting scenes in Greece[7] . . . Art is certainly my forte & I was born a *painter* not certainly an architect . . . I had anticipated your idea of abandoning my mathematical studies for the present & there are more than 6 weeks I have done so . . . I hoped also that you would perhaps give me some further notice of the Wellington Palace . . . the Phygaleia Marbles are hardly to be compared to those of the Parthenon in any way. they should be considered as the sketches of a great artist, calculated for the Temple of a *Province* & done for effect adapted to their situation. they are curious as show-ing the style of thought & work of a great school executed hastily & with all the boldness & liberty resulting from a great practice in the art . . . the idea, composition & style are admirable but the parts as in a sketch neglected & sometimes merely indicated. they must not be regarded as the works of a Phidias & Pericles which were to show how far the refinement of art could reach & the glory of a great nation could inspire & produce . . . they will be highly prized in England. the Marbles of Aegina are much talked of & all agree that their price is a vile one. they are restoring. I mentioned in a note to Mr. Hamilton that my hope that the plaister casts agreed on in both sales will not be overlooked as for the progress of our schools they are equaly interest-ing with the originals, pray press this consideration. I am sure that in any review or newspaper information you would take great care that they should not appear forced or to show off – an impertinent fellow once asked me how much I had paid to the newspaper writers for the advertisement abot: Phygaleia. my blood boils while I remember it.

In 1816 Cockerell removed to Florence. He travelled thither with J. Bartholdy, Prussian consul-general in Rome, and a keen amateur of the arts. Walking together in the Uffizi they examined the famous fourth-century group of the Niobe, the correct restoration of which had long puzzled archaeologists. The figures had been naively assembled with Niobe, the largest, in the centre and the rest grouped in a circle round her. Cockerell,

---

7. Ten of Cockerell's views of Greece can be seen in *Travels in Greece and Albania*, 2 vols, 1820, by his friend the Rev. T. S. Hughes.

fresh from assembling the figures in the pedimental sculpture of Aegina, immediately assumed that the Niobe group had also been designed for a pediment. He spent some time in measuring and arranging the statues and making an etching of the proposed restoration. Though the pedimental solution is not universally accepted today, it dropped like a bomb-shell on Florence in 1816 and was supported by all authorities. Following his restoration of the Temple of the Giants (which modern scholarship has disproved) he was acclaimed as a kind of archaeological Sherlock Holmes.

'I had shown my drawing to several people and amongst the ambassadors and distinguished persons here – of all whom, *de rigeur*, more or less pretend to understand the arts – and it gained universal approbation. It was talked about by all, and written about by Demetrius Schinas and other obscure poets and prose writers. I was flattered, invited, and made much of. Our ambassador boasts that the solution has been proved by an Englishman; others bow and beg to be allowed to send copies of my etching to their Governments, to Metternich, &c. It was formally presented to the Grand Duke, and I have received from the Academy here a handsome letter and diploma of Academician of Florence. It is to be published in the official work on the Gallery. I have presented it myself to Madame de Staël, and my friends have sent it to all parts of the Continent.'

Whilst moving in Florentine society Cockerell saw much of the beautiful Lady Dillon and executed a fine cameo portrait of her (still in the possession of her descendants in 1903). He had learnt the art of cameo-cutting whilst in Syracuse.

An unpublished letter of great interest has survived from S. P. Cockerell to his son written from Westbourne on 7 May 1816, of which the greater part is quoted below. Its particular interest is in its balanced and practical reaction to the 'bohemian' overtones of the letter in which C. R. Cockerell implied he would rather be a penniless artist than a prosperous architect.

Westbourne. 7th May 1816

My dear Robert,
Your letter from Florence dated the 4th ulto. found me ten days ago suffering under one of those langorous complaints which men in the highest health are most subject to. . . . I cannot help observing however that it is the rich variety in Art which excites Your warmest feelings & attachments, and that Architecture, noble as it is & calculated to call forth the graceful the elegant the magnificent & the most stupendous images of the mind, is not

the elder sister with You – perhaps You feel that Yourself, the instances in which You have distinguished yourself & have attracted attention are less as an architect than an artist & in your last letter you speak in that spirit wherein you say 'if I can see & accomplish all I desire in my studies I may look forward to support with success a splendid career as an' – You added *architect* & have blotted out the term & substituted '*Artist*' – if my dear Son this is the real feeling of Your mind, & that alone in which You feel delight & satisfaction, & that the pursuit of Architecture with its constraints & its methodical precision & principles, is dull & unentertaining, I am afraid that you will never count her as Your Mistress with that spirit of fire which is necessary to compleat success ... I hope there are yet objects in Italy unseen by you which may awaken this feeling ... you know enough of the world not to be ignorant that it is the *practice* in Arts on which alone success depends & that the most refined Taste & Knowledge as a 'cognoscenti' is of no value to success in *Practice* ... I now return to Your letter of the 4th & the agreeable communication you give on the subject of the Niobe & family, it seems a most happy & natural arrangement but I have not yet seen your reasonings upon it which your friend Mr. Lapsington Stewart who dined here en famille two days since, informs me are absolutely convincing. he is a very agreeable person & I am to have the pleasure of his further acquaintance, he seems very full of the project of the Vases, the particulars of which he promised to let me have yesterday that I might introduce him to Flaxman but something has prevented his sending it to me.

There is at this moment a subscription proposed in the City for a monument of some sort to the Victory of Waterloo. To this very object the Vase seems applicable & it might be placed either in the State Vestibule leading to the Egyptian Hall at the Mansion Ho: or at the lower end of the great Hall of the Common Council opposite to the statute of the King lately set up at the upper end of that room ... I wish you would send me immediately a sketch of the vase & a pedestal ... Lady Cockerell's sister Mrs. Bowles took great pains as soon as she knew you were going to Rome to write to some particular friends there Natives to show you every possible attention ... the family to whom she wrote ... was Mr. Cheavar son in law to the Duke Bracciani at Rome ... *Friday*: Mr. Stewart sent the drawing of the Vase to Burlington Street & I appointed an interview with Flaxman for yesterday morning but it was broken off ... I find by the Papers today that the City subscription is for another object namely a Piece of Silver Plate to be presented to the Duke of Wellington. It seems that long ago a Piece of Plate (a Shield) was so subscribed for before the Peace of 1814 – the subject of which extending only to the Battle of Hondouras – the later & more important Victory of Waterloo gives occasion for a further subject which is now proposed to be a Pillar 6 feet high against which the Shield is to rest – at least that is the present idea.

I was most agreeably surprized on Wednesday morning soon after eight o'clock by a Visit from Lord W. Bentinck who rode out here in the most unaffected manner without even a Servant attending him & bringing in his hand a roll containing your Print of the Niobe complete & two impressions of the View of Athens with your letter of the 13th April . . . The whole of the building & the arrangements concerning it [i.e. the proposed Wellington Palace] will be left to his Grace's patronage; I know also that Benjan: Wyatt has prepared plans for this purpose being so employed by the Duke, & your friend Hamilton saw them last year at Paris (where B. Wyatt then was) with the Duke of Hamilton, did not think at all favourably of the design. I know too that B. Wyatt has been very long inquiring for a large House in London for the Duke's town residence all which seems to show an election of him by the Duke as his architect. I rather think therefore that the ardour of your noble friends has shot beyond the mark in enforcing your consideration of this subject without any invitation from the principal himself. . . . [though this] may seem to discourage your exertions I by no means wish it to have that effect for I have repeated urged You to some actual exercise of Your mind upon architectural subjects & this is one very fit occasion for the purpose. . . . there are many private persons of rank & fortune in England whose possessions double *all* that the Duke will ever possess – I believe the whole of the public grants together will not produce more than £30,000 pr. ann. If one third of that be taken for residence only there will be so very little left to support the Rank & state he is raised to – & of course the magnificence of the Palace with slender means of support will be ill suited to a comparison with the possessors (innumerable) of superior fortunes . . . we naturally look to Blenheim for a suitable scale to work upon but such an Establishment would in this age swallow up above two thirds of the whole capital given by the Public . . . I have read the article in the Literary Journal & if it were not for your prohibition would publish it in English in the Gentleman's Magazine or some work of that kind, it is a very handsome Testimony of your skill & industry & ought not to rest where it is, much will appear in print upon the occasion of the recent discussions relative to the Elgin Marbles which would give occasion for its introduction to the English public – in the evidence given before the Committee of the House of Commons in the recent enquiry by Parliament into the particulars of the

D

acquisition & the supposed value of those Marbles Mr. Fazakerly gave a very handsome Testimony of your & Foster's liberality in having offered to give up your shares in them to the British Nation & this Testimony is in the minutes of the Committee ... the result of the enquiry is that it will be recommended to be purchased for the nation at £35,000. A great deal of regret has been expressed at the loss of the Egina Marbles. Mr. Galley Knight's evidence as to the Phygalian Marbles is very much in their favour. He thinks them much superior to the Athenian Frieze & tho' not equal to some of the Metopes are superior to others of them & I think the public are well satisfied with the purchase upon the whole tho' the general opinion of Artists is that they are not in the best time of Phidias's School.

It would gratify you to hear the forcible terms in which the Bishop of London speaks of the certainty of your success here ... he thinks your arrangement of the Niobe a proof of refined genius & taste ... my Bro. Sir Chas. tho' he has not the least knowledge or discrimination on subjects of Taste is nevertheless kind & proud of the distinction which this & your etching gives you & is eager to show it to Lord Northwick, Lord Suffolk, Sir Chas. Englefield & every other person of consequence whom he is acquainted with – it would be well if you could find an early opportunity of sending an impression both of the Niobe & of Athens to be presented to the Dilitanti Society as it would assist in establishing your claim there ... I enclose you a letter from Louisa; we are all well here; Pepys not yet begun his legal studies for some reason bearing upon his hopes of success in his views towards a fellowship at Merton – so that he is rather idle at present. My sister's family all well. Chas. Belli ordained abo: 2 months ago & the Bishop has given him a small living abo: 40 miles off in Essex ... adieu I conclude this on the 15th May having been interrupted & delayed by business from closing it sooner – adieu all good fortune & success attend you, so pray, your affectionate Father S. P. Cockerell.

The traumatic experience of designing the proposed palace for the Duke of Wellington (Pls 6–7) is vividly conveyed in the following letter:

My Dear Father,
Altho' my occupation in the Wellington Palace is a very honorable one, & that the study & exercise of invention in the course of it may be profitable, yet I cannot but regret my having been invited to undertake to give any idea for it, from the time which it has lead me to expend in it, & the little it will add to my reputation after all, if I have nothing more to fear – from my being out of the habit of invention & compleating any design for such a

purpose, & having really never attempted anything original, you will easily imagine how an architectural combination so difficult to everyone was to me as a beginner – I consulted by help of books I found here all the works of Europe, as far as incomplete drawings could give them, but I have not found any professional persons of sufficient taste to be able to rely on their advice – I composed several general ideas, & at last fix't on one which I showed Mr. North, Douglas & some others & which pleased, but on going further into detail I found the difficulties increase tenfold, & I soon found impracticable the first vague ideas which made a show of plausibility. All the difficulties of combination of plan & elevation, doors windows &c. followed of course, & I went thro' the pains which no one can be aware who has not experienced them.

I soon filled a portfoglio with sketches in which from day to day I brought my contrivances to perfection & then overturned them. I invented a number of ingenious difficulties to come to a simple end, & compleated at length a set which I showed to Ld: & Ly: Burghersh who were highly pleased with them as were several others but who only judged of the outside or rather did not judge at all.

Remaining at Florence with too large an acquaintance I was a good deal interrupted with visits, invitations &c my wound of which I did not get the better till the end of June, was the occasion of my becoming generally unwell from confinement, & I was obliged to go thro' a course of physic after it – in an occupation of this kind which one is not always in a humour to pursue & which after doing one undoes & which requires reflection & invention (not always to be commanded) the time slips easily away & if the distractions of society are calculated into the bargain, much may be consumed before one is aware of it – & I was so disheartened in the pursuit that I fell more easily into the error, from a desire to relieve myself – I confess that for the first & only time since I left England some days have passed unprofitably.

The discontent with my plans & myself determined me to leave Florence, & I went to Pisa where in perfect solitude I passed a month – then after undoing all I had hitherto done & finding that to do the work worthily much more time & opportunity were necessary, I resolved to make some small sketches, which prettily finished might show that I was in some sort capable – thus I gave up all idea of detail & after economizing, cutting & paring, altering & considering for some time, aware that I could never satisfy myself & that something tho' imperfect must after all be done, I compleated some, of which I send you the rough tracings with a copy of the note I gave with them & a letter to Lady B to whom I addressed them. I dread the thought of your looking over them & the number of errors & insufficiencies you will naturally find – I was always in hopes of receiving some ideas more precise on the subject than those by your letter of May – which altho' infinitely useful to me yet were not what I would have found in your own ideas on the subject. – you will know how to appreciate them & how much a novice must go thro' to arrive even at so little. however I will make no apologies for them or myself knowing that if anyone can excuse them you will. tho' I shall be very anxious to know your real opinion of them.

During all this time I have been extremely happy in the esteem & kindness of everybody Ld & Ly: B have paid me every possible attention & regard & my work on the Niobe has been so far considered beyond its merit that my head may perhaps have been turned by the credit given me from all parties – all which as I know it gives you as much pleasure as it does myself I relate to you & send you the copies of two notices already made of it in Italy. I hear also that it has excited curiosity in France & Germany. I have reaped a great harvest here amongst my country men all of whom who have had any occupation in their travels have really done me great honor, amongst them Mr. Wharton, Sir Thomas Gage, Sr. Robert Lawley, Sr. Thos Freemantle, Col: Keating. The Duchess of Devonshire as at Rome has also been very kind here to me & is one of my greatest protectr,sses. She is occupied in several elegant works which she proposes to execute here in Italy & she has done me the honor of asking me about them & I have even volunteered some slight services – the society here has been even too agreable I have been most kindly received at Ld. Dillon's where the people remaining here & particularly the younger party have associated most pleasantly, I have made some valuable acquaintances, & one of a very estimable young man Mr. Pejou who knows my brother, with whom I shall take my departure for Venice in a very few days & so proceed to Milan, Turin & Genoa & thence here & to Rome to which I shall not arrive till November & my return home will be consequently somewhat retarded.

As Ld & Ly: Burghersh are now in the deepest distress from the loss of their child I have not heard from them in answer to the Portfoglio I sent them a week ago – Philip wrote me a very kind acknowledgement of them Ld & Lady: B are going to Venice on their way home. –

I have been chosen Academician by the Academy here & am addressed as Sigr. Professore. I am also member of the Society called Columbaria – I have been elected at Rome member of the Archeologian Society & am to be made Academician there also – so that I shall return loaded with as many orders as those who sat at the Congress.

I intended to have added much to this letter but Phelps gives me an opportunity of dispatching this immediately. I have again drawn on you for £50 of the date of 9 Sept. – I depart hence on the 12 to Bologna thence to Venice where I shall write to you. – I will add only that I hear from Rome of the return of some travellers arch.ts from Sicily & I have much suspicion & from the time & occupations they have had, having made this journey almost expressly for the Te. of Jupr. Olymps. at Agrigentum that they may publish in which case I may lose the Glory of mine unless I publish it immediately which I have been long ago advised to do. –

My affectionate love to all.
Your affectionate son
C. R. Cockerell.

Florence, 10. September 1816.

The following are some extracts from the lengthy letter of explanation which Cockerell sent to Lady Burghersh to accompany his design for the Wellington Palace:

'It is not possible', he argued rather pretentiously, 'to do justice to such a work without much reflection & if the designs for the gates of the baptistery at Florence a year was allowed to the artist competitors when the arts were so well understood, the palace of the Duke of Wellington can require no less.

'As there exists no original style of archi.e in the present day & as whatever style is adopted must be imitation, there can be little doubt that the Greek as the most classical & convenient should be preferred . . .

'The Palace would be placed on a gentle elevation to give a greater grandeur to the situation & approach. the ordinary defect of those in England is, that they are planted on the ground without the preparatory gradations which give so much effect to a considerable edifice – the elevation of the ground would be divided by low terraces over which the rise is easy – the Principal Front of the Palace should present a simple and grave style of arche in the centre would be a Portico of 8 cols: under which the carriages would drive – in England they serve commonly as ornament only & a long flight of steps which leads to them, exposes those who arrive to the inclemencies of the climate. It would be of the doric of the Temple of Minerva at Athens with a open vestibule corresponding to the pronaos, thus by a second line of cols, producing the extraordinarily rich effect so much admired in that example, and giving at the same time a more secure protection from the weather . . .

'The whole of the Front would be enriched with the same order: at the extremities would be porticoes which would be agreable with lower apartments, give a chearfulness to the general effect & continue the character of the Centre – above the order would be an attic which advancing in the wings only would give a play to the long line of arch.e & break its monotony. The Dome in the centre would arrest this effect & give the whole a variation so desirable in a great mass. The Frontispiece of the Portico as a principal ornament might be enriched with a composition in Sculpture representing some allegoric allusion to the occasion of the building: that the wings might correspond in richness four victories would not inappropriately be placed in the attic. . . .

The door of the Grand Entrance which would have the whole height of the Portico would expose a striking effect of perspective, from the Entrance of the Staircase Hall, thro' the open vestibule, the great Hall, the vestibule of entrance to the suite of apartments. The Staircase would rise very gradually on either side of the great Door. . . . Thro' an open vestibule is the Hall which may be supposed the part of the Palace chiefly dedicated to its monumental character. it is enriched with a corinthian order, the cornice of which would be unbroken in its circumference, above it is an enriched cupola & lantern which lights the whole – at the front of the pilasters are statues of the generals & officers most distinguished in the late wars. – between their Pedestals a marble seat would surround the Hall – above this & nearly rising to the height of the Statues would be a Frieze in bas relief representing their principal actors the manners of their deaths &c. the whole of this in white marble would form a magnificent soubassement above which suspended to the capitals of the Pilasters is an imitated drapery (as in use in the Vatican & elsewhere) on which would be Fresco paintings representing the principal battles. in the Frieze of the order or in the pannels of the Cupola might be portraits, inscribed names, or other subjects allusive to the general object, the pavement (in the centre of which is a large open fire place) would be of mosaic with the plans fortresses, battles &c. or other interesting subjects. –'

The progress of the last months of Cockerell's Grand Tour may be charted by quoting from a number of unpublished letters between him and his father:

Venice. 5 Octr. 1816.

My Dear Father,

My last from Florence will have informed you of my intention to leave that place for my tour thro' the north of Italy. I set out on the 13th Sept. with Mr. Pijou & Pearce who is an old Grecian & friend of John's at college. we reached Bologna on the 15th & staid there but two days. from Ferrara we continued our journey by water embarking on the Po & along the canals to Venice in 28 hours, not a very interesting way but convenient & saving us some time. our intention was to have remained here but a fortnight to see all that was curious but the arrival of my old companion the Baron Stackelberg whom I found here by a fortunate accident in his way to Rome from his country (Reval) has induced me to prolong my stay to three weeks in the hope of his continuing his journey by Milan & Genoa; we shall therefore set out from hence on the 8th for Vicenza & Milan – I abandon my former companions with less scruple as Mr. Pijou has the intention of going to Greece & Pearce to England. I have the advantage of an artist's & an attached Friend's society, & in all probability we shall continue our journey to Rome together.

The examination of this extraordinary city has given me the greatest pleasure, there is much to see & profit by tho' little exactly to imitate. on arriving one is perfectly acquainted with it from Canaletto's Pictures but one feels to have been here before. . . . I have seen no city which contains so perfect a history of architecture as this from the 9th ceny: to the present . . . of course I have been most attracted by the works of Palladio which I was extremely anxious to see & I am happy to find that (as with Michel Angelo) one may safely trust the reputation of men approved by ages . . . Palladio is doubtless the greatest modern architect. I have found in his works many of the leading principles of ancient architecture, you will however smile when I say that still I am persuaded that the Greek remains may leave one a surer road, & that still he is deficient in some of the most important of their rules, but I rejoice in having seen them & I confess that his & the modern architecture is generally more applicable to our purposes, & all that one can do is to apply the ancient principles as far as one can without imagining it possible to follow exactly, for the little essay I have made in the Wellington Palace proves to me the folly & impossibility of close imitation.

I have not yet seen the Palaces of the Brenta & at Vicenza, but I have found much new & interesting to me in every way here & doubt not the profit of this journey. an academy was established here under the French but of little importance. I have made a point of becoming acquainted with the profession of architecture, but I have not thought it worth while to seek any honors here considering Florence & Rome (as the most considerable) enough. ... Sn. Giorgio of which you have the picture by Canaletto brought many recollections to my mind, you will imagine the interest with which I saw it & sought the same point of view. the Venitian school of painting interested me much & as young Beechey told me in his way thro' Rome one cannot duly appreciate it until one has been here. the great scenic pictures which ornamented the public places & chambers could not be taken away by the French, tho' there are but few cabinet pictures left by them & perhaps more Titians & by the great masters (of this kind) are to be found in any city of Italy than here. – they have in general the same character with their architecture, splendid & Theatrical effects & abundance of ornament, even to profusion, & one is convinced that the Venetians in their arts had more money than taste. no city I have seen has so much re-minded me of Constantinople & brought so freshly to my recollections all the sensations I felt in seeing that extraordinary place in my leaving England. its foundation in the sea, its age & architecture of all kinds in such magnifi-cence inspire one really with great respect & the impression of Venice will ever be deep & agreable to me ... no place in Italy has lost more in the modern revolutions than Venice, it is said 60,000 inhabitants in the last 15 years. The Austrian yoke too is much heavier than the French & it is still loosing daily – there is little commerce & the dull influence of this un-enlightened government is complained of everywhere. the French system was really an extraordinary one, all the poor & lower classes were employed & there was a great activity of business, everyone was employed under government, the nobles were oppressed but their wealth was distributed in the country. In the arsenal alone 4,000 men were in constant pay & employ, now there are 500 only. in their 8 years influence here 24 ships of war great & small were constructed. if in Venice so many were built what would not have been the fleet of the French Empire if it had lasted. can it be doubted that they would have devoured us in a few years?

I fear you will have been disappointed by my sketches of the Wellington Palace & the little produced in so long a time & with so much pain. I wait with anxiety your letters on the subject & whatever observations & hints you will have the goodness to send me on them, for from all I hear it is extremely likely my offer of services in the course of this winter in extending them & rendering them more compleat will be accepted, tho' I have not a word from Ld. & Ly. Burghersh, nor can I expect it till thy have recovered further their health and spirits after the misfortune they have felt so deeply.

they showed them to Hopner the Consul in their way thro' this place who complimented me on them. – I foresee what must also be an occupation for me this winter unless I consent to loose one of the most ingenious of my works, that is the T. of Jup: Olymps: at Agrigentum of which I wrote you some time ago; some German architects who have passed the summer on Sicily mean to publish. they will probably have paid much attention to this subject & I may be preceded in an idea which I am sure cannot but do me credit & which they may have robbed me of as I was unwise enough to have several notices in Girgenti, however I shall see that on my return to Rome. Stackelberg has been received with every possible distinction in Russia & thro' Germany, he means to begin some publications immediately and I may probably subscribe something to the edition. I cannot but gain credit by adding my name to his, his first book will be on the vases found at Athens of which I have many drawings & notices. I think I told you in my last that my great Patroness the Duchess of Devonshire has desired my assistance in a work she is about to publish which is views of all scenes spoken of in the Aeneid & of those mentioned by Horace in his journey – the idea is very elegant & I have promised all I can subscribe to it, we have already had some conversations on the subject & we meet at Rome this winter. I met the Duchess on the Appenines in her way to Florence.

Make my love & duty to my Dear Mother & all at home, it is a very long time since I have heard from them & they repay to the full my negligence. I am very anxious to know if Howe was at Algiers. I hope heartily he was – it is making great noise over Italy & is calculated more than anything to put us well with all the continent, the letter of the Admiral Ld. Exmouth is much admired & just what it should be for these countries. I shall write to you from Milan & Genoa. I hope to be in Rome by the end of November. Your affectionate son
C. R. Cockerell.

Pijou has heard so much of the plague in Greece that he puts off his Grecian tour till the spring & is gone to Florence to prepare with reading.

A month later Cockerell wrote another letter to his father which must have dropped like a bombshell on the peace of Westbourne Grove. That the letter should have survived is a piece of singular good fortune, for it reveals more of its author's fastidious character than anything else we have from his pen:

Milan, Nov. 6 1816.

My Dear Father,

... In respect of the House, as I hold independance to be the first principle of every action & good in life I should desire to live in Burlington Street, my own desires are very small & a lodging handsome enough to satisfy my friends is all I desire or deserve. I leave this therefore to your care & only hope that your kind preparation may not frighten by a splendid habitation for so unworthy a lodger. I know that the world expects one to live in some respect as they do but I have no idea of abandoning the obscurity of a batchelor & while I can be independant with the liberty of saving a Friend I care not how circumscribed I may be. Pepys' living with me would be a great satisfaction but even then I know not how we are to occupy an entire house ... I am not a little alarmed at the accounts you & everyone writes me of my reputation – there is no burden so heavy (as Frederick says) as a reputation too prematurely gained. I shall have so little to answer expectations & by my unfortunate timidity so little impudence to back me with that I know not how I am to meet & support it. I am an artist & nothing but an artist, I am a good painter spoilt, for in that road I might have arrived at the first distinction a modern artist could reach – the more I know of myself the more I feel from a positive deficiency of every quality my total incapacity for every other occupation than that of an artist – the more I have seen of Italy the more I am persuaded that I was born a painter – to have proposed such a pursuit after the time & expense & expectation you have had so long would be to disappoint your dearest hopes. I have therefore continued with attention to arche: only & all that is most immediately connected with the beautiful in that art & for this purpose I hope I am in some degree qualified. I state all this merely to impress on you the necessity of my appearing in this & this only – professor of the beautiful in architecture. I am persuaded that my occupation in any other kind would be to lead me to a bad perhaps even a disgraceful figure and to perfect a natural & cultivated talent for which I have already reputation & which may lead me to honor & distinction. I will eat a crust of bread, my wants are as few as the humblest man's can be – but I must be independant of common affairs, I must be artist to be happy, to make an honourable figure in society. I hope this declaration which I make to you from a *long & very solid conviction* may not be too painful to you, you saw before my departure how unfit I was for affairs. You saw how distinguished a natural talent I had, be assured that by my absence both these qualities are much increased. I have neither ambition for distinction in the splendour of the world establishment &c nor an idea of the meaning of interest – hitherto the spoon has been put to my mouth I have never had need to seek it, if that is continued & I am left in my own quiet & obscurity I may produce good works, but I shall be lost. I shall be miserable if I am told to do business, get conexion, get rich. I am afraid this indifference will shock you such as I am & have become I must remain, you must regard me in these respects as an imbecile & out of the common course of persons – but do not interrupt my devotion to art, do not lower my idea of its sublimity & I may still be an honor to my family – perhaps to my country – if common abilities & the opportunities I have had can tell. in a literary country like ours I may remain poor for I can never be otherwise as I despise as much as I am insensible to the value of money, but I shall be highly respected & this is the only & real satisfaction I seek. I earnestly request therefore my Dear Father by all your kindness & all that I have here stated, of the truth of which I have been long & firmly persuaded, that you will not make me a common man of business – do not make interest for any intended buildings or speculations of any kind – if I have any merit I shall be invited to undertake them, if I have none I care not even to ask for them. you will call me wild & an enthusiast, I know all the prudential motives you will so reasonably urge – but I will live on a crust of bread & even relinquish every prospect to indulge this humour in which as I said before I may be at least an ornament to you – in any other be persuaded I am imbecile. I could never apply to be the architect of any building. I cannot submit to a job, a conviction of any merit in me would invite me or I might offer a plan for a subject & might thus gain it but in no other way. I must not be deranged in this simple this oriental way of thinking if I am lead out of my path I am worth nothing – in every other respect I will second your kind views . . . I have not yet heard word from Ld. Burghersh of any kind, I think they cannot but write to me at some time as I know they themselves were highly satisfied. Philips tells me he heard from Paris from them as little better . . . Mr. Pearce will have arrived perhaps in England & he promised to call on John as an old acquaintance & bearing news from me. I shall be glad you should invite him to Westbourne, he is besides an excellent & sensible man a great Traveller. Pigou has continued with me to Parma whence he has returned to Florence. I have however since our departure from Venice been wholly with Stackelberg & have been extremely happy in his society, we have visited every object of interest in this immensely rich country with considerable interest & I trust profit. It would be endless to describe you the innumerable objects which have fallen under our observation. suffice it that tho' the Brenta & Vicenza fell short of my expectation

I am heartily glad to have well observed Palladio & to find that he is not the sublime & inimitable genius one imagines him at a distance – tho' I have profited & observed much in his works & consider him as the first archt: I have seen in every city of this populous & at all times rich country each as a capital contains an infinity of interesting objects. Mantua the Palace of The has the most delighted me Guilio Romano has united all that could elevate one in architecture & interest & please in painting – Parma in its palaces & paintings has astonished me . . . Milan is not the least remarkable we arrived here on Saturday & shall remain until the next, we shall then proceed to Genoa & then return to Rome . . & abo: the beginning of March I shall set out on my return unless you desire it more immediately. – I have recd: letters from Greece of Feby: last, Haller was still at Constantinople but on the point of returning to Athens, he had been so long detained by his occupation for the Prince of Bavaria & a design for a public monument which he has been long employed on. I hoped to have had the happiness of seeing him again in Italy. Linckh is still in Rome, where also Foster & his wife are at present. I know not if his affairs with his father have been accommodated. I know he has suffered extreme ill health . . . I hear the Sothebys are to be at Rome . . .

The last in this series of letters was written by S. P. Cockerell to his son just a few days before his long-awaited return.

Burlington Street,
13 May 1817.

My dear Robert,

As Your Brother leaves us this Evening to meet You at Paris, and it is now many Months since I wrote to You I send a few lines by him merely to mention a few hints as to Your observations (on Parisian architecture) . . . You have raised a name here so high that everything in perfection will be expected from You, at least in all that relates to Taste in the Arts . . . also in *Decoration*, the last is that which calls for the most extensive Employment and You will be surprised to find more importance attached to the decorations of a Saloon than to the building of a Temple; if You can therefore bend to the consideration of what is called the fittings up of the interior of the best Hotels & Palaces of Paris, the graces of their *Meubles* & the harmony of their Colours in Hangings painting & Gilding You may be the general Arbiter of Taste here . . . Percier the Architect is the first in Paris & can tell You what is worthy seeing in Palaces Hotels & the best Houses. Desmalter & Jacob are the first decorators in furniture &c., Desmalter lives at 57 in the

Rue Meslée . . . Your friends Lord Burghersh & Lord Dillon proclaim Your name without ceasing & much is expected from You. The Duke of Gloster has commended me to introduce You to his acquaintance. You have been spoken of at Carlton House where I have reason to think there is a great likelihood of your being noticed advantageously but You must not be disappointed to find very common things occupying the minds of a a large majority of a Nation of Boutiquiers & we must take the world as we find it . . . do not imagine my dear Robert that I am thinking of money only as profitable – I consider *that* as the *last* article, the first a high order of Taste & information, You possess amply – the secondary, to suit in some measure the times we live in & the objects which occupy the multitude. . . . all Your family . . . are now on tip-toe for Your arrival & daily drink their affectionate good wishes to the homeward bound. I cannot feel that any one is behind another in impatience to welcome You to their hearty embraces.

CHAPTER II

The Man and the Diaries, 1821-1828

OCKERELL arrived in London on 17 June 1817, having left it on 10 April 1810. Although his dazzlingly successful Grand Tour had made him probably the leading authority in England on Greek architecture it had in some respects rendered him more unfit than ever for the architectural profession. His researches into ancient architecture were unrelated to the problems of contemporary architectural practice: undertaken for the love of art and scholarship alone they were very different from the continental sketching tours of Victorian architects who always had an eye for the choice detail that would lend novelty to their next commission. His studies, moreover, had been conducted in the company of like-minded artists and archaeologists, not of professional architects. Thus all his natural fastidiousness, impracticality, dislike of financial speculation had been heightened a hundredfold by his seven-year habitation in a palace of art. Like all artistic sons of successful and indulgent businessmen he realized the irony by which the fulfilment of his aesthetic desires was made possible by the financial genius of his father. It was this realization which partly prompted his request in November 1817 to be allowed to repay his father the sum of £950. This sum was the total of the bills he had drawn on his father from October 1813, the date marking the end of the three-year period which his father had originally envisaged as the extent of his tour. His father refused this request partly out of his deep paternal generosity, and partly out of a desire to increase his son's dependence on him at a moment so crucial to the pattern of his future life.

Instead he allowed his son to spend much time on his return in preparing finished drawings of Greek antiquities for exhibition at the Royal Academy and for inclusion in his projected history of ancient art (Pl. 8). This was planned in conjunction with Haller von Hallerstein, whose drawings Cockerell had brought back with him to England, as a final authoritative book on Greek architecture. Haller was to come to London to see it through the press. However, Cockerell seems to have lost heart on the tragic death of Haller in 1818 as a result of congestion of the lungs acquired while excavating at Ambelakia in the Vale of Tempe. The book, so his son tells us, 'was a load on his conscience all his life': a kind of unpaid debt to his dead friends, for Stackelberg died in 1836, Linckh and Foster not long after. When he finally managed to produce *The Temples of Jupiter Panhellenius at Aegina, and of Apollo Epicurius at Bassae* in 1860, three years before his death, it naturally made none of the impact it would have forty years earlier at the height of the Greek Revival.

Our understanding of Cockerell's life and early architectural development has been transformed by the discovery of the diary (Pl. 11) which he began keeping in February 1821. Some of the reasons which prompted him to keep the diary will be suggested below, but it seems appropriate to precede any such suggestions with an indication of what we can definitely learn from the diary of its author's life and character.

During the time of writing the diaries Cockerell was living and working at 8 Old Burlington Street. S. P. Cockerell had the lease of this house from 1802 until his death in 1827. His son continued to work there after his marriage in 1828 until he moved to Eaton Square in 1830.

8 Old Burlington Street was a small early Georgian house, long since demolished, half way down the east side of the street. It also had an entrance from Savile Row, since the greater part of the west side of Savile Row remained undeveloped until the 1830's. The setting of Cockerell's life must thus have been of considerable charm, quiet and spacious, with its long garden and yard running back to Savile Row. From 1832 to 1836 he also had the lease of 34 Savile Row which occupied the site of his garden. He may have built a drawing-office on the site. This part of London was a singularly appropriate setting for Cockerell since it was in these streets that Lord Burlington's protégés, Campbell, Kent, Leoni and Flitcroft, had designed houses for themselves when the land north of Burlington House had been divided into building plots in 1717. The area continued to possess an extraordinary appeal to architects. Basevi and Salvin both lived in Savile Row, and the following all had offices in Old Burlington Street: Joseph Ireland, Robert Kerr, Phené Spiers, W. F. Cave, F. T. Verity, Belcher and Joass, Mewès and Davis, and Richardson and Houfe.

Cockerell's convenient and elegant situation in the centre of the West End with ladies and gentlemen of the highest social distinction as his immediate neighbours on the Burlington Estate, must greatly have assisted his establishment as an architect. Thus as a gentleman, living in a gentleman's residence, he could expect his patrons to call on him, not vice versa; and call on him they did, constantly, to inspect and discuss the progress of their projects, to look over his prints or his drawings of Greece, to dine with him or just enjoy his company. Sometimes, of course, his constant accessibility and lack of privacy irritated him, particularly one day in March 1824 when he 'walked round Park under idea of dissipating illness' occasioned by having 'drunk tea night before on empty stomach'. He had been 'feverish all night [and was] obliged to go to bed after part of day' when his convalescence was rudely shattered by the arrival of the Hon. Robert Clive anxious for news about the progress of his conservatory at Oakly Park. Cockerell records testily: 'Clive came with Mr. Richards into my bed room . . . so does everyone, as if my house were an inn to which people had a right at all hours. not a moment of privacy. settled abo[ut] his conservatory, almost rude, so excessively irritable'.

Cockerell's appearance in these early days is recorded in a water-colour by Chalon (Pl. 10). The boyish grace captured by Ingres is gone and we are presented with a mature handsome man, confident but deeply conscious of the problems that have to be solved. He enjoyed the leisure and freedom of his bachelor days in the elegant, stimulating setting of early nineteenth-century London. The flavour is conveyed in the record of a day in April 1825 when he 'looked at prints & books & so lost all morn[in]g. but the employment of a walk at leisure in morn[in]g', he argued to himself, 'with all the beauties of arch[itectur]e, prints & books & shops & persons & objects afforded by a large city is very great & perhaps more productive to the mind than an apathetic routine enclosure in an office'. He frequently returns to an insistence on leisure and reflection as essential prerequisites of architectural design. Characteristic is the following observation of 30 November 1824: 'good thoughts only come with leisure – if every moment has its occupation either of business or pleasure there can be no leisure for that perfect digestion of the mind necessary to the creation of works. with much thought one can do but little – if one lives in the highway nothing can be done. since the India Ho[use] has left us I have done little or nothing. – I am entirely convinced that dining out is the bane of study.'

Nonetheless he did dine out, and he also gave parties at 8 Old Burlington Street – for example on 16 July 1821, when he 'dressed up my garden with statues & lights – fine night, Blackshaw, Bigge, Collingwood, Mrs Belli, Francos, all our own party, very pleasant, danced till 2 o'clock, all very happy.'

Cockerell, one of eleven children and eventually to be the father of ten, was a devoted family man, and the phrase 'all our own party', in the above quotation, refers to his immediate family circle. Mrs Belli was his aunt and doubtless his sister Anne and her husband would also have been present. In

1815 his sister had married Richard Pollen and from 1818 to 1842 they lived at 6 Old Burlington Street, a house next door but one to Cockerell. Each Sunday when he was in London, Cockerell walked out to dine at his parents' house in Westbourne where there was always a large family gathering. After his marriage in 1828 he moved to 87 Eaton Square but continued to use Old Burlington Street as an office until at least 1830. His father died in 1827 and two years later his mother moved from Westbourne to 6 Stratton Street, Piccadilly. She lived here with her son, Samuel Pepys Cockerell, a barrister with chambers at 7 Old Buildings, Lincoln's Inn. He shared these with the remarkably named Onesiphylus Tyndall and Cockerell made minor alterations to them in 1824.

By a touch of filial piety Cockerell employed as his principal assistant James Noble who was the son of one of S. P. Cockerell's assistants, George Noble (1753–18?). A draughtsman rather than a designer, James Noble was one of the original members of the Institute of British Architects in 1834 and in 1836 published a book called *The Professional Practice of Architects and that of Measuring Surveyors etc., from the Time of the celebrated Earl of Burlington.* Cockerell's devoted assistant from 1833 until his retirement from practice in 1859 was John Eastty Goodchild (1811–1899).[1] He worshipped the memory of his master and in 1889 produced a manuscript scrap-book of *Reminiscences of my Twenty-Six Years Association with Professor C. R. Cockerell, Esqr.*

In the early years of his practice Cockerell employed as one of his assistants an obscure architect called Topple. He does not seem to have been a great success. In August 1825 Cockerell records in his diary: 'told Topple not to over rate his ability – had undertaken a great charge in marrying &c. which he had no right to put on other shoulders. might see he had a mild & easy place here, would get 3 g[uinea]s perhaps for a time p[e]r week – might work his heart out & then be put adrift – that his health required a mild place which he certainly had here – reminded him that I had taken him at once at 2 g[uinea]s p[e]r week & increased it when he wanted it tho' Smirke told me it could only be done for an old servant & under particular circumstances, that I had refused to bind him to his disadvantage when he was desirous to do so on our first meeting & that after 4 years he had already fancied himself perfect & worthy better salary.' In 1833 when Cockerell became architect to the Bank of England he tried unsuccessfully to arrange

---

1. His principal independent work, in a style inspired by Cockerell, was the North British and Mercantile Insurance Offices in Threadneedle Street of 1863. He also published privately *A Study of the Halicarnassian Marbles in the British Musuem* (Walthamstow, 1888) and *A Study of the Marbles from Ephesus in the British Museum* (Walthamstow, 1889).

for Topple to be taken on at the Bank as a resident Clerk of the Works.

Cockerell was in fact too individual and perfectionist a designer to want a large office either of assistants or pupils. He records in February 1822: 'called on Mrs. Tight who wants to make her nephew, natural son of Mr. Tight of Oxford, architect. said had no money to give. told her that I disliked pupils, that premium was 1500 or 2000, that Sir R[obert] Taylor & my Father never took pupils with premium, were bound by indenture &c.'

However, on 20 January 1824 he 'signed articles of apprenticeship with young Will. Clarke for 7 years from June 24. 1822.'

On 20 March 1826 Cockerell notes: 'Clarke wishes to go to Liverpool to see the market & prepare his draw[in]gs in competition for Fleet Market, told his Father that next year I would give him a salary or exonerate him from his bond of Prenticeship supposing it to be the fifth year completed.'

Cockerell gave much employment to a young sculptor he discovered called William Grinsell Nicholl (1796–1871). From the Hanover Chapel in 1821 to St. George's Hall in the 1850's Cockerell was faithful to him. In May 1826 he records: 'glad to find my recommendations had placed Nichol well with Rundel & Bridge at 8 g[uinea]s p[e]r week at 6 hours p[e]r day whenever he likes.'

Cockerell had agreed to pay his father each year from 1817 onwards one third of the profits from his architectural practice in order to pay for his lodging at Old Burlington Street and for his share of office expenses. He worked out in 1825 that his father had received from this source an average of £147. 11. 0¾. annually and that the average sum paid into his own account from the same source, after the deduction of Topple's wages, was £236. 8. 0.

In November 1826 the following account is inserted in the diary which enables us to see very clearly his outgoing expenses:

'J. Noble's Salary	250.	0.	0
G. Noble's D[itt]o	78.	15.	
House, no. 8 Burlington St.	80.	0.	
Coals, J. N[oble] paying 10£ towards Bill	15.	5.	
Maid servant	30.	0.	
Candles	5.		
Stationery	30.	0.	
Repairs & contingencies	———		
Rates & Taxes	70.	8.	9.
	———		
	559.	8.	9'

The character we can build up from close attention to the diaries is romantic and introspective, characterized by a love of religion and royal pageantry, of Beethoven, Turner and Walter Scott. He was warm and generous; he was unpunctual; he suffered indescribably from indigestion. 'I have clearly proved to myself', he wrote in 1827, 'that it is milk in tea that makes it disagree with me . . . also that butter immediately rebels in the stomach especially at luncheon.' He was endlessly tortured by his stomach, though it is hard not to believe that by charting its ever-changing moods in his diary he increased rather than lessened his preoccupation with them. All too characteristic, alas, is the following record of what happened on a visit to Langton in 1824 in connection with the design of the new house for Mr. Farquharson: 'had suffered greater part of Monday and all the night with a violent purging and vomit, occasioned I believe by having eaten macaroni with fried cheese, or possibly by a rich plumb pudding. Mr. F. kindly got me a dose of rhubarb & peppermint.' His appalling stomach troubles may, in part, have been of psychological origin and probably ended, like the diaries themselves, soon after his marriage in 1828.

His unpunctuality, too, was a great source of vexation. On 30 October 1821, for example, he records: 'went by mistake to Mr. W. Hamilton, thinking appointm[en]t at Dowbiggins was for today – gave him the trouble of seeing me to tell me it was for tomorrow. sometimes I forget appointm[en]ts altogether, sometimes I am a day or two beforehand.'

A key to Cockerell's view of the ideal life is found in the charmingly romantic fantasies he indulged when looking through Persian miniatures in the library of East India House. 'Nothing', he considered, 'can convey more agreable impression than the spirit of these drawings. it is study in retirem[en]t under delightful pavilions in gardens. it is conversation with philosophers, uninterrupted enjoym[en]t & conversation of lovers alone in a garden & pavilion, devotional exercises, religious sacrifice, romance, charms of Birds & beasts by beauty, by musick. a manly exercise, hunting, beseiging cities, heroic actions &c &c. never a gross sensuality.'

More characteristic of the romantic spirit of the age was his enthusiasm for the works of Sir Walter Scott though it was, equally characteristically for Cockerell, a qualified one. Of a journey from Bristol to London in September 1822 he records: 'took place in mail £2. 12s. read the fortunes of Nigel. great excitation. I pursued the adventure to the end, chasing the Hero thro the labyrinth of adventures. delighted with their intricacy & could not sleep till I had finished Nigel. cui bono? is the question I asked in reading Kenilworth – novels generally have little use, even much evil may derive but here one is cajolled into a knowledge of the state of our country, history & politics & character of the times which no other mode could give so satisfactorily. – the Pedant King, the bad taste & half learning which prevailed is well conveyed.' On 20 July 1821 Cockerell records: 'took Ld. Elgin to Sir E. Antrobus where I had the pleasure of meeting Sir Walter Scot. found him courteous, well bred, entertaining in a great degree, part[icularl]y in relating stories & choice specimen of his expressions. keen eye, intelligent, sometimes lost & occupied in a thought, but quickly returning to the comp[an]y.'

In December 1823 he 'met Mr. Southey' whom he found 'tall, thin, remarkably gentlemanly in his appearance, mild & intent in his manner. one side of his countenance elevated, the other contracted & depressed. in his expression all that watchful anxious look & that air of alarm common to those gifted with extraordinary perception & foresight of Dangers, with that lively sensitiveness of the present & the past & that unenviable sensibility which enlarging the sphere of our enjoyments encreases in the same proportion our fears & pains. (who would not be rather the easy comfortable housewife than the prophetess Cassandra foretasting what others only feel in its due season. this comparison with genius has always struck me). Southey spoke of his having been 3 months from home hardly sleeping 2 nights in the same bed as if desirous of return[in]g to his studies. talked of Peruvian antiquities, languages, said rhythme precedes rhime in the progress of language. was amused with my acco[un]t of Temple the Giants at Agrigentum, asked my address to call on me. Thought Irving the Prince of Humbugs, that his sermons were the very worst specimens of the very worst style.'

It seems that the poet recognized and found sympathetic Cockerell's keen intelligence and ability to comprehend the stresses of 'romantic genius'.

The romantic, nostalgic side of Cockerell's character which appreciated the dubious mediaeval history presented in Scott's novels also made him particularly susceptible to the 'Gothic' associations of royal pageantry. On 19 July 1821 he went with his sister to Westminster Abbey for the Coronation of George IV. He writes in his diary that day: 'got a seat with Fanny abo[ut] middle of Abbey, 4 arches west of Transept so that [I] saw the procession enter & proceed to altar, perhaps the best point in Cathedral. struck with extraordinary beauty & magnificence of the scene, the dresses, solemnity &c. One seemed transported into history. I never once associated a modern notion with it. fine day, – lucky. think it was desirable first as a piece of internal politicks as occupying the minds of the people for several months, then as distributing bread thro' infinity of channels.' And in Edinburgh the following year the ceremonial devised by Sir Walter Scott for the King's visit reminded him of nothing so much as 'a scene in a play'.

In 1823 he went to Covent Garden more to see the King in his Royal Box than the play. He wrote: 'King in red Marshal's uniform. D. Dorset, D. Wellington, D. Clarence, all stand[in]g except Clarence . . . The King's manner was admirable, his dress & appearance very distinguished tho perhaps hardly with weight & pomp enough – a little affectation of youth, dress & grace not becoming his age & station, but his bow, his complaisant clement look on the crowd, condescending gravely yet considering it his due. nothing meaner than the fiting up of the box. drapery small, low & without meaning. evidently forced into a look of nature & ease – the quantity of gold & yellow lace & tassle on the red velvet & cloth took away effect of the King entirely. the top or roof was on box front above & people were sitting in box above & below him looking between legs of 2 beefeaters which is very unbecoming. beefeaters look well. . . . instead of box lining of red velvet it should be white satin ribbed or spoted with a flower & deep velvet hanging in front should be enriched & lined with the same. the white glossy back would show the various dresses, black, red, blue &c. of lords in waiting & would give them effect of greater size. the box should be lighted in itself with its own chandeliers. back of box should be made to take out & recede back making a room. this full of lords & persons in attendance in long perspective well lighted . . . the King's boxes in foreign Theatres have more dignity. they tell me the King of Sardinia stood the whole time behind the Queen's chair when she went with him (this is truly Italian). he sits only when alone. but it is very important to give all possible dignity to this exhibition of the King to his people & preparation in the building of the Theatre should be made accordingly. in Constantinople the sovereign shows himself to his people in his devotional exercises of religion, then going to the various mosques of a Friday with a certain simplicity very striking, & which he lays aside when reviewing his troops or proceeding to his palaces or thro' the city. in Christendom the sovereign shows himself in his amusements, either at the Theatre or taking his ride. sometimes indeed in a review, never in his humiliation to the ruler of Kingdoms, the only ruler of Princes.'

There are no references in the diaries to contemporary political controversies and personalities, but many which reflect his preoccupation with the panoply and splendour appropriate for the presentation of the sovereign to his people. The concept of the monarch as a glorified country gentleman which has survived in this country from the eighteenth century to the present day was not one which found favour with Cockerell. This explains his grave dissatisfaction with Wyatville's interiors at Windsor Castle which, he considered, were lacking in 'all the parade & pomp & circumstance of a court'. He visited Windsor in January 1827 with his brother-in-law, Goodenough, to attend the funeral of the Duke of York: 'went at 6 to Chapel to get my place. court & approach dark, ought to have been lighted with pitch & Tow in iron baskets on poles. after 2 hours procession entered so[uth] door, [passed] down south aisle wes[t]w[ar]d & up centre nave – first banners, then choir of chanters singing part of service, bier with black pall over it without form, ill carried, procession not orderly, soldiers ill disposed. Guards down aisle, Oxford blues in nave but placed behind a barrier middle [i.e. waist] high hiding half their figures. every other one held a taper. altar painted white & waxed ill & insufficiently lighted. effect of chapel good, reversed light, but chapel looked like chalk quarry, too strong & cold, no painted emblazonments, no gilding. St. George's is a cathedral in little, very small in conception. – anthem, "oh that I had wings like a dove". on the whole thought it very ill considered & unimpressively done. no crown, baton of marshal, insignia of office or royalty, music common place, no serpent, no lights in chapel sconces, no mourning drapery. ended at 11.'

It is not difficult to see that Cockerell's proposals for the ordering of royal ceremonial were guided not merely by a concern for its political implications but by the theatrical imagination of a painter *manqué*.

What was it that prompted Cockerell to begin and maintain a diary on this scale? It would be attractive but erroneous to suggest that it was in imitation of Samuel Pepys, whose nephew's great-grandson he was. After all, his father, one of his brothers and, eventually, one of his own sons were all named Samuel Pepys Cockerell. However, Pepys's diary was not published until 1825 so even if it may have renewed Cockerell's determination to continue his own diary it can hardly be said to have given him the inspiration to begin it.

It is clear that he regarded his diaries primarily as an aid in the management of his own life and profession and unlikely that he ever envisaged their publication in whole or in part. The diaries, then, spring in part from a desire for self-improvement. In an age which, like ours, disapproves on supposedly moral grounds the exercise of discrimination, such a remark is likely to provoke superior smiles. However, Cockerell believed that by self-control and self-knowledge he could raise and refine the standards of his life, not only architecturally but morally and socially. The diaries are thus the records of what he himself called 'the painful anxious pursuit of perfection'. It must never be forgotten whilst we read the extracts from the diaries presented in this book that they are all the result of a process of refinement and discrimination. The comments on his own buildings and on those of others reflect the self-conscious development of a visual and technical training in which the sights were set ever higher and higher.

It is clear that he used the diaries to raise the standards of his personal life. He sometimes notes that he finds his manners in company becoming rough, ungentlemanly and boorish. He attempted to correct this by dining at his three clubs, the Athenaeum, the Travellers', and Grillion's Club to which he was elected in 1822, Grillion's had been founded in 1813 by a group of members of both Houses of Parliament who wished for some neutral ground on which they might meet, politics being strictly excluded. It rapidly became one of the most distinguished and fashionable small clubs of the day, its members dining together every Wednesday during the Parliamentary season at Grillion's Hotel in Albermarle Street. At least two of Cockerell's early patrons, Sir Thomas Acland, Bart. and the Hon. Robert Clive, were members but he seems to have found it rather above his natural social level. For that very reason, however, he made a greater effort to dine there. In a remarkable self-confession in March 1824 he records: 'Never quite at ease at Grillon's club, but . . . [one should] never miss associating with men of instruction & liberality & gentlemen. meet there persons should otherwise lose sight of who may be useful to me – some of my best acquaintances & instruction derived from this club. in company of men of parts & elegant manners one insensibly acquires their habits of speaking & thinking – yet it is always an effort to dine there.' The Athenaeum he found less attractive. His description of an evening spent there in February 1825 shows that some aspects of club life have not greatly altered during the last century and a half: 'dined at Athenaeum . . . staid in room with 6 persons I did not know, some reading, snoring, coughing. this is a disagreable situation for 2 hours together.'

Of all his clubs it was the Travellers' which was to prove of most value to him. One of the founder members at its inception on 5 May 1819, he extensively remodelled its premises in Pall Mall in 1821–22. From the start he was a member of the committee together with Lord Auckland, Lord Lansdowne, Lord Palmerston, the Hon. Robert Clive, Sir Gore Ouseley, diplomatist and oriental scholar, Lt.Col. W. M. Leake, classical topographer and numismatist, and W. R. Hamilton, secretary to Lord Elgin and subsequently Under-Secretary of State for Foreign Affairs. It was Hamilton who, by arranging for Cockerell to carry dispatches to the fleet in 1810, started him on the first stage of his Grand Tour.

As his diaries make clear, the club played a great part in Cockerell's social and intellectual life. That he was determined for its membership to be lively and varied is evident from his reactions to a Committee Meeting held on 27 February 1822 'to elect 60 new members, very aristocratically inclined. Many gentlemanly men already, we want some ungentlemanly.' The club was also a fruitful source of partonage for Cockerell. Three of his fellow committee members, Lord Lansdowne, Robert Clive, and Sir Gore Ouseley, employed his services at this time in remodelling their respective country seats: Bowood, Oakly and Woolmers.

It is evident, too, that he found the diaries of help in eradicating from his life sins of impurity. After discussing with friends in April 1823 the irregularities of Lord Byron's mode of life, he makes the following disarming and rather beautiful observations, beginning by noting a 'distinction between deliberate profligacy & heat of Blood. at a certain age the blood cools as the judgement ripens & mutually aid in the improvement of the character – but our greatest help is absence from temptation.' He notes how he recently 'fell into an error first since Jan.ʸ which makes me distrust the best resolu - tions. Devil steps in when least expected or prepared against. singular beauty of the circumstance that our divine Saviour should be subject to all the passions & errors of humanity & that he should have first said prayed (sic) that we might not be lead (sic) into temptation. that he was so subject is clear from his passion & the effect of his sufferings. be merciful, still be merciful. let not coldness of blood be passed off as the virtue of forbearance & temperence. let us remember errors & be ever mindful of them when we judge others.'

A similar thought occurred to him in April 1827 which he again expressed in the most moving terms. 'I can easily understand how that most religious man Michael Angelo suffered agonies of repentance in his latter days which are strongly expressed in his sonnets & writings generaly. I have when I approached something of amendment felt the same thing – that is the conscience having overcome immediate temptation & the constant daily battle of resistance to temptation ceasing for a moment, the same spirit recurs from present guilt to former sins & feels remorse acutely.'

The most succinct evidence of the role his diaries played in his life occurs in the retrospective notes at the end of the volumes for 1822 and 1823. In 1822 he records:

'I am born an artist. nothing deeply interests my mind but the painful anxious pursuit of perfection. without this I am flat & without ability tho materialy happier. constant daily occupation has obscured my intention & wish of improving myself & occasional indolence & idle habits of being late have contributed to this, as well as habits of indulgence in sensualities to a certain extent which might & must be restrained. certainly the mind like a wheel acquires accelerated strength by effort & accelerated weakness by indulgence of any kind. indulgence is the poison. – I have now been more regular in religious observance.'

He also notes with marked and understandable satisfaction that hand-in-hand with the establishment of his moral character has gone his gradual establishment as an architect of repute:

'Still my plans have progressed, my connection is extended, my experience increased. my trip to Scotland [to design the National Monument in Edinburgh] added materials to my knowledge & reputation as well I think as my contest with the commissioners [over the estimate for the Hanover Chapel] which showed my brothers in the profession a publick spirit & to them a disinterest & willingness to sacrifice to a feeling of principle ... St. Pauls has been a great service to me & admitted me to acquaintance with marked & able men. the work of the Travellers' Club was useful. the competition of Bristol Institution has established my reputation there & given confidence to my steady friend Harford. my introduction to Scotland gave me great eclat. my admission to Grillons' club has been the highest gratification to my vanity indeed to my honor, composed as it is of men so eminently able & virtuous. I can never reap a higher reward than this nor ever have a greater encouragement to merit it. Wellesley's acquaintance has been of use by a great acquisition of acquaintance of design by engravings.

'I have felt my deficiency in science & it has been discovered I must profess the practical artist. Lord Lansdowne's business [i.e. the chapel at Bowood] has been of immense service to me, introducing me to the first persons in the country thro' that Maecenas. I must go on to be more diligent & earlier, more severe. London is dangerous. I have got to undo the habit of working by others, by James N[oble] and Topple [his clerks]. I must avoid indolence which grows apace & apathy which comes from want of elevation moral & religious. surely devotion & ambition should keep me from apathy. I must increase acquaintance with the ingenious & contrive to travel. if poss[ibl]e I must see Holland this year & some parts of England I have not visited. I

must avoid the rock of avarice & its consequent contraction of mind & I
may go on to improve.'

The following year, 1823, concludes with the following confession,
written on a loose sheet, folded in half and sealed. The present writer is
relieved to record that his was not the hand which first broke the seal.

'This year', Cockerell writes, 'I have endeavoured to improve my knowledge of God & to reform myself . . . I have read the Bible for the first time
in my life with infinite gratification. I think to be already sensible of the
benefits of the perusal . . . May God give me good thoughts & true wisdom
& fit me for his habitations when He may think fit if indeed all my sins can
be forgiven . . . I have been constantly pestered with conceited reflections &
have still to accuse myself of great intemperance towards my Father, in
humour but not in deed & I am without control of quick & incitable feelings.
however I have been ready in making reparations.

'My Study has considerably advanced by Practice & by seeing many
objects in arch[itecture] & arts my fame & success proportionately. I
sacrifice every object to this of improving my knowledge in art. I begin to
feel greatly the advantage of these mem[orand]a not only in the important
affairs of business but as a digester of all the circumstances & opinions which,
occur to me . . . I find that moderations in diet has greatly contributed to
quicken me (this since I read B[ishop] of St David's tract on abstinence in
Oct^r). this liveliness of mind & more regular habits have forwarded my
studies much but the latter has made me think much of love & matrimony &
I have thought perhaps these imaginations are timely warning me that I
cannot long be worth a woman's love & that I must prepare at present for
future comfort & all those ties which render the latter days more interesting.' In the summer of 1826 he observed: 'we are commanded not to live
without God in the world. it seems to me it is also as contrary to sense &
nature to live without love in the world. love is the salt of life. without it
where is the enjoyment or motive of it.'

Perhaps the most significant of the allusions in the diaries to their role in
his life is that which occurs in November 1826. Here he weighs up the
advantages and disadvantages of keeping a journal and seems to come to the
conclusion that its tendency to encourage introspection makes it in the end a
destructive rather than a creative occupation: 'In talking over the subject of
journals with young Davis I was considering the advantages & the contrary
– more original motives, 1st that if we are wise by experience how careful
& assiduous we should be in tracing this experience. 2, that memory is

fallacious ... 3, the positive utility in business of minutes taken at the moment ... 4th, that there are few conspicuous men in politics, morals, letters, who have not had this habit. Cicero tells us he wrote at length dissertation on his own conduct. Bacon somewhere says admirable things in this score. Franklin's moral excellence derived from this practice entirely ... Caesar wrote his commentaries, Herodotus & Thucydides ... with regard to the effect on my own self, I have proofs that it has been of important service in business & has saved me from imminent confusion several times. in religion I may say that I may date my little knowledge from the period of my commencem[en]t of this practice. in morals I am sure I have checked almost to eradication one mortal Sin ... I have done more justice to persons & things ... on the other hand I believe it more philosophical than profitable. it takes off the edge of worldly emulation & perhaps spoils that bloom of naivete & simplicity that might otherwise attend ones actions, giving too methodical & systematisation to one's proceedings. it removes me from actual life & does not assist in qualifications for the world. I believe it injures memory & dispenses too much with caution, meditation & trust in oneself. going always to look rather than standing singly on one's own resource. finaly I have sometimes been so doubtful of its benefit that I have in despair discontinued it sometimes. I think it checks action & appeals too often to internal consolation rather than profitable exertion.'

In the end the diaries were given up for a combination of reasons. As we see from the passage quoted above he felt that they encouraged the vice of self-regard, but it was his marriage in 1828 which, in suppressing that vice, inevitably subdued at the same time the self-communing side of his character which had produced the diaries.

Cockerell became engaged to Anna Maria Rennie on 23 March 1828 whilst walking in the grounds of Dalmeny Park, a house by Wilkins of which he strongly disapproved. He was nearly forty, and she twenty-five. Her father was the brilliant civil engineer, John Rennie (1761–1821), whose practice as a designer of bridges was continued by his son, John (1794–1874), who was knighted in 1831 on the completion of London Bridge.

On 29 March Cockerell bought an engagement ring in Edinburgh for £27. 10s. and the couple were married in St. James', Piccadilly, by the Bishop of London on 4 June. The honeymoon began, unromantically enough, in Liphook. The next day they moved on to Chichester where they enjoyed 'very rainy weather', and after that to Bognor where they stayed at the Clarence Hotel which was 'excessively dear.' Their bill for two days and three nights at Bognor came to £5. 18s. The uncharacteristic preoccupation

with economy which seems to have entered Cockerell's life at this moment
may have influenced his decision to move on to the Isle of Wight where he
found at Ryde that 'dinners [were] generally 4s: to 5, sherry 3s., bed 2s.,
wax lights 1.6, breakfast 4s: to 5, addit[iona]l with fish & eggs, 2s.' Crossing
to Portsmouth, he took his bride on a tour of the Royal Naval Dockyard
where it is hard to imagine her sharing his enthusiasm at the 'block
machinery [and] cable manufactory'. On the following day, Saturday 14
June, the last of his honeymoon, he went with Anna to see Grange Park
near Alresford. As we shall see later, this great Greek Revival mansion,
remodelled by Wilkins in 1809, was perhaps the modern house and park he
most admired: 'there is nothing like it this side of Arcadia,' he had written
in 1823. It is not difficult to imagine his delight in showing his young bride
the house which had meant so much to him and explaining to her the design
of the sumptuous dining-room and novel conservatory which he had been
privileged to add to it. Forcibly recalling to his imagination the ruins of
ancient Greek temples and containing interiors which he believed to be the
work of his beloved Inigo Jones, the house wondrously united all his
architectural passions from the 5th century to the present day. That its
associations should now include and culminate in his love for his wife must
have given rise to a joy and satisfaction beyond the reach of words. So we
will leave Cockerell standing with his bride before that vast Greek Doric
portico, lost in dreams of his future career, of his desire to create an architectural language which, in uniting 'the richness of rococo & the breadth &
merit of Greek',[2] might transcend the work of either Inigo Jones or William
Wilkins. How far he achieved that ambition is a question to which Part III
of this book may provide an answer.

2. Cockerell's description, from his diary for 26 January 1822, of the ornament on the plate he had
designed for presentation to General Alava.

PART II

Critic

CHAPTER III

An Approach to English Architecture

A<small>T FIRST</small> sight the extent of architectural information contained in Cockerell's diaries may possibly remind one of Sir Nikolaus Pevsner's celebrated *Buildings of England* series. The analogy is, in the last analysis, dubious because whereas Cockerell's travels were in pursuit of creative selection, Pevsner's are in pursuit of critical inclusiveness. However, Cockerell's outlook was, like Pevsner's, essentially European and his interests were similarly the reverse of topographical, antiquarian or associational. A detached, impartial and ruthless critic, Cockerell was never blinded by sentiment in his search for absolute architectural quality. He did not, however, appreciate what Pevsner has called 'The Englishness of English Art'. The English genius for compromise and understatement failed to impress him. The undemonstrative 'empirical' grandeur of, say, Bath or Hampton Court are typical test-cases. Though he admired the Royal Crescent in Bath, he considered that 'it wants that magnificence & eclat which a frenchman would have given it.' With Hampton Court, which he visited in 1821, he 'was on the whole much disappointed . . . there are no striking features, fine rooms it is true but no striking & beautiful combinations of Rooms, no variety of forms, dispositions & features, no elegant interior architecture – no col[umn]s, no salon, but one room after another but much alike, but leaving no great or agreable impression on the mind. the facade is not well.'

Cockerell was a great traveller. If we have compared his travels in this country with those of Pevsner, then he himself compared those he undertook on his Grand Tour with those of St Paul. In reading the Acts of the Apostles in December 1827 he found that 'the voyages & journies of Paul remind me of mine in those seas & cities, all of which almost I have seen.' His long and remarkably frequent English journeys coincided with the short-lived heyday of the stage coach. Undertaken primarily to inspect the progress of his works, the journeys also enabled him not only to survey and record the whole development of English architecture but also to reflect on his ambitions and character. He rarely complains of the grave discomfort of these costly journeys which he often underwent at night, travelling outside the coach and exposed to the ever variable weather of this country. Indeed, he even seems to have regarded them as welcome periods of relaxation. Thus, on his return from Grange Park in July 1823 we find the following entry: 'chewed the cud of sweet & bitter fancy. great enjoyment of these reveries. the only poetic moments of my life now pass[ed] on top of a coach. the change of scene, the beauty of country, the movement, the variety of character – my constant theme architecture, prospects of improvem[en]t, of honorable distinction, a review of all my various businesses. the mind in repose occupies itself on its favourite topics.'

Although the present chapter and the two succeeding ones will be devoted largely to presenting Cockerell's views of his contemporaries and immediate predecessors, it must not be thought that he did not have a great veneration for the Gothic past. There are many enthusiastic references in the diaries to visits to mediaeval churches and cathedrals – thus in September 1822, he 'rejoiced to be at York considering it to be the Athens of Gothic arch-[itectur]e' – but they have not been cited in this book since they are descriptive rather than interpretative. An exception is his suggestive comment after a visit to Oxford in June 1822:

'remarkable that magnificent Patrons have distinguished themselves by [the] beauty & solidity of the monuments they have left. you will find nothing so good in Oxford as Cardinal Wolsey & Will[iam] of Wyckham's works. a noble ambition seeks the respect of futurity rather than [of the] present thus to give proof of its sincerity by its high disinteredness.'

Cockerell's enthusiasm for William of Wykeham grew with the years and finally found expression in a substantial paper on him published in 1846. We shall return to this study, a model of architectural history, in chapter VIII where it will be related to Cockerell's growth of interest in Gothic proportional systems.

Even in early years what stirred his artistic imagination were not Georgian but Elizabethan and Jacobean country houses. On a visit to Hatfield in 1821 he found the great drawing room, 'the noblest room I have seen'. Burleigh House similarly drew from him almost extravagant praise. Visiting it in September 1822 he wrote: 'aspect grand from extent & quantity & pointed elevations, flat roofs, chimneys in 2 col[umn]s with entablature irregular. looks like the ruins of Palmyra or Balbeck. Vanbrugh must have taken his notion of chimnies from this, making them ornamental elevations.'

For the subsequent development of Cockerell's own architectural style this passage is one of the most suggestive in the diaries. His perceptive comments on Vanbrugh anticipate the findings of modern scholars who have shown how, in his search for a heroic architecture, he looked beyond the quiet reticence of Jones' Palladianism to the splendours of the Jacobean past.

Of Longleat which he visited in the following year he wrote:

'this is said to be the largest palace in England & it has all the air of being so. the aspect in descending the Hill from Warminster is most striking. the facades are finely broken & the roof exhibits a cluster of domes, pinnacles & ornamental arch[itectur]e which fills the eye & imagination. to the East is a river, a fine lawn, bridge & terrace before the windows, to the N.E. a terrace over offices & then an ornamental garden & conservatory having more of the palatial character than anything I know in England. it is throughout architecture of 3 orders, doric, Ionic, corinthian. above frames & acroteria & statues each with pedestal & full entablature ... it must be confessed that the bay windows with 3 pilasters & 2 windows each all alike or nearly so are monotonous. they have interiorly the ill effect of looking into each other. the great quantity of very large windows in all the fronts gives Longleate the air of a great stone lantern, especially at the angles [where] you sometimes see thro' the House. the Hall realizes one's notion of an English nobleman's festive Hall & has all the hospitality, warmth & magnificence which can be desired, in particular the roof, the view into saloon, stairs, musick gallery.'   •

Such was his devotion to this great house that when in Wiltshire in 1825 he wrote: 'so near Longleat would not deny myself the pleasure of visiting it. view arriving from Warminster the most striking I have seen perhaps in any country. imposes on approach by its size but is in effect gothic, the quantity of windows & the seeing thro' the angles gives it all the aspect of a stone cage or lantern. the squareness of the lines fatigues & the ornaments & circles attempt in vain to dissipate the unpleasant effect. the Hall, its chimney piece, window looking in from above, ceiling, Wooton's pictures, buck heads ... emblazonments make it charming. the courts are dull as are the corridores. the bow windows my principal object of the visit satisfied me of their gaiety & convenience. rooms small but not unpleasantly so. could not approve the staircase [by Jeffry Wyatville].'

Longleat, designed by Robert Smythson in c. 1570, was the first of the so-called Prodigy Houses. It was followed twenty years later by one of the

F

most remarkable of all such houses, Longford Castle (Pl. 13) also in Wilt-shire. Triangular in plan it is punctuated by great round towers redolent of Spenserian romance. Cockerell wrote of it on his visit in 1823: 'there is much that interests the imagination. all the graces of Italian arch[itectur]e are imitated tho' badly & there is a sentiment of invention & pleasure about it that is in better feeling than that of your greek simplicity of the present day.' One never fails to be impressed that Cockerell of all people should prefer the heroic romance of Elizabethan architecture to the timid scholarship of the Greek Revival. Longford had recently been remodelled by an architect called Daniel Asher Alexander whose scheme of transforming the house from a triangular to a hexagonal shape had fortunately been arrested in mid-flight. Cockerell, interestingly, pleads for a faithful conservatism in the design of any additions to an earlier structure. 'Abo[ut] 1805 the present lord meant to extend [the] plan & make a pentagon &c. &c. by Alexander. a work half done & much mistaken. Alexander was ignorant of the style, made something vulgar [and] fanciful of his own nasty invention. there is nothing military in Elizabethan domestic arch[itectur]e. an arch[itec]t must be an antiquary when he builds additions or affects an old style of whatever period, otherwise he falls into gross errors hateful to good sense & disgraces himself & his employers ... in Sir P. Sidney's Arcadia it is spoken of as Amphiolus' castle.'

Dating from 1628 was another romantic and symmetrical pile admired by Cockerell, Heriot's Hospital in Edinburgh. When he visited it in August 1822, he found 'the details playful & beautiful' and remarked: 'great effect produced by the tower & lantern system, think Vanbrugh studied it. *effect in architecture.*'

Another building wrongly attributed to Inigo Jones in Cockerell's day was Grange Park and we shall see later how Cockerell considered the top-lighting in the house 'shows how much Inigo was a painter'. Amesbury Abbey in Wiltshire of 1661 was also thought by Cockerell to be the work of Inigo Jones though it is now known to be by John Webb on the basis of an Inigo design. Cockerell's singular devotion to this house, which he was fortunate enough to see before its complete rebuilding by Hopper in 1830, can have been shared by few of his contemporaries. He wrote of it:

'the tower rising above the cupola, corresponding chimney shafts & projection of the Portico is of the best school & contrivance & the genius of Inigo is in few examples more conspicuous. what is surprising is that the proportions are small & yet in the aspect of the whole, especially the Hall, stairs, saloon above, there is an uncommon grandeur which fills & occupies the mind. there are offices below as well as abundant bed Ro[oms] above & I consider that for economy of convenience with proportion & effect it may challenge any Ho[use] in England ancient or modern.'

Cockerell's enthusiasm for Vanbrugh, and particularly for his dramatic skylines, will be described in later chapters. Suffice it for the moment to note how on a visit to Castle Howard he wrote: 'great play & charm in Hall. I *could* not leave it. vast effect, movement in staircases &c. good effect of long passages in entering.'

He could not, however, approve James Gibbs. On a visit to St. Martin-in-the-Fields in 1822 he was 'struck with small effect of interior', and wrote of it: 'col[umn]s short, cieling heavy, terminates ill at altar end.' He wrote of the Senate House at Cambridge: 'thought it low & cieling appeared to sway – not from any defect but from the arch[itectur]e of it.' Years later, in his Royal Academy lectures of 1851, he cited St. Mary-le-Strand as an instance of the solecism of a tower in the form of a parallelogram rather than a square. Yet in the same lectures, in recommending to his pupils the need for 'variety and boldness of form', he pointed as models to the country houses of John Thorpe, Inigo Jones, Wren, Vanbrugh and Gibbs. He regretted that, 'All the expressiveness given by the gable end is lost in England where the roof is always hipped.' As commendable exceptions to this rule he cited Jacobsen's Foundling Hospital of the 1740's and the group of six shops and houses on the east side of Regent Street designed by Sir John Soane in 1820. Here the 'gable end' admired by Cockerell takes the curious form of three attic blocks containing huge semi-circular windows.

It will easily be imagined that to a man of Cockerell's tastes neo-Palladian architecture exercised little appeal. On the same day in October 1825 he visited those two great Norfolk seats, Campbell's Houghton Hall and Kent's Holkham Hall. It is interesting to observe his initial hostility to both houses and to trace a gradual growth of enthusiasm for Holkham. His veneration for Palladio helped win him over to Holkham but the Palladian characteristics of Houghton were obscured for him by the remarkable Baroque corner domes. He wrote of Houghton: 'struck me as too like a publick monument or royal palace ... pompous affected it has anything but grace & ease about it'; and of Holkham: 'not pleased with its exterior first view, all squares, no round or amiable forms. Kent's defect as at Horse Guards. approach too much like a great publick buildg: Hall or stables with its great windows – thought the brick rustic ill judged, little entrance door ill. improved however on acquaintance, especialy the south front which is charming, most pleasingly calm & noble & classical. reminded every moment of Palladio & classic art & countries. rooms not large but well disposed, the gallery new & most pleasing.'

Much less to Cockerell's taste was the High Palladianism of Flitcroft at Woburn. He wrote of it in 1828: 'Total want of imagination in the outline of the House & offices. for size & extent so magnificent, a plain architecture equaly applicable to hospital, museum or anything else. what might be called handsome or neat but conveying no idea of Princely hospitality, sports, country delights – the House seems in a hole, the offices above it.'

On 13 March 1823 Cockerell bought for £5 the two volumes of James Paine's *Plans, Elevations and Sections of . . . Houses . . . executed in the counties of Derby, Durham, Middlesex, Northumberland, Nottingham and York* (1783). He was unimpressed by this great monument to Palladianism, and wrote: 'Paine's taste poor inexpressive, unclassical, a certain baldness & vacancy. must have had sense, was very successful.'

In July 1821 Cockerell inserted in his diary a long and revealing memorandum on the merits of Robert Adam as an architect and planner.

'Mr. Adams's success arose chiefly from his knowledge of detail & his minute & elaborate taste – but he was not an artist of any force nor of very sound judgem^t – he began with details & adapted them to the necessary lines. – I am sure that his imagination did not embrace the whole. first the general design then the parts & then the detail of ornam^t – I am sure his ideas first assembled in ornam^t & decoration – his plans are a labyrinth. he did not acknowledge the effect of the vista nor the good sense of it. in the obvious & palpable disposition of the house your way is never direct sometimes sideways like a crab, sometimes thro' alcove or corner you come into a magnificent room you know not how – instead of its being announced by a noble doorway & a direct way to it you are to look for a concealed handle in the dado of a coved end you then learn to pull down the whole wainscoting of a room that which before was solid is broken into a doorway by the Adamish contrivance of a jib.'

In private Cockerell felt free to attack Adam but when he was discussing his merits with Lord Lansdowne in January 1823 it was rather a different story. 'Lansdowne did not like adams, [but] I said they had much practice, great dispositions & arrangement, that they had done great service in introducing & adapting the architecture of the Roman baths to our purposes.'

He developed this theme in a comparison jotted down four years later between Adam and Palladio: 'Palladio never indulged in any form of Rooms but square or parallelogram – could have seen little of Roman baths or villas. observe his rules of proportion in rooms. Adams from Spalatro & Roman [baths] made ovals, rounds, octagons &c in profusion.'

Cockerell also enjoyed the subtle planning of Sir Robert Taylor which modern historians have been slow to appreciate. In the Goodchild Album is preserved his plan of Taylor's Bank Buildings, an elongated triangular block of *c*. 1781 between Threadneedle Street and Cornhill, whose ingenious planning on an awkward site he praised in his Royal Academy lectures. Demolished in 1844 for the forecourt of the Royal Exchange, the building contained at its eastern end the Sun Fire Office whose premises Cockerell was shortly to rebuild. Taylor had contrived to incorporate no less than nine staircases, many of them in oval or circular wells. In a Royal Academy lecture of 1845 he observed of Taylor's Court Room at the Bank of England: 'the Bank Parlour is one of the most original and scenic in its contrivance, and is peculiar to Sir R. Taylor as he has shewn at Clumber, in his own house in Spring Gardens as well as at the Bank. That contrivance is that you enter the room by lateral corridores from whence the proportion of the room is entirely enjoyed as it were from an external point of view. The order is very small, the ceiling is perhaps a little flat and deficient in dignity of relief.'

Always it was the meagreness of contemporary architecture that lowered his spirits: 'comparing modern architecture with the remains of all former times', he wrote in October 1825, 'we find the art stript of all imaginative beauties, neither sculpture nor painting contribute to it – it is a dry adaptation of proportions without ornament in which the great end in view seems to have been attainment of the negative merit of avoiding errors. to what purpose have the Elgin & Grecian discoveries, the purchases of fine paintings for the ornament of our country & the travels of individuals tended if we are to be quakers in architecture [?]'.

What appealed to Cockerell was the virtue of magnificence. As he observed in 1822: 'something imposing, grand, massive & *high* is wanted in our buildings at present': but in 1825 he noted that the fulfilment of this rich vitality was ever held in check by the peculiar difficulties of the architectural profession. He observed how 'In the practice of the arch[itectura]l profession the artist lapses into the judicial & economical character – the scope of authority required & the weight of responsibility give a severity which sadly checks the artistic & imaginative faculty which is after all a main ingredient in his science – this is the profession that mixes the scientific with the artist & to be perfect in the profession requires a scope of talent which no man can be supposed to possess. – perhaps this with an advancement in years is the chief occasion of the little fertility to my artistic quality & indisposition to it – & it is certainly to this may be attributed the dry manner of some of my Brother arch[itect]s in their works.'

To overcome dryness Cockerell looked for inspiration not only to the Renaissance but also, as we have seen, to the vigour of Elizabethan architecture. He particularly approved 'of the Elizabethan & Italian plan of incorporating the whole offices in the House – so to make imposing front . . . thus sufficient bed rooms would be procured, which are always deficient in modern Houses from that reason. the Elizabethan is truly a romantic style of architecture.'

Romance, however, was not enough. Cockerell had as clear an understanding as Pugin of construction as the basis of design. Cockerell records how on 29 March 1826: 'in talking with Brondsted on the building of the Turks at Constan[tinopl]e I was much struck with the importance of distinguishing the *scheme* or great design & combination of means to be a great end in a Construction – & the *taste*, its proportion & ornament with which that scheme is decorated. in talking of the Turkish mosques all of which are copies of S\ua Sophia he overlooked the merit of the original scheme of S: Sophia . . . in appreciating the proportion & decoration which are naturaly greatly superior in the copies.

'The Scheme of an architectural combination will be comprehended by very few who do not study the subject with intelligence. it is the first excellence, to which proportion & Taste are secondary. in this order of merit Sir C. Wren stood higher than any, either the Italians or the moderns. [Inigo] Jones was the greater man of Taste.'

Despite his stress on what he calls the 'scheme' Cockerell's understanding of architecture was too subtle for him to underestimate the role of taste and imagination. Thus he was not naïve enough to suppose that any problems would be solved by adopting a uniform system of modular proportions. He discussed this in 1828 with his friend, Richard Hey Sharp, an intelligent young architect at York: 'Sharpe says the opening for light in the Pantheon was $1/5$ of the diam[ete]r & that all the dimensions were in relative proportions, as [for example] the great door which was 20×40 high. The Italian arch[itect]s found this system pretty general in the anc[ien]t Roman works & adopted it accordingly in their work universaly as we see everywhere in Palladio, Scamozzi, Sanmichele & all the school. the adoption of a [modular] system was probable in the Greco Roman arch[itec]ts. it is always the case in an established school. system is the result of school, it never obtains in Greek architecture, nor can be with original artists who must ever be directed by feeling, of the circumstances, necessities, & genius loci, by a nice discrimination of these.'

Cockerell would have had sympathy with Lutyens who, though he increasingly depended on modular proportions, worked out a different modular system for several of his late buildings guided entirely by visual or aesthetic considerations.

'The Science of Proportion in arch[itectur]e', Cockerell wrote, is 'delightful but that of construction & the systems adopted in different eras of the world gives the history of the progress of the human mind in all its most ingenious occupations – its utmost efforts of genius, of combination, the discoveries in the use of material.' Cockerell followed this up with an attractively illustrated note on the role of 'supports' in architecture and nature:

'arch[itectur]e address itself chiefly to the understanding, to the reasoning faculties. the principal pleasure arising from the contemplation of a fine building is obviously the proportion of means to the end intended, in the distribution of the parts of support particularly . . . we should be distressed to see a chalk or soft free-stone corinthian col[umn] carrying a heavy weight . . . so in plants, the reed & can[e] tribe & some oriental plants I saw at Lodge's [i.e. Messrs. Loddige's nursery at Hackney] have the most delicate fibres & supports carrying large fruits or heads – these stalks being however exceedingly strong. It is to be remarked that when nature uses these proportions the terminations & joints are generally large, giving great grace to them in form & seeming reasonable to gravitation & space for the working of the joints. The Greeks adopted this principle in legs of chairs & Tables, also in the slender doric col[umn] in which they always gave to the cap[ital] an extraordinary projection . . . Nature must be the great prototype of proportion. Proportions of supports in arch[itectur]e will be regulated by the necessary strengths for the thing supported . . . in spaces, apartment &c. it will be regulated by the uses & necessities of the building – where neither of these essential reasons will serve, proportions in both cases will be regulated by conventional opinion, by the concurrent recommendations of great masters, & general practice of preceding ages. independent of these rules are fashions in proportion. thus in Egypt a fashion prevailed of very low & solid proportion. amongst the Greeks, a great solidity in the doric.'

The classical language of architecture he regarded as being essentially outside fashion. He had an irritating discussion on the subject with his friend Sanford in 1822: 'Sanford's conversation on arch[itectur]e', he wrote, 'the common cant, why should we follow eternaly the same round of arch[itectur]e, why repeat the same thing, why sho[ul]d not genius invent a new order – why, because the materials, necessities & uses, principles of strength & stability must be ever invariable.'

Thus, despite all his lack of enthusiasm for the products of the Greek Revival he remained convinced that Greek architecture must be the starting point for modern design. His visit to France in 1824 where he saw the endless modern imitations of the 'corrupt style' of Roman architecture and of 'all the varieties which the arch has given rise to', confirmed his view that he was right to 'look to the grecian arch[itectur]e as the source & only one whence any originality can be attained . He believed that 'everything else has been done – one can only be original by studying their models. one must hold to a principal, so therefore to the source. one is never more struck with this than when one sees the changes that are rung on old models.'

CHAPTER IV

'Greek Bedevilled':
A View of the Greek Revival

COCKERELL's fundamental doubts about the wisdom of a Greek Revival in nineteenth-century England are set out very clearly in some notes at the beginning of his first diary of 1821:

'Until the attention of the world was drawn to the study of Greece by the spirit of the last century by Barthelemy's Anacharsis & the refinement of English education in the Dead languages & thence to the study of Greek architecture by the researches of Stuart & [Revett] architecture had for its guide in this Country the old Italian masters & their valuable commentaries & publications of the anc[ien]t arch[itectur]e of Rome & Italy. no great enormities could arise under such guidance, but since the rage for Greek has been amongst us all the rules which formerly protected us are now set aside & we are at sea without compass . . . we stick a slice of an anc[ien]t Greek Temple to a Barn which is called breadth & simplicity, than which nothing can be more absurd, as the Greek Houses were certainly of wood & brick & plaister painted & temporary things. I am sure that the grave & solemn arch[itectur]e of Temples were never adopted to Houses, but a much lighter style, as we may judge by the vases, the object being space & commodiousness.'

Cockerell's keen sense of historical continuity and tradition made him reject the archaeological notion of a Greek Revival. He realized that the Renaissance had made its own contribution to the development of the classical language of architecture and that one could not design without reference to this development. He was confirmed in this view by the sight of Dance's College of Surgeons in Lincoln's Inn Fields. Its obvious faults led him to observe: 'What is now most essential is to appropriate the Greek style, engraft it on our wants & recast it for our necessities. the Italian arch[itect]s did this, particularly Palladio.'

The younger Dance, born in 1741, was the oldest of the architects associated with the climax of the Greek Revival in the early nineteenth century. Although later in life Cockerell came to admire the individual 'narrative' character Dance gave to his buildings, the only building by him to which he refers in the diaries is the College of Surgeons. Its unpedimented Ionic portico of 1806 was the first pure Greek portico to be erected in London. Cockerell realized its significance and considered 'the Ionic portico the gravest I have seen & most severe.' However, he judged it 'ill applied to the thin paper front of a Ho[use] with which it has no connection neither by ornamental arch[itectura]l style, solidity, character, lines or material.'

Dance's position as father of the Greek Revival could have been challenged by only one architect, Thomas Harrison of Chester (1744–1829). Harrison was the contemporary on whom Cockerell was most prepared to lavish praise. Refusing to be dazzled by the limelight which surrounded architects such as Smirke and Wilkins, Cockerell turned unerringly to the modest Chester architect as the one contemporary who understood the classical language as a means of construction in stone. He wrote of Harrison's best known building, Chester Castle (1785–1822), 'certainly a great hand is visible . . . [but it] is open to criticism in many points of view. most obviously in the variety of doric orders in the Propylea & court & in the Ionic sides, each seeming of a different hand. the Grecian doric is very imperfect but it is the great intelligence of the masonry that Harrison's merit lies. Cockerell also felt that the North Gate which Harrison designed for Lord Grosvenor in 1808 was 'an excellent work, the effect chiefly arising from the admirable constructive style of the masonry, in particular the arches.'

In November 1823 Cockerell visited Harrison on his return from Ireland. He found him 'grown very old' and with 'a secret exultation in his fine works & his merits, but mixed with great truth and modesty. Harrison has a spark divine, a noble mind, lofty & extensive views, but little improved by study . . . I doubt his capacity for interiors. his merit is external arch[itectur]e as masonry chiefly.' In Harrison's company Cockerell 'walked over Chester [as] always with great pleasure' and felt that there were 'many hints in Chester for the history of English architecture.'

Cockerell's telling summary reads: 'Harrison is undoubtedly the noblest genius in arch[itectur]e we have had in external arch[itectur]e chiefly. Goodwin for raciness invention resource & sometimes for grandeur beats anything but he is certainly not a gentleman in his works.'

Despite his detection of a caddish streak in Goodwin's architecture Cockerell could not help being impressed by his general panache. Indeed in August 1825 he went so far as to write of Goodwin's Greek Doric County

Gaol at Derby of 1823–27: 'saw it with pleasure, he is truly a man of genius seizing the characteristics of a style & applying them in the most powerful manner he is sometimes almost over charged & caricatured but with a bold & striking manner. Cromford stone was said to cost 1:1 pr. foot cube.' He was even prepared to admire a church at Birmingham by Goodwin designed in Commissioners' Gothic, the remarkably pretty Holy Trinity, Bordesley, of 1820–23. Visiting it in August 1825, he found the galleried church with its cast-iron tracery and columns, 'a very excellent piece of work'.

It will hardly come as a surprise that Cockerell had a very low opinion of the most elaborate and famous of all Greek Revival churches, St Pancras New Church designed in 1818 by W. and H. W. Inwood. Cockerell inspected it in July 1821: 'simple Greek Greek Greek – radiates bad taste thro' the whole', he wrote scathingly; 'ignorance & presumption [of] Mr. Inwood attempting to impose on one an idea of his importance.' He returned to the attack the following May: 'Mr. Inwood & his boys . . . have tormented themselves to invent du nouveau & have planned a most minute research into every mould[in]g. wherever their authorities have ceased they as usual have been aground. it is anything but architecture – the inside trite – the aps[e] is flat roofed & whole cieling low & unmeaning. intercol-[umniation]n at sides bad.'

G. S. Repton's St. Philip's, Lower Regent Street, of 1819 did not fare much better. Cockerell wrote of it in 1824: 'corinthian highly ornamented – ill adapted to seriousness of worship, mysterious windows, skylight, one feels to be in a horn lantern, but *style* throughout of ornament moulding – the scagliola col[umn]s most inappropriate – if you scagliola a chapel what is left for a drawing Ro[om]. finery misplaced in a Temple unless it is solid magnificence, in the sense of a sacrifice & glory to God – but fiction scagliola is indecent, it is to be false & flattering to the Deity.' We can hardly fail to observe how strikingly Cockerell anticipates Pugin in this dangerous blend of architecture and morality.

Cockerell found much to criticize in Soane's Bank of England, so much admired today. He noted in his diary: 'the lantern rooms all subject to inconvenience or air descending on the head . . . Corridores are narrow & petites but highly studied & some beautiful effect.' He felt that the impression created was at once 'little & great, the taste sometimes flat, sometimes unreasonably bold.' His views on Soane's Law Courts at Westminster are equally remote from those current today. He wrote of them in April 1826: 'thought them trivial, absurd in their arch[itectur]e. should not expect to hear Sense in such foolish Rooms.'

There are many more references in the diaries to Nash's architecture than to Soane's. The first is to Witley Court, the Worcestershire seat of Lord Foley. Cockerell found the house 'not very striking. Two Towers al'italian with the Portico between to which they are not well connected.' On another visit he considered that Nash had 'some notions very good but ill followed up. instance the 2 towers, very Palladian. very Villa like & pleasing & giving distinction to the Ho: in all views but so little studied. roof overwhelming, extinguishing Towers look like keeps of a castle rather than the pleasant residence of a nobleman. great Ionic Porticoes ill executed . . . nothing can be so dull unsightly as the great stuccoed walls. the rusty brown colour. the flimsy unsatisfactorily substitute for stone . . . wings look like a work ho: 4 windows in height without a string of any kind.'

After Nash had dined with the Cockerell family at Westbourne in November 1822 C. R. Cockerell noted in his diary the impression Nash had made: 'Mr. Nash always same, merry, amusing naive, but making the same quotations, telling the same stories.'[1] On 1 August 1826 we read: 'Mr. Nash called on me & conducted me to see the new Palace of Buckingham Ho: – west front good but many defects. total want of order in the windows of East front. cols: above cols: bad in the Porticoes looking like a scaffolding. his interiors will be dark. has totaly overlooked the upper windows usual in Hall in buildg: in high Ro[om]s none of the rooms of a very just proportion. cast iron doric col[umn]s where stone is to be had. sculptured brackets bad . . . striking effects of iron arched Trusses to carry walls.' Comment is unnecessary for all must realize the justice of Cockerell's criticisms.

Cockerell's opinion of one of Nash's most popular buildings, the scenically placed church of All Souls', Langham Place, is perhaps unduly harsh. He felt in 1824 that the spire 'had an inapposite association, reminding one of a village church & not such as fits a metropolis. for this purpose it is too homely.' In the following year he records: 'went to All Souls new church, had heard the arch[itectur]e praised, think it very good for those who know nothing about it.' Of Regent Street itself he observed in 1821 that it is 'evident that all has been done hastily – hastily thought, hastily executed. Nothing more necessary than a leisurely habit. Festina lente, working at the same time with diligence. nothing profound can otherwise be attained. all must be flimsy & deficient in principle.' No one will be surprised at

1. Nash was a great admirer of the young C. R. Cockerell's talents (see *The Farington Diary*, ed. J. Greig, 8 vols, 1922–8, vol. VIII, 1928, p. 301). Much later in life, Cockerell still spoke warmly of Nash (see *The Builder*, XV, 1857, p. 288).

Cockerell's refusal to take seriously the slap-dash architecture of Nash's Regent's Park terraces. In June 1825 he writes mercilessly: 'The architecture of the Regents Park may be compared to the Poetry of an improvisatore – one is surprised & even captivated at first sight with the profusion of splendid images, the variety of the scenery & the readiness of the fiction. But if as many were versed in the Grecian rules of this science as there are in those of Homer & Virgil this trumpery would be less popular.' Walking through the Park on another occasion he could not help feeling that there was 'something mortifying & humiliating in seeing the profusion of ornam[en]t & badness of the arch[itectur]e.'

On 10 March 1822 Cockerell learnt that Wilkins had won the competition for the United University Club to be built at the corner of Pall Mall East and Suffolk Place. 'Wilkins', he considered, 'has got the building of the university Club by a display of fine drawing & little judgem^t. . . . [Greek] doric Portico. commonplace throughout – low. nothing new or striking in arrangement. no intelligence of general proportions. nothing but detail. I thought Gandy did not draw so well without a great sacrifice of something else [i.e. intelligence?]. has not thought on this subject.'

Downing College, Cambridge, that programmatic monument of the Greek Revival was another of Wilkins' buildings for which Cockerell had scant sympathy. Visiting it in 1822 he found the 'quadrangle too wide, Buildings too sunk, like a string of sausages.' He also complained of the 'miserable deficiency of arch[itectur]e when Porticoes are passed.' Nor did Wilkins' bridge at King's College please him any more. He considered it 'narrow & unnecessarily massive & clumsy.'

However, at Wilkins' Grange Park much was forgiven. Cockerell's venom was reserved for the mealy-mouthed, the mean and the ignorant. Where the conception was bold and manly he was prepared temporarily to overlook occasional infelicities or errors of detail. He paid his first visit to the Grange on 21 January 1823 and the rapturous entry in his diary for that day should be quoted almost in full:

'walked over grounds with him [i.e. Alexander Baring] & his son Mr. Bingham Baring. viewed it from ground opposite to river. nothing can be finer more classical or like the finest Poussino, it realises the most fanciful representations of the painters pencil or the poets description. its elevation on terraces gives it that which is essential to the effect of Grecian arch^e & which no modern imitations possess – it has also dimension so seldom obtained & has thereby that imposing aspect which awes & seems to have a proportionate scale without surrounding objects of nature ... the portico a parallelogram fills & satisfies the eye & beauty & stability of the proportion of the order vindicate the claim of Grecian arch^e to preference over most others. the proportion is indeed so large that on a near approach & living under it, it has something of overcharge & resembles those marked & striking features which have a more than masculine coarseness when near, but the value of which is confessed at a proper distance. as to the Propriety of making a Grecian Temple a domestic habitation, that is a question admitting of much doubt. Wilkins has much credit for the boldness of the conception, the turning the basem^t. into a Terrace, the ground terraces, the sides in imitation of the choragic monum^t. which by the bye in the distance give a squareness quite characteristic of the arch^e are well imagined. but the Parallelogram wants further length. the details then are incorrect in many instances. the cols. present the edge of a flute in centre – for what reason I cannot imagine. the omission of the triglyphs & claping 2 wreaths is vulgar, the entablature of the side porticoes in the internal angles hang in the air. the external angles have a double pilaster & the cornice has the nose cut off octangularly very ill. the cornice over the pediment [the corona] has a double face like the horizontal cornice of which I know no example. the cymatium is altogether omitted in that cornice. what is still discoverable in the interior is sufficient evidence of the great master who contrived it Inigo Jones. the Hall is imposing from its height & cube 27 ft. at the end a corridor very spacious & gallery above lead to the staircase which is also a cube 27 ft. the effect of light by a lantern in the cieling of corridor or gallery above is most pleasing as is also that of those lighted by lamps at night it shows how much Inigo was a painter. the saloon was a cube 27 ft. the taking down of the balcony galleries & the lowering the openings to obtain a continued architrave are done with that presumption which those who are ignorant of & are unwilling to perceive the merit of ancient masters are apt to have. I hold it an axiom that no name which has long & thro various ages & fashions maintained its celebrity can ever be found to be a fraud. it is well to conclude that we have not been able to appreciate their merits when we cannot perceive their rights to celebrity. but I hold those as coxcombs & impertinent who decry Palladio, Jones . . . &c. &c. as some of our professors have presumed to do.'

We learn more of his ambivalent attitude to this remarkable house after a visit in May 1823:

'arrived abo: 12 o'clock at Grange. clear beautiful day. blue sunshine serene with a few cotton clouds, freshness in the air, verdure, flowers, tranquility most exhilerating, a day in which one blessed oneself. . . . strolled abo: in the garden, a steady sunshine upon the building as clear a sky the lights & shades & reflections as in Greece. the rooks & jackdaws in the lime tree avenue sailing & cawing in the air brought home the recollections of the acropolis. the buzzing of the blue flies & the flowers something of the aromatic scent of thyme. nothing more satisfactory than the line of terrace building terminated by the two great piers, the gravel walk beneath the sloping bank, the inclination to the water & the tufted trees finer & more luxuriant than ever grew on the banks of Ilissus. the depth of the portico gives a density to the shade which is most happy & assists the clear expression & ever just & satisfactory effect of the cols & their entablature. the strength yet lightness, the robust yet fine, colossal like the Hercules & yet with traits delicate & elevated shewing a mind within elegant & refined, in the great pilasters this character is most visible, . . . the variety of ground abo^t. affords points of view which remind one of the Villa d'Este & the ornamental character of that villa should be had in view in decorating this. Mr. B wants persuading of its charms, if it were his own child he would feel them more – these works will render it more so & will attach him to it. there is nothing like it on this side of Arcadia, yet full of defects & ill contrivance – in our view from front found it all of a bunch, wants length & that my first plan would have made it. the tail of offices will improve it. want cymatium on pediments sculpture in the highlights. those endless wreaths unmerited in their eternal repetition, tiresome commonplace very unclassical. there is a left-handed wooden-headed arrangemt. throughout the execution which showed the executor but half intelligent in his subject. but there are in the Grange the elements of a great house the vista at entrance even now striking, the other vista staircase, corridore & lady's room very conspicuous but marred. doubt whether portico is quite suited to our climate in the finest day I have a ripresa of that keen & cruel north east wind which I felt in jany:, in England porticos should be loggia porticoes.'

★   ★   ★

In 1824 Cockerell wrote: 'I shall never get entirely out of Smirke's manner in my first works. I appealed to Smirke in all things & nothing but 7 years freedom & travel could ever relieve me from the master's spell.'

Cockerell's self-knowledge is surely extraordinary. His development as an architect was, as we shall see, a slow struggle both to emancipate himself from the Greek Revival as understood by Smirke, and also to infuse his art with a rich vitality derived from wider architectural sympathies than those of his contemporaries. His love-hate relationship with his master, Smirke, is suggested in the diaries by the fact that there are more references to his works than to those of any other architect but that these are almost uniformly hostile. Yet he admired Smirke. He found him 'serene, friendly, communicative'; he was intrigued by his custom of walking 'thro' bye streets to avoid meeting persons who may turn the course of his thoughts & occupations'.

Covent Garden Theatre (1809–10), on which Smirke had been working when Cockerell joined his office at the start of his career, was a work which Cockerell came to dislike a good deal. Perhaps it stood as a symbol of Smirke's dominion over him.

'Nothing can be more obviously misplaced', he wrote of Covent Garden in 1822, 'than the 2 sienna pilasters of proscenium. the base & intercol-[umniatio]n & arch over entablature pierced leaving two ugly square forms which clearly show at how great a sacrifice of convenience they have been thrust in there. they are in contradiction to the first principle of a Theatre – vid: the removing of every possible obstruction to the view.' He argued that for this purpose: 'nothing is so useful or fit as iron supports . . . the theatre is like the inside of a trunk or band box greatly enlarged in which one can discover no solid principle of construction. there is no loftiness either in reality nor by illusion of painting. the colors of ceiling are calculated to bring it nearer to the eye & the confined & choked effect of the house & those wretches within cooped up in the Gallery is still more contracted & bornés. it looks like an attempt to cram more into a box than it can possibly contain.'

Cockerell immediately follows these searching criticisms of Covent Garden with a more enthusiastic description of the King's Opera House in the Haymarket of 1790 by the little-known Polish architect, Novosielski. His high praise makes one regret that there appears to be no adequate visual record[2] of this long-demolished building:

'I have always thought that there is more of greatness in the conception of this work than in any Theatre I ever saw. those mighty beams that show their ends in the proscenium & carry the vault or sounding board look like the giants' hands reaching out of the solid build[in]g to carry the decorations. it is like the hand in Belshazzar's feast. in the form of the sounding board

2. Save for the account in J. Britton and A. C. Pugin, *The Public Buildings of London*, 2 vols, 1825–28, vol. I, 72–9.

there is the motive often employed by artists at Pompeia – the segment. the mode in which this was painted by Angelica Kauffman has remained deeply impressed in my mind & ever will.'

It is interesting to speculate that the origins of the stilted segmental arch surrounding either a door or a window, which became an influential feature of Cockerell's later buildings, may derive from a combination of Novosielski and Pompeii!

Returning to our investigation of Cockerell's views on Smirke we should consider Smirke's masterpiece, the British Museum. On a visit to it in October 1824, Cockerell reflected 'that Exterior arch[itectur]e was an expence much thrown away in this climate, especialy in a corner [i.e. Great Russell Street] so little seen.' He admired, however, the 'fine effect' of the wide steps leading up to the portico from the court. The whole building reminded him 'of the passage in Ld. Aberdeen's book p. 26 [*An Enquiry into the Principles of Beauty in Grecian Architecture*, 1822], "The definition of beauty as given by Aristotle [in which] he says beauty consists in magnitude & order." ' However, in Cockerell's opinion, 'magnitude is purely relative & is made to comprize the whole extent of that scale which the eye is able to embrace at one view.' Visiting it again two years later he wrote in his diary: 'did not like taste of any part of Building of Museum. cast iron corbels used with advantage carrying a plate on which binders were placed – this gives solidity to the wall & shortens the bearings. these I liked much.'

Perhaps the clearest way in which Smirke influenced Cockerell was in the use of concealed cast-iron beams and supports. Smirke had employed these spectacularly not merely at the British Museum but also at the Union Club, Somerset House and even at Eastnor Castle. Though Cockerell followed his example at East India House and several country houses he was not in favour of exposed cast iron and criticized Nash for employing it at Buckingham Palace.

On 22 April 1822 he wrote: 'saw Smirke's elevations for Physicians col[leg]e & Union Club. the flank totaly out of character with Porticoed Front. thin, flat, attempt at play, confused in consequence. & that vicious mode of composition of lapping under & over, a cornice or Frieze sometimes appearing, sometimes concealed, somewhat French in ye composition, square pilasters, 3 wind[o]ws like United Service. want of strength & character, looks like builders' Houses of a better kind ... a something imposing, grand, massive & *high* is wanted in our buildings at present.'

His low opinion of the building was confirmed by his inspection of it

G

after completion in November 1825: 'much disappointed, total deficiency of character, nothing like a publick building, nothing monumental, staircase contracted, none of the rooms proportionate – a dry rigid & insignificant style, in ornament mechanical. nothing worse than the cielings, especialy the lanterns. no coves, circles nor any of those floating amiable forms in which the 17 & 18 [century] schools abounded. the worst is their making a part with the club. no idea more improper than the junction of a college with a club.'

Cockerell returned to this theme in a Royal Academy lecture of 1850 where he observed that:

'In the C16 and C17 a large cove reduced the ceiling to an agreeable parallelogram. as opposed to the so-called Grecian ceiling in which un-measured trabeation, sometimes in a single unbroken sheet of most alarming extent threatens to crack over us.'

It may seem perverse of Cockerell to criticize the British Museum for being too monumental and the Union Club for not being monumental enough. His answer would doubtless be that the site of the club happens to be far more imposing than that of the museum. It is also significant that he should deplore Smirke's elegantly rectilinear neo-classical interiors and look for inspiration to 'those floating amiable forms' of earlier plaster-work decoration. His attempts to combine his enthusiasm for such forms with his enthusiasm for the principles of Greek architecture must be studied in detail by anyone investigating his later stylistic development.

The three major references to this prominent building by Smirke suggest that it represented for Cockerell a text-book example of what had gone wrong with the Greek Revival, of why it had degenerated into 'that vicious mode of composition of lapping under & over'.

A building condemned for its unforgiveable resemblance to the Union Club was Smirke's remodelling of Luton Hoo for Lord Bute in 1826. Smirke had been invited to complete the house which Adam had left unfinished, but it has since been twice remodelled in 1843 and 1903. Cockerell records on 21 March 1826: 'went to O. Tyndale's to see Smirke's designs for Ld. Butes Luton. do not like them, notion of making the House compact, corridores & many parts lighted as if the Ho: was in London, looks packed & contracted, arch[itectur]e large like union club & Coll[eg]e of Physicians, no imagination, dull, no space. the use of large orders seems to me improper in any but sacred & publick edifices. they are a real inconveni-ence, the Portico not giving protection from the Rain & darkening windows, embarrassing the facade.'

A major London interior by Smirke was his remodelling of Dance's library at Lansdowne House, Berkeley Square, to form a sculpture gallery in 1816–19. Cockerell was first privileged to see this grand and remarkable room in 1822 when he called on Lord Lansdowne to discuss his designs for the Bowood chapel. He wrote of it: 'few spectacles are finer than a great assembly of beauty & fashion, but if you have no elevation whence to take a bird's eye view of them you see only those immediately near you. this is most striking in Lansdowne Ho: & one always desires to get upon a chair to have a view of the whole & the statues beyond. for this end I would have raised the platform at the end with steps 3 & pedestals corresponding with the piers & I would have raised the niches for statues & statues themselves. by this means the desired elevation whence to see the company wo^d be obtained the statues wo^d be raised almost wholy above the heads. ... It cannot be doubted that the statues (at least 9 in 10) are copies from great originals designed chiefly as decorations of the villas of Rome, certainly of Gods worshipped or the idol of Temples. they were placed in great hemicycles in niches or disposed on pedestals in the exterior of a Buildg: they were roughly turned out of hand accordingly they are rough originaly meant to be viewed at a distance – they have now the injuries of time & discolourings into the bargain – their real value & merit to us is chiefly as models for the sculpture & even noble decorations to architecture – but positively not as P. Knight says to be considered as furniture. to regard them otherwise or to suppose they can excite admiration in other views but for their merit of antiquity & design, or that uninstructed persons are to feel pleasure in beholding them, is affectation & cant. to bring them into an assembly of gaiety, beauty & fashion is pedantry. you might as well read a lecture on Philosophy in a ball room or introduce an anchorite at a quadrille. the incongruity holds throughout. the marble plinths pose on a parquet floor, a most distressing circumstance. the statues discoloured are opposed to highly finished walls of stuccoe painted & gilt of tender colour in which a spot would have lost the Tradesman his employment. their coarse texture is backed by red drapery of delicate texture. if this is true then all this expence of gilding might have been spared.'

A minor public building by Smirke which Cockerell admired was the Court House at Gloucester of 1814–16. Cockerell saw this in December 1821 and wrote of it: '[The] col[umn]s of Glocester Court House [are] 41 ft. 3 ins. [tall] – simplicity is delightful where the beauty of the proportions compensates for want of ornament – where proportions are very happy, ornam^t. is best omitted. col[umn]s without Entasis look ill & hollow in particular those next pilaster – the high boxes at sides unpleasant in proportion.'

Visiting in January 1824 Smirke's St. George, Brandon Hill, Bristol, of 1823, Cockerell recorded:

'it is wanton to introduce the arch in the Greek. I see it does not accord with the severity & character of the squareness peculiar to the Greek. nothing can look worse than the circular cupola or Tower, common, flat & tasteless. in this situation the Tower might have been omitted with so many steps & so distinct a position.'

On a visit to Sandhurst in June 1822 Cockerell attributed the design of the Royal Military College on stylistic grounds to Smirke. In fact it had been designed in 1807 by John Sanders (1768–1826), Soane's first pupil. Cockerell wrote of it: 'built by Smirke evidently – beautiful arch[itectur]e finely considered & disposed, but no genius whatever, no character of a Coll[eg]e of Military, no vast robust features, nothing to strike or impose. a front much like all other fronts whether a library, a Theatre, a conservatory, a mansion, an Hospital – always Temp[l]e of Minerva [i.e. the Parthenon Doric order].'

Another early Greek Revival building in a distinctly Smirke-like manner are the County Courts at Newcastle designed and built by William Stokoe in 1810–12. Cockerell visited the building in 1822 on his way back from Edinburgh. He found it 'admirably placed – seemingly order of Theseus [i.e. Greek Doric of the Theseum] but many errors – the Attic is ridiculous *unless containing a* story because cornice in Greek signifies & is synonimous with *eaves*. it is obviously a skreen to the roof, a recourse much used by Smirke & in excess. it gives an unnatural weight over the windows, heavy, evidently a subterfuge. it takes away the grace given by swell & outline. in fact it was a means of giving consequence by elevation & is the placing a pedestal on the roof instead of on the ground . . . a *slice* off Theseus same entablature order &c. – it seems to me the greek has hitherto been practised in this country with the same ignorance that Gothick was in begin[nin]g of last cent[ur]y on which Build[in]gs one cannot look without feeling that it is manque & without confessing that one may be very near the thing without success.'

In May 1821 Cockerell visited the Public Baths and Reading Room at Clifton Hot Wells which had been completed the year before from designs by Henry Hake Seward (*c.* 1778–1848). Cockerell's comment was: 'Greek bedevilled – well executed solid – mean confined – the modern always deficient in amplitude & liberality of space & quantity.' The building was demolished in 1867.

Amongst the more mannered and individual of English neo-classical architects were George Steuart (17? –1806) and Charles Heathcote Tatham (1772–1842). In 1821 Cockerell comments unenthusiastically on characteris-ic productions by each of them. Visiting Steuart's Attingham Park, near Shrewsbury, he criticized the gawky portico' for 'serving no purpose', and found its four attenuated columns of 'a disastrous proportion'. His description ends: 'meagre and tasteless beyond description. could not see interior being Sund[a]y, did not regret it.' Rookesbury in Hampshire[3] is one of Tatham's few surviving country houses. It was designed in 1821 for the Rev. W. Garnier. On 1 July that year, Cockerell called at Garnier's house in Albemarle Street and saw Tatham's plans. He noted in his diary: 'large Ho[use] 110 x 76 . . . want of proportion throughout, low heavy wanting relief in the elevations with strange pilasters or piers at angles of no archi-tecture that I know of. a front portico advances before all this.'

3. See C. Proudfoot and D. J. Watkin, 'A Pioneer of English Neo-Classicism, C. H. Tatham', *Country Life*, CLI, 1972, p. 921, pl. 11.

CHAPTER V

'Hercules with the Distaff':
A View of the Gothic Revival

COCKERELL had clear views about the propriety of the Gothic or Castle style for modern domestic architecture. He was forced to take the style seriously if only because his master, Smirke, had been responsible for two of the most prominent houses of the Revival: Lowther Castle, Westmorland, of 1806 and Eastnor Castle, Herefordshire, of 1812.

After seeing Eastnor, more Norman than Gothic, Cockerell wrote: 'a castellated mansion in these days [is] an anomaly, contradiction in terms. it is adopting the character of a fortress to a place assailable from every side, & every window. it is to make a donjon of a drawing Ro: or vice versa. it is Hercules with the distaff – effect [and] ancient patriotic associations induce its adoption. still it is a contradiction, a mockery. the household, the hospitality, the retainers, the hawking & hounds, the House filling & warming can never be reconciled with the ideas of modern economy. the[y']re as irreconcilable as the blue coat & white waistcoat with the Helmet [and] breastplate. it is to make a play scene of your house, when in the great Hall one says where are the retainers, where the band of musick, the numerous guests. – Smirke has done it with more judgem^t. than any one, the effect is great. a character of force is given. a defence might possibly be made.'

After visiting Lowther Castle in November 1823 Cockerell elaborated his views on the subject of Gothic or 'feudal' revivalism even more fully.

'The affection for the old English baronial residence is founded on aristocratical feeling & associations of anct. descent, but I cannot help attaching an idea of ridicule to these mock castles which can never fulfil the notions one has of the times in which they were built or bear any comparison to the remains of buildings of that kind, as Warwick Castle & others. they are an anomaly; affecting all the air of fortress. . . . it is an affectation of a style of buildg: suited to insecure times at a period the most peaceful & secure. it would have been as ridiculous to build an English drawing ro: residence at

Suli or in Morea. such folies do not bear reasoning upon & I think it lamentable that men of taste Adams, Wyat, Smirke, should give in to such miserable affectations which can realy only arise in family pride of possessors & in
nonsensical fanciful notions drawn from novels or *blue* books. If such a thing
were excuseable it seems to be it would be in some romantic site amidst
Hills & lakes & precipices in which a vantage ground might be taken
commanding some striking eagle view over crags & cliffs – terraces &
surprizing hardie effects might be procured from a suite of rooms easily
accessible from courts at the back. I would use the rough walling thrown
together in thick walls producing grand masses all the expence of finishings
reserved for inside. the approach should be thro' courts in which should,
be the offices, producing all that effect of vast establishm^t essential to convey
the just idea of these castles & preparing you thro' a village of offices for the
mansion itself. the anct. Houses were invariably so & the present residences
of the Pashas &c in Turkey are now so. In Turkey you approach the chief
thro' a host of dependants having passed thro' 1 & 2d. court in which you
find his horses saddled & kitchens &c active. you come to a great gallery or
corridore filled with guards some ready to start on distant errands, some a
body guard, some for the entertainm^t. of the Chief, musicians, priests,
clients &c. thro' these you reach the Lord. but how different the economy &
habits of this country where a few well dressed powered & overfed servants
in shoes & stockings supply the place of thin hardy dirty dependants. these
mighty halls are empty, mournfully silent, one discovers no obvious purpose in this magnificence but the misuse of cash & employment for ennui &
mistaken taste. after all I think I have seen nothing so well designed as Mr.
Tracey's house in style of monastic arch[itectur]e. next ranks Eastnor from
the beauty of the site, but the last of all I have seen is Lowther Castle. in
corroboration of this notion Sir E. Carrington quoted Henry VII fining
Ld [Oxford] for having so many dependents when he visited him. see
Hume.'

Cockerell was surprisingly enthusiastic about 'Mr. Tracey's house,'
Toddington Manor in Gloucestershire which his uncle, Sir Charles
Cockerell, took him to see whilst he was staying at Sezincote at Christmas
1821. Toddington is a vast mansion in the Perpendicular style designed for
himself in 1819–40 by Charles Hanbury-Tracy, later 1st Lord Sudeley.
Cockerell considered Hanbury-Tracy had an 'elegant mind' and that the
house was, for the work of 'an amateur, wonderfuly conceived and
executed.' He felt that the 'great advantage of an amateur [is that he] may

do & undo' and that 'a better & more rational taste [had been] adopted than the castellated . . . style.' He praised the 'abundant bay windows, the most delightful of all things, as Bacon says', but felt that Hanbury-Tracy 'appeared not to have conceived the plan, being chiefly subservient to exterior effect.'

Cockerell undoubtedly perceived that Toddington marked a new stage in the Gothic Revival away from mere Picturesque asymmetry to a more rational and disciplined order. The house seems to have influenced Barry's design for the Palace of Westminster.

Considering Cockerell's hostility to the feudal associations of Lowther and Eastnor he was surprisingly enthusiastic about the rather similar overtones of Cassiobury Park, Hertfordshire, which James Wyatt had remodelled for the Earl of Essex in an elaborate castellated style shortly after 1800. Visiting it in October 1825 he found it an 'excellent specimen of a great nobleman's House & hospitality in which is a very great order conspicuous throughout the establishment – there are many excellent Hints in the Taste of the House. he employs a great many hands & always doing something. he has works of all the best modern artists, Turner, Calcot, Wilkie, Landseer, Jones &c. however the faults of all modern houses is here in excess, too much stove heat, too many doors, mixture of too many tastes – too much refinement, nicknacks, conundrums & contrivances, too much of minuteness & sacrificing to these the greater considerations of Taste – a magnificent cieling above (a real work of art) neglected & overlooked, and minutiae attainable by mechanics & ordinary fellows prefered before them & recommended.' It is delightfully characteristic of Cockerell to single out for special praise the late seventeenth-century ceilings surviving from the earlier house by Hugh May (1622–1684).

His embarrassment at 'neo-feudalism' was balanced by his joy at discovering echoes of the real thing. Thus he deplored Adam's 'silk hangings' at Alnwick and longed instead to 'fit up room like Queen Mary's at Holyrood with hangings 15 ft. high & a high frieze with arms, escutcheons &c. even grained stone.' He recorded with real pleasure that 'it is said that old Percys used to pack up all hangings, tapestry, even glass windows & carry them away when they left the residence on waggons. The Percys after their return made a point of keeping up the old forms & till lately there were none but rush chairs & rush carpets.'

A form of discreet neo-feudalism which Cockerell was prepared to countenance was the enchantingly Picturesque group of estate cottages which Nash designed in 1811 at Blaise Castle. Cockerell writes of Blaise Hamlet: 'Nash has always original ideas. he recommended to Mr. Harford to build his alms Houses in a picturesque manner & in a retired spot & not in a row. he says the pride which is natural to men & makes them ashamed of receiving alms is an honorable one & should not be crushed. the bounty you afford should not be dashed by stamping these paupers with their mark of indigence. nor is it well to tarnish a benevolent motive with the blazon of a coat of arms & an inscription seting forth the liberality of the Founder. he built therefore irregular cottages with all those little penthouses for beehives, ovens &c. & irregularities which he found in peasants' cottages & they are so beautiful that it is a sight visited from Clifton & I have always called it Sweet.'

The spectacular remodelling of Windsor Castle by Sir Jeffry Wyatville (1766–1840) between 1824 and 1840 forms, with Barry's Palace of Westminster, the most memorable product of the whole Gothic Revival. Cockerell has much to say on the matter.

His first reference to Windsor on 24 September 1825 is delightfully malicious. He went with a party of friends and 'found Wyatville very civil. [He] shewed us all the draw[in]gs. [We] did not find a single room of regular or good proportions in the new suite, as if proportion signified not. the usual suite of drawing Ro[om], Lib[rar]y & Dining Ro[om] 40 x 25, 70 by 30 &c. like an ordinary country Gent[leman']s Ho[use] enlarged with a bed Ro[om] on same floor & a suite of Rooms for his personal friends & family seperate entrances &c – but nothing like chambre, antichambre, waiting chamber, ministers' Rooms, salle de Huissiers with all the parade & pomp & circumstance of a court. none of those porticoes, galleries, rooms of arms of the bodyguard, museums of art, statues of Kings, or images of great & exemplary men, no room of Waterloo, room of Blenheim, room of Victory, naval room, military, no parade of Horses, nothing chevaleresque, high or striking, poetical, literary, imaginative or gentlemanly – nothing that affects the imagination.'

It is interesting that far from criticizing Wyatville for being too romantic he is criticized for not being romantic enough! Cockerell regarded Wyatville as an architect of limited vision who 'has been eminently successful in restoring small Houses of persons of limited fortune & country gent[leme]n with the eternal set of Lib[rar]y, draw[in]g Ro[om] & din[in]g Ro[om] but scarcely a gent[lema]n. he understands much less what is royal.'

Cockerell considered James Wyatt's 'staircase no great shakes or rather many for the plaister walls are full of cracks, how ignoble plaister! St. George's chamber rather fine, how pitiable to see the King treat lightly the work of his Father & the nephew speak of his uncle's candlesticks of towers.'

James Wyatt's alterations for George III in 1796–1800 included remodelling the north front, adding a new staircase and the Blenheim Tower.

In January 1827 Cockerell returned to Windsor for the funeral of the Duke of York. He 'thought castle at distance had lost its effect by the union of many parts into few great ones by which size was lost. also the interior court uniform & undignified & not characteristic of the style in its elaborate variety & richness. think outside a castle sho[ul]d be massive & defensible, inside sho[ul]d be all ornam[en]t & elaborate with quaint carvings, Galleries, oriel windows &c. like Chambord & other French castles'.

However, on a visit to the castle later in the same year he was 'better pleased with it than before, certainly colossal throughout, rendered voluminous by subsidiary turrets, chimeys &c. disapproved the interior of quad. not understood. neither symetry nor agreable variety, gallery not calculated to view troops or attendants or pageants from balconies in Galleries. they should have been fronted with a rich detailed front, like front of his present office. cannot think he has been equally skilful in interior. no contrivance to obviate the awkwardness of polygonal direction of the rooms & gallery. cielings without skill or beauty, especially draw[in]g Ro[om] proportion of which is quite spoilt. disapprove style of Louis 14th & that of the worst the genius of England should produce something better. no sculpture but of the lowest carvers, no painting but house painting, absolutely mechanical throughout the whole building & destroying Verrio's Gallery to stamp the contempt of fine art.'

Poor Cockerell! He suffered so much through his intense visual sensitivity and his equally intense desire to establish a rich, vivid and manly renaissance of all the arts and crafts which would rival that of the golden years, the sixteenth and seventeenth centuries. This aristocratic vision was constantly being shattered by the small-minded and mercenary preoccupations of his plebeian contemporaries. In this respect Wyatville was particularly culpable. Cockerell met him at Lancaster in November 1823 and had with him a 'long tete a tete, [but] found him dry & barren, no gentleman, vulgar minded, good natured, great boaster. [He] talked of jobs, payment of his acco[un]ts & pecuniary affairs with his employers.'

After Wyatt and Smirke, Wilkins was the principal purveyor of Gothic country houses to the nobility and gentry. Of few buildings did Cockerell entertain quite such a low opinion as Dalmeny Park, Linlithgowshire, designed by Wilkins for Lord Rosebery in 1814 (Pl. 11). He visited it in August 1822 in the company of Lord Elgin and found it 'totaly irregular & confused' and not even made 'extraordinarily pictoresque to supply want of symetry'. He continues: 'running much to chimney shafts like handles to the Ho: like a stalactyte Ho: reversed – all the forms & proportions disagreable, particul[ar]ly windows of no other kind save oriel – totaly barbarous – surprised to find Grecian interior with so much Gothick exterior. all piers in middle of ro: making them smaller, heavy circles in cielings. – stone passages & staircase, a thing never done by ancients. no intelligence of the mode of fitting [i.e. furnishing] practised by the ancients. saw the silk had seen at Dowbiggins – clumsy ill conceived & contrived throughout – this is a barbarous & capricious mode of architecture referable to no rules of proportions of principles of the beautiful in arch[itectur]e & admired chiefly by its association with a good historical period & somewhat interesting from the quaint elaborate style, but to be discarded by those who study the beautiful – convenience can be the only excuse offered it.'

Nor did Wilkins' exercises in the Gothic taste at Cambridge appeal any more to the severe Cockerell. In October 1825 he visited King's College, where he 'totaly disapproved of all Wilkin's proceedings, narrow Huddled ill contrived ill conceived. the whole system is conceived in a servile spirit of imitation & that of a limited period [i.e. the Perpendicular] – also without an extended acquaintance even with that – for he is always the same. Kings Hall is a gross imitation of Crosby Hall. there are no open porticoes, no staircases of merit, on the contrary nothing worse contrived – the rooms are ill lighted, all sacrificed to the exterior.'

CHAPTER VI

A Visit to Paris

O N SATURDAY, 2 October 1824, Cockerell sailed from Dover to Calais in a small party which included two of his younger unmarried sisters, Susan and Louisa. One of the first buildings they visited in Paris was the Invalides. Cockerell preferred the sober arcuated courtyards by Libéral Bruant to the magnificent chapel by J. H. Mansart. He wrote of it: 'pleased with fine proportion & simplicity of the arches of first court & ill effect of subsequent ornaments of coats of mail for dormer windows, the furious horses at the angel (sic) of cornice as acroteria, purpose to which sculpture should never be applied in such confusion & dimension. admired chapel just completed – absurd baldachino, flat & ill effect, spotted gilding.' Later he found some harsher things to say about the chapel: 'architecture of Invalides is purely ornamental. it is a mask put up against the building having no reference to the anatomy of the construction & not describing it in any way. there is no constructive sense or understanding in it & [it] is calculated to dazzle the eye only & not satisfy the mind. it is directly contrary to the spirit of Greek arch[itectur]e, or rather of sense & nature, and the first of all rules, that the decoration should seem to grow out of the natural form and construction.' It is a fascinating comment on the complexities of architectural theory that Cockerell should here justify classical architecture using exactly the same arguments with which Pugin was so soon to defend Gothic.

Cockerell amplifies his sister's view of the Invalides: 'Louise says truly it is frenchified' – by pointing out that 'there are no two intercol[umniation]s alike. sometimes col[umn]s are coupled, sometimes stradling & occasioning a difficulty of construction & consequently liability to decay.' However, he thought that the 'building seems well put together.'

He visited on 8 October not only the Invalides but St Sulpice, and felt that both churches shared the same defect in the handling of the orders so as to produce an effect of complexity without coherence. He disapproved the elliptical vault and thought that as a whole the church had 'little merit except its vastness & its façade in which are some fine lines.' With its twin classical towers, the façade might be considered to bear some relation to Cockerell's Hanover Chapel, but Cockerell found 'the arch[itectur]e of towers also corrupt. pediment & circular tower on this.' As we shall see in chapter VIII his views on the merits of this church changed over the years.

On the same day he 'visited Notre Dame at time of evening services, saw mummeries of processions, incense &c.' and noted particularly the 'harsh organ, [and] fine effect of serpent.' Earlier in the day he had visited Ste. Geneviève and the chapel of the Ecole Militaire. Soufflot's magnificent church of Ste. Geneviève, restored to Christian worship again after its desecration as the Panthéon from 1794 to 1814, was a programmatic monument in the early history of neo-classicism. It was intended to be an exercise in rational structure based on load-bearing columns and was approached through a vast Corinthian portico of twenty-two columns. Cockerell, however, was 'struck with the poverty of Ste. Geneviève in facade, the maigneur of the col[umn]s, enormous width of the intercol[umniation], congregation of col[umn]s at the ends, poverty of cornice, platitude of the enrichments, Fronton &c. a poor doorway & a style of arch[itectur]e by no means correspond[in]g with the vastness of the scale. Portico 112 by 36 deep. a congregation might listen to a sermon under its cover.' Inside the church, Cockerell 'was much more sensible in this visit of the beauty of the plan, its classical intention & the infinite richness & variety of the views, in particular of the entrance this may be remarked. but the cielings of stone descending in the pointed spandrils leaving the little pavillions over the square projection of the col[umn]s is weak & looks as if a window were blowing up the air like a parachute & in the same affected hardiesse which prompted the attempt of the dome & will be followed with the same failures after a time. the great windows of 20 lights is a striking example of disproportion (See my chapter thereon) and so lessens the rest of the arch[itectur]e as to have destroyed my former impression of the beauty of this building.'

Another temple-style monument to neo-classical stylophily was Brongniart's Bourse of 1808. There were many features of this bold cube, such as 'the depth of Front Portico', which Cockerell admired, though he 'did not like attic'. He praised the 'beautiful staircase, [and] Interior Hall 100 x 55, Hypethral [i.e. top-lit], [with] floors & roof in pottery & Plaister.' His account continues: 'visited cieling done in plaister & sculptured like stone, would not have sufficient effect by any other mode, rainwater pipes well contrived with great appareil for lighting – whole covered in iron of construction & copper tiles imitation of antique superbly done. room with octagon ceiling well [done]. large coved ro[om] beyond not agreable in cieling. there are 14 col[umns] in front, 20 at sides. well raised on pedestal.'

Amongst the most striking of all neo-classical contributions to Paris was the series of dramatic 'barrières' designed by Ledoux in 1785–89. These bleak visionary monuments, many of them incorporating the then revolutionary Greek Doric order, had naturally an immediate attraction for Cockerell. On 9 October he records having seen two out of the whole number of forty-six. One of these two was, in some ways, the finest of them all: the Barrière de la Villette or de St. Martin. He wrote justly: 'there is a prodigious greatness in the style of these monuments & they are placed with great advantage.'

On 18 October, Cockerell 'went by an order of Mr. Visconti . . . to see new apartments of the minister of finance, M. de Villette . . . des Tailleurs archit[ect], the most expensive & tasty production of the day.' The Ministère des Finances, built in 1824 from designs by F. H. Destailleur and L. T. J. Visconti, was a continuation of Percier and Fontaine's Rue de Rivoli with its round-arched colonnade on the ground floor and its continuous metal balconies on the first and third floors.

Cockerell also saw the remarkable iron dome which F. J. Belanger had added in 1805–13 to the Halle au Blé. As designed and built in 1763–9 by Legrand and Molinos, the vast circular Halle had been provided with a wooden roof which had been destroyed by fire in 1802. Belanger's roof, calculated by Cockerell to have a diameter of one hundred and twenty feet, was regarded as one of the triumphs of the age. It cost 700,000 francs and was, alas, demolished in 1855.

Other works of engineering admired by Cockerell in Paris were the bridges over the Seine. One of the most remarkable of these was the Pont de Neuilly constructed in 1766–72 by Perronnet. In the design of this revolutionary and influental bridge, Perronnet contrived to diminish the size of the piers whilst increasing the span of the arches. It was an austere unadorned monument with plain and solid parapets. Cockerell admired its 'beautiful simplicity' and the presence 'in parapet [of] a stone said to be 42 ft. long', but added as a loyal Englishman, 'but our Ballustred Bridges are certainly beautiful.' He was also attracted by the Pont d'Iéna executed under Napoleon in 1806–13 from designs by Lamandé in a bold Empire Style. He was particularly 'struck with the cornice as forming the chief relief & beauty of this bridge, seting off its great simplicity with uncommon delight.' He particularly admired the 'lightness of its piers, [and] plaines of parapet.'

On the whole Cockerell was not impressed by modern French architecture. He makes the fascinating observation that 'the french have had no arch[itectur]e since the school of Louis 14 & 15, for Percier & Fontaine have done nothing but fit up – there is nothing but the Hotel Marboeuf which can be called modern arch[itectur]e. in the meantime, 30 years, the school of Adam & Wyat & Smirke have done much in this country worthy [of] observation of which the French have no idea.' Absence seems to have made Cockerell's heart grow fonder! But it is interesting that he should single out for special praise the Hôtel Marbeuf. Built by Lassurance or J. J. Gabriel, it had been acquired by Joseph Bonaparte in 1803, but what attracted Cockerell's attention was the remodelling of the entrance front and the interiors in a dazzling Empire style by Legrand and Molinos in 1789. Like Paulina Borghese's subsequent residence, the Hôtel de Charost (now the British Embassy), the Hôtel Marbeuf was evidently a key monument of the proto-Empire style, and its destruction in 1886 was a major disaster. Cockerell wrote of 'the prettiest arrangement & proportion of rooms I have seen at Paris – salon 22 by 28, very gay & agreable, pretty cieling coved.' This room, and the library, were illustrated in Krafft and Ransonette's celebrated publication of 1801–2 of *Plans . . . des plus belles Maisons et des Hôtels construits à Paris.* With its colonnade, sphinxes and colossal caryatids the façade evidently recalled that of the Théâtre Feydeau designed in the same year by the same architects.

However, Cockerell did not view the Théâtre Feydeau with quite the same rapture. He does not mention the celebrated curved exterior with its row of seven round-headed windows divided by Erectheum caryatids but remarks of the interior that it 'cannot be called in good arch[itectur]e. it bears not the test of reasoning or any classical view of the subject. [it] may have been done by an ingenious but not a reasoning or classical mind.' He criticized 'the great [proscenium?] arch bearing on such a small order as if to crush it . . . the nearness of the stage & consequent precipitancy of the boxes & height of the theatre, cieling a foolish star meaning nothing.' He considered that there was 'too much green used in this Theatre & [that] oriental alabaster & gold do not ally well – looks like a cork model gilt.' What most distressed him was the decision by Legrand and Molinos to articulate the interior with the classical orders. 'The attempts to make the orders subservient to Theatres subjects them to many inconveniences & affects solidity which must be destroyed & is incompatible within a great vase of noble arch[itectur]e. I think nothing but galleries or balconies will do.'

He had no higher opinion of the Théâtre Français constructed from 1787–90 as the south-west wing of the Palais Royal from designs by Victor Louis, architect of the magnificent theatre at Bordeaux.

His judgement on the Théâtre Français was that 'this theatre is one of the striking examples of the ecarte from rational constructive arch[itectur]e practised in time of Louis XV. Why', he asked, 'in the present day that we have attempted to (ramener) recal[l] arch[itectur]e to its original simplicity of construction, has the theatre francais rebuilt so lately been exactly imitated from the old or former theatre[?]'

On his visit Cockerell was able to meet many of the architects who were busy transforming Paris. Visconti was one of the more important but he also met Hittorff. He records on 19 October: 'called on Hittorf, rec[ieve]d me politely, told him it was a great object with me to secure the little merit I had in the discovery of the arch[itectur]e of [the temple of] Jup[iter] Olym[pius] at Girgenti. He assured me that he had attributed the discovery of it to me in his work,[1] that he agreed in my view of it, &c. &c. satisfied me fully.' Another archaeologist-architect whom Cockerell met was F. Mazois who published the *Palais de Scaurus* in 1819 and the *Ruines de Pompei* in 1812–38. On 18 October, Cockerell 'called on Mazois, found him more deaf, saw Mad[am]e & 2 children [and] his old Father who lives with him & his sister. going on with his work, shewed me many private Houses, villas, &c. projets after Italian model, open & ill calculated to our climate – sacrificing interior to exterior, always symetric.' These must have been the minimal arcuated projects all too familiar from the pages of Durand's *Précis des leçons ... donnés à l'école Polytechnique*. Mazois 'defended the drainage of Paris & objected to sewers as inapplicable to the Seine, & only so to London because of tides.'

Amongst the other architects Cockerell met were A. M. Chatillon, whose church of Notre Dame de Bercy he visited, Auguste Famin, J. N. Huyot, M. P. Gauthier, Surveyor of Hospitals, and the stage-designer Ciceri. He met the Baron Vivant Denon on more than one occasion and passed some time at 'Durand's gallery of bronzes, vases, antiquities of all periods, fine M[ar]cAntonios, faience which I am told are for sale.' On the 22nd he 'went to Hotel de Ville to dine with the Prefet [who] had the complaisance to invite Chatillon & Gaut[h]ier to meet me. I sat by the Countess, a sumptuous dinner – Barriere, de Fresne, Daubanton, M. Walkner, M. de l'Isle – very complimentary to me on Jup[iter] Olympius, my Travels, &c.'

1. J. A. Hittorff, *Architecture antique de la Sicile*, Paris, 1826.

Returning to England on 29 October, he noted in his diary: 'remarked the smallness of all objects, buildings, want of design, without grace of brick & wood but great cleanliness, small houses all in comfort, all well off – new painted with small gardens – bien etre universel. men looked pale, none of that rich warm color so common in France . . . struck with the width of the streets of London, beauty of squares as if we had deprived the houses of courts in favour of the streets – the trottoir – abundance of gas light, want of design in shop fronts – quantity of glazing. arrived at Westbourne abo[ut] ½ past 7. found all well. Mr. Boyle & Pepys dining there. everything looking exquisitely clean & happy.' He noted again the following day the 'bad arch[itectur]e of new streets & monstrous irregularities, showing that this is not the natural soil of taste.'

Cockerell would probably have agreed, on reflection, that nowhere is taste 'natural': it has always to be acquired. He did feel, however, that 'It must be owned that France has given the mode in arch[itectur]e and fine arts in northern & western Europe. It is a greater centre than England can be from its geographical position. the love of imitation & ease procured to the mind by catching at what others have produced has been inducem-[en]t with other countries to adopt everything French. even so original a man as our Wren has copied age of Louis XIV & so no doubt in former times Henry IV gave the ton. by a sort of prevention France has been allowed the lead in all fine arts & only the force of genius here & there in other countries has sometimes emancipated us from them.' He markedly disapproved, however, modern French architecture 'taken from a corrupt style', i.e. Roman, '& all the varieties which the arch has given rise to.' The French are now on Roman & the renaissance – & the Greek in sculpture & painting.' He disliked their tendency 'to overlook many other noble models' and thought that 'nothing can be more dry or less effect than all that has been done at Compiegne [by Gabriel] & here [i.e. Paris].' On the other hand, the 'model of Louis 14 is extraordinary, has great merit & bears a stamp of grandeur very considerable.'

In other words, exactly as with English architecture, he preferred the richness of the seventeenth century to the dryness of the eighteenth-century neo-classical reaction. The French love of symmetry he saw sometimes as part of this dryness, sometimes as a virtue. 'With them symetry is everything – they have no idea of planting a House according to the natural slope & grace of the Ground in the manner of the English parks – they carry their town Houses into the country with them, nor have the French any conception of a rural life, or that of an English gent[lema]n.' On another occasion

H

he wrote: 'The Symetry of all the arrangements whether of gardens, architecture or roads & woods is as a general observation very striking to an English eye in France – as our extreme irregularity must be to them. I doubt not that we have carried our picturesque mania & love of irregularity in forms of architecture & landscape much too far, so that the form of architecture has often a caprice which is contrary to its genius.'

CHAPTER VII

Painting, Sculpture and Music

Painting

KNOWING less about painting than about architecture, Cockerell was more prepared to praise contemporary painters than contemporary architects. The apocalyptic John Martin (1789–1854) was a special favourite, partly because of his elaborate architectural backgrounds. The bold romance, dramatic imagination and vigour of his works somehow echoed Cockerell's plea for an architecture more gripping than that commonly associated with the Greek Revival. There are several references in the diaries to paintings by Martin but the finest description is that prompted by the sight of "Adam and Eve entertaining Raphel" which he saw exhibited at the British Institution in March 1823:

'Martin's Eden. wonderfuly poetical conception of the delights of landscape, of all the varieties of lawn & dale, of pool & lake, islet & mound & glen & wood, forest & mountain, precipice & waterfall plain & sunny bank & terrific elevation clothed in eternal snows, an atmosphere ecstatic serene & clear, that the eye expands in beholding the space & infinity described in the picture. in the foreground is a deep cool grotto in which are Adam & Eve discoursing with Raphael. they are strangely drawn but round about are flowers in gorgeous profusion & fruits, spotty sugar plums. Some oriental plants are introduced with great judgement & effect. Martin has a vast genius but is deficient in taste & instruction.'

In the same month Cockerell went to view Haydon's 'Raising of Lazarus' at the Egyptian Hall in Piccadilly. He wrote of it: 'Haydon's picture contains parts of extraordinary merit & execution as well as fine conception. the Lazarus, the Magdalen, the brother & mother of Lazarus nearest the scribes. the Christ as usual fails. his placidity is not the placidity of intelligence & divinity but of insipidity. his head has extraordinary shape, narrow, the neck thin & like a neck cloth. it has none of the sorrow nor the suffering of Christ, none of the fasting & praying. it is less intelligent than any other head in the picture. the other sister of Lazarus in the foreground with the pocket handkerchief is trite & common place . . . the distance of the picture is well managed, it imposes. this is vast genius.'

There are no further references to Haydon and only one to Wilkie. He records in June 1825 that 'Wilkie is suffering under a nervous malady from having worked too hard. for 4 months he has been unable to do anything in painting whatever – cannot fix his mind – cannot read more than 20 pages a day – like a soul on the borders of Styx he is unable to occupy himself or find rest. Wilkie has reason to be out of sorts, has lost his mother & 2 brothers, his intended Bro[ther] in law died in his House, a brother has turned mad & left 4 children on Wilkie's hands.'

Despite his enthusiasm for the grand manner, only to be expected from an architect with his classical training, Cockerell had the breadth of imagination necessary to be able to admire Turner. In this, it seems, he differed from that great neo-classical patron, Thomas Hope. He records his marvellously sensitive reactions to Turner in 1821:

'saw Mr. Fawkes' collect[io]n of draw[in]gs by Turner. great Poet. the accessories exceedingly characteristic – in view of the ho[use] had given the young ladies looking out of the wind[o]ws & a kite on the lawn, a hare in the foreground scudding across. the air of his pictures look[s] beaming with light, heat & vegetation. they seem to breathe the exhalations after a shower on a summer's day. a ship of war taking in stores wonderfully characteristic. at first it seems like the perspective of a fortress with towers at the terminations – you discover it is the poop & cabin &c. wh[ic]h gives that effect. the Colliseum in wh[ic]h he has given all that mystery wh[ic]h the view of that ever gives. Venice, the Rialto in which all one ever saw of Venice is recalled, Canaletto, the masques, Gondola, an old debaucher, a Venetian noble . . . all the splendour of Venetian commerce, silks, velvets, gold & colouring of their school – Turner is a great poet.'

In May 1821, visiting Sir John Leicester's Gallery he makes the single splendid observation, 'Turner transcendant.' A year or so earlier he had commissioned Turner to execute a watercolour of the temple at Aegina based on rough sketches drawn by himself. Thornbury records that the sum of thirty-five guineas which Turner asked for this 'was thought by Mr. Cockerell to be an exorbitant demand from an old friend.'[1]

A minor artist admired by Cockerell was John Frederick Lewis, R.A. (1805–1876). His later work has pre-Raphaelite overtones and was much

---

1. W. G. Thornbury, *The Life of J. M. W. Turner, R.A.*, 2 vols, 1862, vol. 1, p. 390. Thornbury also notes that Cockerell was one of Turner's executors.

admired by Ruskin. In April 1826 Cockerell 'called on Lewis & saw a pretty portrait with landscape, a beautiful combination of the two in wh[ic]h tho perhaps deficient in taste there is great truth, no vice, much colour & novelty – but portrait painting is evidently not his genius. he does well therefore to support it by landscape.'

Lewis came to mind on 1 October the same year, when Cockerell was travelling cheerfully through the Welsh landscape. In a beautiful passage in the diaries we read:

'much delighted with autumnal tints of the Hills & vegetation on the road to Lampeter, especialy with the heath which was rich deep green, pink flowers, a yellow okerish blossomed faded & the black of shade forming a harmony inconceivably rich & beautiful in the banks of the road. the briar & blackbery is admirably in color, form & poetry. the leaf is especialy fine in form & the rich deep purple of the ripe berry & the crude red of the unripe often on the same stalk are especialy favorable to pictoresque – it strikes me painters do not enough observe these beauties which would tell greatly. I think the seasons might be represented in a rural simple manner with children as decorative painting in a room, by Lewis for instance. Autumn might be children picking blackberries, their little sun burnt faces & hands somewhat stained with the fruit, a wanton abundant look might be given to the groups – back ground the orchard, the trees laden with rosy golden fruit as we now see them propt with sticks to prevent the bows breaking.'

It is interesting to see Cockerell and Ruskin united in their admiration for Turner and Lewis and to see Cockerell anticipating the near hysterical attention to brightly coloured detail of the Pre-Raphaelites in, for example, his description of 'the rich deep purple of the ripe berry & the crude red of the unripe often on the same stalk.'

One of Cockerell's closest friends was his exact contemporary Simon Jacques Rochard, who was born in Paris in 1788 and who had settled in London where he became successful as a painter of portrait miniatures. It may have been through Rochard that Cockerell came to know Géricault of whose work he was a keen admirer. There exist a number of tracings by Géricault of drawings of the Bassae frieze which seem to have been based on plates in a book published in Rome in 1814 entitled *Bassorilievi Antichi della Grecia o sia Fregio del Tempio di Apollo Epicurio ... designato ... da Gio. Maria Wagner, ed ... Ferdinando Ruschweyh.* It is natural enough that on his visit to London in 1820–21 Géricault would wish to meet the original discoverer of the Bassae frieze. Cockerell's descriptions of Géricault constitute the only known references to him by one of his English friends. The first reference occurs on 8 April 1821: 'Gericault and Rochard called. smoked in my garden.' On 24 November Cockerell 'went in even[in]g to see Gericault lithographs – was much struck with the uncommon energy of his works. at the same time the mind he shows in the pathetic, the paralitic woman, the piper & poor beggar – when works of art attain their utmost perfection they are eminently calculated to awaken thoughts of energy and virtue.'

In the following month Cockerell records: 'bid adieu to Gericault on Tuesday. great admiration of his talent. his modesty so unusual & remarkable in a Frenchman, his deep feeling of pity, the pathetique at same time vigour, fire & animation of his works – solemn *tetro* at same time. profound and melancholy. sensible. singular life – like that of the savages we read of in America. lying torpid days & weeks then rising to violent exertions. riding, tearing, driving, exposing himself to heat, cold, violence of all sorts. came to England chiefly to abstract himself from the idlness & no. of persons. company – fear he is in a bad way – often said that England was the best place for study he had seen. the air contributed & the habits of the People– . Gericault has not produced 10 works before the Publick. yet his reputation is great everywhere – Remark that a name derives not from the number but the excellence of works – therefore we lose ourselves if we drible away attention on 1000 things and adopt a method that will dry up our faculties.'

Cockerell also met Delacroix on his visit to London in 1825. He and Rochard dined with Cockerell on 10 June and Cockerell records: 'de la Croix says Ingres has l'air glaciale – a good phrase descriptive of that coldness the phisiognomy takes by contemplation – particularly that of artists, very often.' Cockerell notes a few days later that he went with Delacroix and Rochard to look at the Marquess of Stafford's collection at Cleveland House. This note, incidentally, establishes for the first time that Delacroix had visited this celebrated gallery.

Although Cockerell was enthusiastic about the works of some of his contemporaries there are few sustained references in his diaries to works by the old masters. In May 1824 he upholds a view characteristic of the most austere phase of neo-classicism but hardly one which he can have maintained for very long. He affirms that he is 'persuaded that the purest sources of art are in the earliest works, more of poetry less of convention commonplace & manner – works of Cimabue, Giotto, early Greek when objects significant were placed & speaking a sort of Hieroglyphic poetry. after that a common-place loose style, mechanical, when painters cease to be Poets & became workmen.'

This approach accounts for his unfavourable judgement on Sebastiano del Piombo's 'Raising of Lazarus' (1517–19), now in the National Gallery. Cockerell inspected this vast Michelangelesque canvas on 15 April 1823 when it was in the collection of John Julius Angerstein. He wrote: '[I] cannot agree in the immense value of Raising of Lazarus. the action seems double. Christ is in the moment of performing the miracle, but Lazarus has been revived at least 10 minutes, more than half his wrappers are already loosened & those immediately around have recovered the shock of surprize & are congratulating him & each other on the event. in the distance are some discoursing on the miracle, plainly showing that the event has passsd. the trite notion of holding noses is introduced. I should say that the pomp of design & elaborate execution, truth of the heads & drawing & colour, in short the pedantry of academy prevailed in the mind of Sebastiano del Piombo by much over the poetry & dramatic feeling of his art. the figure of Lazarus is a remarkable instance of the scientific draw[in]g & muscolatura, & that of the Christ of fine position & grand composition, also the heads around remarkable for truth & sometimes colour. it seems to me quite in the pedantic character of the French school to have induced Buonaparte to offer such immense sum for that picture. it is a fraud. Haydon tho' full of errors & bad taste has more poeticaly conceived the action.'

Cockerell's observations, as so often, are so challenging that they send the modern reader back to the works of art or the buildings described. The comparison between Sebastiano del Piombo's and Haydon's treatment of the same subject matter is surely an arresting one. If a man of Cockerell's extreme intelligence and sensibility could prefer Haydon with all his obvious faults to Sebastiano with his equally obvious virtues then, we feel, it is time for us to inspect and clarify our own easy assumptions. As a romantic Cockerell was distrustful of the academic note he detected in Sebastiano's blind worship of Michelangelo's figure drawing: and yet who could be more merciless than Cockerell when he discovered errors of scholarship in the works of his fellow architects?

He could also admire the elegant Mannerist work of Francesco Parmigianino (1503–1540). After spending an evening looking over etchings by him in 1822 he noted perceptively: 'Parmegiano's style, grace, ornamental, voluminous. his single figures & small groupes are surprizing & best suited to sculpture. I think Jean Goujon & the French School studied Parmegiano.'

The singularly attractive account of Claude's seaport scenes in April 1823 will be referred to elsewhere in this book for the light it throws on the design of the Hanover Chapel. Here is the whole lively and evocative account:

'went with S.P.C. [i.e. his father] to see Angerstein's pictures . . . much flattered at Claude's pictures & finding in 2 of the 5 pictures in this collection the idea of the two turrets repeated at the entrance of a building as in my chapel. I have little doubt that the idea of this adoption arose in my mind from having seen these pictures & engravings. in these wonderful pictures one feels the balmy rosy atmosphere of the Mediterranean, that agreable air . . . which I so well remember in those parts. the ripple of the water & one feels the movement of the ships & waves. his arch[itectur]e tho in bad style, profile & perspective very often is that which conveys as much as possible the idea of pleasant palaces & nobles dwellings, loggia portico, hanging gardens over the sea, vine bowers, terraces with orange trees in pots ranged along . . . they are enchanting. when painting arrives at this perfection a moral & a positive pleasure are excited. the mind is soothed & transported to the scene & to me, half a mediterranean, where my earliest days of liberty were spent, few pleasures can exceed this.'

Sculpture

In 1807 Lord Elgin installed the sculptures of the Parthenon in a shed at the back of his house in Park Lane. This extraordinary event roused the interest of some though by no means all artists. The young Cockerell was one of those who, like Haydon, applied for permission to make drawings of the sculpture.[2] These were done before his departure for his Grand Tour in April 1810. The impact of Greek sculpture on his emotions is powerfully conveyed by his reactions to seeing the casts of the Aegina pedimental sculpture installed in his Literary and Philosophical Institution at Bristol in February 1825:

'greatly struck with the sight of my Aegina casts. consider them calculated greatly to inflame an artists imagination – where else can be seen such a groupe of living statues – their vigour, energy & beautiful drawing. – I enjoyed a day dream illustrative of their beauty & history there – in a

2. See W. St. Clair, *Lord Elgin and the Marbles*, Oxford, 1967, pl. VII.

lecture room sufficiently large to receive the groupe & pediment compleat abo[ut] 7ft. from floor. above the spectators a kind of moveable glass light moving by clock work casting a strong light & revolving so as to give all the variety as from sunrising to sunset, occasioning a great variety of light & shade & views of the figures. in the first instance all these covered with a curtain – the lecturer with his back to curtain would describe Aegina, the gulf, the surrounding country, something of its history. of our curiosity objects, history of excavation, exhibit drawing of the island, views of the Temple first distant, then nearer, elevation of Temple restored. then the curtain would rise & exhibit the statues, the light would revolve & then a critical dissertation on the style, composition &c. would be read. I cannot doubt such an exhibition in London would produce money & fame if I had time to attend to it.'

It is impossible not to see in Cockerell's astonishing day-dream the birth of the concept of 'Son et lumière'; and the present writer has stressed in another book how much this concept was anticipated in the neo-classical mania for living in museums.

Cockerell thought he detected in Michelangelo's sculpture something of the roughness and vigour he so much appreciated in the early Greek sculpture of Bassae and Aegina. In March 1823 he saw the uncompleted tondo of the Holy Family, or Taddei Madonna, which had been acquired the year before by Sir George Beaumont. 'Great treat at Sir G. Beaumonts', he recorded on 28 March, '– the holy Family of M. Angelo. more striking in its unfinished state than if entirely compleated. the parts of greatest beauty & interest are brought out & wrought with the very soul of love & genius. the inferior are left but sketched or scarcely discernible or in the native rock. the subject seems growing from the marble & emerging into life. it assumes by degrees its shape, features from an unformed mass. as it were you trace & watch its birth from the sculptor's mind as you would an animal in its birth, the chicken breaking thro' its shell. I have seen nothing but this that conveys the idea in the Greek epigram of a sculptor who says I have no merit but discovering the form which lies within the marble. one feels in beholding it to desire still to go on discovering, still to disclose more. It would be a curious metaphysical question to trace the pleasure which derives from an unfinished sketch & which is confessed by all the world – doubtless M.A. knew this well & calculated on the value of his works as not lessened by it. admiration mixed with regret – if "he had finished it what a fine thing it would have been – was he disgusted with its failure, did he cut too deep or make mistake, did he die prematurely in the progress of the work, was he idle." he knew the mind would trace the progress of the sculptor's mind with more interest . . . [if it entered] into the pursuit with the artist. he sees the unformed rock beside the half finished work, he feels & confesses the difficulty of the art. the contrast convinces him of it, the contrast too gives additional effect to the work. Set a spectator before a finished work, he compares it with its prototype, nature – he finds it inferior – but show him first a wet or plain canvas, let him watch the artist who out of this blank creates a living groupe & animates a vacancy – he will confess there is merit & his mind enters into the contest or pursuit.'

This perceptive and, of course, intensely romantic appreciation of Michelangelo explains why he found the sculpture of Canova so unacceptable. His views on Canova have been quoted in an earlier chapter but we are now in a position to understand them in their context. What he said in 1815 was that 'Canova by the very nice & laboured finish he gives to his works has deceived and captivated all the world, nobody ever *worked* the marble as he does. his is certainly art, but is nothing but art – & Tasso says that is truly art where only art is not seen. One single idea of grace he has & . . . he puts the soft & tender into everything, man, woman & child . . . when he attempts the sublime he is perfectly absurd . . . Canova is no poet.'

It was Flaxman to whom Cockerell handed the laurels, Flaxman to whom he devotes as much space in the diaries as to any other artist or architect living or dead, Flaxman whom he considered 'as far superior [to Canova] as a poet in the comprehension & elevation of his art as "Hyperion to a Satyr".' In January 1824 Cockerell asked Flaxman, then in his seventieth year, 'why he had not illustrated sacred history. he said because he had not been employed . . . Mrs. Naylor had employed him on Homer, Mr. Hope on Dante – these are the works by which he will live and here is a striking example of the efficacy of patronage . . . clearly the fruit of Flaxman's life as an artist are those works.' However, in November Cockerell records: 'Flaxman had received £600 for the composition of Athamas and Io – but the marble, time and expences had cost so much more to Flaxman that this work "had beggered him" (his own phrase).' On 26 April Cockerell notes: 'Saw at Flaxman's a beautiful composition of a monum[en]t to 2 charitable ladies put up in Yorkshire[3] – this is his best manner, another to a widow & 6 orphans done in marble 20 years ago but never put up.'

---

3. Perhaps this is the monument of 1799 to members of the Smyth family in St Peter's church, Kirkthorpe, Yorkshire.

Cockerell was moved by the grace and piety[4] not only of Flaxman's works but also of his character as a man. On 18 September 1824, he took Flaxman and his friend Brøndsted on a visit to his as yet uncompleted Hanover Chapel. He records:

'Brondstedt was delighted with Flaxman and was struck with the agreableness of his person, countenance & manner – the extraordinary activity of the mind in a person so unhappily formed by nature. his notion that the noble pursuits of the mind are to form the occupation of those blessed souls who are to inhabit Paradise & where they are to attain in them that perfection which we vainly seek here. he said it should appear so by the revelations but on questioning him I found he could point out no passage, but by inference ... his benevolence & exact integrity in all his sentiments & dealings very remarkable. his love and kindly friendship – he would not put on his hat in my chapel tho' not finished. his voice in contemplating the build[in]g betrayed the tenderness of his piety.'

Cockerell was always ready to listen to Flaxman's views. He notes on 7 November 1824:

'Flaxman says truly one may collect too many materials & authorities, & habituate oneself to rely too little on ones own resources. he accuses the French of this. He was pleased with my quotation from "as you like it", "Base authority from books." when I told him how much his originality had been copied & appreciated he said they would do well to seek those beauties as I have done in the works of God.'

Cockerell welcomed Flaxman's opinions on architecture as much as those on sculpture and notes in January 1824 that, 'Flaxman discoursed very learnedly upon anc[ien]t architecture.' In the following month we read: 'I showed Flaxman my views of Greece. expressed himself much pleased. disapproved the overhanging of entablature in an angular view of Doric Temples, also small projection of cornice – quoted Stothard who said it looked like a hat with brim cut off.' On the visit to the Hanover Chapel later in the year, Flaxman 'admired the fitness which he said was the Greek compliment & the highest he thought he could make, one he had made to

4. Cockerell seems to anticipate Pugin's opinion that, 'Had Flaxman lived a few years later, he would have been a great Christian artist' (*An Apology for the Revival of Christian Architecture in England*, 1843, p. 42, n. 26).

no other arch[itectu]re. approved ionic for ecclesiastical purposes. disapproved Smirke's Doric in the Theatre.'

On 3 March 1825, Cockerell called on Flaxman to inspect progress on the chimney-piece for his new dining room at the Grange. A melancholy but beautiful note in his diary reads:

> 'found he had done little to Baring's work, very feeble & slow, his lamp is expiring, little fruit can be expected from so old a stock however golden its former productions – his religious, learned & contemplative mind is too little of this world to feel powerfully the attractions of art & this will still diminish as he draws nigher to the object of his thoughts.'

Flaxman died on 7 December 1826 and Cockerell, as an act of piety, wrote a charming note on him for the *St. James's Chronicle*.[5] It would be uncharacteristic of Cockerell, however, to lavish unqualified praise on any artist, and it is not surprising to find a memorandum in his diary in 1823 in which Flaxman's lectures as Professor of Sculpture at the Royal Academy are heavily censured:

> 'Flaxman's lectures are literaly but the exposition of beautiful drawings. there are no analytical or critical definition, no luminous explanations of the principles of design amongst the ancients or moderns, none of that poetry or perception in his lectures which are so abundantly displayed in his works. so true is it that the critic & the Poet are separate beings not to be united. a beautiful work is performed by a magical operation – it is madness, a charm which vanishes when it is attempted to define it. I have seldom heard a lecture from which I gathered less. generaly one is disappointed in his lectures & one's opinion of him as an artist is diminished but as a man he is endeared to one, his great piety, his purity & simplicity of mind, his great benevolence, or what he often averts to himself as the charities of society, his modesty too is so remarkable that I have some doubt whether he has not restrained himself from giving his notions of principles on this account. as Wellesley said very neatly he does not illustrate truths by his ideas of principles. in him exists what I have remarked universaly in genius of arts, which is a mind which like a fine coloured mirror reflects all things in the most favorable light & the most beautiful point of view. Desnoyers who does not understand English

5. Cockerell's letter, signed 'PALLADIO', appears in the issue for 7 to 9 December, 1826.

observed on his eternal recurrence to the word beautiful, "Je l'ai conte sept fois dans une minute".'

It must have been a great pleasure for Cockerell late in life to co-operate with Professor Donaldson in the design of the Flaxman Gallery at University College, London. Here was displayed Flaxman's collection of casts of his own works in a setting where, in the words of a contemporary critic, 'The architectural arrangements and decorations contribute effectively to the harmony of the scene, and the spectator becomes impressed with the feeling that he is in the presence of the artistic spirit, whose immortal genius is so well expressed in the works around.'[6]

Of that great triumvirate of Regency sculptors, Rossi, Chantrey and Westmacott, Cockerell had a very low opinion. He called on Rossi in January 1822, when he was executing the monument to John Deverell to Cockerell's designs. Rossi was engaged in 'burning the terra cota for the Pancras church' and Cockerell found him 'sleepy & ignorant' and 'all his works cold tho' having some shape & proportion'. His inadequacy as a portrayer of human emotion partly derived, so Cockerell felt, from the fact that he 'knows nothing but Thompson & Milton'.

Westmacott he dismissed in July 1821 as an 'uncouth affected' figure, and Chantrey fared little better. Cockerell found Chantrey 'good fellow talkative & free' when he met him and his wife on 25 August 1821, but felt that 'every man too much accustomed to incense of flattery is disagreable.' A year later he wrote: 'Chantrey is an excellent workman. he will copy you every wart & wrinkle but he has no more idea than a turnip.'

We should include, finally, an investigation of the fruits of Cockerell's admiration for Gothic sculpture which he developed much later in life. In a lecture of 1842 at the Royal Academy he argues that though Rheims is better as architecture than English Gothic, the sculpture at Wells 'surpasses anything in Europe.' Considering that the work at Wells was completed before the Pisani he is amazed that it should be so neglected. With characteristic energy and determination he set himself the task of undertaking the first systematic study of the sculpture at Wells. He presented the results to the world in a substantial volume illustrated with eight extremely attractive lithographs (Pl. 12) from his own drawings, published in 1851 as *Iconography of the West Front of Wells Cathedral with an Appendix on the Sculptures of Other Mediaeval Churches in England.*

It seems that Cockerell first came to know Wells as the result of the

6. *The Architect and Building Gazette*, II, 30 November 1850, p. 568.

invitation of his brother-in-law, Dean Goodenough, 'to advise on the application of the funds munificently raised by himself and the chapter for the repairs of the fabric.' His study of Wells only encouraged his conviction, gained in Greece, that 'Sculpture is to architecture what the countenance is to the human frame, or what the voice and gesture are to it; namely, the expressive index of the soul which animates it various members . . . Architecture, like Music, may excite the loftiest, but at the same time the most indefinite emotions, while Sculpture explains and details them in plain and distinct terms.' (Appendix, p. 2).

A good number of Cockerell's guesses at the identity of some of the figures portrayed on the west front have been rejected by modern scholarship, but the book still maintains its position as a landmark in the appreciation of English Gothic sculpture. It contains much beautiful and perceptive writing, particularly in the introduction to the Appendix, on the religious and artistic quality of mediaeval art. Indeed the book was reviewed enthusiastically in *The Ecclesiologist*.[7] Another admirer was Cockerell's friend Prosper Mérimée (1803–1870), the novelist and Inspector General of Historical Monuments. He told Cockerell that his book on Wells reinforced 'ma thèse favorite – c'est que la belle sculpture gothique se rapproche fort de la sculpture grecque.'[8]

Another important though slighter contribution was his paper on the sculpture of the Angel Choir at Lincoln Cathedral, delivered in 1848 and published two years later.[9] Again, the originality of Cockerell's work must be stressed. No one before him had either properly illustrated or attempted to identify the figures in this, one of the most beautiful of all English interiors. The article is illustrated with eleven lithographs, prepared by Alfred Stevens, showing thirty figures of which twenty-two were from drawings by Cockerell and the remainder by Stevens. Cockerell was so struck by the exquisite beauty of the Lincoln sculpture that he wrote of them: 'all the freedom and naturalness attributed subsequently to Giotto, who was but an infant when these works were executed, are here anticipated, and strike us in every instance.' Another and most remarkable proof of his love of this sculpture are the splendid angels with outstretched wings with which he filled the spandrels of St. George's Hall, Liverpool (Pl. 160).

7. Vol. XIII, 1852, pp. 419–21.

8. In a letter dated Paris 26 Mai (no year), in the collection of Mrs B. J. Crichton.

9. 'Ancient Sculpture in Lincoln Cathedral', *Proceedings at the Annual Meeting of the Archaeological Institute of Great Britain and Ireland at Lincoln, 1848*, 1850, pp. 215–40.

Music

For the man of taste one of the many delights of life in London in the 1820's was the concerts given regularly by the Philharmonic Society. The founding of this remarkably civilized society in 1813 had established London as one of the most important musical centres in Europe. It enjoyed the closest contacts with many of the most brilliant composers and performers of the day, including Beethoven and Weber. Indeed, in commissioning a symphony from Beethoven in 1822, it can justly claim to have given birth to the Choral Symphony. In 1825 this was given its first performance in England by the society to a baffled audience which included Cockerell. It would be a mistake to assume that artistic life in London was as smooth and unemotional as the stuccoed terraces which formed its setting, at a time when one could hear new works by a composer of the stature of Beethoven. The thrill could scarcely have been exceeded by that of attendance at the first performance of the plays of Shakespeare.

Annual payment of four guineas entitled one to attend the eight concerts given each year between February and June in the Argyll Rooms in Regent Street, immediately opposite Cockerell's Hanover Chapel. Built for the society in 1819–20 by John Nash, the rooms were a prominent feature of the new street with their domed corner pavilion.

Cockerell was a regular attender and was present at no less than thirty-six of the fifty-six concerts given between 1822 and 1828. From his recorded reactions it is clear that his preferences were overwhelmingly for Beethoven. Not only was he privileged to hear the first performance in England of Beethoven's 9th or Choral Symphony but also that of his Piano Concerto in C Minor. After hearing this concerto on 8 March 1824, Cockerell wrote simply: 'Beethoven great composer.' The Choral Symphony was performed on 21 March 1825 and can only have been partially comprehended by either performers or audience. Cockerell's only comment was, 'extraordinary Sinfonia last 1 hour 10 minutes by Beethoven.' The next month he heard Beethoven's 2nd symphony which he found 'fine . . . wild, original'. In May he admired the Eroica Symphony and a septet for strings, clarinet, horn and bassoon. In the following year the 4th symphony was 'superb', the 7th 'very fine', the overture "Egmont" 'fine'.

He was present on 3 April 1826 when before a great crowd Weber, on the point of death, conducted a concert which included four works of his own composition. Of these Cockerell mentioned only the overture to *Der Freischütz* which he did not greatly care for. However, he seems to have

become accustomed to Weber's proto-Wagnerian language for he found on
1 May his overture to *Oberon* very fine. He considered this 'the best concert
of the year.' It included, apart from Weber's overture, Beethoven's 5th
Symphony, Haydn's Symphony in E flat and a violin concerto by Charles
Auguste Beriot and Pierre Rode which Cockerell thought 'very fine'.

His praise of the many composers inspired by Beethoven was not indiscri-
minate. Though he admired Romberg, finding his work 'grand and masculine', he had the discernment to disapprove that of the enormously popular
Joseph Mayseder (1789–1863). 'Modern sickly music without harmony,' was
his verdict on Mayseder. In April 1825, he heard a piano concerto by Ignaz
Moscheles (1794–1870) 'of which I could not make head or tail, music
without character.' Mozart, not surprisingly, always pleased with his
'delightful . . . fluty fine tones.'

Cockerell was no great musician but it is attractive and impressive to
watch his critical judgement at work, endlessly discriminating and discern-
ing in a field unfamiliar to him. Of the scores of contemporary architects,
painters, sculptors and musicians whom Cockerell discusses, Beethoven and
possibly Turner alone receive unqualified praise. It is tempting to suggest
that he found in Beethoven that 'magnificence & eclat', that personal
heroic romance contained within a sure classical discipline, for which he
looked in vain in modern architecture.

CHAPTER VIII

The Royal Academy Lectures, 1841–1856

'WE ARE identified with time; we ourselves become a part of history.' So Cockerell argued at the Royal Academy in 1843 in moving words which show his profound historical sense of belonging to a great tradition. This timelessness is a basic though almost inexpressible part of Cockerell's grand and mysterious appeal. It was his conviction that 'Architecture belongs to history. With her a hundred years are but as a day. Calculated for endurance to the future she *must* be founded on the principles of the past.' He attempted to convince his pupils that the study of architecture was a more humane and valuable occupation than the history of politics which often showed men at their worst. 'Architecture', on the other hand, 'is one of the most powerful enigmas of human civilization, combining every step in moral discipline and social order, every discovery in mathematics and physics, every concept of ideality.'

Cockerell had been elected Professor of Architecture at the Royal Academy in September 1839 on the death of Wilkins. The duties of the Professor as laid down at the foundation of the Academy in 1768 were to 'read annually Six Public Lectures, calculated to form the taste of the Students; to instruct them in the laws and principles of composition; and to point out to them the beauties and faults of celebrated productions.' Of Cockerell's four predecessors in this office, Sandby, Dance, Soane and Wilkins, only Sandby and Soane had seen fit to deliver the lectures required of them. We know that Soane spent three years, 1806–9, in the preparation of his course of six lectures; Cockerell spent less than half that time, delivering his first in January 1841.

In general character and subject-matter – the history, theory and practice of architecture from the ancient world to the present day – Cockerell's lectures resemble those of Soane which he had certainly heard as a young man. Soane's lectures[1] were the straighforward and workmanlike compilations

---

1. Published in 1929 under the editorship of A. T. Bolton as *Lectures in Architecture by Sir John Soane* (Soane Museum Publications, no. 14).

of someone who, though a designer of genius, had not travelled widely, had written little, was not a man of ideas, but who had read painstakingly and extensively so as to accumulate sufficient information for his course of public instruction. Cockerell's, by contrast, are equally obviously those of a man of huge intellectual and emotional vision who was ideally suited to the task before him save that he knew far more than could ever be contained within such a course of lectures. He had seen more, studied more and thought more than any of his fellow architects. We have observed, as his audience had not, how at the start of his architectural career in the 1820's he had been unconsciously preparing himself for an opportunity of this kind by filling his diaries with rapid critical appreciations of the buildings he saw as he travelled about the country. By the time of his appointment in 1839 he was at the height of his powers as an architect: at work on the Ashmolean Museum and the Royal Exchange and about to begin the branch Banks of England.

Cockerell's lectures from his first in 1841 to his last in 1856 were delivered in the room provided for the Royal Academy at the eastern end of the National Gallery in Trafalgar Square. The Academy moved here from Somerset House early in 1837 and remained in Wilkins' cramped quarters until 1868 when it moved to the newly-remodelled Burlington House. The lectures, which 'excited more than usual attention',[2] were immediately successful. 'It was impossible not to feel warmed by the fervour of the Professor's manner at frequent times', wrote an obituarist; 'Never has a lecturer in the Academy collected round him more attentive listeners.'[3] Another admirer records 'the passion, amounting almost to a prejudice, with which he views and entertains everything pertaining to architecture. A little more and his very self would be lost in the pursuit of this all-absorbing object of his devotion.'[4]

Two years after the start of Cockerell's lectures appeared the first number of *The Builder*, a journal which was destined to have a profound influence on the development of Victorian architects and architecture. The report which it carried in its first issue of 13 February 1843 of Cockerell's lectures at the Royal Academy was the first of a series which became a regular feature of the journal each January and February. Indeed, the account of the lectures given in this chapter has been compiled not merely from the original lecture notes preserved at the Royal Academy, the R.I.B.A. Drawings Collection and Trinity College, Cambridge, but also from the summaries

2. *The Athenaeum*, 1841, p. 114.
3. *The Builder*, XXI, 1863, pp. 683–5.
4. Ibid., I, 1843, p. 44.

in *The Builder*.[5] It is the editor of *The Builder* who tells us how Cockerell illustrated his lectures:

'Such a display of illustrative drawings, so laboriously compiled, as were exhibited by the learned lecturer, it has never before been our good fortune to see brought together . . . Two large sheets, or rather assemblage of sheets, were hung up, shewing in comparative juxta-position most of the famous structures of antiquity, the one in elevation, the other in section . . . But there were others whose assemblage and lengthened treatment would make up volumes, some embodying the ingenious speculations of the professor, but, in the main rigid and critical delineations of the buildings of the ancients from measurement.'

On 11 March 1843 *The Builder* reproduced a large chart prepared by Cockerell listing chronologically the names and dates of buildings, one hundred architects, and architectural authors, and great events, from Noah to Blondel. 'Such a table', argues Cockerell, 'presents at one view the religious and moral, the political and technical influences which have guided and developed the art.'

To illustrate this chart Cockerell prepared a huge drawing, fourteen feet by ten feet, which showed sixty-three of the most important buildings of the world all standing on a common base. He called this his 'drop-scene' and hung it up at all his lectures. Over four hundred other drawings were produced, and Goodchild tells us how scholars of the day supplied Cockerell with valuable information: 'Mr. Owen Jones, Mr. Arrundel, Mr. Arthur Hakewill, Mr. William Hamilton, Professor Willis of Cambridge and other well travelled artists and gentlemen lent their drawings and sometimes assisted in the work and by their conversation made the work always interesting. Mr. Cockerell had an excellent architectural library of his own . . . He also used those of the Travellers' and Athenaeum clubs, we had in the office two Italians and Arthur Hakewill was [i.e. spoke] French and Italian too.' They also had in the office in 1845 Jackson, son of a Wisbech clergyman, who had served his articles with Lockwood of Hull. He made the finished drawing of the Tepidarium at the Baths of Caracalla, based on the reconstruction in Abel Blouet's book.[6]

5. The lectures were also reported in *The Athenaeum*, and in the *Civil Engineer and Architect's Journal*, VI, 1843, and VII, 1844, where we learn (VII, p. 25) that Cockerell refused permission for them to be published verbatim. They were reported at length and sharply censured in *The Ecclesiologist*, III, 1843, pp. 37–44.

6. *Restauration des Thermes d'Antonin Caracalla à Rome*, Paris, 1828.

Cockerell threw himself with such selfless energy into the preparation of these lectures that his practice must inevitably have suffered. Every year from the middle of November to the middle of the following February, 'professional work had to give way to the lectures', in Goodchild's words. They were, moreover, very inadequately paid. Cockerell received sixty guineas a year for six lectures which had sometimes cost him over £200 to prepare. Nevertheless, he never repeated the same course exactly. Soane, on the other hand, read the same course year in, year out, sometimes even employing his assistant, George Bailey, to read the lectures for him.

We have already compared Cockerell to Pevsner in an earlier chapter and the range, liveliness and evident popularity of his Royal Academy lectures all support the comparison. Cockerell must be counted amongst the earliest of modern architectural historians: he is not writing a treatise like Alberti or pure archaeology like Canina, to name two of his favourite authors; he has the imaginative grasp of Winckelmann but exceeds him in archaeological knowledge; he has the religious fervour of Pugin but is generous where he is fanatical. Despite his belief that through the use of the orders 'We are identified with time; we ourselves become a part of history', Cockerell devoted much time to an extremely productive and original study of Gothic architecture. This is in itself an indication of his pioneering role as a detached observer of architectural history. The popular image of him in old age, isolated like the Psalmist, 'an owl in the desert, a pelican in the wilderness',[7] is a false one but only because he was no more isolated in old age than he had been in youth. His indifference to the fashions of his day had always set him apart from his contemporaries. The investigations he undertook in later years of Gothic proportional systems and of Gothic sculpture opened up a field which was surprisingly unexplored by Pugin, Ruskin and Willis and in which there still remains work to be done today.

For Cockerell, however, architecture meant first and foremost the creation of order, which is why he was able to investigate impartially both Greek and Gothic. 'A work of order', he exclaimed in 1851, 'is like an oasis in the desert, or the temple of Apollo in Arcadia . . . Order, disposition and repose, then, are the great ends for art to achieve, for after all our pranks, we find tranquillity the great element of satisfaction to the eye, as in the forum of Nerva restored by Palladio, the library at Venice, and the palace at Naples.'

The creation of order was achieved most naturally by the use of the orders. 'The orders', he argued in his first lecture of 1842, 'are not only

7. Psalm CII, v. 6, from the *Book of Common Prayer*.

Roman and Greek but Phoenician, Hebrew and Assyrian.' He went on to cite the words of his beloved Wren: 'Architecture is founded on the experience of all ages, promoted by the vast treasures of all great monarchs, and the skill of the greatest artists and geometricians, every one emulating the other. And experiments in this kind being greatly expenceful and errors incorrigible, is the reason that architecture is now rather the study of antiquity than fancy.' Cockerell particularly censures the notion of individual fancy and as an example of what he calls 'the delusiveness of fashion in architecture' cites the 'Greek Revival of 1790–1820'. Fashion is not to be confused with taste which is essential for good design. Genius, he argues, is a gift, 'but taste is rather the fruit of *learning and study*.' Architecture is thus a fine art, and 'when the architect retreats from consideration of beauty he departs from the example of our mistress, nature.'

For the purposes of lecture courses Cockerell divided his vast subject into three main categories: firstly there was 'a broad illustrated survey of the major monuments of all periods', secondly 'the laws and principles of composition', and thirdly a bibliographical approach which can only be described as the history of the history of architecture. This third course, which was first given in 1842 and subsequently repeated several times, was the most interesting from an historiographical point of view. Nothing of quite this sort had been attempted before, nor is there even today a reputable book on the subject. Cockerell argued:

As well might the lawyer or the divine dispense with books, as the architect. In the very dawn of literature the architect required to be learned. In the Memorabalia of Xenophon, Socrates, inquires "But what employment do you intend to excel in, O Euthedemus, that you collect so many books? is it architecture? for this art, too, you will find no little knowledge necessary".'

As evidence of the practical value to the architect of studying books, he cites *Le Premier Tome de l'architecture de Philibert de l'Orme*, Paris, 1567, a favourite work. Professor Willis had recently shown that the whole theory of the *coupe des pierres*, the vaulting systems and the architectural nomenclature of the Gothic architects was set forth in Philibert de l'Orme, and that had modern historians only known this they could have been spared much needless research. Cockerell demonstrated, too, that 'In Philibert de l'Orme (lib. II, c, xi) you will find the specification for concrete corresponding precisely with the recent so-called discovery of this method of securing foundations.'

Dividing architecture into sacred, civil and domestic, Cockerell dwells lovingly on the biblical origins of sacred architecture in the account in Exodus 26 of the raising of the Tabernacle in the Wilderness by divine inspiration. He was struck by the resemblance between the sacred architecture of all periods, even noting that the instruction to raise five columns at the entrance to the tabernacle found its echo in the disposition of Gothic portals with their central *trumeau*. He reminds his audience how,

'In discussing the form and proportions of temples, we hold in veneration those noblest motives of the heart, which we recognise alike in the Grecian, the Druid, the Hindoo, and the Christian temple, and so finely expressed in the Book of Psalms. In excavating the foundations of the temple at Aegina, the remains of burnt woods and bones were discovered, mixed, doubtless, with tears and aspirations as warm as those of David; – at Selinus, the steps of one of the temples were worn down almost to an inclined plane by the devout.'

This passage shows two characteristics of Cockerell's approach which help lift his lectures above the common level: one is his essentially numinous vision and the other, which counterbalances this, is his insistence on architecture as a setting for life.

The description of the building of Solomon's Temple in the First Book of Kings with its reference to the 'great stones' shows, so Cockerell argued, that the Hebrews understood the importance for sacred and public architecture of magnitude of materials. Criticizing much modern practice in this respect, Cockerell complains that,

'the noble material which nature furnishes we contrive by our petty contrivances of art and we make a merit of enfeebling those fine blocks which left alone would convey ideas of energy and beauty . . . the builder has outgrown the architect and while we reproduce old things in antiquated scale he has prepared his materials for a more enterprising and gigantic style than we are capable of inventing. He points at the large and noble blocks lying in the quarry or even in his yard which we proceed to subdivide into what we are pleased to call architectural proportions. When the quarries of Pentelicus had displayed the magnitude of their materials, the architects Ictinus and Mnesicles took the utmost advantage of them . . . Pausanias, 550 years after, described the Propylaea as the most memorable work up to the present time for the enormous marble ceiling, for the length of the stones as for the beauty of their order &

execution. Ten marble beams 19′ 3″ long sustained the eastern ceiling; fourteen beams 18′ 9″ sustained that in the hall. Wren adopted the double external order at St. Paul's because the quarries would not furnish scantling of sufficient dimensions for the cornices of the Great Model design. Aristotle says that the effect of architecture derives from magnitude and order, the magnitude being also that of the parts.'

This interpretation of the double order at St. Paul's, derived from Wren's *Parentalia*, is a favourite with Cockerell and one which he returns to and elaborates several times in the course of his lectures. Again and again the magnitude of ancient architecture makes a profound impression on him. He notes that some Greek capitals consist of single stones fourteen feet square; elsewhere he records the temple at Baalbec where three stones measure together 199 feet. He reminds his audience, too, of the grandeur that a comparatively small building can achieve if built with stones of sufficient magnitude. Thus it is 'difficult to believe the small size of the Pantheon and Carnac till they are drawn to the same scale as the cathedrals of Antwerp or Salisbury.' In modern times Smirke and Harrison were to be commended for their handling of materials: 'Since the days of Trajan or Hadrian no such stones have been used as have recently been employed at the British Museum where eight hundred stones from five to nine tons weight form the front. Even St. Paul's contains no approach to these magnitudes.' He records that 'At Chester six monoliths of ten tons each were placed on their pedestals one night by Mr. Harrison before the Court of Justice', and adds that the effect next day on the magistrates was so great 'that they allowed him to carry out certain matters in which his taste and judgement might otherwise have been over-ruled.' Another anecdote concerns one of his own buildings, the Edinburgh Parthenon. He remembers at the laying of the foundation stone in 1821 his surprise at the 'indifference of the assembled dandies to the three great stones employed, each weighing two tons or more. They had no minds capable of appreciating the large masses used by the Greeks in their glorious erections.' Indeed the stones were better appreciated 'by intelligent tradesmen, artificers and labourers than by the educated.'

His worship of the large scale of ancient architecture leads him to admire particularly the Tuscan order for its 'agreeably wide intercolumniation.' As good modern examples of this he cites not merely Inigo Jones' St. Paul's, Covent Garden, but also two less well-known examples, Wyatt's St. Peter's, Manchester of 1788 and Henry Garling's Corn Market at Guildford of 1818. He even goes so far as to point out that buildings of this type occur in the backgrounds of paintings by Poussin and Le Sueur. The use of cast-iron beams is recommended in the construction of the long stretches of un-supported entablature required in the Tuscan order. Indeed, the combination of cast-iron beams and stone produces 'elements of strength, size and duration which are to produce new architectural combinations, new beauties and arrangements of a boldness, hardihood & mastery unprece-dented.'

His admiration of the easy grandeur of the Tuscan order led him to censure as 'pure pedantry' the crowded columns of Lord Burlington's Assembly Rooms at York. He also considered that in modern street architecture the columns are always put too close together, being imitated from temple fronts, and argued that since street fronts are always seen in perspective the columns should be wider apart thus leaving more space for windows. The pediments, too, will also be wider, and as a happy example of this Cockerell cites Vardy's Spencer House, Green Park, of 1756. The wide intercolumnia-tion of this building was justified by the fact that Vitruvius' rules for inter-columniation applied only to free-standing not to engaged columns. Cockerell showed in subsequent lectures how the proportions of the orders should vary in sacred, civil and interior architecture. This, he states, is a point 'lost sight of by the moderns, though Palladio seldom enjoys the whole entablature in interiors and uses the architrave only with a small cornice making it at most 1/5 of the column.' He drew attention to the fact that in the design of the recently uncovered Tabularium or Record Office in Rome, the column and entablature were much lighter than those of the nearby sacred buildings at the Capitol and Forum. He notes in passing the strong modern objection, as exemplified in Milizia, to employing features proper to external pediments and cornices in interiors. The stern neo-classical Milizia obviously intrigued Cockerell and he recommended him to his pupils as 'an author extremely well worth consulting for the bold and original views he indulges.'

The author whom Cockerell recommends more than any other is, of course, Vitruvius. He mentions the twenty-three commentaries on his work which had appeared since 1520 and also emphasizes the fact that Vitruvius himself refers to no less than forty-one Greek authors whose writings on art and architecture are now lost. He takes his pupils through the seven fundamental principles of architecture as laid down by Vitruvius in Book I, Chapter II: Order, Arrangement, Eurythmy, Symmetry, Propriety, and Economy. In outlining the concept of Arrangement or 'Diathesis', Cockerell pointed, not without some apology, to a work of his own, the Taylor

Institution and University Galleries at Oxford. Though the longest part of the site was in Beaumont Street, it was obvious that the more important elevation was that greeting travellers from the north in St. Giles's. Furthermore, the far end of the Beaumont Street front was terminated by a terrace of imposing houses, forty feet high. It was thus clear that the site demanded a wing at least forty feet high at the end of Beaumont Street and another equally impressive wing in St. Giles's. The customary 'disposition, therefore, was reversed, the lowest part of the building being in the centre; the edifice was disconnected from its ordinary neighbours by raising the whole site on an artificial terrace of eight feet high . . . This disposition, though unusual, had, after due deliberation, been preferred by the judges. So the victory (if so it was) had been achieved like that of Trafalgar, by reversing the ordinary tactics.'

Economy he described as the combination of beauty and fitness which we find in the productions of nature herself. It also, of course, described the ability to provide the largest possible accommodation at the smallest cost. Again, he referred to the example of the Taylor Institution and University Galleries which had provided an area of 38,000 square feet at a cost of only £52,000.

Propriety or character and fitness of style (Thematismos) could, in Cockerell's view, be particularly well understood from study of Palladio and Dance. 'Palladio never repeated himself unless the purpose and use were repeated'; while Dance 'shewed himself the most complete Poet architect of his day – no one can doubt that Newgate is a prison, that St. Luke's is an asylum, prison or place of milder confinement for the unhappy and bewildered in mind, nor that the front of Guildhall, though anything but Gothic, is still the metropolitan and magnificent place of Government and civil authority.'

However, it is always to the use of the orders that Cockerell ultimately returns. Apart from the subtleties of the individual members of the orders, there are a number of points about their general combination which Cockerell feels are of especial importance. He categorized these under four headings: (1) the gradation of orders in different dimensions in the same building; (2) the combination of the arch with the orders; (3) suiting the object to the angle of vision; (4) partial concealment. Knowing that Palladio would be more familiar to his listeners than Roman architecture itself, Cockerell explained what he meant in these four points by referring to the work of Palladio since 'all of these were great principles which Palladio gathered better than any of the masters of the revival from ancient Rome.' From

Cockerell this is praise indeed. His interpretation of Palladio as primarily a handler of the orders is markedly different from that of Burlington and his followers which had dominated so much English eighteenth-century practice.

Cockerell described 'the gradation of orders or of similar parts in different dimensions which Palladio constantly practised in all his works; the interlacing, as it were, of orders of different dimensions so as to give scale and composition.' He had in mind particularly Palladio's brilliant Loggia del Capitaniato at Vicenza which, as we shall see in subsequent chapters, was to be a potent influence on the development of his own mature style. The first instance cited by most modern architectural historians of the uniting of two storeys with a single order is Michelangelo's Capitoline Palaces. Cockerell specifically mentions Michelangelo in this respect but, interestingly, argues that his work at the Capitol is inferior to the Loggia del Capitaniato in that the minor order is unrelated to the major. He noted that the combination of two orders 'had been employed by the ancients in the adjustment of side porticoes to the temple and in the Propylea of Athens. In this last the subordinate being ten, the principal is fifteen. In Palladio's Casa del Capitano, it is ten to sixteen-and-a-half, the same in the Basilica, in the Casa Valmarana ten to twenty-and-a-half.'

Cockerell's second point, 'the combination of the arch with the orders', leads him to a eulogy of one of his favourite building types, the triumphal arch. As minor but novel examples he cites to his audience the Porticus Octavia in the Forum and Soane's Lothbury Gateway at the Bank of England. His own preoccupation with this theme culminates in his magnificent project for the Royal Exchange which we shall investigate in Chapter XII. Compelling evidence for the organic connection in Cockerell's career between history and practice is afforded by the beautiful preliminary sketches for the Royal Exchange which he made on top of one of the pages already covered by lecture notes. Once again, Palladio is praised for his understanding of the combination of arches with the orders. He cites as an instance of this Palladio's reconstruction of the Forum with the Temple of Nerva at the far end in the *Quattro Libri*, book IV, pls 24–27. Here Palladio shows the Corinthian temple front linked by arches to the adjacent buildings. Though this composition 'may be criticised for not being trabeate, it has a beautiful effect at the New Exchange in Glasgow.' It seems that Cockerell knew the curious temple at Bordeaux, illustrated by Perrault, where the Corinthian order supported an attic of round-arched columns, for he refers to 'an ancient market portico which I believe was at Bordeaux.' We shall see in Chapter XII how the temple as depicted by Perrault was almost certainly an influence on the design of the St. Giles's front of the Taylorian. In connection with the Bordeaux portico Cockerell mentions the 'magnificent new palace for foreign affairs on the Quai d'Orsay, showing the application of the order on the pier and spandrel of the arched system.' The sumptuous Foreign Ministry was executed from 1814–38 from designs by Bonnard and Jacques Lacornée, but though Cockerell approved the rich effect of its superimposed arched orders he could not but 'remark the ill effect of the abrupt termination of the arched front without due fortification of the angles, as in the Farnese palace.'

Cockerell's arguments for his fourth point, 'partial concealment', are of especial interest: 'The Parthenon was partially concealed by the Propylaea and the walls. The best distance from a building is one equal to about three times the height of the elevation. When we get within the enclosure [on the Acropolis] we find this best position. The imagination is excited by partial concealment. If, according to the modern practice, the building be stuck ostentatiously before us, we see at once the whole of it and we are tired before we approach. There is nothing to be imagined or discovered.'

He claimed that the Romans frequently deflected the angles of the great colonnaded streets which crossed their cities at right angles, 'so that their extent was never seen.' An example of this, he believed, could be found at Palmyra. To provide another instance of his principle of 'partial concealment', he stated that 'If the buildings were removed from around St. Paul's Cathedral, the effect of the building would be lessened.' He claimed, too, that the principle 'prevailed in Gothic architecture equally. The introduction of the organ at the east end of the nave, sometimes complained of in our cathedrals, is surely advantageous to the effect.'

Closely related to the principle of 'partial concealment' was what he called, 'suiting the object to the angle of vision – a great art.' He understood by this a painterly understanding of perspective. He believed that 'The successful architect must be a painter' and took confidence from the fact that so many men had combined the two professions. For example, 'Servandoni was a great scene painter and was employed to build St. Sulpice, certainly the most effective modern work of Paris' – a more sympathetic view than that of 1824 cited in Chapter VI. Vanbrugh was another architect who understood the perspective of architecture and who bore in mind in designing and placing his buildings the changing position of the spectator. Cockerell describes him as a man 'whose whole genius was theatrical.' A church in Belgium which Cockerell particularly admired in this respect was 'the Grand

Beguinage at Brussels which had much loftier columns in the choir and transept than in the nave; and great ingenuity was manifested in the connection of the whole by one entablature. The perspective effect produced by this interior arrangement was deserving of careful study; for whilst the near columns, on entering the church, were sufficiently large, those which were more remote, together with the high altar and other distant objects, were seen to much greater advantage.'

Related to this is the fact that features employed inside a building will always seem larger than the same features employed outside: 'Thus the uninitiated are often deceived by the greater apparent size of the columns in the interior of St. Paul's, when compared with the lower external order; although, in fact, the size of both is alike.' Cockerell was evidently a pioneer in the appreciation of what Gombrich was subsequently to call 'Art and Illusion', and St. Paul's furnishes another example of this. Cockerell argues that 'The mind naturally desires expansion as a means of escape from the limits imposed by the walls of a building; and nothing can more effectively help carry the eye forward than the judicious use of painting.' In redecorating the cathedral in 1822 Cockerell discovered that the pilasters at the east end of the choir, then painted to imitate Sienna marble, had originally been painted blue by Wren in imitation of lapis lazuli. Cockerell believed, as he told his academy students thirty years later, that 'the admirable effect of distance produced by the original blue colour was totally destroyed by the supposedly warmer tint.' Anticipating the 'archaeological' approach of modern decorators such as Mr John Fowler, Cockerell insisted in March 1822 on the pilasters being painted blue in the face of some opposition. He consoled himself in his diary with the thought that: 'we must after all appeal to principles – if in painting them blue we are wrong, Sir C. Wren is wrong.'

We have briefly touched on Cockerell's third point, 'suiting the object to the angle of vision'. Bound up with this is his fundamental principle that 'Proportion should alter with the magnitude'. Unfortunately, the commentators on Vitruvius give no consideration when determining intercolumniation to the vital point of the height of the whole building. They all draw their orders to different scales which are sometimes determined by the height of the page. Sansovino's *loggetta* at the base of the campanile in Venice, though only thirty feet high and at the foot of a building three hundred feet tall, 'yet has dignity through a low compressed character contrasting with the tower'. Cockerell concluded that 'Beauty of proportion arises from inequalities.' He did not believe that rules for good proportion could be drawn up, for the deceptiveness of the eye could play havoc with rules and, as we have seen, proportion must alter with magnitude. Thus he noticed that by varying the height of the capital one could make the column itself appear taller or shorter. At Paestum the Doric columns had twenty-four flutes; at Sunium, where an effect of breadth when viewed from the sea was all important, they had only sixteen. With large columns one should increase the number of flutes and decrease the size of the capitals. For the increased flutes there was a biological analogy, always a favourite with Cockerell, which was that while the bark of the young oak is smooth, that of the old is corrugated.

Concluding his account of his four principles Cockerell passes immediately to an account of the Baths of Ancient Rome where, he believed, many of them had been given their most brilliant expression. Of their spatial quality, 'Greenwich, Chelsea and Blenheim give something of the effect.' In defining the character of the Baths in terms of architectural space Cockerell antici-pates an approach developed by German art historians in the late nine-teenth century and popularized in this country by Geoffrey Scott and Pevs-ner. He saw that a building of early Imperial Rome which shared their complex and dramatic spatial character was the Domus Augustiana or Palace of Domitian on the Palatine. In his lectures of 1845 he described in some detail this remarkable building, still too little known today. He was particularly impressed by its south front looking on to the Circus Maximus with its 'segmental plan on a high terrace with noble arcades below and orders above, an open temple of Belvedere high in the centre for the Emperor to look at the Games in the Circus Maximus.'

He described the Baths as 'the most remarkable buildings the world has ever seen', and admired especially the Baths of Diocletian, speaking of 'the effect produced by the vistas in this extraordinary pile.' The dramatic effect was heightened by 'the magnificent Exedrae, which occur in the plan, 60 feet high, with a semi-dome, 84 feet in span.' Applauding Bramante's use of this feature in the Belvedere Court at the Vatican and Vignola's at the Villa Giulia, he wondered why it had not been more widely imitated. Another greatly admired building was the Ulpian Basilica with its domed apses set behind two-storeyed screens.

He recognized that the Great Hall of the Baths must have inspired Alberti's splendid vaulted space at S. Andrea, Mantua. He recognized, too, the tremendous significance of this church for the whole history of Renais-sance architecture and seems to have felt a special sympathy for Alberti, the scholar-architect. Sensing the essentially pedestrian character of Vasari's mind, Cockerell resented his implications that Alberti was merely a theoretician and dismissed him with the delightful, memorable phrase: 'Vasari seeks to bring everyone to his own level.' The notes on Alberti from Cockerell's fifth lecture of 1842 should be quoted at greater length since, though they may have been amplified in delivery, they suggest the liveliness, originality and arresting range of reference characteristic of his approach:

'At S. Andrea, Mantua, Alberti did not build one of our commissioner's churches but reflecting deeply on all the principles applicable . . . produced a design which became the parent of the nave of St. Peter's. A vast arch the whole height externally expresses the order of the interior . . . no one who has visited Mantua will ever forget its effect . . . We can see the same idea at Peterborough Cathedral. I made a humble imitation of it at the Hotwells church, Bristol. Bramante and Peruzzi could only copy what Alberti had done. The source is the Ephebeum or the Great Hall of the Baths.'

Cockerell's skill in formulating these rapid vignettes or 'character impressions' of buildings is one of his most endearing and enviable abilities. Having described in some detail the plan and disposition of Alberti's S. Francesco, Rimini, he sums the building up as, 'impressive, grand and melancholy'. The Pitti Palace he thought memorable chiefly for its great stones, some eighteen to twenty feet long, and 'of a dusky hue'. Its style, he found, had 'all the grave and gigantic character . . . highly characteristic of a republican high-minded people.'

His fertile mind is ever throwing out to his audience suggestive *aperçus* relating to his favourite topic, the use of the orders: 'Vignola used entasis, a novelty in his day; he also invented the cornice partaking with the frieze used by Wren at St. Paul's . . . this had appeared at Baalbec but Vignola could not have known this'; 'Raphael probably invented the balustrade, unknown in antiquity'; 'the use of coupled columns, unknown in antique architecture, was a present made to posterity by Bramante and Raphael'; 'there is no artist of his day more worthy of study than Sansovino . . . he proportioned the height of the cornice of St. Mark's library to that of the whole building, not merely to that of the upper order, displaying a kind of judgement in design not now usually given.' To the student of Cockerell's own buildings the interest of such quotations is doublefold. Thus he uses Vignola's great bracketed cornice himself, most notably at the Ashmolean; while at the Sun Assurance Office we can see him carefully proportioning the crowning entablature to the whole building not merely to the Corinthian order which supports it. He was aware, too, that Peruzzi had innovated in this field and observed of him: 'Peruzzi was the first to render his orders homogeneous with the structure and his giving to the entablature of the upper order (especially in the Farnesina) a proportion suited to the entire height of the two [storeys].' He noted on the other hand that 'San Gallo was remarkable for the dignity which he gave to his buildings without the aid of the orders, especially in the Palazzo Farnese. The verticality which is . . . usually conveyed by the orders, he communicated to his buildings by rustic quoins which carry the eye up and enable it to embrace the whole front. This invention which appears to be wholly his own became popular and universal.'

This essentially visual or painterly approach is surely Wölfflin before his time. Indeed, in Cockerell's delicacy of observation and the strength of scholarship on which it rests, he seems sometimes to exceed Wölfflin in quality. We find him elsewhere remarking that: 'Vignola by subordinating the parts gave apparent vastness to the whole. His doors and windows are remarkably small, the latter 3' 8" by 7' only in Caprarola.'

In the light of Cockerell's enthusiasm for Italian sixteenth-century architecture, it is interesting to observe his attitude to Michelangelo. He mentions only two works by Michelangelo in his lectures, the Capitoline Palaces and St. Peter's, and these are cited not for their virtues but for their errors. We have already noted his criticism of Michelangelo's handling of the orders at the Capitol; and he often censures St. Peter's for failing to make use of its enormous size. His view that we do not appreciate the dimensions of the building until we are actually told them has, of course, been shared by many. However, later in life he seems to have reached a maturer estimate of Michelangelo's genius. He co-operated with his old friend, John Scandrett Harford of Blaise Castle, in the production of a book entitled, *Illustrations Architectural and Pictorial of the Genius of Michael Angelo Buonarotti*, 1857.

The only building illustrated in the book is St Peter's. Cockerell and the brilliant Luigi Canina had prepared a number of plates which reconstructed Michelangelo's plans for the church, showing how they differed from both Bramante's and Maderno's. Cockerell produced a twelve-page essay to accompany these illustrations. He was much impressed by Michelangelo's decision to reproduce externally the huge Corinthian order established internally by Bramante. The dimensions of the great portico would have exceeded by one-fourth those of the largest temple of antiquity, the Temple of the Sun at Baalbec. To Michelangelo's contemporaries, it 'seemed beyond the powers of execution.' The double dome, too, particularly appealed to

Cockerell since he saw in it the 'novel application of the cellular system exhibited universally by nature in the animal and vegetable creation.' Michelangelo had learnt from the Duomo at Florence where Brunelleschi, as an anatomist, had himself learnt by observation of the double shell of the human skull. Referring to San Gallo's model for St. Peter's, Cockerell observes with much truth and clarity: 'San Gallo and M. Angelo are, in fact, the exponents of two opposite systems of design, alternately professed in all ages, the one producing impression by the multiplicity of parts and features, the other by colossal magnitude of fewer parts and features ... Both are to be respected.' He does not describe Maderno's nave in the book, although he several times refers to it in his lectures as a striking example of how not to use the orders: 'The facade of St. Peter's exhibits a total absence of order, the spaces between the columns being all of irregular width. The columniation, originally intended to be open, was subsequently filled up and presents the appearance of a compressed bas-relief.'

He ends his account of St. Peter's with a few references to other works by Michelangelo. He now considers the Capitoline Palaces to be 'entirely worthy of the Capitol of Rome', though adds that they still leave 'something, perhaps, to be desired in the purity of detail.' The Porta Pia is 'perhaps one of the most eccentric of his production', while 'The library and staircase at Florence are singular and remarkable.' Cockerell had early been attracted by the romance of Michelangelo's sculpture, and we have seen in an earlier chapter his poetic account of the unfinished roundel of the Holy Family. However, his devotion to the orders and his knowledge of what happened when lesser architects imitated the licences Michelangelo had taken with the orders, prevented him from fully appreciating Michelangelo's own architecture. He was moved by the depth of Michelangelo's religious feeling; impressed by the fact that he 'raised the Beautiful and the Sublime almost into a worship'; impressed but also a little alarmed by his realization that 'Originality was the character and aim of Michelangelo'; and certain that his example was a dangerous one to follow.

Throughout the lectures there are a number of hostile references to Borromini as one of the most culpable of Michelangelo's followers. These are but passing references and merely follow the current trend, but as soon as he came to study in detail the lines of Borromini's buildings his mind was sufficiently open to perceive their merit. In a remarkable lecture of 1851 he showed that the combination of rectilinear and curvilinear lines, both in the plans of buildings and in their mouldings, was a basic part of the appeal of all the most sophisticated architecture. Having established this point from a study of ancient architecture he could not but deny that 'the same principle was carried to a great extent by Bernini and Borromini and by it much grace of composition, with a great variety of light and shade were attained.' It is a remarkable and perceptive tribute and antedates by many years the general reinstatement of the Baroque. Elsewhere he praises the subtle handling of perspective in Bernini's Scala Regia at the Vatican.

It was the English seventeenth century, however, which for Cockerell marked the climax of Renaissance architecture. Wren towers above Cockerell's lectures like a great beacon, the radiating light from which clarifies and sets into perspective the troubled waters of architectural history. He regarded Wren's many different buildings as each displaying fundamental principles. In attempting to define this quality he observed, in a phrase of much beauty, that each building 'may be called the Patriarch of a great race.' In 1838 Cockerell had made Wren's remarkable progeny the subject of a famous water-colour, *A Tribute to the Memory of Sir Christopher Wren* (Pl. 9), which depicted all Wren's major works, including thirty-three of the City churches. It is ironical to reflect that this may have given Pugin the idea of depicting twenty-four of his own buildings in a similar composite view in the somewhat coarse etching which accompanies his *Apology for the Revival of Christian Architecture*, 1843. Ten years after Cockerell's *Tribute* of 1838, his pupil John Clayton dedicated to him his great folio-volume on *Wren's City Churches*. The story will be told in a later chapter of how Cockerell fought to preserve and re-use the fittings of Wren's St. Bartholomew Exchange, which he rebuilt on a new site.

Another indication of Cockerell's veneration for Wren and English seventeenth-century architecture is the remarkable observation, made as late as his last lecture of 1856, that 'nothing in Paris can compare with Greenwich.' Apart from Mansart's domed chapel, 'the Invalides is nothing.' Wren's domes, on the other hand, were miracles. That of St. Stephen, Walbrook, is 'a mere bubble of unexampled lightness which has stood more than 150 years and not yet blown away'; while at St. Paul's he considered that the cone and dome had been derived from the Baptistery at Pisa, the plan from the Cathedral at Siena. The last lecture is made the occasion of a final panegyric upon St. Paul's. For Cockerell, 'St. Paul's is without a rival in beauty, unity and variety'; as evidence he cited the placing of the consistory and morning chapels; the apsed bays of the aisles; the making of the dome equal in width to the nave and aisles, and not merely to the former; and the extraordinary arrangement of double windows in the apse 'allowing the light to penetrate as in Gothic churches' by an arrangement

K

which has 'all the strength of a pier, all the grace of an apse and a lightness which appears unique – for I have found such a combination nowhere else.' He found endlessly fascinating the essentially Gothic character of the cathedral, and returns again and again to his discovery that the building is 'a gothic structure clothed in classic garb.' Apart from the use of a higher nave and lower aisles linked by flying buttresses, Cockerell could adduce in support of his view not merely the apse windows and the obvious inspiration from Ely in the plan of the crossing, but the fact that Wren had been a member of a masons' lodge at the last moment when the lodges had architectural significance. We shall return to this important point when discussing Cockerell's approach to Gothic architecture.

On the whole, Cockerell's later lectures seem to have become more personal and unpredictable – an impression which is aided by the increasing scrappiness of the notes. Professor Aitchison, who had heard the lectures, recorded forty years later that, 'The students hung upon his utterances; and while lecturing he would often pause and then say, "and so on" – he had dropped the thread of his discourse, forgotten his audience and the lecture room, and was in Athens admiring the Parthenon and communing with Pericles and Phidias.'[8] Favourite topics in these later years were at once broad and specific: the biological analogy, and the subtlety of line and form in classic architecture.

Obvious examples of the former were to be found in Gothic architecture: 'In the cornice of the nave of York cathedral we found an ornament which was, in fact, the common savoy cabbage, without disguise.' Classical architecture offered more profound examples of natural analogies and we have already noted his interpretation of the domes of Brunelleschi and Michelangelo in terms of the human skull. A page of lecture notes is adorned with a beautiful cross-section of an elephant's skull, for now Cockerell animated his lectures by making rapid drawings upon a blackboard. Another favourite instance was the construction of the steeple of Wren's St. Bride's, Fleet Street. This reminded him of the delicate convolutions of a snail's shell, an analogy which, though characteristically novel, is also apt. The steeple appears to consist of four diminishing octagonal storeys of round arches, capped by an octagonal spire. The construction, however, is very different for, as Margaret Whinney observes, 'the centre of the steeple is not a cone but an open stone staircase from which compartments radiate to the outer face.'[9] Cockerell could not, in fact, have chosen a happier example

8. *R.I.B.A. Transactions*, new series, VI, 1890, p. 261.
9. *Wren*, 1971, p. 73.

of the parallel between architecture and nature. Another parallel, perhaps less suggestive, was between egg-shells and domes. He was struck by the strength of both despite their apparent vulnerability and described how in the transporting of eggs 'from Scotland in boxes containing 1,400 each, no greater allowance for breakage is made than thirty or forty per box.'

He moves rapidly on from these considerations to the importance of the natural setting in the design and placing of a building. This is illustrated with a simple but telling sketch showing the relationship of the horizontal lines of a Greek temple such as the Parthenon to its mountainous setting. His sketch and the beautiful descriptive phrase that 'The Grecian Doric order on the Acropolis seems to grow out of the rockwork itself', will remind us of the theme and illustrations of Vincent Scully's study of Greek temples and site planning, *The Earth, the Temple and the Gods: Greek Sacred Architecture*, 1962. So strongly does Cockerell feel this organic connection that he argues that the Greek Doric, 'when placed in our modern streets and combined with vertical lines appears out of place, like an elephant in a cage.' Thus in this country it 'can only be properly employed in such situations as Edinburgh and similar elevated spots.'[10]

From here his mind reaches out to the relationship between the lines of movement of Greek sculpture and the framework or setting within which it is contained. In pedimental sculpture, he argues, one requires lines that are winding not parallel – and he illustrates the point with a sketch of his pediment at St. George's Hall, Liverpool. Similarly, in square metopes the lines of the figures will be predominantly diagonal. Indeed, 'the Greeks carefully avoided placing any perpendicular or horizontal line in sculpture that would be placed in conjunction with architecture: particularly in the Phigaleian sculptures and those of Halicarnassus.'[11]

He argues that 'The happy contrast of curved and straight is essential', and shows with sketches how this applies even to the human face: thus his drawing of a face where every line is curved is repulsive. It was exactly this contrast which 'constituted the soul of beauty in the composition and contour of Greek mouldings. Hogarth's "line of beauty" is identical with the profile of the Greek cymatium.' His raptures on the effects of these contrasts in the torus and cavetto mouldings, or in the juxtaposition of column and pilaster, can only be compared to the subjective visual aesthetics

10. He is obviously anxious to excuse his own version of the Parthenon on Calton Hill, Edinburgh.
11. This theme was elaborated in a lecture he gave at the Architectural Museum on 'The Distinctive Characteristics of Greek and Mediaeval Sculpture as applied to Architecture', which was fully reported in *The Builder*, XII, 1854, pp. 457–9.

of Adrian Stokes. It leads him naturally to a discussion of entasis and the use of parabolic curves where, characteristically he gives all the credit to Professor Penrose not mentioning that it was he himself, in 1810, who for the first time noticed and recorded the use of entasis on the columns of the Parthenon. Curiously, he never seems to have followed up his early investigations and analysis of entasis does not form a prominent part of any of his lectures. For a full presentation he referred his students in later lectures to Penrose's *Investigations of the Principles of Athenian Architecture* of 1852. One of the most important archaeological publications of all time, this remarkable study which came as the climax of a century of English scholarly interest in Greek architecture should, one feels, have been written by Cockerell himself. However, there is a sense in which the generous and wholehearted way in which Cockerell threw himself for fifteen years into the task of enlightening the young and uninformed by lectures, prevented him from pursuing his independent researches. Thus he had to be content in his lectures with throwing out suggestive hints like the following:

'Vitruvius had overlooked one important feature of the Doric order, namely the steps forming its stylobate. In the main steps, the Greeks introduced a sinking in each riser, which gave its due effect of shade to every step, and but for this expedient the steps would have presented the appearance of an unbroken mass of light when the sun shone full upon them.'

As a modern and rather different example of 'the happy contrast between curved and straight' he cited the huge arch at the entrance to the Hôtel Thélusson in Paris by 'the eccentric Ledoux'. In a lecture of 1845 he had already singled out this splendid archway as an object 'perfectly scenic and theatrical' and exquisitely placed so as to frame the view of the house itself. He had recommended that the entrance to a railway terminus might be marked by such an arch, seventy foot in diameter, sixty feet high and thirty feet deep with offices contrived in flanking wings.

'The happy contrast between the curved and the straight' goes a long way to explaining the peculiar merit of Cockerell's own architecture in which there is a great predilection for curved forms. In his lectures he attempted to build this into a great system, arguing that the triangular form is Gothic, the square and circular Greek: 'in triangular forms there must be absolute light contrasted with absolute darkness; whereas in square or circular compositions an exquisite gradation of light is obtained.' He was enchanted by the circular forms of the Colosseum, Pantheon and Castel

Sant'Angelo, Jones' Persian Court at the Palace of Whitehall, the curves and counter-curves of Wren's steeple at St. Vedast, Foster Lane, and the splendid drama of the crescent at Bath – all these, he felt, together with 'the column in all its varieties, the rainbow arch of the bridge and the vaulted ceiling were alike wonders of structure, strength, suavity of form, gradation of light and shade and beauty of effect from every point of view.' He considered that 'The less the elevation of circular buildings, the better their effect; their proportion should be rather that of the single or double Gloucester, than of the Stilton cheese.' He passes from a consideration of the circle to its offspring, the spiral line: 'In treating the spiral line we should admire the fossil relic, Cornua Ammonis which, if it had been a work of art discovered amongst the ruins of Greece or Ninevah would have been the theme of general admiration, but as a natural phenomenon was altogether disregarded. Tacitus claims that Venus was worshipped in Cyprus under the form of the cone said to have fallen from Olympus – as if the worshippers of beauty had recognized its principal element in that form.'

This feeling for geometry, for the language of sphere, cone and cube, combined with his search for order, had a profound effect on the revolutionary interpretation of Gothic architecture which he elaborated in the mid-1840's. To this major aspect of not only his lectures but of his whole scholarly output we should now address our attention.

The references to Gothic in his earliest lectures are brief and hostile but round about 1845 his views changed dramatically as a result of discovering that in his edition of Vitruvius, published at Como in 1521, Cesare Cesariano had chosen to illustrate the proportional theories of Vitruvius with sections of Milan Cathedral. This opened up to Cockerell the attractive notion that Gothic architecture might be found to be governed by a series of proportional relationships as sophisticated as those which he had discovered in Greek temples. He immediately set about testing this hypothesis by measuring William of Wykeham's chapels at Winchester and New College and gave the remarkable results to the world, or rather to the members of the Archaeological Institute of Great Britain and Ireland, in September 1845 at the Annual Meeting of the Archaeological Institute at Winchester.[12] His researches formed the basis of his course of lectures the following year at the Royal Academy.

Cockerell worked in association with the great Robert Willis (1800–1875), to whose discoveries he frequently refers in his lectures and whose methods

12. Published in *Proceedings at the Annual Meeting of the Archaeological Institute of Great Britain and Ireland at Winchester, 1845, 1846*. It was reviewed in *The Ecclesiologist*, VI, 1846, pp. 222–7.

revolutionized the study of architectural history. Willis' painstaking studies of the fabric of English cathedrals, published in the 1840's and '50's, have never been equalled, still less surpassed. Both he and Cockerell were pioneer figures in the Archaeological Institute and published their findings on mediaeval subjects in its *Proceedings*. Thus on the same morning in 1845 Willis delivered his brilliant paper on Winchester Cathedral and Cockerell his on William of Wykeham; in July 1848 at Lincoln, Cockerell read a paper on the sculpture of Lincoln Cathedral and Penrose on the system of proportions in the nave; in 1849 Cockerell spoke on the sculpture of Salisbury, and Willis on the architecture; and similarly in 1851 Cockerell spoke on the sculpture of Wells and Willis on the architecture.

Archaeological interest in Gothic architecture had, of course, been growing since the middle of the eighteenth century but by the late 1830's scholars were interested not so much in acquiring more descriptive information but in discovering the principles or systems which, they felt, constituted the 'secret' of mediaeval design. J. W. Papworth and R. W. Billings published important investigations into proportional systems in 1840 and 1847 respectively but Cockerell's contribution was possibly of more significance. Penrose, as we have seen, also took up the topic. It is no coincidence that Penrose and Cockerell were both trained observers of the proportion and entasis common in Greek architecture and both interpreted what they saw in the same way. Thus both the Gothic proportional methods observed by Cockerell and the entasis observed by Penrose were originally employed as a means to an aesthetic end. However, in writing about them, both men tend to interpret the means as the end. This is particularly true of Penrose for whom entasis and the whole Greek employment of parabolic curves were nothing more than a predictable practical device for correcting optical illusions.

The six lectures which Cockerell devoted to explaining his views on Gothic architecture at the Academy in 1846 began with a brilliant and revolutionary survey of the Gothic Revival – revolutionary in its understanding of the Gothic intentions which lay behind French neo-classicism. These were not generally uncovered until Dr. Robin Middleton wrote his remarkable thesis on Viollet-le-Duc in 1958.[13] Cockerell spoke of the researches and influence of Batty Langley, Walpole, Wyatt, Grose and Bentham, and realized that James Essex 'had done more in the examination of

13. *Viollet-le-Duc and the Rational Gothic Tradition*, unpublished Cambridge Ph.D. dissertation, 1958.

principles than anyone of his day'; he spoke, too, of the great trio of Carter, Britton and Willis who 'belonged to that class of patient investigators of whom Wren was the head.' We have already seen Cockerell's interpretation of St. Paul's in essentially Gothic terms. Here he writes: 'The principles of the architecture of Wren were those of the middle ages which that architect was well acquainted with and greatly venerated. The Panthéon [Ste. Geneviève in Paris, by Soufflot, 1757] was built in imitation of St. Paul's Cathedral, but in the constructive part the imitation of mediaeval architecture was carried to too close a point; the supporting piers had been too weak and a failure had been the consequence. Soufflot had collected together many drawings of Gothic buildings in France.' Cockerell concluded that 'at present we had done little more than collect the materials for correct analysis, but from which it could be shown that no random or caprice entered into the fundamental principles of the style.' It was a realization of this last point which made him impatient with the Gothic Revival. As he told his pupils, he had 'always greatly admired the style but we merely copied the forms and did not possess the principles.'

What then were the principles? Certainly not social, moral and theological like those of Pugin. Cockerell observed in a delightful, dismissive way: 'The Cambridge Camden Society had discovered itself in the pursuit of other objects than those of art, and consequently had been put down'! Cockerell's approach to the principles was, as we have already hinted, through his discovery that mediaeval architects had known and sometimes venerated Vitruvius, but, because the diagrams to Vitruvius' work had been lost the mediaeval architects substituted their own interpretation. The rules discovered by Cockerell were those set forth by Cesariano in his Commentary (folios xiv and xv) on the Ichnography, Orthography and Scenography of Vitruvius (lib. i. c. 11) which he illustrated by the plan, section and elevation of Milan Cathedral of 1386. The first rule ('a Trigono') establishes the respective proportions of the length and breadth of the cruciform body of the church. These are included within two arcs of 120° constructed according to the first proposition of Euclid and forming in shape the 'Vesica Piscis', the ancient anagram symbolical of Our Lord, the form of which is so familiar in mediaeval art. The 'Vesica Piscis' also enables the architect to set out a right angle and an equilateral triangle upon the ground.

The second rule ('a Pariquadrato') determines the position of the columns or piers and the external walls and buttresses by dividing the area contained within the 'Vesica Piscis' into commensurate squares or bays on the intersections of which the columns and piers are placed.

The object of the third rule (also 'a Trigono') is to establish the height of the building by equilateral triangles, of which the sides correspond with the diameter of the entire plan or its commensurate parts.

Cockerell later published a diagram (Pl. 14) showing the application of all these measurements to the design of an imaginary cathedral. His clear and simple diagrams of the application of the rules to the chapels at Winchester (Pl. 15) and New College are memorable and convincing. He notes that both chapels are divided longitudinally by seven equal parts and transversely by four. He is fascinated by the recurrence of the number seven, 'a number of perfection': 'accordingly we find the number seven employed in the following remarkable instances, sometimes in the nave and sometimes in the choir: In the cathedral churches of York, Westminster, Exeter, Bristol, Durham, Lichfield, Paris, Amiens, Chartres, Evreux, Romsey church, Waltham Abbey, Buildwas, the Norman portion of St. Alban's, Castle Acre, St. George's Windsor, Roslyn, &c. &c.'

Cockerell's forty-six page pamphlet on William of Wykeham, which we have considered in conjunction with his Academy lectures on Gothic, is a model of architectural history in its combination of the general and the particular, its presentation of the social, political and religious setting, its analysis of the structural, aesthetic and symbolic aspects of Wykeham's buildings and their relation to the character and aims of their patron.

If in the 1840's Cockerell's lectures were lent piquancy by his unexpected discoveries concerning Gothic proportional systems, the arrival of the Crystal Palace in the 1850's was another event which could not but influence the direction of the lectures. It is at first sight surprising to find Cockerell sharing the general bourgeois enthusiasm for the Crystal Palace. On the whole, the finer minds of the nineteenth century disapproved the new ferro-vitreous architecture, and on the whole they were right: a limited constructional technique, lacking in human warmth or expression, it had already played itself out by the end of the century.[14] However, Cockerell was looking beyond the superficial appearance and had seen the ordered system that lay behind. Just as it was the pursuit of such a system that had first led to his enthusiasm for Gothic, so now it was to lead to admiration for the Crystal Palace.

On 22 February 1851, he proudly announced to his audience that he had

14. The tone of his comments altered slightly towards the end of the decade when, speaking in praise of Owen Jones' use of interior colour, he argued that, 'Without his assistance the Crystal Palace would have been but an overgrown green house' ('On the Painting of the Ancients', *The Civil Engineer and Architect's Journal*, XXII, 1859, p. 90).

been the day before to a private viewing of the new Exhibition Building. His first words of description were: 'Commensuration (which was a part of the Greek definition of symmetry) is the great feature of it. We all know that every proportion of it is a multiple of eight ... William of Wykeham especially formed his ground plans upon the equality of spaces or multiples of them.' One can only marvel at the freshness, independence and perception of a man in his sixty-third year who has been lecturing for a decade on the same general topics. Who, knowing nothing of Cockerell but the conventional picture of a dogmatic preacher of a set of classical rules, increasingly out of touch with the spirit of his age, would ever think of attributing to him this bold conjunction of New College chapel and the Crystal Palace?

He returned to the theme in his last course given in 1856. Surveying the development of iron as a building material, he praised Rennie's revolutionary Southwark Bridge of 1814–19 with its three cast-iron arches, Smirke's use of iron for trabeation at the British Museum, and Sidney Smirke's dome at the British Museum Reading Room. 'But', he added significantly, 'the engineers have kept ahead of the architects from Mr. Rennie to Messrs. Stephenson in displaying the powers of iron. But recent experiments since 1851 in England and France show plainly that iron will revolutionize architecture and will give to the art in the nineteenth century that characteristic style which we have long been whining about as the desideratum and the deficiency of our age.' Iron was attractive both because it 'was cited in Deuteronomy as the essential and last fruit of the promised land' and also because it was analogous to the forms of nature, as the palm, cane or reed. It could be governed by similar proportions to those of these natural forms and could also be decorated and made susceptible to a similar system of classification as divided the Doric, Ionic, and Corinthian.' He argued that the architect should be Janus-headed, displaying reverence for authority on the one side – to which the Ecclesiologists adhered too fanatically – while 'the other face is young, looking only forward, enterprising, prospective, for ever taking advantages of the discoveries and appliances of the day.' In a memorable phrase he observed that 'Iron might be termed the osteology of building.' He elaborated this by arguing that, 'Hitherto, the architectural system had proceeded on statics and the equipose of molecules, as if the human frame had been built without bones. Now our buildings would have bones, giving unity and strength which never before existed.' Considering that it was not iron which ultimately revolutionized architecture but concrete reinforced with steel, it is remarkable that he passed immediately on to a discussion of the use of concrete. He reminds his audience of the concrete

Pont de l'Alma 'raised these eight months in Paris, a new and admirable development where three arches of about 140 feet span form one vast stone from pier to pier cast directly on the centreing.' He considered that, 'ranking among the gigantic novelties of the day', it is 'a great hope for the future if it stands.' He cannot resist reminding them further that the 'so-called Temple of Peace at Rome was ceiled and vaulted with a similar form of concrete.'

He thus concludes that, 'It need never be doubted that the year 1900 will display in architecture that which never before was dreamt of, characterizing the century in a manner worthy of its extraordinary progress in civilization.'

His last words to his students, however, were concerned not with the uncertainties of the future but the educative splendours of the past. He dwelt finally on St. Paul's, where within seven years he was to lie himself next to its architect, and on the Parthenon where 'the sculptor treats the architecture as the mere framework and enclosure to his work'; his last three words were, 'Study, study, study.'

In a late portrait of Cockerell by Boxall (Pl. 170) we see the ethereal face the Academy students saw. To these young men, caught up as they must have been in the Ruskinian passion for Gothic, Cockerell, with his burning eyes and hollow cheeks, must sometimes have seemed as remote, as archaic and as awe-inspiring as the ancient Greeks themselves. Yet he must surely have convinced them – to quote the words he had used as a young man to his father – that he had devoted his life to being a 'professor of the beautiful in architecture'. In 1855 he had praised Ruskin's *Seven Lamps* but had pointed out that 'his Lamps are not of architecture but of ethics' and had proposed instead lamps of Wisdom, Power and Beauty. Though Cockerell invented no new analogies between art and morals, as Pugin and Ruskin were doing, he was sufficiently a child of his time to accept some of the inherited assumptions about the later Roman Empire. The following passage, rather untypical of Cockerell, appears in 1851: 'It is proved by history that architure and public morals decline simultaneously. To any philosophic student, comparing the history of the age of Augustus with that of Justinian that the architectural works of the former period must of necessity be elevated, and those of the latter debased. The student should be guarded against the meretricious graces of Spalatro, Baalbec, Palmyra and the Byzantine works described by D'Agincourt.'

He is typical of possibly the best in his age in his complete acceptance of the Victorian code of the gentleman. It is a concept which no one should deride who surveys dispassionately Cockerell's life and career. In 1849 he told his pupils:

'I must congratulate you on the choice of a profession so entirely that of a gentleman; for as my German friends truly say, 'no man can be a thorough gentleman unless he has something of the artist in him; and no man can be a thorough artist unless he is (in mind and character at least) a thorough gentleman' . . . He stands before Princes as their counsellor and confidential friend, and holds their purse strings; and he takes by the hand the humblest artificer . . . he becomes the keystone of the social arch.'

One of the aspects of architecture which made it a fitting occupation for a gentleman was that it involved the art of contemplation. 'Architecture', he believed, 'is an art which requires as much thought as observation, and more might be done in four walls than by galloping all over the world. It is possible to have seen everything and to have learnt nothing . . . Travel should not be the rushing down to Greece and Italy and losing ourselves in sentimentalities; but we ought first to see every part of our own country, and next rather the north of Europe than the south, and lastly, Italy and Greece. Some of the best architects, Wren, never travelled at all.'

Cockerell's vision, of course, went beyond the gentlemanly and in 1850 he gave clear advice to his pupils:

'Always be great and let the lamp of Power be ever before you. We may be great on little occasions. A work of architecture should strike us as a moral deed. All my life I have desired to achieve something grand – but never have succeeded, except once, in the scraper of the north door of St. Paul's which I put up. I hope you will do me the honour to look at it.'[15]

These words well convey the quality of Cockerell's lectures: the arresting combination of the general and the particular.

Perhaps what we remember most about the lectures is their amazing freshness, novelty, and variety: a variety both of approach and of subject matter. The approach thus reminds us now of Pevsner or Wölfflin, now of Scully, Venturi or Zevi; the subject-matter, too, is continually unexpected, ranging from egg-shells to the Crystal Palace and from whale-skulls to Peterborough Cathedral; we are stopped in our tracks by his cogent references to Alberti and William of Wykeham, to Ledoux and to Pugin whose gateway at Magdalen College, Oxford, is praised for its masterly use of polychromy.

---

15. This is evidently Cockerell's idea of a joke. His scrapers survive outside the doors in the north and south transepts. Though now in a state of decay they can never have been impressive.

Inspired by the 'drop-scene' which Cockerell produced in 1840, he prepared in 1848 a similar composite view of the great buildings of the world which he called *The Professor's Dream* (Pl. 16). This was smaller in size than the 'drop-scene', over six feet long by nearly five feet high, and differed further in that the buildings are not on the same level but ranged on four terraces thirty feet above each other. This strange romance, these pyramids, porticos and domes, is surely the idea, years before its time, of Banister Fletcher's celebrated *History of Architecture on the Comparative Method*. One can only envy Cockerell for having lived before the invention of stylistic labels by architectural historians. Thus, unhampered by considerations of whether a particular building was 'Baroque' or 'Neo-Classical' he could dart from one period, place or person to another in pursuit of what Sir John Summerson has called 'the Classical Language of Architecture'. In marveling at his skill in pursuit and the over-riding belief in order which impelled him to undertake it, I am reminded of the words of that great historian, F. A. Simpson, who described how 'the mind of man can range unimaginably fast and far, while riding to the anchor of a liturgy.'[16]

16. In *A Commemoration of Benefactors*, Great St Mary's Church, Cambridge, 1932, reprinted 1972.

PART III

Architect

CHAPTER IX

The Hanover Chapel and Some Early Works

ODDLY enough, Cockerell's first executed building was not Greek but Tudor. The irony must have amused his father who had gone out of his way to tell him the year before that despite his 'high order of Taste & information . . . [he must learn] to suit in some measure the times we live in.' The mood of the day demanded the Gothic not the Classic style for educational buildings. Thus when the headmaster of Harrow, the brilliant Dr George Butler (1774–1853), invited Cockerell to design new buildings for the school in 1818, he provided a skilful pastiche of the Tudor style which doubtless continues to deceive the majority of visitors today (Pl. 17). The same can hardly be true of any other building of its date.[1] His first work, then, prepares us for an architectural career only marginally related to contemporary fashions.

What Cockerell did at Harrow between 1818 and 1820[2] was to add a balancing wing to the original Speech Room building, providing the resultant skyline with the twin crow-stepped gables which are the most memorable visual experience of the whole school. In fact, they *are* Harrow. Visiting the new building in March 1823 he wrote in his diary, 'pleased with Harrow, something, collegiate and striking. the gates good piece of work [and the] chequered wall. throughout there is a diligence & elegance.' In a similar 'Jacobean collegiate' style he provided an attractive chapel at Harrow in 1838 (Pl. 18).

Though he received few architectural commissions before 1821 he designed a number of funerary monuments of which the most splendid, not executed, was one of 1818 for Princess Charlotte (Pl. 20). The drawing for it

---

1. Mr Howard Colvin reminds me, however, that Cockerell was not entirely alone in his gift for pastiche. The church of SS. Peter and Paul, Kirton-in-Holland, Lincolnshire, was skilfully rebuilt in 1804 by William Hayward, and the church of St Lawrence, Meriden, Warwickshire, contains much deceptive work of 1826–27.

2. E. D. Laborde, *Harrow School, Yesterday and Today*, 1948, pp. 69–70.

shows the quite exceptional elegance of his draughtsmanship, the rich fertility of his imagination. A year later he was commissioned to design a monument to Admiral Lord Collingwood in the church of St. Nicholas (now the Cathedral), Newcastle-upon-Tyne (Pl. 19). It was executed by John Rossi (1762–1839). When Cockerell visited in in September 1823 he wrote, 'sorry to see my Mon[umen]t of Ld. Collingwood, felt the head was too large & whole too sunk.'

Throughout his life Cockerell had a genius for the design of metal-work and two sharply contrasting designs of these early years well convey the range of his invention. Plate 21 shows a remarkable project of 1819 for a hammer-beam roof constructed of cast-iron, while Plate 22 is a sumptuous neo-classical candelabrum designed a year later.

By this time, the building expansion of the post-Waterloo years was well under way. Two of the most characteristic products of these newly-serious years were the Commissioners' Church and the Literary Institute. Any young architect would be lucky to begin his career with commissions for either of these, and it was Cockerell's extreme good fortune to be invited to design both: the Hanover Chapel in Regent Street and the Literary and Philosophical Institution at Bristol.

For seventy years the unforgettable twin towers of Cockerell's Hanover Chapel enlivened the skyline of Nash's Regent Street (Pls 27–29). Designed in 1821–22 for its cramped site on the west side of the street, just south of Oxford Circus, it was executed from 1823–25 and demolished in 1896. St. George's, Regent Street, known as the Hanover Chapel since it was a chapel of ease to St. George's, Hanover Square, was Cockerell's first important commission. He probably owed it to his father who had been appointed Surveyor to the Parish of St. George's in 1774. With its prominent position in London's newest and most fashionable street it could hardly fail to attract the attention of all those whose opinions were of consequence in the social and architectural world.

Though an early work the Hanover Chapel is highly characteristic of Cockerell's idiosyncratic architectural aims and of his leisurely introspective process of design. From the start it was clear that it was going to be quite unlike any other of the Commissioners' churches. Indeed, Cockerell's buildings are nearly always unlike the works of his English contemporaries. His abhorrence of the common-place and of the easy solution saw to that. In fact it almost seems that where there was no problem he was not happy till he had created one and then solved it in at least half a dozen original ways. Certainly at the Hanover Chapel the problems were many and grave, the most important being the extreme awkwardness of the site. Cockerell himself observed that 'a site less favourable for the purpose . . . can hardly be found, the western end being so much contracted by the premises on the south, and by a right of carriage-way on the north, as to give to the ground the form rather of a wedge than a parellelogram: the buildings also by which it is surrounded, preclude in a great measure, the power of obtaining light from the sides.' To these unavoidable difficulties the Commissioners added two of their own creation: a demand that the chapel should seat the un-realistically large number of fifteen hundred persons; and that the communion table be placed at the east end which, since the chapel was on the west side of the street, was necessarily the end from which public entry to the chapel had to be gained. Furthermore, the Commissioners of the New Street decided, after the foundations of the portico had been laid, that the pavement had to be widened. Thus, since the portico passed over the pavement, the portico itself had to be enlarged while the building was in progress. Other difficulties included Cockerell's painful battle with the Church Commissioners over their insistence on architects entering into a bond that their estimates would not be exceeded. At first Cockerell strongly resisted this demand but later had to withdraw ignominiously from his position.

The many problems and complications which attended the erection of the Hanover Chapel can only have confirmed Cockerell's early suspicions that he would find the architectural profession both demanding and uncongenial. It could hardly be said, however, that lack of funds was one of the problems he was called upon to face. The Hanover Chapel cost £16,628, a figure exceeded by only eighteen of the six hundred new churches built by the Commissioners between 1818 and 1856. Furthermore, it was built of Bath stone, not stucco.

The cramped site of the chapel meant that every inch of it had to be used. The problem which faced Cockerell, therefore, was that of designing street architecture, not an isolated monument. His façade thus continued the frontage and the architrave line of the adjacent houses and shops (Pl. 29). It was a model of architectural good manners, yet no one could deny its distinctive impact in an already unusual street. What gave the church its memorable stamp of originality was its twin towers. These were originally objected to by the Commissioners when they saw the plans in June 1822. Cockerell was adamant. He would not consent to a tower 'growing out of roof' and felt that without his twin towers the church 'may be Theatre or any other building'. Evidently he was anxious to avoid what he felt to be the illogical form of the typical English classical church, established by Gibbs at

L

St. Martin-in-the-Fields, in which a central tower rose incongruously above a pedimented portico. His solution of placing a single tower on either side of the portico where it also formed a logical termination to each aisle is, in a sense, a Gothic notion. Perhaps it is significant that in his diary Cockerell usually refers to the towers as 'turrets', a word with definitely Gothic or mediaeval overtones. He did, however, observe that this disposition of a west front was common on the continent and it is unlikely that in making this remark he had mediaeval architecture in mind. There had been Grand Prix competitions for twin-towered churches in 1802 and 1809. Related to these was Gisors' St. Vincent at Macon of 1810, a church with which Cockerell may have been familiar: in March 1822 his friend the architect Sharp promised to send him details of a French church similar to the Hanover Chapel.

A very definite source is provided by the background buildings in some of Claude's famous seaport paintings. The day before the foundation-stone of the church was laid Cockerell visited the Angerstein collection of pictures where he was 'much flattered at Claude's pictures & finding in 2 of the 5 pictures in this collection the idea of the two turrets repeated at the entrance of a building as in my chapel. I have little doubt that the idea of this adoption arose in my mind from having seen these pictures and engravings. in these wonderful pictures one feels the balmy rosy atmosphere of the Mediterranean ... which I so well remember.' The art historian cannot fail to notice with interest that here the artist has become conscious of his source only *after* he has employed it. That the source of inspiration should, in this case, be a painting by Claude shows the quite extraordinarily persistent influence of the Picturesque on English neo-classical architecture.

Cockerell discovered that his towers were an unconscious echo of yet another earlier source: Vanbrugh's Town Hall of 1716 at Morpeth in Northumberland. When he saw this building in July 1822, he noted that it was 'picturesque *like my chapel.*'

The twin towers, however, were not universally admired. Forming a feature as unforgettable as Maderno's 'asses' ears' at the Pantheon, they could not escape becoming, for some, an object of affectionate ridicule. The opinion of the architect Foster seems to have been a fairly common one: Cockerell records on 15 February 1825, 'Walked with J. Foster to see my Chapel, said there was something wanting in the Turrets, did not like them, this is every one's opinion'. In the following year he describes how 'Smirke talked of the skyline as the silhouette or contour made on the air by an object as my towers at Chapel for instance to which he objects'. There was considerable comfort, however, from the ageing Flaxman, 'who approved my chapel greatly especially in the turrets'.

The dramatic skyline was balanced by an equally bold handling of the façade itself, in which interest tended to be concentrated towards the top. Thus the walls were smooth up to the sills of the windows; above this point they were heavily rusticated, as was the attic itself. The windows and the side doors within the portico were kept deliberately small so as to emphasize the 'remarkable breadth and solidity' of the front as a whole. He seems to have considered taking the design for the doors from those in the Baptistery in Florence, and notes in his diary in June 1821: 'thought of having the gates of my church cast from those of Florence [with] a niche on either side.'

The general proportions of the portico itself were based on the temple of Athena Nike at Athens. The design of the entablature of the whole façade posed some problems. As late as August 1823, Cockerell 'adjusted entablature, lowered it, endeavoured to give it character and expression. found Teos one of the most characteristic with strength given to the details. Priene not so much so, tho very beautiful. in Aphrodisias there is less distinction given to the parts, evidently of lower time. endeavoured at the finesse & expression of real Greek, breadth boldness finesse.' A single entablature united organically portico and towers, the distinction between these parts being adequately emphasized by their different orders. The Ionic order of the portico was that of the temple of Athene at Priene; the pilaster capitals of the side wings were taken from those at the temple of Apollo Didymaeus at Miletus. These great temples of the Hellenistic and later periods in what is now Turkey had rarely been imitated by English architects, but Cockerell felt strongly that the Asiatic Ionic, on account of the grandeur and size of Eastern temples, was often more appropriate for modern use than the smaller and 'graceful examples of Attica' popular with English architects. The grandeur of conception of the Didymaean temple was combined with a rich peculiarity of detail in a manner irresistible to a man of Cockerell's tastes. He wrote in his diary for 29 April 1821: 'Upon the chapel New Street all day hit upon the double pilaster to carry tower & Portico. gives grandeur. chose Asiatic Ionic not yet seen – the cap[ital]s of Sardis, the pilasters of Miletus. T[empl]e on Ilissus & Min[erv]a polias in Acropolis used to excess and abused. [Inwood] ... has employed it at St. Pancras an imitation for which the arch[itec]t sent his son to Athens. Scale always mistaken. Smirke has employ[e]d T[empl]e on Ilissus in more than twice the size. Mr. Inwood nearly twice.'

The immense and solitary doorway of the chapel contributed greatly to the aloof dignity of the façade. Cockerell emphasized how this 'doorway, in conformity with the Vitruvian precept (too rarely observed), is proportioned to the whole frontispiece, and reigns alone within the portico . . .' It was on 6 July 1821 that this idea first occurred to him. 'There does not exist', he noted on that day, 'a single portico correctly copied in this respect: we affect the col[umn]s of a portico of the ancients but we neglect the door which formed so striking a part altogether. this may arise from its rarity as it exists only in the Pantheon . . . 3 mean doors lead from Portico to Chambre des Deputes – think it must have a great effect.' An early project for the façade (Pl. 29) shows how much of grandeur is lost by substituting for this single great doorway a trio of smaller ones. The building as depicted in this sketch makes a feebler impact than as executed for a number of other reasons, of which the most noticeable is probably the absence of rustication; also the openings in the belfries are filled with conventional louvres in place of the striking cruciform arrangement eventually adopted, and the prominent dentil cornice of the portico is not continued on the entablature of the side wings which are thus less firmly linked to the centre of the building. In the final designs this dentil cornice was extended to the side wings where it was, however, appreciably smaller than in the portico: a subtle way of lending greater emphasis to the portico. The dentils were entirely omitted from the raking cornice of the pediment since Cockerell felt that in that position they were 'always attended with a crowded and graceless effect'. So as to fill the space which a dentil cornice would have taken up in the pediment Cockerell advanced the whole plane of the tympanum. Further adjustments to emphasize the portico are indicated in his diary in January 1823: 'settled with J. Noble mode of granate Plinth to Chapel. made a good hit in imagining the Pilaster of portico to have base like col[umn]s so to distinguish itself from other pilasters & by advancing to place basement wind[ow] in centre of Plinth. I think cap[ital] of Portico pilaster should be enriched the others not. settled to make lower plinth only of Granate, upper of Portland according with Plinths of Col[umn]s.' The extremely slow and thoughtful nature of Cockerell's process of design can be appreciated from the fact that when this entry in his diary was written the foundations had already been laid of some of the columns of the portico. More remarkably, it was not until December 1823 that he finally determined on a rectangular outline for the top of the towers. On 18 December he notes: 'walked with Anne [his sister] to St. George's chapel. she felt there was more of greatness & originality in the square topped towers & persuaded me accordingly.

after much consideration on the spot I decided & gave draw[in]g to Hancock.'

The nervous introspection of which this slowness was in part the product is made clear in a quotation from his diary for 19 April 1821 in which he turns over in his mind the difficulties he has experienced during the day: 'Worked at the Chapel in Regent St. – could not bring myself to put it on paper till the last moment. – hard worked at it on Sunday. & brought myself to the conclusion of the 2 col[umn]s the fancy is wayward, could not work it but was more idle than usual because so pressed still bearing in mind the work. find that one required *échauffement* in order to force one to produce and to induce those vaporish & confused notions from whence as if shaken in a sack something new & unexpected derived. – "tell me where does fancy dwell." '

In this building Cockerell first introduced a feature which was to be a hall-mark of all his finest work: the magnitude of the blocks of masonry. The sheer physical size of the stones he employed always gives his buildings an unforgettably compelling presence, a bold and silencing weight. At the Hanover Chapel some of the stones making up the portico architrave were fourteen feet long. This characteristic Cockerell had observed for himself in the temples of the ancient world; he had seen it confirmed in the pages of Vitruvius; and in the Bible he found a third justification in the description of the building of Solomon's temple in the Third Book of Kings. This concept of sacred architecture meant much to him and he rejoiced greatly in bending to Christian aims pagan and Jewish religious traditions. It was a theme which he developed in a more personal manner in the interior of the chapel. To the interior and to the plan (Pl. 30) we should now address our attention.

Despite the irregularities of the site, Cockerell contrived to produce an alternative plan for the church which was wholly rectangular save for the projections of the two towers and of a shallow segmental apse at the west end. This dull plan was rejected in favour of one of a complexity which must be unique amongst English churches – indeed one could hardly wish it other than unique. Its curious diminution or shrinking towards the west as it edged its way uneasily between a projecting house to the south and a carriage-way to the north was effected by two successive re-entrant angles. As a result the west wall was barely more than twenty feet long: a baffling anticlimax after a street frontage of seventy feet. A natural assumption from reading the plan would be that this small shallow western projection was the chancel. This, however, was not so. As was mentioned earlier, the

Commissioners insisted that the altar be at the east end. Moreover, the pre-Oxford-Movement Anglican church had no need of a chancel. In the Hanover Chapel attention focused not on the communion table but on a monumental centrally placed pulpit. Every other inch of space was taken up by pews, and of course there was no choir. Cockerell's extremely Evangelical views on church planning were expressed in a letter he wrote much later to Sir Thomas Acland: 'ours at present is the most incongruous that perhaps exists. a popular & perhaps superstitious attachment to the Roman form the lengthened nave & aisles is tacitly admited by the Commiss[ione]rs of churches, the *low* altar . . . are all cherished to the ruin of the purpose & of the architecture. The fact I *boldly* believe to be that our church saw its flock going so fast to the wolves that they built folds without ever caring about the manner such was their haste. Whereas in Queen Anne's time Sir C. Wren & the commissioners laid down rules adapted to our wants for auditories, which have been followed by the Dissenters whose churches have after all the true form for the Protestant church.'[3] However, a later age than Cockerell's, in which the provision of choir-stalls and an 'English altar' with decent riddel-curtains assumed more importance than correct orientation, turned the Hanover Chapel back to front, removed the western galleries and in their place formed a chancel with traditional choir-stalls.[4]

As an exercise in mental geometry Cockerell's treatment of the problems posed by his site was masterly, even if when translated into reality it must have been a rather crowded and overpowering space in which to worship. That he realized this himself is perhaps suggested by his emphasis on the plan of the ceiling in the account he wrote of the chapel for Britton and Pugin's *The Public Buildings of London* (1825–28). He even included a diagram of the ceiling (Pl. 31), arguing that it was the ceiling, and particularly its 'intersecting trabeation' which connected the several parts of 'the whole into one harmonious figure'. Indeed, the 'Ceiling, addressing itself perspicuously to the view of the spectator, will at all times be the best index of the design, as respects the geometrical arrangement of the edifice.' The 'geometrical arrangement', of which he was so proud, was briefly this: the widest part of the site allowed for a cube of about forty-three feet which was supported by four columns and pilasters. Outside the long sides of this area, that is the north and south, ran narrow aisles separated from the central area by piers. West of this opened a similar smaller space, though lacking the aisles; and west of this again was a yet smaller projection framed by pilasters answering

3. Letter to Sir Thomas Acland, Bart. of 30 November 1836, at the Devon County Record Office.
4. See *The Architect*, XLVII, 1892, pp. 29 & 45.

the westernmost columns of the central area. This central area Cockerell likened to the atrium of the classical house, that is, the central courtyard containing an impluvium or tank. He fancifully argued that his glazed dome corresponded to the impluvium. Certainly the great dome of glass and iron, combining the offices of lantern and dome, was a remarkable creation for its date. Cockerell himself claimed uniqueness for it, although he pointed out that the sides of the spire in the Anatomical Theatre at the College of Physicians in Warwick Lane were pierced with windows. He had also essayed a similar dome over the staircase at the house in Pall Mall which he had remodelled for the Travellers' Club. At the Hanover Chapel the dome was supported not directly by the four central columns but by a trabeated system resting on the architraves of the columns. This emphasis upon construction in space is vital to an appreciation of the chapel. Very early in the process of design he notes: 'my chapel the atrium impluviatum in interior – shewing the beams.' The aim of 'shewing the beams' is fundamental to his style: he wanted the eye to see and the mind to take pleasure in the constructional reality of beams and members, joists and trabeation – a desire as rare in English as it is common in French architecture. Unfortunately, in the executed building the presence of pews for fifteen hundred people tended to counteract any effect the display of beams might have had. In order to appreciate that effect fully we must look at Cockerell's striking drawing (Pl. 32) with its wonderfully satisfying grid of beams and piers, pilasters and columns. This, however, is only a preliminary sketch and Cockerell was forced to depart from it by introducing a second gallery (Pl. 33) – the realization that this would be necessary must have been an unhappy moment. However, he managed to incorporate it organically in a way of which he was justly proud and which we should allow him to describe himself: the 'collocation of the columns and pilasters determines the situation of the respective galleries; the lower advancing to the columns, the upper to the pilasters; and by thus receding, the theatrical appearance produced by double galleries is effectually obviated.' (Pl. 34). Another departure from the interior as depicted in the sketch affected the dome. In the sketch the glazed openings rest directly on the cove but in the final design 'a choir of cherubim' was interposed between these two areas. Perhaps this daring innovation owed something to the great ring of caryatids supporting the lantern in Soane's Consols Office at the Bank of England, but I think it more likely that Cockerell's source was biblical. There are notes from the Third Book of Kings in his diary in 1823 on the construction of Solomon's temple. No one who reads that description can remain unaware of the prominent role played by the cherubim in the iconography of the greatest of the Jewish temples. Only second to it in importance was the representation of the palm. Thus as the cherubim appeared below Cockerell's dome, on the apex of which appeared a symbol of the Trinity, so the palm-branch was carved on the capitals of the four Corinthian columns. Also on these remarkable capitals were great carved doves, the work of the sculptor Nicholl. By a stroke of Cockerell's strange imagination these biblical overtones were contained within an Early Christian setting, for the Corinthian order of the interior was generally based on that of the Golden Gate at Constantinople erected under Theodosius II in the first half of the fifth century. Cockerell's nervous, fertile genius, taut with recondite allusion, may occasionally have led him to concentrate more in a small space than might have been permitted by a more relaxed and successful designer. Nor have we yet exhausted exploration of the chapel's stylistic echoes. Its interior, Cockerell claimed, had 'frequently been compared with that of St. Stephen's, Walbrook, one of Sir C. Wren's most admired works.' Except in the broadest terms the comparison is not a very relevant one. Moreover, when Cockerell visited St. Stephen's in February 1822 he recorded in his diary: 'did not so much like it, the oval lights all ways disagreeable – thin unsolid in the arches so in the angles – coarse in the taste of the ornaments of the Dome.' In Wren's design all is subordinate to the effect of the dome; in the Hanover Chapel, compartmental rather than Baroque in composition, the dome is merely an incident. Hawksmoor's St. Mary Woolnoth, with a suggested rather than a constructed dome, is surely a closer parallel than St. Stephen, Walbrook. In June 1821 Cockerell visited Hawksmoor's St. Anne, Limehouse and St. George-in-the-East, making careful plans of the former.

Cockerell took many of his friends to see the completed chapel. He notes in June 1825: 'took Lord & Lady Lansdowne to see my chapel. had realy great pleasure in doing so. they see & understand with half an eye. nothing escaped them. organ was playing, pleased to hear him sing to it.' A year earlier he had been working 'early at Chapel [and] met Sir T. Lawrence riding. he walked into Chapel, remarked on the want of ornament in the cap[ital]s, want of completion in the Frieze of cherubs by representing other wings. very polite & satisfied. like the chimney sweep on ship board he looked for a place for a picture.' These experiences naturally made Cockerell conscious that the complexities of his design might with advantage be explained to the visitor. The first suggestion of this seems to have come in September 1824 from a perceptive friend who 'said it was desirable to publish an expose of the motives of the design of my new chapel because otherwise these things are often misunderstood, mistaken, get an ill name illfounded – or may be totaly overlooked.' After a meeting five months later with the Vestry Committee at which Cockerell was called upon, as usual, to explain numerous points of design, he 'proposed even to write an article for their better understanding.' His determination can only have been strengthened by the attitude of Committee members when the final financial reckonings came to be made. There were awkward moments. On 10 February 1826, he 'passed all morn[in]g with them [but] did not justify all my extras, thought it very cold & did not know why. I could throw away my pains in the cieling & on the Dome &c. or anything else in outside decoration. [they] said not one in a hundred could see the Dome & one in a thous[an]d only was arch[itec]t enough to care abo[u]t it . . .' However, an opportunity soon came for initiating the philistine into the architectural mysteries of his chapel. In 1826 he was fortunate enough to be asked to contribute a short article on the chapel to Britton and Pugin's elegant and scholarly publication on *The Public Buildings of London*.

With a distinguished church in the centre of the metropolis and an illustrated account of it published in a handsome form, Cockerell was for the first time before the eye of the public as an architect. He was now nearly thirty-nine: characteristically, he had not rushed things.

The other major project of these early years was the Literary and Philosophical Institution at Bristol. The moving spirit here was John Scandrett Harford (1785–1866) of Blaise Castle, a scholar and collector of whom Cockerell was to see much in the coming years.[5] He had reacted from the Quaker religion of his father, a Bristol banker, and had been baptized an Anglican in 1809.

Cockerell's designs for the building were completed in the spring of 1821 (Pl. 35). A substantial though simple building, its most striking feature is the entrance portico. This rather self-conscious exercise is characteristic of his attempts in his early buildings to incorporate references to his recent discoveries in Greece. Thus, though the idea of the circular portico is taken from Soane's favourite Temple of Vesta at Tivoli, the order is that of the single Corinthian capital which Cockerell discovered in the cella of the temple at Bassae. He discussed his portico with Smirke in September 1822, and wrote afterwards: 'called on Smirke, serene, friendly, communicative. said my col[umn]s at Bristol would be better fluted.' Certainly the glum little façade is in need of all the animation it can get and a few flutes would

5. See A. Harford, ed., *Annals of the Harford Family*, 1909.

probably be better than nothing. No one will be surprised to learn that Cockerell was early struck with the lack of integration of the portico with the façade behind. He records on 19 June 1823: 'passed an hour at Bristol. my impression of the elevation always unfavourable in respect of Portico inharmoniously attached to the Build[in]g.' The year before, he visited Bristol to inspect progress and noted in his diary on 3 May: 'col[umn]s look slender but graceful. basem[en]t remarkably well . . . on reflection am convinced that the horizontal lines should have been avoided as making the deformity of the descent more obvious than the perpendicular lines. thus I should say in all cases as a general rule, on a slope avoid horizontal lines in arch[itectur]e & rather lead the alteration by perpendicular ones.'

One cannot but agree with Cockerell that the lines of his building draw attention to, rather than conceal, the considerable declivity of its site on the corner of Park Street and St. George's Road; but like all architects he had to learn by his mistakes.

Cockerell's doubt about the building were shared by his contemporaries. He must have been disappointed not to have been elected to the Royal Academy in 1823 and to learn from Flaxman in February that his 'drawing of build[in]g in Bristol disappointed them, the academicians, that it was little better than a shop front.'

If the composition of the façades was not wholly satisfactory, the interior planning on an awkward site was masterly. For the Pickwickian activities of the Institution Cockerell contrived to provide a lecture-theatre and laboratory with, on the second floor, a large library and a top-lit exhibition gallery. The attractions included casts of the pedimental sculpture from the temple at Aegina, though it is not clear what position in the building these occupied. The drawing exhibited at the Royal Academy shows classical friezes in both the entrance portico and the circular vestibule to which it gave access, but there is no suggestion of groups of pedimental sculpture. The frieze in the portico was carved and donated by Edward Baily (1788–1867), the successful Bristol-born sculptor and pupil of Flaxman.

In 1819 S. P. Cockerell had contrived to secure for his son the surveyor-ship of St. Paul's Cathedral, a post which he had held himself from 1811. It is not clear what qualifications the young C. R. Cockerell possessed to fit him for this high office, but since it was in the gift of the Archbishop of Canterbury, the Bishop of London and the Lord Mayor, it is likely that Dr. Howley, who was Cockerell's first cousin by marriage and Bishop of London, played a large part in the negotiations. In October 1818 S. P. and C. R. Cockerell had drawn up plans for a substantial house for Howley at 32 St. James's Square. With its prominent and subtly-articulated Palladian windows on the first floor, this building was executed under C. R. Cockerell's supervision from 1819–21 at a cost of £11,087. In 1821 he replaced the cross and ball[6] at St. Paul's and in the following year redecorated the interior and introduced both stoves and the doubtful benefits of gas-lighting.

Cockerell was at work once more at Bristol in the late 1820's where he designed in 1828 the now rebuilt church, Holy Trinity, Hotwell Road (Pl. 36).[7] Its striking south entrance, set in a huge concave reveal which is dramatically coffered so as to heighten the perspective illusion, recalls the ground-floor windows of the west towers of St. Paul's. Indeed we may regard the building as, in a sense, the fruit of his surveyorship of the cathedral. The interior of the church (Pl. 37) betrays Cockerell's experience of Wren's churches as much as does the exterior. A central domed space carried by four columns is extended to east and west by two more pairs of columns, thus creating a happy compromise between a centrally and a longitudinally planned church. Favourite Cockerell motifs are the Greek Doric columns with fluting confined to the top of the shafts, and the prominent cherubim clinging like giant moths to the capitals of the four eastern pilasters.

Cockerell's enthusiasm for Wren could also have been derived from his father whose interior at St. Mary's, Banbury, of 1790, was ninety feet square with twelve Composite columns forming an inner square and supporting a shallow dome. Though remarkably Wrenian for its date it lacks the directional emphasis characteristic of Wren which C. R. Cockerell achieved at Holy Trinity, Hotwell.

St. Mary's, Banbury, was consecrated in 1797 but funds proved inadequate for the provision of the western tower and portico originally envisaged.[8] The completion of these was thus delayed until 1820–22 by which time S. P. Cockerell had handed over to his son the responsibility for their general design (Pl. 38). C. R. Cockerell replaced the coupled Roman Doric columns of his father's curved and somewhat elephantine portico with

6. Wren's ball was acquired by the proprietor of the Colosseum in Regent's Park where it could be seen by the curious.

7. See *The Builder*, vol. 199, 9 December 1960, pp. 1062–4. After bomb damage in the 2nd World War the exterior was restored but a new design by T. H. B. Burrough was adopted for the interior. Mr Burrough subsequently argued that this was done 'so as not to falsify history.'

8. See N. Cooper, *The Building and Furnishing of St. Mary's Church, Banbury* (reprinted from *Cake and Cockhorse*, Autumn 1972), where S. P. Cockerell's original design is reproduced.

single columns. He also considered carving the metopes of the frieze. The principal change in the design of the tall circular tower rising above the portico was the introduction of the Bassae Corinthian order in place of his father's Ionic.

Cockerell worked much for the Church of England in the 1820's. Further evidence of the flourishing churchmanship of these neglected years is afforded by his commission to design St. David's College, Lampeter, in 1822 (Pl. 39). The college was founded largely through the energy of the powerful and scholarly Dr Burgess (1756–1837) who had been translated to the See of Llandaff in 1803 and who subsequently became Bishop of Salisbury. Despite popular belief, it was founded as a university college not as an Anglican theological college. Another moving spirit was Cockerell's friend and patron at Bristol, John Scandrett Harford, and it was through him that he obtained the commission. Harford and his brother owned property in Wales and they donated the twenty-one-and-a-half-acre site together with a subscription of £500.

Lampeter, like Harrow, is in a Tudor style, and the excuse, exactly as at Harrow, is that the building was educational in character. The woolly-minded sentiment produced by nearly a century of Picturesque theory had produced a climate of opinion in which it was inevitable that an Anglican college such as Lampeter would be Gothic in style. It was, ironically, this climate of opinion which, though Picturesque in origin, was shortly to prove so susceptible to the fantasies of Pugin.

Cockerell paid his first visit to the remote Cardiganshire village of Lampeter in December 1821. When he showed to Bishop Burgess his first bird's-eye perspective and plan of the college, the bishop exclaimed, according to Cockerell, 'this is magick, here is more done in a few days than many years have accomplished . . . I have been 18 yrs. on this work & rejoice that I have not quited St. David's because I see my way thro' it.' Schemes for the college had apparently been proposed by other architects since the bishop claimed that 'the draw[ing]s he had seen [previously] were stables. Prisons, anything but colleges – here was a college of three hundred y[ear]s back.' Cockerell records how Burgess 'kept his eyes on the draw[in]g with delight & after a time he said I sho[ul]d be tempted if I see this accomplished to say the words of Simeon – Lord now lettest thou thy servant depart in peace &c. &c. his enthusiasm was venerable & striking.'

The Bishop's remarks were perceptive, for in observing that 'here was a college of three hundred years back', that is of about 1620, he had isolated the peculiar and characteristic charm of Cockerell's design. Like his work at

Harrow, and unlike the more spectacular college buildings by his contemporary, William Wilkins, it is somehow genuinely collegiate in character. From a position outside the Gothic Revival, Cockerell felt able to design a college based on the modest seventeenth-century vernacular seen at its best in, say, the garden front of St. John's College, Oxford. Indeed, when Cockerell visited Brasenose College, Oxford, in June 1822 he was interested to discover that the quadrangle was the 'same size at St. Davids [and] much resembles my conception in dormers, entrance Tower, size of Chapel &c.' Similarly at Oriel College he much admired the 'very pretty arrangem[en]t of Hall & chapel with auriol wind[o]ws much size of mine.' In the same year he visited Heriot's Hospital in Edinburgh, which he believed to be the work of Inigo Jones, and was 'delighted to find some arrangem[en]t of staircases' [i.e. a projecting spiral staircase in each corner] 'as I had adopted in College of St. Davids.'

Cockerell's first scheme of December 1821 provided for a cloister walk round all four sides of the quadrangle. This scheme was modified in the following year and the cloister restricted to the north range. Entrance to the college was through a substantial gate-tower in the middle of the south range. The south, west and east ranges were taken up with undergraduate rooms on the staircase plan. The little wooden stairs with their Jacobean-style newels have considerable charm. The two-light Tudor windows have cast-iron heads through the mullions and sills are of wood. The west half of the north range was devoted to the chapel and the east to the hall with a long library on the first-floor between them and at right angles to them. The hall, which survived unaltered till 1972, had a remarkably 'authentic air', but the chapel was completely remodelled in the nineteenth century. Both rooms were originally on the first floor, following much Oxford precedent, but the chapel floor was lowered in the rebuilding. The north-west angle of the quadrangle was occupied by the Principal's lodgings, and there were further lodgings for the Vice-Principal and for the Rev. L. Llewellyn. Just to the north-east of the college Cockerell provided in 1827 a simple Tudor house, recently demolished, for another of the professors, the Rev. A. Ollivant.

Despite his classical tastes Cockerell derived a surprising amount of pleasure from designing and visiting Lampeter. He doubtless found working for clergymen and scholars congenial. Inspecting progress in December 1823 he considered that the college 'presents itself well from road [from] Llandovery. – turrets give it distinction of publick build[in]g – else it would be but a row of alms Houses.' He had prepared a print of the college as part of a campaign to encourage donations and when he visited the building in 1826 he was delighted to find 'how far it surpasses the print in magnificence of character.' It is certainly curious to find him so far carried away by enthusiasm as to be able to describe his low rough-cast walls as possessing 'magnificence of character'.

Considering the remoteness of Lampeter from London and the grave inconvenience of travel Cockerell was able to inspect the progress of the work during construction with remarkable frequency: at least eight times between October 1823 and the consecration of the chapel in August 1827. Indeed part of his success in these early years must have been due to his willingness to travel across the country to inspect the progress of his commissions. It is clear that his frequent visits in which rapid decisions were taken on the spot after consultation with workmen, contractors and clients, inspired confidence and enthusiasm all round. In January 1823 he recorded in his diary: 'I have never visited a building in progress that I have not found something to learn & always something to reprove & correct. superintendance is of the utmost import.'

St. David's College is the oldest university institution in the country after the two ancient universities. In the same year Cockerell received another highly unusual commission though, again, one that was characteristic of the improving spirit of the age. This was the Scottish National Monument (Pl. 40). There had been discussion since at least 1817 of erecting in 'the Athens of the North' a great memorial to those fallen in the Napoleonic Wars. Some thought this might also become a national Valhalla, a place of burial for Scotsmen of fame and distinction. In January 1822 an appeal was launched for £42,000 'to erect a facsimile of the Parthenon'. The notion of a Valhalla was a *leimotiv* of neo-classicism. Two had already been proposed in recent years, one in England and another in Germany. A Valhalla which might take the form of a church had been envisaged in the instructions issued in 1809 to architects entering the competition for the improvements to Marylebone, later Regent's Park. In Germany, where neo-classicism had long centred on the tomb and the monument, a similar movement was under way. The idea of a Valhalla to commemorate celebrated Germans had originated in 1807 with the Crown Prince Ludwig of Bavaria. In the year following Napoleon's defeat at Leipzig in 1813 the Prince announced a competition which stipulated Greek forms because the Parthenon, it was argued, had been closely linked to the Greek victory over the Persians from which Greek unity derived. Prince Ludwig's architect and Cockerell's close friend, Haller von Hallerstein, sent from Athens in 1815 a project based on Gilly's celebrated competition design of 1796 for a Monument to

Frederick the Great on the Leipzigerplatz in Berlin. In 1829 Prince Ludwig re-framed the competition and his new architect, Leo von Klenze, erected the great Greek temple-Walhalla above Regensburg on the Danube in 1830–42. Turner's dramatic painting, *The Opening of the Walhalla* of 1842, is a compelling reminder of the romance which lies at the heart of neo-classicism.

Calton Hill, rising above Edinburgh, is similarly dominated by a great temple, Cockerell's uncompleted version of the Parthenon. It came as the culmination of an astonishing variety of monuments and public buildings which had been spreading over the surface of the hill from 1776. Cockerell notes in his diary in July 1822: 'rec[ieve]d invitation of Com[mitt]ee for national monum[en]t at Edinbro' to assist in choosing site &c. answered Lord Elgin that was much engaged but in a national concern of this importance thought I might engage to come down in a week.' He arrived in Edinburgh on 2 August and learnt from Lord Elgin how it was that he had been invited. Elgin had seen Lord Aberdeen's book, *An Inquiry into the Principles of Beauty in Grecian Architecture* (1822), and had consequently sought his opinion of Cockerell's merit as an architect. Lord Aberdeen, who knew Cockerell as a member of the committee of the Travellers' Club, 'confirmed his opinion of my ability.' Aberdeen was later, in February 1824, recorded by Cockerell to have 'commended very highly my Bowood chapel & my St. George's, [Regent Street].' However, Elgin had acted prematurely and without the full knowledge of the committee, many of whom were anxious to appoint a Scottish architect,[9] but on 5 August the committee agreed to allow Cockerell to officiate at the laying of the foundation stone. This was to take place in a few days' time on the occasion of George IV's visit to Edinburgh. The ceremonies of this important visit had been stage-managed by Sir Walter Scott and marked the beginning of the Highland 'takeover' of Scotland. The king's bogus tartan was echoed by the shift in the subject matter of Scott's novels away from seventeenth- and eighteenth-century Scotland about which he knew so much, to mediaeval Europe about which he knew so very much less. It is highly suggestive that the backcloth of the opening scene in this romantic drama should have been Cockerell's uncompromisingly Greek temple.

He explained his plans for the temple to the committee on 10 August, and on the next day inspected the stone at the Craig Leith quarry two miles

9. From Cockerell's correspondence with Burn, Playfair *et al.* (preserved at the National Library of Scotland, Edinburgh, MS. 638), it is clear that Burn would have liked to work with Cockerell though Cockerell probably preferred the meticulous and deferential Playfair.

from Edinburgh. His drawing was now 'gaining great prosyletes [sic] – D[uke] of Montrose, D[uke] of Athol saw it . . . Ld Wymes [i.e. Wemyss] & his son Lord Elco called to see my drawg: of the Parthenon. [I] had seen Ld. Elco at Lady Westmorelands at Florence.' On 15 August 'The king landed at 1 oclock. salutes from ships, fort & Salisbury craggs. procession from Leith. fine day. from Princes St. to Holyrood Ho: saw the whole from Calton Hill. like a scene in a play. much pleasure in the people who called it *awful*. no noise or clamor but a collected satisfaction. King had a *sandy wig* wh^h delighted them. smiled & bowed. very gracious. charity children were brought to see it. Scotch cherish recollections, politic visit of the King.'

There was still strong feeling that the Scottish Archibald Elliott should be appointed architect of the Monument but Cockerell told his friend the architect William Burn on 22 August 'that it would be impossible that Elliott & I would agree being of different age, unacquainted &c.' Conflict became so bitter that on the 27th Cockerell wrote to Lord Elgin offering his resignation. On the same day the foundation-stone was laid, prematurely as it turned out. Cockerell attended wearing a cocked hat, white stockings and 'black Clothes' and feeling that, despite undertones of embarrassment, 'this was proud day for me because tho' not positively appointed I stood here as not unworthy of the post. [I] dined with Ld. Elgin.'

He spent the next two days in preparing drawings for the Monument. It is interesting to note that from the start he had 'felt the necessity of setting forth the Parthenon as a *free Translation* of the original'. He was also naturally anxious for sculpture to play its part in the building, but Lord Aberdeen had told him on 24 August that he 'thought it might be difficult to apply sculpture to the church of Scotland. [we thought it] better not at first to bring this matter forward but let it creep on.'

In the following year, 1823, Cockerell was definitely appointed architect, though with W. H. Playfair (1789–1857) as assistant resident architect. Cockerell's remuneration was to be three hundred guineas. Playfair came to London in May 1825 for discussion with Cockerell, and the working drawings were completed on 9 June.

The construction of the building proceeded very slowly and in 1829, when the money ran out, ceased altogether. One of the reasons was undoubtedly the cost of handling stones which weighed ten to fifteen tons each. Cockerell adored large stones and the building was described in 1828 as exhibiting a 'durability and splendour perhaps unequalled in the history of masonry';[10]

---

10. In a report made at a Directors' meeting, 17 April 1828, National Library of Scotland, MS. 638

but it required teams of twelve horses and seventy men to haul these stones to the top of Calton Hill. Thus all that Cockerell and Playfair were able to achieve was the erection of fourteen columns supporting merely an architrave and not even a frieze.

The painful incompleteness of these bleak dispirited columns[11] symbolizes the comparative failure of the Greek Revival itself and can only have confirmed Cockerell's antecedent lack of enthusiasm for it. Though the fragmentary building on its dramatic hilltop site may have a certain Picturesque appeal for us, it is not clear that Cockerell himself would have felt this. Indeed, after dining with William Burn in Edinburgh in August 1822, he noted that Burn's 'architecture [was] totaly irregular' and came to the conclusion that 'symetry is the distinct character of architecture & whence it derives it chief effect, compared with the fortuitous accidents of the distribution which nothing but an extraordinary pictoresque can excuse.'

The Scottish National Monument was only partially completed. We shall end this chapter by investigating Cockerell's designs for two more public buildings which never got off the drawing-board at all. Both in London, these were for University College and the Houses of Parliament.

In 1825, a band of radicals and free-thinkers brought to this country from Germany the alien notion of a non-sectarian metropolitan university. In that year Brougham and Jeremy Bentham acquired a site in Gower Street for the new university and advertised for architectural drawings in the press. On 4 November, Lord Auckland called on Cockerell bringing the plan of the site and expressing pleasure at his decision to submit plans. Here, again, Cockerell's standing in society was as valuable to him as his skill as an architect, for Lord Auckland and Lord Lansdowne – both committee members, like Cockerell, of the Travellers' Club – were on the building committee of the new college.

Cockerell's first-floor plan and a bird's-eye view of the whole building survive at the Victoria and Albert Museum (Pl. 41). It is a handsome varied composition with two great quadrant wings with circular-ended lecture-rooms opening off them. These seem to derive from a plan for a college published by Durand in his *Précis des leçons donnés à l'école polytechnique* in 1802. Cockerell records in his diary on 9 November: 'was very early in the morning at 5 devizing university. looking over various books for hints of university.' It would be surprising if he did not search for hints in Durand's standard manual of monumental neo-classical design. Indeed

11. William Hamilton referred to their 'hard and cowed appearance' in a letter to Cockerell dated 30 June 1829 (National Library of Scotland, MS. 638).

M

there are extensive notes on Durand in his diaries in January 1822. The only book he mentions by name in connection with the design of the university is Palladio. A very characteristic entry in the diary is that for 30 November 1825: 'on university. studying Palladio &c. on the Propylea. thinking closely on my work as usual on those occasions lethargic, confined at home, restless but sleeping much early & late.' Cockerell's propylaea consisted of a Greek Doric entrance gateway set dramatically in the centre of a long, absolutely bare wall. Behind was an attractive inner courtyard or cloister framed by long low colonnades leading towards the huge portico in antis of the main building. Behind this was a monumental staircase giving access to the large hall. At this point in Durand's plan there is a chapel but that was expressly disallowed in the godless college devised by Bentham and his associates. On 2 December, Cockerell rather unwisely showed his designs to McKenzie, the draughtsman who was employed by Wilkins and Wyatville to make the final presentation drawings of their plans for the college. McKenzie, equally indiscreet, told him that his plans differed considerably from two of the others – presumably Wilkins' and Wyatville's – about which 'there was a remarkable similarity.' However, Cockerell's plan shared with Wilkins' a great hall lying behind the central entrance portico. Ludicrously, when Wilkins' designs were finally built the hall was omitted so that the magnificent portico leads to nothing.

Cockerell worked on his plans in the early part of 1826 and submitted them, at the last possible moment, on 18 March. On 27 March he was called before the six members of the building committee, including Lords Lansdowne and Auckland to explain his designs. The estimated expense of his buildings was £160,000 which, he discovered from seeing the drawings of his competitors, was the lowest of all since the others had all 'adopted more magnificence than myself.'[12] In writing his account in his diary of this interview he enlarged on the merits and drawbacks of the architectural competition: 'the advantage of a competition to the employer', he wrote, 'is that it furnishes him many ideas & puts the competitors to the best of their ability & induces great effort on their part. but it has its disadvantages, the comp[etito]rs think rather of the contest than the subject & in the desire not to be outdone consult much less the real purpose & interest of the employers. & some of them in showing what they can do quite overlook

12. This is not substantiated by a comparative analysis of the six plans submitted by Wilkins, Gandy, Atkinson, Davies, Wyatville and Cockerell (University College, London, Records, Document 1167, part 15), in which it is claimed that Wilkins' estimate was £70,000, Wyatville's £250,000 and that Cockerell did not provide an estimate at all.

the main question & run into all sorts of extravagances proposing many things for glory's sake which in sober judgement they would not have thought of – observe too that when there is no responsibility to employers these works will be but loosely considered & there is this difference that thus the employers are obliged, but when a professional man is employed 'tis he who is the obliged person & in great alarm to preserve his reputation & keep himself in their good graces. I think it would be well to have the opinion of each on the other's works. thus a clear definition of the leading principles of each design would be obtained.'[13]

Cockerell's sceptical but acute remarks about the dangers of architecture by competition were to be wholly justified by the appalling chaos of nearly every major nineteenth-century competition. Cockerell himself, needless to say, lost almost every competition he ever entered.

The results of the University College competition were announced on 1 May 1826. The entry for that day in Cockerell's diary concludes rather touchingly: '... Wilkins's were chosen. dined at home on rice pudding & went to Philharmonic. Beethoven's symphony, fine overture of Oberon.'

Another and much more important competition which Cockerell failed to win was that for the Houses of Parliament in 1835 (Pls 42–43). Here, his rejection can scarcely have come as a surprise to him since his designs, though fascinating, deliberately flouted the condition that they should be in either the 'Gothic or Elizabethan' style. 'If in prescribing Elizabethan architecture', Cockerell boldly announced in the legend on his design, 'the Honble. the Committee will admit the AGE in which that Queen reigned, we shall find that the greatest Architects of Italy were then flourishing – from 1558, her accession, to 1603, were living MICHAEL ANGELO, PALLADIO, VIGNOLA, SANSOVINO, GALEAZZO ALESSI, SCAMOZZI, &c. &c. Elizabethan Architecture cannot be defined, the examples all differing – as Burleigh, Hatfield, Audley End, Houghton Conquest, &c. &c. These examples exhibit an union of Old English Architecture with a reflection of Italian (ill understood) and occasional Moorish and Venetian ornaments and features of oriental origin. Its Bay Windows introducing much light allowed great convenience internally and great luminousness suited to Offices and Committee Rooms for business; and producing great effect of light and shade exteriorly. The advantages of Elizabethan Architecture are that it unites Ancient English Architecture and National Associations with good

13. He later elaborated his views on competitions before the Select Committee on the Arts of 1836. See *Reports from Committees*, 1836, vol. III, Question 2195.

Italian Style and proportions, and with the modern system of structure and arrangement.'

The argument that had Elizabethan architects been better trained they would have designed as well as their Italian contemporaries is an entertaining one and Cockerell doubtless enjoyed twisting the tails of the committee by proposing it. However, it is not the way to win competitions, as he also doubtless knew: but his design was remarkable for another feature, which the committee were probably right in the end to reject but which shows Cockerell's astonishing sensitivity to the past. His proposed new buildings were grouped so as to frame not only Westminster Abbey but also far more of the surviving mediaeval fragments of the old Palace of Westminster than any of the other competitors had envisaged retaining. Barry's first scheme, indeed, made nonsense of Westminster Hall by raising its roof to the level of his own.[14] Cockerell proposed retaining not only the Hall but also St. Stephen's Chapel and its cloisters as well as the House of Lords, the great thirteenth-century Painted Chamber and even Soane's dramatic Royal Gallery. Since the mediaeval buildings occupied most of the western fringe of the site Cockerell had to make them, together with Henry VII's chapel towering above them to the west, the focal point of his composition. This meant completely abandoning the conventional disposition of a monumental building on this scale which would be to work up to a central climax from lower subsidiary pavilions. Thus Cockerell's building modestly fades away in the centre creating a visual effect which, it must be confessed, would be appreciated only from the correct axial position on the south bank of the Thames, directly opposite the east end of Westminster Abbey. From any other position Cockerell's extraordinarily effacing and dislocated composition would have been a visual disaster. It is part of the success of Barry's design that it took advantage of the fact that the buildings would normally be seen in sharp perspective.

The visual accents of Cockerell's composition were three: the two balancing pavilions containing the House of Lords and the House of Commons, capped by squat French domes, and slightly to the west a tall Gothic campanile which was 'St. Stephen's Bell Tower restored'. Cockerell pointed out how by raising a tower at this point 'the ridge and roof of Westminster Hall is thus broken and will be less objectionable and unsightly – the ancients probably had the same reason for so placing it.'

The long ranges which Cockerell placed along the river-front contained

14. A. Barry, *Memoir of the Life and Works of the Late Sir Charles Barry, Architect*, 1867, p. 245.

committee rooms and residential accommodation. These incorporated the bay windows for which he particularly praised Elizabethan architecture and displayed skylines indebted to those of Longleat. The two great domed pavilions were recessed in a plane considerably behind these ranges and were linked by an open cloister-walk of round-headed arches a little reminiscent of that at the south front of Hatfield.

Though Cockerell's plans were not preferred, he later put to good use at the Ashmolean the unconventional *parti* of large flanking pavilions overwhelming the central wing. At the Ashmolean, too, he claimed a functional reason for this striking departure from customary practice – but consideration of this will have to wait till Chapter XII.

CHAPTER X

Country Houses

URING the 1820's Cockerell was busy with the preparation of a huge volume of drawings which he entitled portentously, *Ichnographica Domestica*.[1] This constitutes a record of the plans of all the country houses, of whatever period, which he admired as he travelled about the country. It is curious that despite the interest in domestic architecture revealed by the production of such a book, his gifts did not seem to lie in the design of country houses. Langton, Lough Crew and Derry Ormond are the only major houses which he designed *de novo*. Everywhere else he was merely remodelling or adding to other men's work.

The reason for his comparative lack of success as a country-house architect lies in the unsuitability of the Greek Revival style to domestic architecture. Clearly a 'public' style like the Greek was most appropriately employed for public buildings. Moreover, the principal country-house architects in the first half of the ninteenth century were Blore, Salvin, Barry and Burn and the styles popular with them and their clients were Gothic, Tudor and Picturesque Italian. In the country, it seemed, Cockerell's sober but allusive classicism would be quite out of place. Thus, after his experiments of the 1820's we find him more and more directing his talents to city buildings and particularly to the premises of banks and insurance companies. At the moment when the country gentleman was at last discarding the mantle of classicism Cockerell was there waiting to pick it up and drape it comfortingly round the shoulders of the new city magnates.

However, at the start of his career he was anxious to establish himself as a country-house architect. His opportunity came in 1819 when he began work on a very complex commission which was to exercise his ingenuity on and off for the next twenty-one years. This was the remodelling of Oakly Park near Ludlow, seat of the Hon. Robert Clive (1789–1854) whom he had met

1. This is the companion volume to another album called *Ichnographica Publica* containing the preparatory drawings for Cockerell's *Tribute to the Memory of Sir Christopher Wren* of 1838. Both volumes are in the possession of Mrs B. J. Crichton. The plans in the *Ichnographica Domestica* were published by John Harris in the *Journal of the Society of Architectural Historians*, 14, 1971.

on the committee of the Travellers' Club. It is necessary to explain in some detail Clive's family history since until it is clarified it is impossible to understand why Cockerell's chance acquaintance with him should have led to commissions at Oakly, Walcot and Wynnstay.

Robert Clive's mother was something of a genealogical curiosity since she was at different stages in her life both the daughter and the wife of an Earl of Powis. Born Lady Henrietta Herbert, sister of the last Earl of Powis of the first creation, she married in 1784 the son of Clive of India. Her husband was created Earl of Powis in 1804 and his father had bought from her father the Oakly estates, although he already owned two large Shropshire properties, Styche and Walcot. Thus Oakly ultimately descended to her second son, Robert, on the death in 1817 of his grandmother, the widow of Clive of India; whilst the Powis estates descended to her elder son from her brother on the condition that he changed his name from Clive to Herbert. In 1817 her daughter, Henrietta, married Sir Watkin Williams-Wynn, 5th Bart., of Wynnstay.

Oakly Park had been several times modernized in the eighteenth century, culminating in a remodelling by the elder Haycock for Lady Clive in the 1780's. When Robert Clive inherited the property in 1817 Haycock's son presented a new scheme in a style at once timid and austere. This was rejected and it was not until 1819, the year of his marriage to Lady Harriet Windsor, a daughter of the 5th Earl of Plymouth, that Clive turned for plans to his friend Cockerell.

To match the existing house Cockerell was forced to employ a red brick of a rich hue which inevitably gives the house more of a Georgian than a Greek Revival character. He sensibly moved the entrance from the south to the west front and placed before it a four-columned one-storeyed portico (Pl. 45). In the middle of the west front he placed a dining-room of unusual plan with a screened vestibule at either end (Pl. 44). Several years later, in 1836, he remodelled the portico, duplicated it at the north end of the façade (Pls 46 & 48), and advanced the outer wall of the dining-room between them so as to connect them, supporting on an iron joist the wall of the existing bedroom above. Though an ingenious way of enlarging the dining-room, the result is an irregular and ambiguous space which is lacking in axis or direction: the room is thus a hybrid that appears to be neither rectangular nor square. Outside, the intriguing Doric columns of Cockerell's porticos are unfluted save for small bands of fluting at the top and bottom. This feature is imitated from two archaic temples he had seen in Sicily, the Olympiaeum at Syracuse and the Temple of Hephaestus at Girgenti, which had already exercised influence in the ancient world on the Hellenistic temple of Apollo on the island of Delos. This 'Delian Doric' had been employed in 1766 by Nicholas Revett at Standlynch at the beginning of the Greek Revival.

The southernmost of the two porticos opens into a circular entrance vestibule which survived from Haycock's house. Cockerell adorned its shallow saucer dome with diagonal coffering which may have been inspired by coffering supposedly used at Bassae and illustrated by Donaldson in his publication on the temple in 1830.

The top-lit staircase-hall (Pl. 47), into which the circular vestibule leads, is a remarkable neo-classical symphony composed of themes drawn from Cockerell's travels and, above all, from Bassae itself. Below the elegant glazed dome runs a cast of part of the Bassae frieze supported by columns with lotus capitals derived from those of the Tower of the Winds in Athens. The Bassae theme is echoed on the opposite side of the hall by columns of pale grey marble on the ground floor. These are based on the remarkable Ionic order of the cella of the temple at Bassae with its beautiful curvaceous volutes. Most surprisingly, the original drawing for the hall, dated 1823, shows Roman Doric not Greek Ionic columns at this point. The estimate for the columns, less their capitals, submitted in March 1824, came to £54 each.

The immediate antecedents of this spare, noble room are easily found in the work of Holland, Wyatt, in Dance's now demolished staircase at Ashburnham of 1813–17 and Wyatville's at Bretton Park of c. 1815. At this time glazed domes were a preoccupation with Cockerell. He was providing them not only at Oakly but also at the Hanover Chapel and the Travellers' Club.[2] Indeed, it may have been seeing the domed staircase at the Travellers' which prompted Clive to ask Cockerell to provide something similar at Oakly. It is clear from his diaries that Cockerell was very proud of his staircase at the Travellers' and often brought people to see it. In disposition and effect it cannot have been dissimilar to that at Ashburnham House, Westminster, then attributed to Inigo Jones. In fact when Cockerell visited Grange Park (another house then attributed to Jones though now known to be by Samwell), he 'was much flattered to find Inigo Jones using the same dome lantern I have adopted at the Travellers' but I think not so well contrived.' It is one of the intriguing paradoxes of Cockerell's stylistic

2. The Committee minutes of the Travellers' Club were kindly made available to me by the Secretary, Mr. R. P. McDouall. They contain evidence (overlooked by the L.C.C. Survey of London, *The Parish of St. James Westminster, Part 1, South of Piccadilly*, 2 vols, 1960) which confirms Cockerell's extensive alterations to the club's premises at 49 Pall Mall.

development that he sometimes discovers the sources for his buildings only *after* he has designed them! Another feature of Cockerell's Travellers' Club which may have inspired Oakly was the presence in it of casts of the Bassae and Parthenon friezes.

The handsome railings of the cantilevered staircase at Oakly are of brass. This is an unusual feature in an English country house and Cockerell doubtless took the idea from Irish country houses. Plate 49 shows his sketch of the brass bannisters at Castletown near Dublin. Where the railings on the landing meet the north wall of the staircase-hall at Oakly they are curiously returned inwards to make room for an enormous canvas by Benjamin West depicting *Lord Clive receiving from the Mogul the grant of the Duanney*. This had been commissioned by Clive of India to hang at Claremont whence it was brought to Oakly with much more of his fine collection.

On the right at the foot of the stairs is a strange truncated column of the same cool grey marble as the complete column of the adjacent screen. This abruptly terminated column, which is nevertheless an integral part of the structural and ornamental system of the whole room, is perhaps the one European architectural detail one would select as expressing more elo-quently, poignantly and simply than any other the romantic paradox at the heart of the neo–classical movement.[3]

In May 1821 Cockerell prepared designs for remodelling the south front so as to incorporate Haycock's three-bay centre-piece with its central niche. He also extended the façade three bays to the east so as to provide space for a library. In December he visited the house and 'saw with great satisfaction the effect of the south front & balcony, also well executed. passed morn[in]g considering the next operations. determined . . . on sinking bookcases in library.' The recessed shelves in the library (Pl. 50) are one of the most subtle features of a subtle room. The ledge separating the lower shelves from the upper is made of the same dove-grey marble used in the hall. The library chimney-piece is a striking composition in which columns with lotus capitals stand out dramatically against panels of green marble. Made from Cockerell's designs by Messrs. Browne and Company, there is an interesting reference to it in Cockerell's diary for 10 May 1823: 'finished Clive's Chimney Piece, sent it to Browne's with instructions to see lotus in Museum Of E[ast] I[ndia] Ho[use].' Cockerell had himself made drawings of a lotus in the museum on 6 May and had found the 'resemblance of Hindoo or

3. Cockerell repeated this truncated column at the Ashmolean Museum. The motif had been anticipated in James Playfair's Cairness, Aberdeenshire, 1789, where the portico is flanked by truncated columns.

Indian & Greek art striking.' However, when he visited Oakly in October 1823 he noted: 'did not like chimney piece. coarsely considered, hurried, but is liked & looks handsome.' The library itself he found of 'very handsome proportion.' His judgement was sound and the room today is perhaps his finest surviving unaltered domestic interior.

In April 1822, Cockerell wrote to Clive recommending 'him to continue his line of Fascia & portico of south Front & build conservatory against it.' The working drawings for the conservatory were not prepared until two years later, by which time it had been decided to set it at right angles to the south front where it would mask the earlier office-wing. Cockerell sent Clive many variant drawings for the curvaceous metal supports of the conservatory. These and the glazing were provided at a cost of £460 by the remarkable firm of Jones and Clark from Birmingham, about which more will be said later. When he visited the completed conservatory in August 1825, Cockerell found that with its elegant cast-iron columns it looked 'very classical . . . like a Pompeian paint[in]g.' At the same time he 'saw the House with great interest & on the whole satisfaction . . . but [felt that] some things are objectionable & not in the truly classical taste, which after all should be sought as the best.' He does not specify the 'objectionable' items but may have had in mind the Indian capitals of the library chimney-piece. One wonders whether Clive may have asked for these to remind him of the exploits in India of his father and grandfather.

In 1826 Cockerell designed the Bromfield lodge (Pl. 51) which bears in miniature all the characteristics of his style. In red brick with stone dressings, it is a variant on his favourite theme of an arch breaking into a pediment. Like his other lodges, it is brilliantly sited and plays an essential role in concentrating attention on the otherwise rather insignificant entrance to a park which, though of considerable antiquity, has never been very dramatically landscaped. The lodge forms the central accent of a long curved composition and is flanked by the entrances to two separate drives.

The final word on Oakly must be Cockerell's, for we have an attractive and characteristically idiosyncratic account of the house sent by him in 1838 to his friend Sir Thomas Acland: '[I] was induced & half obliged to go to Mr. Clive's where we have just finished a work which is the very picture of himself having been molded by our joint labors these 10 or more years. it is substantial, of very handsome intrinsic material, almost unadorned, except by minor features, beside those solid proportions, shewing a refinement that would escape vulgar eyes like those almost female delicacies which accompany the robust magnificence of a Hercules, or a very strong but high bred horse. of low proportion & Doric in all its character. & I was happy to find him in high good humour.'[4]

In 1828 Cockerell made some minor alterations to Clive's London house in Tilney Street. He also worked for Clive's father, Lord Powis, at Walcot in Shropshire which had been built for Clive of India by Sir William Chambers. Here in 1826 Cockerell added a Venetian window to the picture gallery, but the wing containing it was demolished during substantial alterations to the house in the 1930's. In 1823 he had designed, though not executed, a 'Gaze Tower' for the park at Walcot based on the Tower of the Winds in Athens. In August 1825, he was invited to Walcot but does not seem to have found the experience a very enlivening one: 'Party all walking & sunning themselves', he records; 'much yawning after a time & difficulty to get over it – this is a real source of evil to such a party as I am now in but this should never happen with those who can regulate their time. the ladies sat at work after dinner, the gents sat & dozed – the true English evening in these Houses is lamentable dullness – we may boast of our domestic tastes & love of the country but where dullness is habitual & constitutional it is the true element. I imagine it much otherwise in continental society & there the temptation to its follies is great – here there is none & no merit therefore [in] abstaining.'

Cockerell was at once appalled and attracted by the country-house world of which, though not born to it, he frequently gained glimpses. He records at some length his impressions of his Clive patrons at Walcot and Oakly: 'In Lord Powis was much of the virtu, horseracing & debauched style of the gentlemen of that day. monstrous extravagance, 1200£ for two carpets. Day had taken him in for 2200 for a restored Luini or Leonardo da Vinci, Salviati, Gavin Hamilton, Weenix, Carlo Dolci. great conservatory [since demolished] (at Walcot) 220 feet long, aloes Indian which had blown 25ft. high, produced infinity of suckers. little conservation . . . touch of the Nabob about him. woods brought from India made into doors of the very worst taste, coach House doors looking like the great particolour doors of accomodation at an Inn to throw one room into another & make a Ball Room [a free-standing building which still survives at the back of the house], giving an idea of great weakness from the large & wide opening. *his own* architect, spoiling a decent house with ill conceits . . . told me an obscene & dirty story at which he laughed heartily, & asked me an *architect* to send him some book on arch[itectur]e from which he might take some hints for building

4. Letter of 7 December 1838 at the Devon County Record Office.

lodges & cottages – Lord Clive & Robert Clive of the modern school, bred in diplomacy in the midst of all the exertions & efforts made in the late wars, companions of Castlereagh & Wellesley, educated in the constant anxious employm[en]t of the East 10 y[ea]rs. no corrupting leisure of Italy or India, no vicious virtu, both married early, both in the conversation contemplating higher persons & excellencies. great respect for all that is truly great & respectable, accompanied with a great simplicity & innocence peculiar to them. cautious & dry & careful as their education, punctual, economic, seeing things too much divested of that splendor & decorum which should accompany rank, & with a certain dryness & hardness which considers most things as humbug. looming up to & esteeming distinguished men & their pursuits. somewhat rough in conversation & bearing, tho often concealed by their high family & breeding.'

In 1827, when most of the work at Oakly Park had been completed, Cockerell was invited by Robert Clive's sister to provide a new dining-room and a lodge at Wynnstay in Denbighshire. The dining-room was completed in the late summer of 1828 and on 13 September Sir Watkin Williams-Wynn held a great ball in it. The house was destroyed by fire in 1858 but Cockerell's remarkable lodge[5] (Pl. 52) still survives on the main Chester to Oswestry road near Ruabon. The two-mile drive leading up the hill from the lodge to the rebuilt house is long since disused, which is scarcely surprising since there are other lodges on roads far closer to the house. Cockerell's lodge and drive thus appear to have been conceived in a mood of Picturesque grandeur.

Though small, there are few surviving buildings by Cockerell which convince one more forcibly of the brilliant vigour of his independent genius. It is thus worth analysing in some detail. Firstly, there is its remarkable siting. It lies at right angles to the main road from which it is set well back on a sharp corner. The obvious position would have been on the flat ground above the river Dee on the opposite side of the drive, and indeed drawings survive to suggest that this was the site Cockerell originally envisaged. However, he could not resist the unorthodox solution and thus embedded the lodge into the base of the steep hill on the opposite side of the drive from the river. This in turn suggested the architectural form of the lodge which is, as it were, a substructure or crypto-porticus with its three massive arched supports. The huge rustication is reminiscent of Giulio Romano but the disposition of the whole building forcibly recalls Ledoux's *Barrières* which

5. See P. Howell, 'Wynnstay', *Country Life*, CLI, 1972, p. 853.

Cockerell had admired in Paris in 1824, whilst the sarcophagus-tops of the piers are distinctly Soanean. The lodge thus contrives to be at once cyclo-paean, antique, Mannerist and Neo-Classical. This goes with an un-compromising attitude to construction and materials: thus in the entrance archway there are immense stones four feet long, and in the interiors the vaulted ceilings are of exposed concrete.

After Oakly Park Cockerell's next major commission for work at a country house was also given him by a fellow-member of the Travellers' Club committee, Lord Lansdowne. In the summer of 1821 he was invited by this great Whig magnate to remodel and extend the long Adam wing at Bowood in Wiltshire.[6] What this meant in practice was the addition of a chapel (Pl. 53) running north from the centre of the Adam wing, the con-version of a room at the east end of this wing into a library and the remodell-ing of the existing library adjacent to this room. He also provided a small breakfast-room. Of these improvements the chapel and remodelled library (Pl. 54) survive intact as handsome examples of his decorative skill.

The library bookcases are particularly fine with their slender brass colonnettes and black marble shelves. Also by Cockerell are the pelmet cornices which surround Adam's large round-headed windows and the pattern of the ceiling with its deep coffered coving. When Cockerell visited Bowood on 18 January 1823 the chapel appears to have been complete save for the glass. He thought 'the Chapel looks well, considerable breadth & relief, cieling also beautiful and paving steps to altar, also the doorcase. but arch at Altar end is entirely mistaken & has worst effect, crown coming so near frieze, also does not accord with the square character of the style which is strikingly maintained in the other parts.' As so often, we agree immediately and instinctively with Cockerell's visual judgement and it is surely fascinating to watch this sensitive but inexperienced architect learning slowly by his mistakes. One wonders, however, why the possible incongruity of the arch above the altar had not struck him earlier when there was still time to do something about it. Similarly, it only occurred to him very late in the day that the pronounced horizontal string-courses of his Bristol Institution served to emphasize rather than minimize the sloping site.

The windows did not in the end give complete satisfaction. Inspecting the chapel in 1824 Cockerell 'saw Ld. Lansdowne who said it was perfect excepting the windows from the thick colour of the glass.' Cockerell even grew to dislike the round-headed windows themselves. Inspecting the

6. See J. Cornforth, 'Bowood, Wiltshire, Revisited', *Country Life*, CLI, 1972, pp. 1448–51, 1546–50 & 1610–13.

building in 1824 he wrote: 'If I had to do this again would avoid circular headed wind[o]ws. never will use them again with Greek – could not reconcile myself to the circles of glass. shall always regret them.' However, when he showed the chapel to his younger brother, Richard Howe Cockerell, 'Howe said it looked solid but elegant. this is the true Greek character.'

Cockerell designed an organ for the chapel in 1823 but the present organ is clearly later in date. The elegantly Greek pews must be Cockerell's and the Early Christian arrangement of ambones or twin pulpits. Cockerell was pleased to discover that his slightly quattrocento-style altar rails were similar to those in Pietro Lombardo's church of the Madonna dei Miracoli in Venice of 1480.

On his final visit in January 1824 Cockerell records: 'Ld. L. seemed highly satisfied tho' sparing in expression & certainly too short. dismissed me with a short audience. invited me to dinner to meet Mr. Bowles. Lady L: also short & cold. neither encourage one to familiarity, perhaps rightly.' Elsewhere in the diary he gives us telling character sketches of both Lord Lansdowne and his wife: 'Lord Lansdowne excellent man of business part[icularl]y for keeping men to their duty, severe with himself, exact, accurate & scrutinizing, nothing escapes his penetration wh^h is ever minute & sharpened by occasional irritation in small degree. regulated in all his affairs never has more than 2 coats in wear, servants on board wages the moment they quit the house, exact economy, if anything is lost they replace it. his Waggoner once lost a parcel, was obliged to pay the amount. Lady L. disciplined & regulated in same way. not a poor cottage in Calne she does not visit, passes an hour in her own girls school. or has 2 girls in her house to teach – a sempstress in her ho: who makes coats skirts &c. for poor. did so in case of distress in Ireland to great amo. Ld. L. sent provisions. I never knew anyone who put such pointed questions & ascertained the truth from you as he does. no false complaisance. does not spare. looks directly at you & reads your soul.'

The 3rd Marquess of Lansdowne was not, in fact, the inheritor of a great fortune so that the economies described by Cockerell were enforced as much by circumstance as by personality. Nevertheless with Barry's help he eventually gave to Bowood the character of a great Victorian country house. To Barry, indeed, is due the cupola which today surmounts Cockerell's chapel.

Cockerell's role at Bowood was a minor one but shortly before he began to work there he was invited to Ireland to design a new country house of some magnitude, Lough Crew (Pls 55–57). His patron at Lough Crew was a James Lennox William Naper (1791–1868) whose descendants still own the estate which is situated near Oldcastle in County Meath.

The story of Lough Crew is tragic and profoundly Irish. The shadow of a curse is said to hang over the house which has been thrice burnt within a hundred years and twice rebuilt, though only a few stones stand today. The sole surviving wall of the great house rises from a medley of fallen capitals and immense stones strewn across a noble landscaped setting, breathtaking and remote. One can imagine oneself at a Greek site. Dropping away before one are the remains of the great terraces which were constructed in 1821. Cockerell loved to place his houses on these huge stepped grassy platforms, and created an equally striking effect at Derry Ormond.

The planning of Lough Crew bulks large in the diaries for a number of years since not only was it his largest commission of the decade but Naper was an informed and demanding patron who had strong ideas, sometimes in conflict with Cockerell's, about almost every aspect of the design. Cockerell visited the site frequently and in October 1823 records: 'saw with much interest Lough Crew, work on which I had spent so much time and thought. all masonry done except upper cornice – roof finishing – proportions seem just but very plain, too bald, after all it is but a square house. admirably executed. all hands seem satisfied.' The next day he adds: 'still think it is sadly plain. will never again use Athenian order except in small scale. col-[umn]s look just & well.' The following morning was 'so bad that there was no stiring. remained at home writing & forming a plan of more spread & extent than Lough Crew which in its squareness left me an unpleasant impression . . . it would have been well to rusticate between the pilasters.'

The implication of all this is clear: that the building which established Cockerell as a master of the most austere phase of the Greek Revival was criticized by him at the moment of its completion for exactly those short-comings which modern critics, such as Summerson, find in this style. He thought it bald and square; he found the Athenian Ionic of the portico too miniscule to enliven a monumental building; he regretted the absence of the movement and shadow which features such as rustication and acroteria might have provided. Evidently his restless mind was already seeking wider horizons. How characteristic it is of him that at the moment his work nears completion he should begin 'forming a plan of more spread & extent'!

In its bleak astringency the house owes much to Cockerell's old master, Smirke. The huge masses of unadorned masonry, the powerfully articulated corners with their giant double pilasters, the bold rectilinear clarity, all these confirm the truth of his remarkably perceptive confession of 1824 that, 'I shall never get entirely out of Smirke's manner in my first works.'

In 1823–25 Cockerell added the extensive office wing which stretches out in a long arm to the north-east. At the end of this is an elaborate conservatory of which the two end pavilions survive, both of the finest masonry construction. Beyond this to the north-east lies the huge stable yard with broad roofs cantilevered out so as to form a covered way round the perimeter. This handsome and convenient arrangement, which he repeated in the stable-yard at Langton House, may possibly have been inspired by one of the Paris *abattoirs* which he had admired in October 1824.

Cockerell's designs for the lodge (Pl. 58) were approved on 3 August 1825. The lodge must be considered as one of the most brilliant small monuments of the Greek Revival. No photograph can convey the compelling, almost imperious presence of this tiny building in the midst of a vast landscape, nor the manner in which it dominates the whole journey down the long drive from the house to the entrance gates. It stands not timidly flanking the gates but facing them centrally from the opposite side of the road. Cockerell brilliantly contrived to make of the public road at this point a kind of piazza or Baroque enclosure by lining it with railings which curve forward towards the road at each end of the enclosed space. The absolute inevitability of the lodge is achieved not only by its masterly siting but by its blending of Doric and Tuscan forms. It does not give the impression of a sacred Doric temple caught unawares in a landscaped park because the broad eaves and the absence of a frieze give it the authentic vernacular or rustic stamp of the Tuscan order. Yet the Greek Doric is hinted at in the curious fluting which ends abruptly just below the capitals.

Lough Crew was an expensive house, though Cockerell calculated that labour and materials were about twenty-five per cent cheaper in Ireland than in England. In September 1827 he noted that the total cost of the house amounted to over £22,000 – that is, nearly £6,000 more than the Hanover Chapel.

In June 1821 Cockerell designed a new school (Pl. 59) to be erected at Oldcastle under Naper's patronage. The building still survives and with its excellent siting and varied composition is undoubtedly the most distinguished building in the town. An extremely handsome master's house is flanked by two lower wings each containing a large school-room with ingenious timber vaults.

Concurrently with Lough Crew Cockerell was remodelling for William Dutton Pollard (1789–1839) a much smaller country-house at Castle Pollard seven or eight miles away. Here he added a small Greek Ionic portico (Pl. 60) and an elegantly cantilevered staircase with brass rails leading up to a spacious bedroom lobby – another Irish feature – lit by a coloured glass dome. At the same date in England he was enlarging Woolmers Park, Hertfordshire (Pl. 61), for Sir Gore Ouseley, a fellow committee-member of the Travellers' Club. Between 1821 and 1823 Cockerell provided a fine new dining-room and a long colonnade of unfluted Greek Doric columns.

It is fitting that Cockerell, whose name will always be associated with the discovery of Greek marbles, should have prepared architectural designs for Lord Elgin himself. Elgin, however, collected almost as many architects as marbles. Between 1796 and 1828 he commissioned designs for the completion of Broomhall, his Fifeshire seat, from no less than fourteen architects.[7]

By 1796 the greater part of Broomhall had been completed to designs by the distinguished Greek Revival architect, Thomas Harrison (1744–1829). In that year, prompted by Harrison, Lord Elgin set out on the famous mission which ended with the acquisition of the Elgin Marbles. It was his dissatisfaction with two parts of Harrison's building – the low side wings and the semi-circular entrance-porch – which led to his commissioning designs for their replacement from thirteen architects. Cockerell, incidentally, had already referred to Broomhall in his diary in April 1821 as an 'ugly house & bad.' His turn to suggest improvements came in 1822, by which time the Earl's study was littered with unexecuted projects from amongst many others, Holland, Porden, Smirke, Wilkins, and Burn. On 31 May 1821 Elgin invited Cockerell to prepare a design for a hexastyle Ionic portico and a west conservatory communicating with the dining-room. Three weeks later Lord Elgin called and was 'much pleased with his plans.' It must have been an entertaining interview for Cockerell was under no illusions as to the fairy-tale character of the world inhabited by the eccentric Earl. 'His object', Cockerell remarked tartly in his diary, 'is to collect various plans as amusement to discant upon & with no other view. Smirke is dissatisfied with him as are all the arists. – he said I must not ruin him, my answer that he would not execute it that it was all well to look at & consider. – this was letting the cat out of the bag. & he was very anxious to convince me of his sincerity. sometimes not ill to let a man know you are up to him.' In this case Cockerell's policy was certainly successful for, in the

7. See J. M. Crook, 'Broomhall, Fife', *Country Life*, CXLVII, 1970, pp. 242–6.

very next month, he received the invitation from Lord Elgin to design the Scottish National Monument.

Cockerell provided a variety of designs with Ionic porticos of four, six and eight columns. These do not exist beyond the stage of sketches and suggest a rather bald treatment reminiscent of Lough Crew. The conservatory seems to have been destined as a repository for casts of the Elgin Marbles.

The next architect tried by Lord Elgin was J. P. Gandy (1787–1850), who had travelled in Greece at the same time as Cockerell and whose researches were published in 1817 by the Society of Dilettanti as the *Unedited Antiquities of Attica*. His first work was the United University Club in Pall Mall East designed in 1822 in collaboration with Wilkins. Cockerell called on Gandy to see his plans for the club-house on 14 May and found them 'commonplace throughout, low, nothing new or striking in arrangement, no intelligence of general proportions, nothing but detail.' Two years later he records disconsolately: 'I have no doubt Ld. Elgin has consulted Gandy abo. Broom Hall – he is amazingly bitten with University Club – he took up Smirke, Wilkins, myself & now Gandy – but it is folly to imagine that artists have any other right to their patrons than that founded on their pencils or talents. We like bravos live by our sword. When this fails we sink into insignificance. there are few who like Harford give their friendship & patronage at the same time.'

Cockerell need not have envied Gandy's patronage by Elgin, for hardly was the ink dry on his drawings when he was replaced in the Earl's affections by J. B. Papworth (1775–1847). In fact, the entrance front of Broomhall did not receive its portico and its wings until 1865 and 1874 respectively – long after Lord Elgin's death.

The commission to which Cockerell refers more frequently than any other in the early 1820's, apart from the Hanover Chapel, is Grange Park. It is significant that this should be so for, in terms of quantity, his work there was not of enormous extent. He evidently found a compelling fascination in the task of adding to what was, probably, the most remarkable neo-classical house in Europe. Such was his devotion to it that, as we have seen, he took his bride to see it on his honeymoon.

It had been remodelled by Wilkins in 1809 to combine references on a daunting scale to the Theseum and the Choragic Monument of Thrasyllus in Athens. Its vast bleak portico was set dramatically above a lake in the middle of a landscaped park of singular beauty. The house was, moreover, the kind of conundrum which appealed vastly to Cockerell, for beneath

Wilkins' Greek Doric shell survived intact a superb late-seventeenth-century house then attributed to Inigo Jones.[8]

Such was the house which in 1817 was bought from its creator, Henry Drummond, by Alexander Baring, later 1st Lord Ashburton (1774–1848), second son of Sir Francis Baring of Stratton Park. The two estates were adjacent and it was the Greek Doric portico which Dance added to Stratton for Francis Baring in 1803 which prompted Drummond's remodelling of Grange Park. Alexander Baring was not content with the accommodation afforded by Grange Park which, in its bones was, after all, still only a seventeenth-century house. Thus he employed Dance and, shortly after, Smirke to extend the house westwards in the form of a low narrow wing. Smirke's contractor, Harrison, proved a trial to everyone and at the beginning of 1823 Baring turned to S. P. Cockerell for assistance. Cockerell entrusted the commission to his son.

In January 1823 C. R. Cockerell proposed two schemes for Baring. Firstly, the duplication at the west end of the house of Wilkins' great portico. Secondly, the replacement of Smirke's wing by a larger addition containing the dining-room, conservatory and extra bedrooms which Baring desired. The first scheme, then, was visual in origin; the second practical. Baring chose the second. However, Cockerell still considered that 'It is well in offering design to propose the noblest & most magnificent as well as that which is more practicable & economic. it makes a show of genius & people like to talk of a fine design. many will content themselves more with this privilege than with the enjoyment of a noble design in execution. this I did at the Grange.'

In August 1823 Cockerell set to work in earnest on the designs for Baring's dining-room (Pls 62–64). It is clear from the diary that he was obsessed by a desire to make of this room a *tour de force*, a composition matching in distinction and originality the architecture of the house itself. It is fascinating to trace through the terse telegraphic hints in the diaries his intensive quest for a solution. Earlier in the week he had visited for the first time Thomas Hope's extraordinary house, the Deepdene in Surrey. Hope, in a similarly self-conscious way, had attempted something that would be at once novel and archaeological. Cockerell's reaction was that 'Novelty has a vast effect in arch[itectur]e. we are sick to see the same thing repeated & over again what has been seen any time these 100 yrs. The Deepdene attracts

8. See J. M. Crook, 'Grange Park Transformed', *The Country Seat*, H. Colvin & J. Harris, eds., 1970, pp. 220–8. For the earlier history of the house, see E. Mercer, 'William Samwell and the Grange, Hampshire', ibid., pp. 48–54.

in this respect exceeding, but if the Pompeian style can be so cultivate[d] as to practice well it may supersede the Templar style in which we have so long worked.' It is interesting to note that, as we shall see, Cockerell contemplated a Pompeian source for the Ionic order in his dining-room.

On 23 April he writes: 'On Baring's dining Ro: turned over every book of decoration I have. read Potter on symposia, asked Millingen for hints. wish to make this room as pure in architecture as poss[ibl]e as classical by figures recalling such associations. drove at novelty, to avoid common place. made out Ionic of Pompeia, inferior to angular volutes of Phygaleia, but these show how common the angular volute was.' Again on the 24th he spent 'all day on Mr. Baring's Ro[om] abandoned myself to the work. searched all my books [for] novelty, originality of conception – yet appropriate. hardiness, unfettered fancy. composed Chimney piece symposium.'

The room which Cockerell finally produced was one of the most elegant and scholarly rooms of the whole Greek Revival. Based ultimately on the cella of the temple at Bassae, it achieved that jewelled, casket-like quality which we know Cockerell felt was characteristic of Greek design. As at Bassae the entablature was supported on free-standing columns of the novel Bassae Ionic order placed close to the outer walls. Above was a segmental coffered vault delicately patterned with painted decorations of Pompeian character. The columns were an expensive luxury: the estimate for the shafts came to £118.2.6., and for the white scagliola capitals £45. Like the columns in the staircase-hall at Oakly Park, they were executed by Messrs. Browne and Company of Tottenham Court Road, a firm of marble workers employed by Nash at Buckingham Palace.

A further luxurious adornment was the chimney-piece (Pl. 64) adorned with two serpentine columns already in Baring's possession and a bas-relief specially commissioned from Flaxman. Cockerell's pupil Clarke, called on Flaxman on 20 January 1824 with Cockerell's drawing for the chimney-piece and a letter explaining that Baring did not want to spend more than £150 on the frieze; Flaxman considered that a frieze four feet eight inches by fifteen inches 'would cost all that money.' Cockerell explained in his letter how his aim in designing the chimney-piece was that 'the sculpture (the main object) may be made more principal . . . I have attempted (though very lamely) a sketch of a groupe from Millingen's vases and some tracings of mine in Italy.'[9]

The curtains in the room were arranged and hung by Dowbiggin's,

9. British Museum Add. MS. 39781, f. 198.

the fashionable Regency firm of decorators and upholsterers. Dowbiggin 'was struck with curtain behind col[umn] as like the *fond* of pictures.' This arrangement of curtain and column evidently found less favour with Mrs. Baring than with Mr. Dowbiggin, for Cockerell records an interview with her in July 1823 marked by 'much heat & violence abo[u]t the furnishings of dining Ro[om].'

The dining-room was approached through a small apsed ante-room opening off a half-landing from the main staircase at the west end of the house. Beyond it Cockerell provided some private rooms for Mrs. Baring which were ready in May 1824. His major addition to Grange Park – apart from the new dining-room – was the conservatory for which designs were first drawn up in June 1823. Adjacent and at right angles to Mrs. Baring's apartments, it was approached from the east by a tetra-style Ionic portico (Pl. 65) delicately answering in miniature Wilkins' giant portico on the east front of the house itself. This portico concealed the large conservatory which, remarkably, had been manufactured entirely from iron and glass in Birmingham and then, transported to Hampshire, had been reassembled on the spot in the autumn of 1824 as though in a trial run for the Crystal Palace. Cockerell had spent two days in December 1823 discussing the design of the conservatory with Mr. Jones, co-proprietor with a Mr. Clark of a firm of metallic hothouse manufacturers of Lionel Street, Birmingham. Cockerell found Jones a 'coxcombe but having judg[e]m[en]t & taste.' The conservatory was the subject of much comment. It was believed at the time, probably correctly, that it was 'not surpassed by anything of the kind in the United Kingdom.' (Pl. 66). A rectangle eighty-one foot ten inches long, forty-eight foot seven inches wide and eighteen foot ten inches high, it was constructed entirely from cast-iron framing with sashes of rolled iron and copper sash-bars. The frames of the side lights and doors were of mahogany filled with British sheet glass. Three barrel-vaulted aisles, anticipatory of Paxton's great transept at the Crystal Palace, were separated from each other by two ridge and furrow roofs. The cast-iron columns supporting the roofs were hollow and thus ingeniously served as drain-pipes, conveying rain-water into a large subterranean reservoir for the supply of the house.

The firm of Jones and Clark was one of the most remarkable of the nineteenth century and it is curious that despite the almost obsessive attention paid to the development of ferro-vitreous construction by propagandists of the Modern Movement in architecture its achievement should have been overlooked. Founded in 1818, it had already produced in the first fifty-odd years of its existence a variety of metallic conservatories and forcing-houses at over two hundred and fifty country houses, as well as providing hot water apparatus for numerous churches and public buildings. Cockerell was one of the firm's earliest and most enthusiastic patrons and we find it, for example, providing mahogany sash windows with bronze mouldings for Lough Crew.

As revolutionary as Cockerell's employment of prefabrication at Grange Park were the formal Italianate gardens which he laid out in 1825–26 before the south and west fronts of the conservatory. With their fountains and balustrades, these elaborate terraced gardens anticipated the Italian revival of Nesfield and Barry. The present writer has discussed in detail elsewhere the relationship of this revival to the established corpus of Picturesque theory in early nineteenth-century England.[10]

We have already seen that, despite Cockerell's enthusiasm for Wilkins' Greek Revival masterpiece, Grange Park, he was more critical of his own work in the same vein at Lough Crew. In 1823 he designed a house that one can only interpret as a conscious reaction against Lough Crew. This was the now demolished Derry Ormond in Cardiganshire.

Cockerell's patron at Derry Ormond was John Jones (1780–1835) who was on the committee of management of St. David's College, Lampeter. Jones had recently inherited from his father a house and estate at Derry Ormond, about three miles from Lampeter, and in 1823 he invited Cockerell to design him a new house on a different part of the property. The materials from the old house were to be sold for re-use at St. David's College. Indeed Mr. Taylor, clerk of the works at the college, was to perform the same task at Derry Ormond.

Cockerell enjoyed this commission and found 'nothing so confident, liberal, modest & gentlemanly as Mr. Jones.' The site, though small, is spectacularly beautiful and is set high up in a fold of the hills. Cockerell considered that one should not provide 'a place of any scale nor does the estate demand it as he says, but for small mansion know nothing that offers better.' He placed the new house at the east end of a long existing terrace some way to the east of the old house. The south front of his house followed the line of this bank which was cut into to allow for basement offices. Not content with the existing terrace he created two more beneath it.

The west, or garden, front (Pl. 67) consisted of two large bay-windows linked by a portico and adjacent to the north of the house was a substantial office-wing. The house itself was comparatively small, basically three bays

10. D. Watkin, *Thomas Hope (1769–1831) and the Neo-Classical Idea*, 1968.

in each direction, but the planning (Pl. 68), particularly of the top-lit staircase-hall, was ingenious. In September 1825, Cockerell was considering the interior decoration and spent 'half day in looking over the loggia of Raphail & other motives of ornam[en]ts for his cielings – on the idea of selecting such as would have character of antique, simple but speaking & characteristic & new – or old in a new light.' On an earlier visit he was pleased to find 'masonry well done [and] some stones 5 ft. long.' The very few stones which survive on the site of the house confirm this estimate of their size. The body of the house, however, was constructed of local, rendered slate. The plinth and dressings were of stone as probably were the giant double pilasters at the corners of the house. He had already adopted pilasters in this position at Lough Crew. On the whole, however, Derry Ormond is a somewhat dislocated composition compared with Lough Crew. Its indecision results in its being neither wholeheartedly Greek nor Picturesque despite the superb terraces on which Cockerell placed it. The Greek details, such as the Delian Doric order of the entrance porch on the east front (Pl. 69), fail to lend tone or coherence to the lumpish forms of the house itself with its prominent gables and bay-windows. A rather dull offspring of Derry Ormond is the house Cockerell designed at Caversfield (Pl. 70) in Oxfordshire in 1842 for the Warden of Merton College, the Rev. R. B. Marsham, whom he had met in the course of designing the Ashmolean Museum.

In June 1826 Cockerell was 'at Derry marking out lodge, water, bridge &c. &c. showed Mr. Jones approach & drives round the place, showing beauties of which he was not before aware ... enjoying most delicious weather & fragrant air, the cuccoe & doves & birds filling the air with life & love & murmur.' Since the lodge on the Lampeter Road, which still survives, was visible from the house Cockerell rather neatly designed it to echo in miniature the forms of the house itself with a pediment or gable containing a lunette window on each of its four fronts.

Cockerell's next house after Derry Ormond marks the climax of his career as a country-house architect. This is Langton House near Long Blandford in Dorset which was designed in 1824 and executed in a slightly altered form in 1827-32. Alas, like both Lough Crew and Derry Ormond it has recently been demolished.

On the whole Cockerell was fortunate in his choice of patrons but the squire of Langton, Mr. Farquharson, was an exception. A man of no very great intellect he was also indecisive and procrastinatory by temperament. Cockerell paid his first visit to Langton in April 1824 to prepare a scheme for remodelling the existing house which had formerly been a parsonage. When he left a few days later he had persuaded Farquharson to build instead an entirely new house to cost £10,000 and for which he had already made a number of drawings. When it came to choosing the site of the new house in June, Mr. Farquharson's nerve failed. Cockerell paints a vivid picture of wandering about the grounds with the Farquharson family in a state of near desperation wishing they had never seen the place. Cockerell was amazed at the shattering effect of making a decision 'on people unused to mental exertion'. He realized that the decision would have to be his and was anxious to raise the house on terraces as at Derry Ormond. In laying out the grounds he called on the services of W. S. Gilpin, the landscape gardener from Sheen in Surrey with a London office at 50 Upper Berkeley Street.

In February 1825, Cockerell was summoned once again to Langton to discuss the site of the house. So little progress was made on this occasion or, indeed, in the course of the next few months that in September, Cockerell decided to recommend Farquharson to revert to his original scheme of merely extending his present house. However, in May 1826, Farquharson announced that he intended to begin building the new house shortly, though he 'wished to reconsider the plans in June.' Even after settling the site of the house in June there was to be another year's delay before the construction actually began. Work proceeded slowly until 1832 though the body of the house was largely finished by 1830.

The general form of Langton House (Pl. 72) reflects Cockerell's enthusiasm for Palladian architecture – an enthusiasm which was rare in the 1820's though the architect Thomas Hopper had some facility in the style. The garden-front with its projecting pedimented towers is a type much favoured by the English Palladians, deriving ultimately from the Villa Trissino at Cricoli, designed by Palladio's master, Giangiorgio Trissino. The blank but beautifully balanced and satisfying composition of the south-east front (Pl. 74) with its central Venetian window is a little reminiscent of, though much more subtly modulated than, the south-east front of Lord Burlington's villa at Chiswick. A note of subdued novelty is struck by the slight recession of the central bay which the eye expects to be advanced. In his diary in December 1827 Cockerell records how 'Sharpe reminded me of the beauty of Palladio's proportions of rooms, 5/3ds. of the width – so my rooms 22 ft. wide will be 36.8 long at Farquharsons.'

The only two drawings which survive are undated sketches for the colonnaded garden front and for the entrance-front (Pls 71 & 73), on paper watermarked 1822 and 1823 respectively. These early projects, probably dating from 1824, relate closely in general disposition to what was finally executed, but are so much more pedestrian in detail that they seem at first sight to be for a different building. Thus, in the house as built, the central window of the entrance-front and the two end-windows of the garden-front are set in shallow, arched recesses adorned with lively and freely-flowing carved swags. This unexpected decoration which lends character to the entire building seems to be derived from Wren, though it is hard to point to a precise source. It does not appear in the early sketches for the house nor does the florid iron-work which replaced the stone balustraded balconies of the first project. Another departure from the early drawings which makes the house as executed look like a work of *c.* 1840 rather than of the mid-1820's is the elliptical heads of the ground-floor windows. Normally associated with early Victorian architecture this must be one of the very earliest uses of this not very pleasing form.

When the house was demolished the stable-courtyard (Pls 77–78) was happily spared. It bears all the stamps of Cockerell's genius and is as carefully controlled a spatial experience as, say, a comparable group of stable buildings by Lutyens. Indeed, Cockerell's elemental approach to the classical vocabulary in the Langton stables is in some ways anticipatory of Lutyens. Its immediate source, however, is undoubtedly Vanbrugh. The Farquharson family, indeed, had owned the remains of Vanbrugh's great house, Eastbury, since 1806. It was only a few miles away from Langton and on one of Cockerell's early visits to the Farquharsons in June 1824, he 'rode over to Eastbury . . . [where] every minute part bore a character of magnificence quite extraordinary, seeming like conception & habitation of a superior order of beings.' Something of this almost superhuman 'character of magnificence' he perhaps achieved himself in the stables at Langton.

We should remember, finally, that Cockerell built a number of Gothic or Tudor houses of which the most substantial were Hinchwick of 1826, North Weald Basset parsonage of 1827 for his brother, and Enstone Vicarage of 1832.[11] All three of these survive, the most successful being Hinchwick (Pl. 79) near Sezincote, a large farm-house designed for his uncle, Sir Charles Cockerell. It is a remarkably skilful pastiche in the style of a Cotswold manor-house. Cockerell may have had these houses in mind in making a small but significant correction to the manuscript of a proposed biographical notice sent to him in January 1860.[12] He altered the phrase, 'He has chosen to follow the classical style', to, 'He has chiefly followed the classical style.'

11. See Bodleian Library, Oxford Diocesan Papers, 103, no. 2b.
12. British Museum, Add. MS. 28509, f. 336.

Perhaps the most interesting of all his departures from the classical tradition was the conservatory he designed in 1839 for Mr Battersby at Stoke Park near Bristol (Pl. 80). This was octagonal with a dome and cupola carried on intersecting ribs inspired by those in the fourteenth-century Kitchen at Durham Cathedral. Messrs. Jones and Clark constructed a model for this conservatory contrived from brass rods and bent glass. It must have been one of the most remarkable of all tributes to Cockerell's idiosyncratic inventive genius.[13]

A related project was the remarkable chapel of the Holy Evangelists at Killerton, Devon (Pls 81–82), designed in 1838 in imitation of St. Mary's chapel (sometimes called St. Joseph's) at Glastonbury Abbey. Dating from the 1180's, St. Mary's chapel is an unusual example of the Norman Transitional style and is a free-standing aisleless rectangle with prominent corner turrets, anticipating in form the late mediaeval Royal chapels.

Cockerell had been in consultation with Sir Thomas Dyke Acland, Bart. (1787–1871) as early as 1824 about a new private chapel at his Devon seat, Killerton, to replace the existing chapel a mile or so away at Culm John. He may have been introduced to Acland by their common friend, John Scandrett Harford, and would also have met him at Grillion's Club. This cultivated autocratic head of an ancient Devon family must have been a stimulating companion for Cockerell. An active landlord, he found time to bring a remarkably independent mind to bear on problems of politics, education and religion. In 1836 he renewed his discussions about the chapel which Cockerell, obtained a licence to build in 1837, and in the following year settled the rather curious form the building was to take. The decision to base it on the Glastonbury chapel was evidently his and not Cockerell's, though Cockerell certainly admired the building. Thus we find him writing to Acland in 1838:[14] 'If this finds you at Killerton & still bent on Joseph of Glastonbury, do not think of neutralizing, castrating & emasculating the copy of that noble building, & flattering yourself that you have what will be worthy of the original – either have an original work altogether or a correct reproduction – a good copy, but let us not have half measures . . . or we shall have a ψευδο Gothic, not worthy of you or any one concerned.'

13. Though brother to, and partner in the same bank as, Cockerell's friend, John Harford of Blaise Castle, Mr Harford-Battersby did not treat Cockerell with the respect to which he was accustomed at the height of his career. Thus Goodchild relates how Cockerell abandoned this commission on learning that he was expected to do the journey from Bristol to Stoke Park and back on foot!

14. I am grateful to Lady Acland for bringing to my notice the correspondence between Cockerell and Sir Thomas Acland at the Devon County Record Office which is quoted here, and for putting at my disposal her knowledge of Killerton and the Acland family history.

To Cockerell the moment of the Glastonbury chapel was 'the Augustan period of the middle ages', and in that period he could 'find nothing superior to Glastonbury.' Nonetheless, when submitting three different designs to Acland on 1 June 1838, he could not help observing: 'I hope you will not think me a peremptory Fellow for having an opinion on the subject & in differing from your fixt determination, as stated by Mr. Harford, to prefer No. 3 [i.e. the Glastonbury model]. should you remain unshaken in this opinion I will do the best I can in assisting that preference.'

When it was clear that nothing would make Acland change his mind, Cockerell entered fully into the spirit of this archaeological exercise. It was he, however, who suggested to Acland in 1839, when the walls were already rising,[15] a definite departure from the Glastonbury model in the form of a rose window at the west end: 'after much consideration of authorities & beauty breadth boldness & originality of character', he wrote on 21 January, 'I am induced to offer to your consideration the rose window. it is in the spirit (at least) of the Prototype & its Period – it is more beautiful than the three congregated windows [of Glastonbury] . . . you have seen many such abroad – see Hope's Specimens throughout, of that date.' It is interesting to see the direct influence of new architectural publications such as Thomas Hope's *An Historical Essay on Architecture* (1835) on building types in the 1840's. The *Rundbogenstil* in all its many forms was especially characteristic of these years offering, as it did, a non-Gothic solution to those who had grown weary of neo-classicism. In designing Killerton chapel Cockerell consulted personally two of the key figures associated with the literature of the *Rundbogenstil*: Baron Bunsen (1791–1865), who published *Die Basiliken des Christlichen Rom* from 1823 to 1843, and Henry Gally Knight, of whom he wrote to Acland on 5 August 1840: 'I saw some details of S. Ambrogio at Milan belonging to Mr. Gally Knight much to your point yesterday. he is about to publish all his anc[ien]t Ecclesiastic arch[itectur]e of 8th to 15 cent[ur]y or thereabouts.'[16] Later in the same month Cockerell drew Acland's attention to an English source, the rose window of the Norman church at Barfreston in Kent, from which he derived the trefoil-like shape of the cusps in the Killerton rose window.

15. His reluctance to provide definite working drawings and the many changes of plan made possible by the absence of such drawings, contributed to the exceeding by over £1,000 of his original estimate of £2,909. The chapel was built of a combination of local stone and of Whitby stone, but Cockerell complained in a moment of exasperation in 1843 that 'granite would have been cheaper, as far as execution goes.'

16. H. G. Knight, *The Ecclesiastic Architecture of Italy from the Time of Constantine to the fifteenth Century*, 1842–44.

Cockerell also had to contend with advice from Sir Thomas' young son, Henry, who had been a freshman with Ruskin at Christ Church in 1836 and was to be the prime mover of the celebrated Oxford Museum from 1849 onwards.[17] Henry asked Cockerell for a detailed drawing of one of the capitals in the interior of the chapel. Cockerell sent him a rough sketch and, with a pleasing reference to Henry's Ruskinian views, wrote of it to Sir Thomas on 23 July 1840: 'I left him one in June which Stead has & can put into detail for him, always with the help of living lillies.'

The Stead to whom Cockerell refers was a Ludlow stone-mason whom Cockerell had employed at Oakly Park and for whom he secured the commission for the stone carving at Killerton. Cockerell's delight on discovering him reminds one irresistibly of Ruskin's reaction to the work of the O'Shea brothers at the Oxford Museum: 'I can without fear of contradiction say', Cockerell wrote in December, 1838, 'that as an artist mason he is the best *I ever met with*. he is worthy of Royal & Princely employment. his work is such that you cannot refrain from passing your hand over its surface & mouldings as perfect & realy lovely – he is the only mason I ever met who worked in the true sense of the word "con amore" – he has consequently always been distressed, loving his work more than himself; & such a quality cannot be appreciated in a provincial Town, perhaps no more in this Babylon.'

Despite his enthusiasm for Stead, Cockerell was concerned that he should restrict himself to abstract decoration and not attempt the more difficult art of figure sculpture. Rather reluctantly perhaps, he wrote to Acland in December 1840: 'we must be absolutely *arabesque* & true Mahometans in this respect in protestant countries, abhorring images – ignorant therefore of the practice of drawing the human face or form divine.' This led Cockerell on to the question of the figures of the Evangelists in painted glass with which it was proposed to fill the windows of the apse. He had a low view of the talents of Thomas Willement (1786–1871) whom he was employing at this time for heraldic glass at Cambridge University Library. Willement, who worked in association with Pugin, undoubtedly had ability as a designer of heraldic decoration in both Gothic and Classical veins but his figure drawing left much to be desired. Cockerell wrote scathingly of him to Acland in 1840:

17. Henry subsequently wrote of the Oxford Museum, '. . . there is on all sides evidence, both in material and design, of a rigorously restrained expenditure, just as in respect of material and finish the direct contrary may be noticed in another great structure, recently built for the University by my esteemed friend Mr. Cockerell – the Taylor Institution' (H. W. Acland and J. Ruskin, *The Oxford Museum*, 1859, pp. 25–6).

'I believe Willement incapable of doing them as a gentleman should desire to have them ... with all submission they should be drawn by learned hands, such as Dyce's or Eastlake's.[18] English eyes (even of gentlemen Protestants) are commonly ... ignorant in the human form divine. how other wise would we see such horrors done as would be scouted in any catholic (Roman) country of Europe? If the *drawing* were made & superintended by a learned hand, the color & paint may be done by Willement, but permit me strongly to recommend that the holy Evangelists be worthily drawn – or turn we to arabesque, safe in our ignorance & absence of pretension.'

Here, as so often with Cockerell, we are in the presence of a man who speaks with authority. His uncompromising belief in 'everything or nothing' reminds us of Pugin who wrote a letter a year or so later to his patron, Lord Shrewsbury, rebuking him for modifying his proposals for the dining-room at Alton Towers: 'I know my design was quite right, and again I entreat of your lordship to carry it out, or to leave the present building unaltered ... I have nailed my colours to the mast, – a bay window, high open roof, lantern, two good fire-places, a great sideboard, screen, minstrel-gallery – *all or none*. I will not sell myself to do a wretched thing.'[19] Allow for the transference of style and this, surely, is the authentic voice of Cockerell. The point is confirmed in an anecdote told by the architect John Brydon (1840–1901), 'of how Stanfield the painter,[20] being anxious to introduce Cockerell and Pugin did so one day, and left the two to have a chat together. Afterwards, he asked each of them what he thought of the other. Cockerell said, "Pugin is the most earnest and enthusiastic man in his profession and has the greatest belief in it of anyone I have ever met." And Pugin said of Cockerell, "The man is a great artist, though I don't believe in the style he works in." '[21]

We may appropriately end this chapter by leaving Cockerell and Pugin in each other's company, for in the early 1840's they were both employed in improvements at Peper Harow House in Surrey for that eccentric architectural amateur, the 5th Viscount Midleton. Cockerell's additions to the Georgian house were minor; Pugin's Gothic buildings in the grounds more extensive. But according to Goodchild, 'Lord Midleton wanted a Gothic

18. William Dyce, R.A. (1806–1864) and Sir Charles Lock Eastlake, P.R.A. (1793–1865), with both of whom Cockerell was associated at this time over the Government School of Design.

19. Quoted from B. Ferrey, *Recollections of A. N. Welby Pugin*, 1861, p. 120.

20. Clarkson Stanfield (1795–1867), the popular marine and landscape artist.

21. Quoted from R.I.B.A. *Transactions*, 3rd series, VII, 1900, p. 351.

doorway by Pugin in the churchyard wall and opposite a Grecian classic entrance with columns to Chambers' conservatory, and between them a door into the kitchen gardens to be based on Inigo Jones' York stairs gateway. Cockerell submitted designs for the two doors but could not enter into Midleton's eclectic spirit and the work was not executed.' Shortly after this disappointment Lord Midleton's wife, who had started life as his mother's laundry maid, left him. The double blow proved too much for him and in 1848 he took his life at Peper Harow by asphyxiating himself with charcoal fumes. One can only hope that in the meantime he had enjoyed to the full what Phoebe Stanton has rightly called 'a quite dazzling juxtaposition of personalities.'[22]

22. P. Stanton, *Pugin*, 1971, p. 173.

CHAPTER XI

The Path to Greatness: Cambridge University Library

ONE OF the most important stages in the evolution of Cockerell's mature style is represented by his designs for the Cambridge University Library. Had these been executed Cambridge would have had a monument to rival the Ashmolean Museum at Oxford, for which, incidentally, they may be regarded as a preparatory exercise.

Extension of the Library had been much discussed in the eighteenth century and culminated in a proposal by Robert Adam of 1784 for replacing all the existing buildings with an extravagant composition entered by a great portico in the middle of the south front facing King's chapel.[1] The buildings Adam proposed to destroy were the uncompleted mediaeval court of King's College and, immediately adjacent to it on the east, the fifteenth-century Old Schools quadrangle which contained the University Library and served as both the administrative and educational centre of the University as opposed to the colleges. After the completion of Wilkins' new buildings for King's College, the college agreed in 1829 to sell its now unwanted mediaeval court to the University. The growth of interest in the Natural Sciences, for the teaching of which there were wholly inadequate lecture-rooms, and the chance to extend the site of the Schools buildings, gave new impetus to the old ambition of extending the accommodation of the University Library. On 6 May 1829, a Syndicate was appointed to consider methods of realizing this ambition, thus opening the first chapter of a long and distressing story marked both by chronic indecision and lamentable irresponsibility.[2]

By 2 July 1829, the Syndicate had formulated the University's building requirements as follows: Museums for Geology, Mineralogy, Botany and

---

1. See A. Oswald, 'The Old University Library, Cambridge', *Country Life*, LXXVI, 1934, 416–21.

2. This summary of the competition is based on the lengthy account in R. Willis & J. W. Clark, *An Architectural History of the University of Cambridge*, 4 vols, Cambridge, 1886, III, pp. 97–128, and on the eight contemporary pamphlets, referred to below, published in 1831–35.

Zoology; Schools for Divinity, Law, Physic and Arts; a Model Room for the Jacksonian Professor and an Apparatus Room for the Plumian Professor; an Office for the Registry; and rooms for the Librarian and the Syndics of the University Library. These should be placed round four sides of a courtyard covering the whole site of the two existing courts which should be demolished. The whole of the first floor of the new building should be devoted to the Library. It was further agreed to hold a limited competition in which the following architects would be invited to submit designs to the Vice-Chancellor by 1 November 1829: C. R. Cockerell, Decimus Burton, William Wilkins, and Rickman and Hutchinson. The Syndics decided not to prescribe any 'particular style of architecture', though demanded that the building be finished externally in stone. So as to incommode as little as possible users of the existing library the new building was to be capable of being erected in two separate stages. Most surprisingly, no hint was given as to the extent of the funds available for the whole enterprise.

Cockerell accepted his invitation and visited Cambridge on 24 July in order to discuss the plan with Mr John Lodge, the University Librarian. He was again in Cambridge at the end of September with his assistant, Topple, and spent the following month preparing the designs for what was by far the largest and most important project of his career so far. Working to a deadline never suited his introspective temperament, and we find the following characteristic entry in his diary after 1 November:

'heartily glad to have got rid of the Cambridge business – these pressing and anxious competitions, as any other too exacting business, prevents one's attention to one's worldly & spiritual affairs of any other kind. a racing business is contrary to all mental improvemt. & nothing tends more to a groveling habit.'

Poor Cockerell – little did he know that the trials of this interminable competition had hardly yet begun! However, on 25 November his designs were selected by the Syndicate in preference to those of his competitors. Alone amongst the competitors Cockerell had taken the liberty of sending down not one but two designs for the new buildings. His second and more ambitious design (which was not that selected by the Syndicate) was evidently that which had particularly engaged not only his attentions but also those of a powerful member of the Syndicate, the Rev. George Peacock, a Fellow of Trinity College. On 7 January 1830, Cockerell visited Cambridge to confer with Mr Peacock and, as a result, spent much of January and February in preparing new designs (Pl. 84) based on his earlier alternative project. In the meantime, there was much unease in the University concerning both the extent of the destruction which the erection of the new library would entail, and also the funds – or rather the lack of them – available for such a course of action. Consequently, in February 1830 the Senate confirmed a Grace to appoint a Syndicate to report on the funds of the University chest. In March Cockerell sent his new plans privately to a member of the first Syndicate, presumably Peacock. By this time, 'so extraordinary a degree of excitement prevailed in the University respecting the different plans, and in opposition to the Report of the (first) Syndicate, that the new plan in question could neither be publicly shewn nor impartially considered.'[3]

The solution adopted was the appointment of a new Syndicate in June 1830 to organize what was, effectively, a second competition though limited to the original architects. The new instructions stipulated 'the Grecian style' of architecture and made it clear that the only part of the whole scheme which was likely to be carried out in the near future was that on the site of the old court of King's College. The cost of erecting this part was not to exceed £25,000.

After some hesitation Cockerell agreed to send in new designs as requested. The views of George Peacock, with whom he discussed the matter on 14 July, were probably a powerful persuasive. He worked on his designs during August and September, the closing date for the competition being 10 October. The second Syndicate now absurdly reversed the decision of the first and on 10 December selected the designs of Rickman and Hutchinson on the grounds that Cockerell's had departed from the instructions. These departures consisted principally in the provision of a Zoology Museum, which was not required by the Syndicate, and of an entrance into the courtyard from Trinity Hall Lane opposite Clare College chapel; and in the separation of the museums from the lecture-rooms.

What Cockerell must have suffered on learning that the banal and clumsy designs of Rickman and Hutchinson were now preferred to his own, we can only imagine. However, he was not without his supporters. On 1 January 1831, George Peacock published a pamphlet entitled *Observations on the Plans for the New Library &c. by a member of the First Syndicate* which reproduced the plans of both Cockerell and of Rickman and Hutchinson, enlarging eloquently on the merits of the former and the offensive defects of the latter. This brought forth a rather indecisive response in the form of a pamphlet 'by a Member of Both Syndicates', William Whewell, a

---

3. G. Peacock, *Observations on the Plans for the New Library*, 1831, p. 18.

distinguished authority on German Romanesque architecture and a tireless advocate of the merits of the Natural Sciences who later became Master of Trinity College. The fight was now taken up in Birmingham where Messrs. Rickman and Hutchinson published anonymously an attack on Peacock's pamphlet in which the virtues of their own design were artlessly brought forward to the detriment of Cockerell's which, they claimed, had been inspired by their own entry in the first competition. However, support for Cockerell was now forthcoming from another quarter in the form of a pamphlet 'by a Member of neither Syndicate', the Rev. H. Coddington, Fellow of Trinity College. This was closely followed by another and – at this stage, one would have thought – needless effusion on Cockerell's behalf from George Peacock. The University was further entertained by two pamphlets by William Wilkins published respectively in February and April 1831 in which alarm was expressed at the possibility that the University might be tempted at this stage to resolve the matter by allowing the Senate to choose between the designs of Cockerell and of Rickman and Hutchinson. Wilkins was careful to emphasize the tempting economies which he had been able to effect in his design by leaving intact the principal east front of the Schools quadrangle.

There, almost unbelievably, the matter rested for nearly three years. The report of the second Syndicate was never even presented to the Senate. The long silence was eventually broken in 1834 by the report of a Syndicate appointed on 14 March to confer with the long-suffering architects. This Syndicate hit upon an original way of dealing with the problem by announcing that the University had been compelled to abandon altogether its intention of building a library. In compensation it invited the architects to accept the sum of one hundred guineas each. He would be guilty of considerable ignorance of human nature who supposed that a man of Cockerell's calibre would be tempted by such paltry blandishment. Alone of the competing architects Cockerell spurned the hundred guineas. Now the puissant Peacock came once more to his aid and published a pamphlet early in 1835 making the modest, if realistic, proposal that a library be erected along the north end of the site leaving untouched the remainder of the two existing courtyards. Although this is, in effect, what was eventually decided on, the University went through the motion in November 1835 of inviting the four architects to submit further designs, having first decided that the necessary funds could be raised by subscription.

The plans in this, the third competition, were to be submitted by 18 February 1836. On 11 May, those by Cockerell were selected by a large majority. This by no means marked the end of the whole tiresome affair, for Cockerell's refusal to promise to keep within the suggested £25,000 limit caused such alarm that demolition work on King's Court was suspended in June 1836, and the third Syndicate was re-appointed for further conference with Cockerell. In December, a building syndicate was appointed to discuss with Cockerell how far the existing structures on the site could be incorporated into any new building. This syndicate reported on 8 March 1837 that no old walls could be used structurally and that it had proposed a number of alterations to the architect which he had since embodied in a new set of plans. It further recommended that work now begin on Cockerell's whole North range instead of proceeding with the West and parts of the North and South ranges. This was at last confirmed by the Senate and work began later in the same month, the foundation stone being laid at a small ceremony on 29 September 1837. The contractors were Messrs. J. & C. Rigby of London. By the beginning of 1840 the whole was substantially complete, the interior fittings being finished by November 1842. The cost of the whole, confirming Cockerell's initial suspicions, was in the region of £35,000.

To trace the development of Cockerell's designs it is necessary to disentangle the random drawings[4] which survive so as to relate them to the three competitions of 1829, 1830 and 1835–36. This is a difficult task since not only were the designs frequently amended between the competitions, and most importantly in 1836–37, but also most of them are undated. Where dates are provided they are often in a later hand. Moreover there has been confusion about the dates of the competitions themselves so that a set of drawings at the Victoria and Albert Museum is catalogued as having been 'submitted at the first competition in 1830.' In fact, no drawings survive from the first competition and none of any consequence for the building as executed. However, we have the explanatory letter which Cockerell sent to the Vice-Chancellor on 31 October 1829 to accompany the eight drawings which he submitted in the first competition. The principal feature of this design was the impressive colonnade along the East front 'imitated', so Cockerell tells us, 'from the celebrated Western portal of St. Paul's Cathedral by Inigo Jones.' The order adopted, however, was Greek, taken from the Temple of Athene at Priene which Cockerell had drawn and measured on the spot. The attic storey was derived from another favourite of his, the Forum of Nerva in Rome, while the arrangement of raked benches in the principal lecture-theatre was inspired by that in the College of

---

4. These consist of thirty-three drawings in the University Library, Cambridge, Add. MS. 6630, and sixteen sheets of drawings in the Victoria and Albert Museum, E. 2069–2084 – 1909.

Physicians in Warwick Lane believed by Cockerell to be the work of Sir Christopher Wren. Since designs in either Greek or Gothic were allowed, Cockerell felt it advisable to stress of Gothic that though 'a temporary celebrity has attached of late years to this style, it has never been esteemed in comparison with Grecian at periods in which fine art has been cultivated.' To defend himself from any possible criticisms of over-crowding on a small site he adopted an interesting argument, ultimately Picturesque in origin, which he was later to develop in his Royal Academy lectures:

'most of the remarkable buildings in Rome were placed in confined situations, or . . . with porticos or walls surrounding them . . . the skills of the great masters in architecture has been chiefly observed in the proportion of their edifices to the space [which surrounds them].'

He went so far as to suggest that the Hall and Chapel of Trinity College would be more effective visually in a more crowded space and that their grandeur is, in fact, diminished rather than enhanced by their being seen across the vast empty spaces of Great Court.

Of Cockerell's alternative design for the 1829 competition we know only that it departed from the programme laid down by extending the building to the extremities of the entire site and by more or less duplicating on its south side the Senate House by James Gibbs. This, of course, was but to realize the original proposals of Gibbs himself – proposals which had nearly been effected in 1791 by Sir John Soane.

Cockerell accompanied his proposals with a detailed estimate of their cost. This amounted to £64,615 – 19 – 7d. and was accounted for in fifty-six separate items.

We have a clearer picture of Cockerell's entry in the competition of 1830 since a number of drawings survive and it is described in some detail by Peacock. A highly finished water-colour (Pl. 85) dated 9 October 1830, shows the east front flanked by curious Greek Doric stoae relating rather uneasily to the Senate House on the north and to nothing in particular on the south. However, the principal innovation consists in the suppression of the splendid Greek colonnade in favour of a Corinthian portico. This, Rickman and Hutchinson claimed, was inspired by the portico in their entry in the 1829 competition. However, Cockerell's portico achieves a rich drama altogether beyond the scope of Rickman's talents. It is, in fact, a double portico within which the principal staircase begins at either end between the two rows of columns. Peacock cites as a source the first of all Baroque staircases, Longhena's at S. Giorgio Maggiore, Venice, or Bartolomeo Bianco's at Genoa

University. It is by no means unlikely that it was Cockerell himself who suggested these stylistic comparisons to Peacock. To them one might add Schinkel's Altes Museum in Berlin of 1823. Further richness is achieved in Cockerell's portico by the fact that it opens into the internal courtyard from which in turn an archway leads into Trinity Hall Lane. Thus there would have been an uninterrupted axial vista from the tower of Great St. Mary's Church to the Chapel of Clare College.

The atmosphere of uncertainty and unreality characteristic of the conduct of the competition aggravated Cockerell's natural tendency to lose himself in a welter of alternative schemes. Thus there are a number of sketches showing the east front flanked by squat domed towers, and one which shows it with neither colonnade nor portico. This last is pasted on to a sheet dated 1830 (probably not by Cockerell) and is related to three more (dated 1835 in the same hand) which show the front with two towers, a shallow central dome and a colonnade. These are more Renaissance in tone than any of the other projects executed or unexecuted. Characteristic is the lovely drawing (Pl. 84) of sensuous wall-surfaces handled with a positively Genoese richness, though with hints of a subtlety derived from late works by Palladio such as the Palazzo Valmarana at Vicenza.

The sequence of great rooms round the first floor of the courtyard would have formed one of the noblest libraries in Europe. The mighty splendour which Cambridge lost can be appreciated in the ravishing drawing, dated 1830, which is reproduced in Pl. 86. This shows one of the circular vestibules which were placed at the angles of the court as a solution to the problem of turning corners with rooms containing book-cases projecting at right angles to the walls. The high drama of Cockerell's solution is produced by his characteristic blending of antique and Renaissance themes. The screens of columns framing vistas down barrel-vaulted naves echo the Roman baths but the design of the circular vestibule is perhaps based on Sanmicheli's Cappella Pellegrini at San Bernardino, Verona, or on the interior of Palladio's chapel at Maser which has the same Corinthian columns between broad, arched recesses supporting an uninterrupted circular entablature with a sumptuous frieze and a modillion cornice; and the same winged victories whose full-blown forms amply fill the spandrels over the arches. How like Cockerell to hit upon this mannered, little-known and inaccessible work by Palladio! The ground-floor, treated rather like an undercroft, contained a series of bold and simple lecture-rooms. The view of the Divinity School (Pl. 87) shows load-bearing Greek Doric columns of stone carrying iron beams which in turn supported the iron cores of the larger wooden columns in the library above.

The quality and subtlety of Cockerell's plan is made the more apparent by comparison with that of Rickman and Hutchinson which was, so grotesquely, preferred to it in this second competition. In Rickman's design there is an unhappy handling of changing ground-floor levels; there are frequent diminutive courts, culminating in the principal court which is narrow, deep and studded with windows of all sizes and in all positions; there are two needlessly large staircases designed so that the eye could never see both together and so that they both led into two points in the same room which were out of reach of window or skylight and blocked by book-stacks. George Peacock summed up the design as one in which all rooms were sacrificed to exterior display and which was characterized as a whole by waste of space and want of light. He contrasted its thirty-eight exterior columns, its pediment filled with statues, its enormous entablature and its seven hundred and fifty feet of figured frieze, with the twelve columns of Cockerell's portico and the one free-standing column at each corner of his exterior, which together constituted the building's sole adornments.

None of these designs relates very closely to the wing finally erected in 1837–40; nor, surprisingly, does the majority of those which can be connected with the third competition of 1835–36. We have a ground-floor (though not a first-floor) plan (Pl. 88) relating to this competition which shows the reinstatement of the colonnade of his original design of 1829 in place of the costly double portico. Both storeys of the north range of the court are now given over to the library, the ground floor of which is somewhat inconvenient of access. Grave economies have effected sad changes elsewhere: there is now only one staircase and that not beginning grandly in a portico but tucked into a room of its own. Moreover, the whole front is variously punctuated by four ambiguously-placed doorways. Of these the principal one is inevitably asymmetrical to the colonnade which thus becomes a decorative adjunct unrelated to what lies behind it.

However, we have three particularly fine elevations for the interiors of the courtyard. That for the north range (Pl. 89) corresponds, save for the attic storey, fairly closely with what was eventually erected on this site (Pl. 102). Pilasters with extremely beautiful Corinthian capitals divide the façade into seven bays, the ground-floors of which are filled with broad windows containing slender metal mullions with exuberant heads in the form of swans. A decisively French note is struck by the extravagant centre-piece in the attic which derives from sources such as Lescot's Square Court of the Louvre of 1546 or the Luxembourg Palace of 1615 by Salomon de Brosse. Indeed, Cockerell's whole façade has something of the bold

Mannerist feel of a building like the Hôtel Lamoignon of 1584 by Baptiste du Cerceau. More plastic than the north range is the east range with attached Corinthian columns instead of pilasters, but the west range (Pl. 90) is yet more characteristic of mature Cockerell, showing him in his boldest and most idiosyncratic mood, gloriously independent of what any other architect was doing in Europe at that moment. Its themes were powerfully amplified in its corresponding western front (Pl. 91) on to Trinity Hall Lane which thus forms, in a sense, the climax of the entire building – an arrangement which will come as a surprise to anyone at all familiar with the lane's cramped and devious course. These remarkable façades are amongst the first statements of the theme which was for long to obsess Cockerell: the powerful and strange combination of the column supporting an arch, complicated by the interposition of a varying entablature. Cockerell gave it its most mature statement in the St. Giles' front of the Taylor Institution at Oxford. An antique source for the columns linked in the attic storey by three great arched windows can be found in a Roman temple at Bordeaux (Pl. 92). This had been drawn by Perrault shortly before its demolition and published by him in 1684 in his edition of Vitruvius. As we have seen in Chapter VIII, it was known to Cockerell, and it has been proved that it was known to his hero, Hawksmoor. Indeed there are striking hints of the Vanbrugh-Hawksmoor world in the West range of Cockerell's courtyard, in the form of the arches which surmount the end bays of its east front and the centre of its west front. The skyline heroics provided by these arched chimney-stacks derive directly from aspects of Vanbrugh's work at Blenheim, King's Weston and Eastbury which are the subject of enthusiastic comment in Cockerell's diaries. Cockerell also admired Heriot's Hospital in Edinburgh designed in 1627 by William Wallace. Referring in his diary to the roof-line of this building – which he believed to be the work of Inigo Jones – he spoke of the 'great effect produced by the tower & lantern system – think Vanbrugh studied it.' When in the same year, 1822, he visited the vast Elizabethan mansion, Burghley House in Northamptonshire, he similarly enthused over the 'aspect grand from extent and quality and pointed elevations, flat roofs, chimneys in two columns with entablature irregular, looks like the ruins of Palmyra or Balbeck. Vanbrugh must have taken his notion of chimneys from this, making them ornamental elevations.' This is one of those wonderfully illuminating remarks which tells us much about Elizabethan architecture, about Vanbrugh and about Cockerell – and particularly about the skyline of the west range of his University Library. Arched chimney-stacks had already assumed a peculiar prominence in a weird semi-Elizabethan project by Cockerell of 1832 for a house at Falkland in Fife (Pl. 93) for a Mr Bruce. The strange confluence of influences which marks such schemes as Falkland House and the University Library seems to derive from an ability of Cockerell's to step back into the past, as it were, and to remould past events according to his own ends – as though a modern Summerson instead of writing books of architectural history should erect buildings to prove his stylistic points.

Of the extravagant design of the west front of Cockerell's west range there is no hint whatsoever in a calmer and more conventional elevation for this front which is appended to the plan already discussed (Pl. 88). It is possible, therefore, that this plan was produced after the third competition in response to the demands of the building syndicate appointed in December 1836. Two further designs were definitely produced after the closing date of the third competition in February 1836, though before Cockerell's plans were chosen three months later. These are both dated 13 April 1836 but, attractive though they are, do nothing to clarify our understanding of the evolution of the whole project. One of them shows a superb two-storeyed library interior (Pl. 94) bearing no resemblance to any other design for any part of the building. The other (whose whereabouts is now unknown) shows an east front which corresponds in many, though by no means all, particulars with that appended to the plan reproduced in Pl. 88. It also shows that the design of the east front of the north range as finally executed was not even dreamed of by Cockerell as late as April 1836 – that is to say less than a year before its first stone was laid and nearly seven years after the first design was prepared.

As we turn our attention to the executed north range it must again be emphasized that we have no drawings of any significance for it, though Le Keux's engraving (Pl. 99) shows how it would have been related to the colonnaded east range. The principal innovation of the north range consists in the application of the triumphal arch motif to its eastern front (Pl. 95). This is evidently derived from the pavilions which flanked the west front of the west range in an earlier design (Pl. 91). Thus on to one elevation for the east front of the north range, preserved at the Victoria and Albert Museum, Cockerell pencilled a number of additions including a tall arched window which broke into the attic and was flanked by free-standing Ionic columns. It is not impossible that he placed this new emphasis on the design of this front when it became increasingly likely in 1836 that the north range was the only one which would ever be carried into execution.

In the façade as executed, the free-standing columns have been replaced by a screen of four Doric pilasters. The huge entablature which these pilasters support is bisected and the two separated halves linked by an arch set in a rusticated attic. It is worth digressing on the history of this motif since it is fundamental to Cockerell's architecture. It originates in late Roman architecture in Syria and Asia Minor where the entablature itself is bent upwards to form the arch. Characteristic examples of the application of the motif in this form are seen at Termessus, Palmyra, Baalbek and the Palace of the Emperor Diocletian at Spalato, whilst a rare post-antique example can be seen in Pietro da Cortona's remarkable church of Sta Maria in Via Lata, Rome, of 1658. The first post-antique application of the motif in the form in which Cockerell employed it is Alberti's San Sebastiano at Mantua (Pl. 100). Hawksmoor, with his 'almost morbid obsession with classical archaeology',[5] managed to combine the motif in both its forms on the west front of his extraordinary Christchurch, Spitalfields of 1723 (Pl. 101) whose upper stages seem to be echoed in the east front of Cockerell's library.

Cockerell's brooding triumphal arch is given a plastic Baroque twist by containing a shallower arch, or reveal, of concave form. This represents a personal development of the Wren-inspired false perspective enclosed within the entrance archway of his church of 1829, Holy Trinity, Hotwells. In front of the library window which the great arched recess contains there is a rather odd iron balcony manifestly of Cockerell's design, though earlier designs show a conventional stone balustraded balcony. Beneath this window is now a modern doorway inserted in 1904 to designs by W. C. Marshall.[6]

The north front (Pl. 96) in Senate House Passage – for which no drawings exist at any stage – is a complex grid of panels and antae subtly recessed and advanced. This rich surface modelling is particularly noticeable since the façade is always seen in sharp perspective. It is eloquently distinguished from the white Portland stone of the east front by being constructed – save for the easternmost section – of a reddish-brown Whitby stone. No one who passes down Senate House Passage can fail to be moved by the austerity and magnitude of this façade. We are humbled by its tall stylobate – swelled slightly by a Greek entasis – consisting of rusticated stones of an immensity that was close to Cockerell's heart. The dazzling splendour of the north and east fronts, showing clearly their relationship to the never-executed eastern colonnade, is emphasized in a strange engraving by Le Keux published in his *Memorials of Cambridge* (Pl. 99). The crumbling ivy-clad buildings of Caius Court are strewn like a child's playthings at the foot of the gleaming

5. Sir J. Summerson, *Architecture in Britain, 1530–1830*, 4th ed., 1969, p. 179.
6. Information from drawings in the Cambridge University Archives.

triumph of Cockerell's intellect. It is like an architectural parable on the theme: 'but when I became a man, I put away childish things.'

The delicate wooden mullions dividing the lower windows of the north front were, until a recent cleaning, visually indistinguishable from cast-iron; and as cast-iron they are described by the Royal Commission on Historical Monuments.[7] Now, alas, a coating of sticky brown varnish has deprived them of both illusionary and visual quality.

The west front of the library is no front at all but merely a brilliant way of turning a corner and providing a staircase. Its bare sculptural forms rising high into the air never fail to astonish by their bold abstraction, their functionalist poetry. It is hard to believe that the library behind contrives to have a symmetrical rectangular end.

The Library (Pl. 103) is perhaps the noblest interior Cockerell ever executed. At either end stands an open screen of coupled Ionic columns derived from those in the cella of Cockerell's beloved Temple of Apollo Epicurius at Bassae with their flared bases and the remarkable curvature of their unique capitals.[8] These columns frame the splendid vista down the long central nave of the library with its uninterrupted semi-circular barrel vault. The false jointing skilfully painted on to the surface of the vault suggests that it is of masonry construction but in fact it is of brick rendered with plaster. The ceilings elsewhere were also of vaulted brick and this was claimed at the time as 'a matter of no small exultation as we have the first example of a fire-proof library hitherto executed in this country.'[9] The vault of the library is also panelled with diagonal coffering, bold, memorable, but very peculiar. It is just possible that it may have been inspired by some diagonal coffering which was supposed to have been employed in the Temple at Bassae and which Donaldson had illustrated in his publication of the Temple in 1830. In the spandrels below the vault are wreaths derived ultimately from antique sources such as the Choragic Monument of Thrasyllus at Athens. The broad flat ribs of Cockerell's vault are curiously channelled and a number of their inter-sections are unexpectedly punctuated by large gilt stars. Would it, perhaps, be too far-fetched to suggest a Baroque source for these stars? The star, after all, is very much a hallmark of Borromini. Gilt stars adorn by the score the breathtaking vault of his church of Sant'Ivo della Sapienza and reappear at the Palazzo Propaganda Fide both in the

---

7. *An Inventory of the Historical Monuments in the City of Cambridge*, 2 vols, 1959, I, p. 18.

8. Thus Pevsner's description of them as 'characteristically impure' (*The Buildings of England, Cambridgeshire*, 2nd ed., 1970, p. 204) is not wholly just.

9. *Cambridge Advertiser*, 29 July 1840.

chapel and elsewhere in the building. To push this surprising comparison further, close analogies can be drawn between the rib vaults in the Propaganda Fide chapel and those in the large vestibule at the east end of Cockerell's library and in the two galleries opening off the north and south sides of this vestibule. The south gallery still retains its original brass and cast-iron railings. These elsewhere have had to be replaced with the introduction in 1896 of new book-stacks designed by T. D. Atkinson which have done much to obscure the noble lines of the room as a whole.

The greater part of the ground floor beneath the library was originally designed as the Woodwardian Museum of Geology. It is a simple groin-vaulted undercroft divided into nave and aisles by two rows of free-standing Greek Doric columns. It has been refitted for the purposes of a library on more than one occasion, and most extensively in 1935 by Murray Easton to whom we owe the introduction of the elegantly adorned architraves[10] separating the aisle bays. Today it houses, like the great first-floor library above, the Squire Law Library.

Were the surviving building not so huge, so cerebral, so aloof, its manifest incompleteness would be almost touching. An extraordinary engraving showing it in a state of partial completion was made by Goodchild under Cockerell's direction for the *University Almanac* of 1839 (Pl. 98). The picturesque fancy which installs books in an as yet unroofed structure might be regarded as the final fling of that neo-classical aesthetic which impelled Soane to commission views of his buildings as they would appear when in ruins. It will also be observed that the coffering of the vault is disposed in a quite different pattern from that executed only a year later. Constant modification of detail whilst the building was in progress was, of course, something with which many of Cockerell's clients became familiar.

Cambridge, ever more elusive than her sister university, chose to dispose on a central site of much obscurity this arcane monument, uncompromising, intellectual and aristocratic, and further hidden from the general view behind a fortuitously preserved patchwork of mediaeval and later buildings; the associations evoked by the whole complex perhaps recalling Pater's characterization of English education as teaching the classics in a Gothic setting.[11]

10. These are generally thought to be the work of Cockerell. That they are not is made clear in 'The Old Library and Schools Buildings, Cambridge University, an Account of their conversion to new uses', *R.I.B.A. Journal*, XLIII, 1936, pp. 925–35.

11. In *Emerald Uthwart*, privately printed for the King's School Canterbury, in 1905, where he describes how boys are taught 'their pagan Latin and Greek under the shadow of mediaeval church-towers' (p. 10).

On the completion of the Library in 1840 Cockerell wrote to his friend and patron, Sir Thomas Acland: 'have mercy on my Library – consider it a fragment of a great Quadrangle . . . a vast vaulted fire proof enduring plain building. observe the large stones & the attempt at a *large* manner. it being as difficult to be large & noble in arch[itectur]e as it is to be large & noble in morals.'[12] There could surely be no more adequate or moving summary than this of all that we find arresting about Cockerell's career.

12. Letter of 11 July 1840 at the Devon County Record Office.

CHAPTER XII

Maturity Achieved: The Ashmolean Museum and the Royal Exchange

ON 10 JUNE 1839, Dr Philip Bliss, the Registrar of Oxford University, signed a document announcing the University's intention of erecting new buildings for the University Galleries and the Taylorian Institute.[1] A new building was made almost inevitable firstly by the overcrowding of the Bodleian precinct with the Bodley, Selden, Arundel, Wheler and Tradescant collections, and secondly by the benefactions of the late eighteenth century from Sir Roger Newdigate and Dr Francis Randolph. Randolph's bequest was specifically for the purpose of a gallery to house the Arundel marbles and any other works of art the university might own – which was in fact little more at that time than the collection of portraits from the Bodleian gallery. What was rather less than inevitable was the decision to unite such a building with an institution destined, in its founder's words, for 'the teaching and improving the European languages' – the founder being the architect Sir Robert Taylor who, dying in 1788, left the bulk of his considerable fortune for this purpose though it did not become available to the university until 1835. The decision to unite these two institutions under a single roof was surely a curious one and must be in part responsible for any incoherence in the design of the building which Cockerell gave us. The document of June 1839 which announced the architectural competition for the new building drew attention to the fact that the buildings housing the Museum and the Institute were distinct both in their objects and in the funds by which they were supported, and that it would consequently be necessary for them to be entirely distinct in their internal arrangements. Yet at the same time it was considered desirable that externally the two buildings should harmonize and if possible form parts of one architectural design. It was an almost impossible programme for an architect. Not only was the university determined to kill

---

1. The committee minute books relating to this competition, Smirke's report, and a large collection of Cockerell's drawings are preserved in the Oxford University Archives.

two birds with one stone – it was also determined to have its bird and eat it.

By the closing date of the competition on 19 October 1839 altogether twenty-seven sets of designs had been sent in. The list of competitors seems almost purposely contrived to unite all that was most obscure and provincial in English architecture at that moment.[2] This can only be seen as a reflection of the rising tide of the Gothic Revival in which was to be produced nearly all that was most distinguished and imaginative in English architecture for the next half-century; it also serves to emphasize Cockerell's all but unique position in the architecture of his day. Amongst all his competitors there was only one, apart from Elmes, from whom we would antecedently expect a design of quality comparable to Cockerell's; and that, significantly, is an architect normally connected with the Gothic Revival, Anthony Salvin. However, he was to show how sensitively he could handle the classical idiom in his additions to Trinity Hall, Cambridge of 1852 – influenced perhaps by the example of Cockerell's University Library which they face across the street. It is most unfortunate that Salvin's design for the Ashmolean is lost. Indeed the only competition design, other than Cockerell's, whose whereabouts is known is that produced by the united skill of G. Gutch and E. W. Trendall. It is a dull design, indeed, exceeded in dullness only by the building which its architects all too obviously took as their model, Smirke's General Post Office of 1824. No attempt is made to express the division of the building into two parts each housing separate institutions. Indeed, Cockerell's was almost the only design which did so, if we are to believe the notes on the Ashmolean written by his principal assistant, Goodchild.

By 19 November 1839, the Delegates had prepared a short-list of five from amongst the twenty-seven designs entered in the competition. They then agreed to submit these five to the superior judgement of Sir Robert Smirke, probably the most successful architect of the day and, as architect of the British Museum, a particularly appropriate adjudicator for this competition. An appropriate choice, too, for Cockerell since not only had he been a pupil of Smirke but he was almost the only contemporary architect whom he was prepared to take seriously.

The delegates had arranged the five designs of their choice in the following order, presumably an order of merit: C. R. Cockerell; George Mair and E. H. Browne; John Plowman; Henry Hakewill; and Anthony Salvin. The

---

2. See Bodleian Library, MS. Top. Oxon. a. 9. The complete list of competitors, who included James Elmes and T. L. Donaldson, is in MS. Top. Oxon. c. 202.

precise role which the delegates intended Smirke to play is not absolutely clear. He was not invited to select which he thought the best in so many words, but to comment on all five designs from the point of view – to quote from the delegates' infelicitously phrased instructions – 'of their practicability, adviseableness, durability and probable amount of expense.' Smirke's report, dated 28 December 1839, is brief and on the whole uninformative. Perhaps he himself felt – as was probably the case – that he had been called in merely to whitewash or give authoritative support to the decision already made by the delegates. He did not in the end make any individual recommendation but confined himself to short comments on the designs in the order in which they had been submitted to him by the delegates. Cockerell's he found an 'excellent Example of that style of Grecian Architecture which is seen in the best works of Italian Architecture of about the sixteenth century.' He commented on the fact that Cockerell had sent in no designs for any of the interiors. The plan by Mair and Browne was impractical in that it assumed a larger site than was then available to the university. John Plowman's design suggested to Smirke 'a distinguished residence rather than a collegiate establishment.' His comments on Salvin's designs, are, alas, uninformative.

It was just five days after the date of Smirke's report – in fact on the 2nd of January 1840 – that the delegates voted unanimously in favour of recommending Cockerell to Convocation as architect of the Taylor Institute and Randolph Galleries. It was agreed to grant the premium of £100 to Cockerell and the second premium of £50 to John Plowman. With characteristic generosity Cockerell, so his devoted assistant Goodchild records, immediately made over the whole of his premium to the assistants in his office, and later made a further gift of £50 each to the three assistants who had played the greatest part in preparing the designs. In his letter of thanks to the delegates, Cockerell observed of this commission that: 'My ambition knows no higher attainment. It confirms to the full that assertion of an early Friend that my Profession was one which offered the peculiar advantage of being a rising young man at fifty.'[3] Cockerell did not use words lightly and he undoubtedly regarded this commission at the time and probably later, as the high point in his career. To be invited by a body of scholars and gentleman to provide a large and costly building for the housing of books, paintings and sculpture in the heart of one of the most

3. The letter is preserved amongst Cockerell's correspondence of 1840–45 with the Rev. P. Bliss. British Museum, Add. MS 34, 573. f. 409.

beautiful cities in Europe, must constitute for any architect a happy experience and for one of Cockerell's temperament, an experience of rare, indeed unique, felicity.

By December 1840, the delegates had received tenders for construction from seven builders of which they had no hesitation in selecting the lowest. This was for £49,373 and came from Messrs George Baker & Son of Palace New Road, Lambeth. In February 1841 it was agreed to divide this sum between the two institutions as follows: £30,992 for the Randolph Galleries and £18,381 for the Taylor Institution. The Clerk of the Works was Henry Case, a pupil of Wilkins. Both the contracting firm of George Baker and the principal ornamental sculptor for the Ashmolean, William Nicholl, were at this moment working on the construction of the Fitzwilliam Museum at Cambridge where, in four years' time, Cockerell himself was to join them as architect. However, the links between Cockerell's work at the two universities are not between the Fitzwilliam and the Ashmolean but between the University Library at Cambridge and the Ashmolean.

The Baroque strength of the Fitzwilliam is certainly echoed at the Ashmolean though in each case this full-blooded vigour is antique in origin. Its uncompromising nature is emphasized at the junction of the Taylorian and the Ashmolean in the corner of the courtyard (Pl. 108) where pilaster bumps into column with a sense of dislocation which, for better or worse, Cockerell clearly intended us to feel.

There are very considerable differences between the design with which Cockerell won the competition and that finally executed. Indeed, even in the process of execution an illustration of the building was published in a form from which it eventually departed. This is a woodcut by Orlando Jewitt (Pl. 106) from a drawing by Cockerell now at the Victoria and Albert Museum. The most striking change is that which deprived the attic storey both of its windows and of the continuous frieze of heavy swags immediately below the cornice. As late as 1840 there is yet another variant for these swags in the working drawings; but the swags had to go – as also, by special request of the delegates, did the round-headed niches on the central wing. The frieze of rumbustious swags was derived perhaps from Wren or from exuberant Cinquecento works such as Sansovino's St. Mark's Library in Venice or the interior of Palladio's chapel at Maser. A major building of Cockerell's own day which boasted a similar frieze was Labrouste's Bibliothèque Ste. Geneviève in Paris of 1843.

The problem of how to treat the upper stages of the building was evidently one which greatly exercised Cockerell. Amongst the drawings and

sketches for the building preserved in the Print Room of the Victoria and
Albert Museum there are at least five separate schemes for the treatment of
the attic storey. This indecision is occasioned by the complex problem of
dealing with what are, effectively, two parallel cornices;[4] and this problem
is itself occasioned by the decision to break the arch into an attic and not into
a pediment in the manner of Alberti and Pietro da Cortona. In the competi-
tion-winning design, attention was concentrated upon the upper cornice
not only by emphasizing it with swags but also by leaving the frieze of the
giant order absolutely plain and by stopping it where it met the arched
windows. In the final design, the prominent swags are omitted and instead
attention is concentrated on the frieze which is now allowed to run in
front of the windows. If anything, then, the ambiguity or duality of the
parallel cornice motif is actually heightened in the final design. The eye is
attracted now by the elaborate bracketed cornice, now by the frieze which
has assumed an unprecedented sculptural quality of its own. First of all it is
a pulvinated frieze, that is to say it is convex in section, then it is carved into
a deeply-cut woven plait. Now this plaited form Cockerell took, I think,
from a number of Asiatic Hellenistic temples in Turkey, and in particular
one of them which was as extraordinary in its way as the Ashmolean itself.
This is the Temple of Apollo Didymaeus near Miletus, one of the most richly
imaginative, not to say eccentric, of all Hellenistic buildings. The plaited
motif appears on the lower torus moulding of the great antae at this temple.
It also appears on the Temple of Zeus at Euromas and the Temple of
Artemis at Sardis. There are enthusiastic references to two of these buildings
in Cockerell's diaries. However, so far as I know, there is no precedent in
any antique building for the use of this plaited motif in any position so
prominent as a frieze.

What further gives added movement and vehemence to the building as
finally conceived is Cockerell's change to the use of the Bassae Ionic order.
Given his fondness for this form it is surprising that it was not an essential
part of his vision of the building from the start, yet the early designs
(Pl. 110) show a conventional Composite order for the principal entrance
portico and a Roman Ionic for the Taylor Institution. Similarly, the drawings for the Sculpture Gallery show Roman Doric columns not the Greek
Doric finally executed. This shift from Roman to Greek contradicts what
the books tell us about the development of Early Victorian architecture.
He may have hesitated before adopting the Bassae Ionic for the exterior of

---

4. Goodchild argues that there are not two cornices since the cornice of the order is treated as an
impost, and the crowning cornice is proportioned to the height of the whole building.

the Taylorian since at Bassae this Ionic was used only in the *interior* of the temple; and the Ashmolean is the only work by Cockerell where he dared employ the Bassae Ionic on the *exterior*. The Bassae volutes swing forwards in a licentious way which Borromini himself might envy, and this Baroque vigour is capped by the wonderful posturing maidens who, sensing the excitement of the building, have now stood up to declare that excitement to the world – whereas before they were sitting dumped down on their chairs. The precise significance of these maidens is not very clear. They are intended to represent the languages of France, Spain, Italy and Germany, but in fact the only way we can deduce this is because the names of some of the principal authors of those countries are carved on the sides of the plinths behind the maidens. If the delegates had had their way the statues would have been male and not female. On receiving in March 1844 Cockerell's sketches for these figures – each taken, so Cockerell claimed, from an antique example – the delegates asked him to furnish them instead with designs for four *male* figures 'intended to represent the four countries, literature or national character discarding any peculiarity of national costume that he may himself deem objectionable.' And it was not until a year later that the delegates finally and reluctantly succumbed to Cockerell's insistance on the female rather than the male sex for his figure sculpture.

The theme of the whole building (Pl. 112), of course, is sculptural, from the astonishingly elaborate bracketed eaves cornice – derived perhaps from Vignola's Villa Farnese at Caprarola – to the sensuous tactile mouldings somehow Mannerist or Michelangelesque in character, particularly in the handling of the entrance. Then there are the little balustrades deriving perhaps from Vasari's balconies at the Uffizi; and the superb panels in the attic by William Nicholl depicting griffins, possibly based on reliefs at the Temple of Apollo Didymaeus. These panels were an afterthought and when the delegates first saw the drawings for them in 1843 they specifically requested Cockerell to justify their presence.

The general architectural disposition of the façade is inspired, I think, initially by a work Cockerell had admired in Dublin in 1823: the back of Gandon's Customs House capped by a line of statues. Cockerell's obsession with arches above columns, particularly columns with statues on them, can be traced to the Roman temple at Bordeaux (Pl. 92) which we have seen in Chapter XI. It is also likely that Perrault's illustration of this building was known to Cockerell's hero, Vanbrugh. Both architects occasionally used skylines of arches. The theme of free-standing columns, each with its own entablature breaking over it is, of course, *also* an antique one. It appears at the so-called Library of Hadrian at Athens and, more dramatically, at the Forum of Nerva in Rome, which Cockerell restored in a drawing for use in his Royal Academy lectures. It is rare in post-antique architecture until the revival of the triumphal arch in the age of neo-classicism where it was used by Adam at Kedleston, Lewis Wyatt at Hackwood, Soane at Pitzhanger and the Lothbury Courtyard at the Bank of England, and Daniel Robertson at the Clarendon Press in Walton Street, Oxford, of 1826, a little-known building which Cockerell must have seen.

However, in this monumentally bold creation Cockerell goes far beyond his immediate predecessors. The drawing for the St. Giles' façade shows that the bases of the central columns rest on an immense stylobate containing no less than five courses of rough-hewn masonry. He always had in mind the rocky base of the Greek temple, he loved these huge ponderous stones, and could never bear Greek Revival buildings where the columns came straight down to the pavement. Moreover, he particularly emphasized the different parts and character of the building by his choice of building stones, though the effect has in part been obliterated by a recent 'restoration'. For the massive plinth and retaining wall he chose a reddish-brown Whitby stone which unfortunately did not weather well.[5] For the principal façades he chose the bright golden Bath stone known as Box Ground. The Ashmolean is an early instance of the use of Bath stone in Oxford; it seems to have been introduced in Beaumont Street which, begun in the 1820's, was scarcely completed by the time of the announcement of the Ashmolean competition. His use of Portland Stone for the columns, pilasters and entablatures was far more revolutionary. He seems to have been the first to use this stone in Oxford, and was indeed almost the last. Cockerell's feeling for stone and the part that its selection and cutting could play in classical composition was rare amongst English architects of his own or any date. It was of the very essence of French classicism, as Sir William Chambers had learnt before him; and yet it is possible that the strong polychromy of the Ashmolean derives from the precedent of Inigo Jones. For at the Banqueting House in Whitehall, Jones had hit on just such a combination of stones: he chose browny-red Oxfordshire for the basement; yellowish Northamptonshire for the upper parts; and white Portland for the orders and the balustrade.[6] With Cockerell, as we have seen, this understanding of stone was linked to a

5. W. J. Arkell, in *Oxford Stone*, 1947, p. 107, suggested that the podium might be of Mansfield stone. It has recently been replaced with Portland stone.

6. It is not clear whether Cockerell was aware of Jones' polychromy, for the rebuilding was refaced over a long period by Chambers, Soane and Smirke.

strong feeling for the use of architectural sculpture. Not the least remarkable feature of the museum is the seething, organic sculpture in the principal pediment (Pl. 114). There is a sketch for this in Cockerell's hand dated March 1843 (Pl. 113) and it was executed – like the rest of the sculpture on the building – by Cockerell's favourite assistant, William Grinsell Nicholl (1796–1871). Nicholl was, to some extent, Cockerell's own discovery and he owed much to Cockerell's patronage. The amazingly fecund, swirling forms of the pedimental sculpture have a hot exuberance which verges almost on the Indian. However, most things about any Cockerell building are nearly always quite unlike the details of work by his contemporaries, and to the visitor who comes upon the Ashmolean suddenly in the sunlight it can seem the most exotic building in the whole of Oxford.

Another personal yet antique touch was provided by the roofs which were covered with large slab slates an inch thick and about three feet six inches by five feet. To give a Greek touch the joints were covered with ribs and fixed with copper bolts.

The contrast on which, rightly or wrongly, Cockerell insisted between the design and character of the University Galleries and of the Taylor Institution was extended to their interiors. The exterior of the central wing of the galleries is chaste, austere and elegant, as are the interiors. The large spare staircase-hall (Pl. 115) is particularly impressive with, almost inevitably, its cast of the Bassae frieze lit from above as it had been at Bassae itself. With their crisp low-relief plasterwork, the interiors of the original sculpture galleries on the ground floor (Pl. 116) represent to some extent a survival from a stricter neo-classicism – just as the exuberant exteriors of the flanking wings look forwards to the lush hey-day of High Victorianism.

The Taylor Institution, however, is as rich inside as it is out. There is no doubt that this is the part of the whole commission on which Cockerell lavished the greatest care and interest. The great, galleried first-floor library of the Institution is one of the noblest, though least-known, English nineteenth-century libraries (Pl. 117). Its splendid chimney-piece, (Pl. 118), with a rotund vehemence which recalls the Baroque, represents the only moment in the interior of the entire building which captures the plasticity of the exterior. Its exuberant sculptural forms are enriched by the two spandrels of beaten copper worked into a fantastic, almost Celtic interlace. This metalwork, for which a drawing survives by Cockerell, was carried out by a Mr Potter of South Molton Street, Mayfair. The library designed by Cockerell at this time for the Fitzwilliam Museum at Cambridge contains a chimney-piece of similar design (Pl. 152), though the library itself is a simple rectangular space. The Taylor library, on the other hand, though almost square in ground-plan assumes as it rises an octagonal shape defined by the lines of the iron gallery and of the octagonal ceiling which is supported by almost excessively prominent cornice brackets. Both in the design of these brackets and of the railing to the gallery there are definite echoes of the exterior of the building. The brackets strongly recall the great eaves cornice outside, while along the gallery railings runs a continuous narrow frieze of just that plaited, woven form which, on a larger scale, forms so memorable a feature of the external frieze. As I have hinted before Cockerell's work reminds us of the progress of some splendid piece of polyphony endlessly recalling and developing a fixed set of themes, now pulling out all the stops in triumph, now echoing the theme in miniature and unobtrusively. It is remarkable that this splendid room should have been spared – as so many libraries have not – the intrusion of additional and unsympathetic shelving, and it is greatly to be hoped that having survived for so long the room will now escape any major remodelling.

The interiors of the two galleries for paintings at the other end of the building from the library, that is, in the south wing, presented particular problems of their own. Cockerell himself, as Smirke had pointed out in his report on the designs, had given little or no indication of how these were to be treated. Moreover, the 1830's and '40's were years in which different methods of hanging and displaying pictures in public galleries were being hotly disputed. Thus in 1840 two great connoisseurs of the early Victorian art world – Sir Charles Eastlake and William Dyce – were invited to submit a report on the lighting of galleries in general, with particular reference to Cockerell's proposals. Their report, dated 17 December 1840, contains letters from the celebrated Dr Waagen on the display techniques at the Altes Museum in Berlin designed by Schinkel in 1823, from Professor Schnorr on the Pinakothek at Munich designed by Leo von Klenze in 1826, and from Baron de Friesen on the arrangements adopted in the Dresden Gallery. However, the reliance on German specialists did not produce absolute conformity of opinion, though there was a measure of agreement between Waagen and Friesen. The latter went so far as to reject top-lighting altogether in favour of side-lighting. Waagen declared himself content with the high side-lighting which, combined with screens placed at right-angles to the walls and windows, Schinkel had pioneered in the Altes Museum closely followed by Klenze at the Hermitage in 1839. Disagreeing with Waagen, Dyce considered Schinkel's scheme suitable only for small canvases and argued that large paintings could still be successfully lit only by top-lighting. Eastlake's and Dyce's attempts to apply these views to Cockerell's plans were hampered by the complete lack of information as to which pictures were to be hung in which galleries. All they could affirm was that the two rooms over the sculpture galleries in the north wing would be suitable for the display of small pictures if provided with screens, and that the large room occupying the top two storeys of the west wing would be totally unsuitable for the display of any pictures at all, punctuated as it was by no less than nine side-lights of greatly varying dimensions.

This searching criticism confirms the point made at the beginning of this chapter that the attempt to combine in a single building two institutions so different in function as the Ashmolean and the Taylorian was bound to result in serious conflict at some stage. Eastlake and Dyce put their finger on this by pointing out that the presence of the nine windows of differing sizes was determined entirely by the need to answer symmetrically the window openings of the library and lecture rooms of the Taylor Institute. The point is irrefutable; and, significantly, the room was divided internally in 1923 and is not now used for the display of pictures but of the decorative arts.

We have already noted in the Introduction the exceptionally high opinion of the Ashmolean entertained by the influential Victorian critic, James Fergusson. His intelligent comments on the way in which Cockerell attempted to overcome the problems inherent in the commission should be quoted in full:

'Of his other buildings, perhaps the most important was the Taylor and Randolph Institute at Oxford. It consists of two wings, three storeys in height, connected by a long gallery of singularly elegant and Classic design. But as this has no apparent windows, and is lower than the wings, it certainly is a mistake; so, too, is the mode in which the windows of the upper storey break through and interrupt the lines of the principal cornice. In spite, however, of these and other defects which could be pointed out, there is perhaps no building in England on which the refined student of Architecture can dwell with so much pleasure. There is not a moulding or chisel mark anywhere which is not the result of deep study, guided by refined feeling. If there are errors in design, inseparable from the problem he was trying to solve, there are so few in detail, that it is quite re-freshing, among the barbarism of both ancient and modern Gothic Art in that city, to be able to dwell on something so pure and elegant as this.'[7]

★　　　★　　　★

7. J. Fergusson, *History of the Modern Styles of Architecture*, 2nd ed., 1873, p. 349.

The works of Cockerell's maturity are so intimately related that we cannot properly appreciate the Ashmolean designs without studying the project on which he was engaged at the same time: the Royal Exchange.

In 1563, Sir Thomas Gresham offered to build at his own expense a great Bourse in the City of London. His handsome Exchange in a Flemish Renaissance style was replaced in the 1660's by a building designed by Jarman which provided a home during the eighteenth century for a great number of ancillary activities. Thus, the second Royal Exchange eventually contained Lloyd's Coffee House, the Merchant Seamen's Offices, the Gresham Lecture Room, the Lord Mayor's Court Office and the Royal Exchange Assurance Offices. The outside shops contained lottery offices, newspaper offices, watch-makers, notaries and stockbrokers, while the vaults were let to bankers and to the East India Company for the storing of pepper. This whole curious complex was destroyed by fire in January 1838, whereupon the Gresham Trustees decided upon the building of a new Exchange on an enlarged site, the architect to be determined by open competition. The Treasury was to provide the money though its attempts to control the whole project were successfully resisted by the Trustees. The Royal Exchange had in fact reached that characteristically English position of being effectively nationalized but administered by trustees independent of the state. In fact, its administration was considerably more complicated, for the City Corporation and the Mercers' Company, in whose Hall the Gresham Trustees were accustomed to meet, were also involved in the competition of 1838. The combination of overlapping authorities and strong personalities helped make of the competition the fiasco of the century.

The Gresham Trustees determined that the building should be fronted with stone and in the 'Grecian, Roman or Italian style'; that all entries should be anonymous and should be submitted by 1 August 1839; that no models should be allowed; that neither their own retained architect nor any of his pupils should compete; and that three professional assessors, bearing in mind the Treasury's price limit of £150,000, should select the five best designs to three of which the Trustees would award the three premiums and one of which they would select for execution. The three assessors chosen were Sir Robert Smirke, Sir Charles Barry and Philip Hardwick. Barry declined and Joseph Gwilt was appointed in his place.

The designs submitted were exhibited to the public at the Mercers' Hall, and on 2 October 1839 the assessors presented their rather unfortunate report to the Gresham Committee. Of the designs capable of being erected for £150,000 they felt unable to recommend any to the Committee. Thus, 'Under these rather embarrassing circumstances' they made a 'selection of eight designs for their consideration, rather, however, as works of art than as designs which we can certify in their present state to be practicable and capable of being made durable edifices.' They considered that even 'in the best designs ... whole suites of apartments are placed in upper stories without adequate support ... [and] passages are shewn without the necessary light.'

The names in order of merit of the five architects selected by the jury of assessors were William Grellier (1807–1852), a pupil of the Surveyor of the Mercers' Company; Alexis de Chateauneuf (1799–1853), a pupil of Schinkel from Hamburg; Sydney Smirke (1798–1877), brother of Sir Robert Smirke; James Pennethorne (1801–1871); and Hardwick's pupil, T. H. Wyatt (1807–1880). The Gresham Committee, therefore, duly awarded premiums to the first three but at the same time announced that it was not prepared to execute any of their designs.

Cockerell's position was a very curious one. Understandably distrustful of competitions he had not intended to enter this one. However, H. B. Richardson, a former pupil of his, had applied to him for help with a design inspired by Palladio. The potentialities of this roused Cockerell's interest and he turned it into the design we know today. He insisted that it be submitted under Richardson's name and that its dual authorship should only be disclosed in the event of its being selected. Although it was not, as we have seen, amongst the first five selected by the jury it did appear in a list which they were subsequently asked to draw up of those which they considered best but which exceeded the price limit of £150,000. These three designs were, in order of merit, those submitted by Thomas Leverton Donaldson (1795–1885), H. B. Richardson, and David Mocatta (1806–1882), a pupil of Soane. Cockerell now revealed what some had long suspected, that he was the prime author of Richardson's design.

The committee attempted to resolve the deadlock by inviting the jury to submit a plan jointly taking into consideration the designs of Donaldson Cockerell and Mocatta. This grotesque suggestion came to nothing and in the meantime these three architects protested at the jury's decision that their plans had exceeded the price limit of £150,000. They were, therefore, allowed to appoint their own estimating surveyors who would work in collaboration with George Smith, the surveyor to the Mercers' Company. Cockerell made the mistake, as it turned out, of seeking the help of William Tite (1798–1873) who had not previously competed but who had many connections in the city and was a friend of Richard Lambert Jones, the chairman. Cockerell's assistant, Goodchild, describes the situation thus:

'Mr. Cockerell had made two errors, first in allowing the design to be sent in only in Richardson's name, second in seeking the aid of Tite as a friend for his opinion with reference to the alleged excess of cost . . . Mr. Tite's opinion and help was readily and at first honestly given, but knowing his position in the city and his connection with Mr. Jones, his subsequent action led us to look upon it as working with a view to bring about a similar arrangement with Mr. Cockerell as at the London and Westminster Bank. Richardson was uneasy at this and failed in the exercise of wisdom and discretion . . . This was the opinion of our office staff but Mr. Cockerell did not share in it and rebuked us very severely for entertaining such an idea.'

As a result of Tite's help, George Smith found that of Cockerell's, Donaldson's and Mocatta's designs only Cockerell's fell within the accepted price limit. The committee now complicated the issue further by inviting Cockerell in February 1840 to compete with Barry, Sydney Smirke, Tite and, ludicrously, with two members of the jury, Hardwick and Gwilt. Barry, Hardwick, Smirke and Gwilt all declined, thinking the arrangement unfair to Cockerell. Tite, however, called on Cockerell suggesting a collaboration whereupon Cockerell insisted that he was engaged to Richardson. Tite, as Goodchild records, suggested that Richardson might be induced to stand aside 'for a consideration'.

The committee thus invited Tite and Cockerell to engage in a limited competition of their own. The two architects accepted this invitation and drew up their final plans in April 1840. Cockerell prepared a model but the committee did not officially see this since the odious Tite had persuaded them that it would be unfair for them to do so since he had not sent in a model. The committee voted in favour of Tite's design by thirteen votes to seven. It was a shattering and probably unexpected blow for Cockerell. The reasons for the decision are obscure, and it seems likely that the choice of the jurors at this stage would have been in favour of Cockerell. It can be established from Gwilt's manuscript notes[8] that he was a strong supporter of Cockerell: as early as 11 September 1839 he had made a sketch of Cockerell's elevation describing it as, 'a very extraordinary and fine Composition and drawing.'

We do not even have the model as compensation. Constructed of wood to

8. In his MS. volume, *Papers relating to the Royal Exchange*, Guildhall Library, MS. 4952.

a scale of half an inch to a foot it was nearly twelve feet long and raised high on a platform so that the spectator could put his head into the courtyard. Even the carved decoration was accurately reproduced, the sculptured figures modelled in wax by Nicholl and the ornamental carving in plaster. The committee sent Cockerell a hundred pounds for the trouble he had taken over it and in compensation for the whole fiasco, but he returned the money, suggesting that it be 'applied to some really charitable purpose'. Goodchild records the melancholy end of this splendid model: 'After all the labour and disappointment, but little care was afterwards bestowed upon it. it was left in an empty house under a skylight which became dilapidated and broken letting in the weather so that the model gradually dropped to pieces, and by degrees for the want of space was broken up.' Tite subsequently made several approaches to Goodchild in the hope of persuading him to enter his office, each time with an increased salary. Goodchild did not find it difficult to resist the temptation for, in the words with which he concludes his notes on the Royal Exchange, '*I did not like him*'.

The complex but flaccid articulation and banal portico of Tite's Exchange are poor substitutes for the powerful imaginative genius of Cockerell's design. His original plan covered rather less of the awkward site than Cockerell's so that some of his shops were only five feet deep, also his false use of shadow in his perspective of the west front increased the apparent depth of the portico. This octostyle Corinthian portico was probably inspired by the very similar feature on Donaldson's design which had, after all, been preferred by the jury in the first place. The towers were, in like manner, copied from those on Cockerell's design. The plan submitted by Alexis de Chateauneuf, incidentally, was in a Florentine *rundbogenstil* which would have been popular in Munich but was scarcely suitable as a neighbour to the Bank of England and the Mansion House.

Cockerell's project for the Royal Exchange (Pls 119 and 120) is one of the great triumphs of his career and hence of the whole of nineteenth-century architecture. Its superb panache and vigour are the mature climax of his growing preoccupation with the triumphal arch motif at the Cambridge University Library and the Ashmolean Museum. Unlike Donaldson and Tite, he was not content to clap a conventional portico on to the Exchange behind but was concerned with integrating structure, function and adornment into one triumphal whole. His arch was not a motif but a constructional reality, and in the report which accompanied his design he argued that his scheme represented the 'Triumphal arch expanded and rendered habitable by floors' – a just, if simple, explanation. What he has done is to extend the customary four-columned triumphal arch by two columns, thus producing a long façade which recalls the Library of Hadrian in Athens and the late first-century Forum of Nerva in Rome. The latter was a particular favourite of Cockerell's and, as we have seen, he had prepared a reconstruction of it which he used in his Royal Academy lectures. He felt it was particularly appropriate for the Royal Exchange since he envisaged the space in front of it as the 'Forum Londinium'.[9]

Another source which Cockerell specifically mentioned by name is Palladio's Loggia del Capitaniato at Vicenza (Pl. 122), though this will come as no surprise to anyone who has studied his earlier commercial buildings. Other Italian architects who had developed similar themes were Sanmicheli in the lower storeys of the Palazzo Grimani in Venice and Nicola Salvi whose Trevi Fountain in Rome of 1732 was also based on the triumphal arch motif. Nearer at home there was Soane's triumphal arch in the Lothbury Courtyard of the Bank of England which, as Cockerell's diaries show, was almost the only feature of Soane's masterpiece that he was prepared to admire. His perspective view of the Royal Exchange includes a considerable stretch of Soane's screen wall at the Bank and it seems probable that the subsidiary order in the Exchange was incorporated in order to echo the height of Soane's columnar screen. Without this tactful gesture the contrast in scale between the two buildings might have been overpowering.

Cockerell's manipulation of this columnless Doric frieze which weaves its way in and out behind the great Corinthian columns is absolutely masterly. The frieze is, as it were, bent inwards through the central archway, and here for the first time we see its Doric columns silhouetted dramatically against the vast top-lit courtyard. It then becomes the order of the entire courtyard (Pls 124–5) and we can understand from Cockerell's view of the courtyard how the central arch of the entrance façade was repeated as the entrance to the court itself. A continuous barrel-vaulted triumphal way led between these two arches, flanked by Doric columns which framed a series of changing lateral vistas. That the columns should be an idiosyncratic variant of Greek Doric is eminently characteristic of Cockerell's independence of contemporary fashions of the 1840's.

Cockerell's firm interpenetration of his major Corinthian with his minor Doric order, and his use of the Doric order to create a complete correspondence between exterior and interior, forces us to recognize how in his mature buildings the order is a kind of sculptural growth, a rich linear weave. He

9. According to A. E. Richardson in *Monumental Classic Architecture in Great Britain and Ireland,* 1914, p. 79.

emphasized this concept of growth in one of his Royal Academy lectures by observing that: 'In the treatment of orders above orders, care should be taken that they should seem to grow one out of the other – and not as in the portico of Buckingham Palace.' He spoke, too, in connection with Greek temples, of 'the sculptor being a more important person than the architect who only furnished the framework for his brother artist. The lines of the sculpture contrasted with the right lines of the architecture to the improved effect of each. In the pediments the sculpture often projected beyond the mouldings, breaking their lines.' Thus in the Royal Exchange we can almost see the whole building as a kind of framework set in motion by sculpture and rich carving and by Cockerell's characteristically organic ironwork. The large female figures surmounting the six Corinthian columns of the façade were intended to represent the four quarters of the globe together with South America and Australasia. A particularly remarkable feature of the sculptural adornment is the two ground-floor windows flanked by consoles supporting statues.

Perhaps the least happy feature of the building is the four corner towers. They are not well related to the structure of the building as a whole and were incorporated, so Cockerell tells us, to compensate for the destruction of two Wren churches each with towers, St. Benet Fink, Threadneedle Street, and St. Bartholomew Exchange. The site of the former church, with its remarkable decagonal plan, was needed for the Exchange, and that of the latter for the new premises of the Sun Fire Office. Despite its imminent destruction Cockerell includes the tower of St. Bartholomew's in his perspective view of the Exchange. The church, which he rebuilt on a new site in 1849, had a feature of which both he and Vanbrugh before him were particularly fond, an arch on the skyline. To the right of his view Cockerell includes Hawksmoor's Gothic tower of St. Michael, Cornhill.

Cockerell's perspective drawing differs in one respect from the fine lithograph made of it in 1840: it omits the great attic which is such a feature of the lithograph and which would have been visible from the point at which the drawing was made. The attic concealed the coving of the amazing roof of the Exchange courtyard. The coving was filled with the vigorous diagonal coffering Cockerell loved so much, and above it the cut-away roof was open to the sky. The execution of this in 1840 would have been something of an engineering triumph, and it may have been apprehensiveness about the difficulties involved which encouraged the Gresham Committee to reject Cockerell's scheme. In fact, his drawings show what he called 'dragon trusses' forming a 'V' pattern at each end of the ceiling to support the cove. He wanted the space to be glazed, not left open, but this was disallowed by the committee. Even Tite's courtyard as first executed was open to the sky and was not glazed until 1880.

Cockerell claimed that the width and the height of his courtyard bore the same relation to each other as those of the Guildhall, and that they were identical to those of the Paris Bourse by Brongniart of 1808. Cockerell had, of course, visited the Bourse in 1824 and we have already quoted his enthusiasm for Brongniart's monumental top-lit hall with its fire-proof earthenware construction.

Though Cockerell was denied the privilege of executing his designs for the Royal Exchange, his career in the 1840's was dominated by the production of monuments of commerce. To the development of this important aspect of his life's work we shall turn our attention in the next chapter.

CHAPTER XIII

The Purple of Commerce

OCKERELL's premises in the Strand for the Westminster Life Office of 1831 are of consequence not only as marking the beginning of his fruitful career as a commercial architect but also as formulating for the first time the stylistic themes which later became the hall-marks of his well-known branch Banks of England.

The development of life-insurance in eighteenth-century Europe was a largely English phenomenon. The Royal Exchange Assurance and also the London Assurance were granted authority to do life business in 1721, though little use was at first made of their new facilities. Success was delayed until the second half of the eighteenth century, by which time a professional middle class had been established in England which tended to have incomes only for life. On the continent, on the other hand, life-assurance hardly appeared before the 1820's. The short-lived Equitable Life Assurance Society was founded in 1762 but it was not for thirty years that another appeared on the scene. This was the Westminster Life Office whose directors invited Cockerell to provide them with new premises on the corner of the Strand and Agar Street in 1831.[1] The building was erected in the following year and survived until 1907 when it was demolished to make way for an equally brilliant classical composition, Charles Holden's British Medical Association headquarters.[2]

Amongst the surviving drawings for the building is one of the Strand front (Pl. 127) which is either an alternative version or an early scheme. With its applied Greek Doric order it is a rather flat and tame composition though the segmentally-headed ground-floor windows with minimal use of glazing bars are remarkably proto-Victorian for 1831. In the design for the building as executed a profound change has taken place (Pl. 128). It is

---

1. S. P. Cockerell was a Director of the Company in the 1820's, which may account for the choice of C. R. Cockerell as architect.

2. In 1863 the Westminster Life Office was absorbed by the Guardian Assurance Company which is now part of the Guardian Royal Exchange Assurance. Unfortunately, none of the Westminster Life Office records appears to have survived.

conceived now as a temple but in a sculptural, rather than a literal, sense. Avoiding the mere application of figured friezes or porticos, such as would have satisfied Smirke, Wilkins or Burton, he has imparted to the whole building a fully-moulded depth and vigour, a plastic, sensuous and tactile quality, so that here the Greek Doric order, far from being employed as decorative pilasters as in the early project, becomes with the two vast sentinel columns the constructional and aesthetic *leitmotiv* of the whole. This new and powerful emphasis has been described as 'Baroque' but I suggest that 'Mannerist' is a more appropriate label. In so doing, I want to point to two late works by Palladio which help explain the direction taken by the architecture of Cockerell's maturity. These two buildings, the Villa Barbaro at Maser of the late 1550's (Pl. 126) and the Loggia del Capitaniato at Vicenza of 1571 (Pl. 122), are exceptional in Palladio's *oeuvre* for their sculptural exuberance. Needless to say they had not been amongst those of Palladio's buildings which had been held up for imitation by Lord Burlington and his circle. Moreover, they were probably little known since the Loggia had never been illustrated and the woodcut of the Villa Barbaro in *I Quattro Libri* was inept and unrevealing. We know that Cockerell toured the neighbourhood of Vicenza in search of Palladio's works and he may have hit with delight upon these two buildings. He seems to have regarded them as somehow occupying a position of similar independence from the rest of their architect's work as the Temple of Apollo at Bassae did from the other major fifth-century Greek temples. The Westminster Life Office of 1831 is the first work in which he blends these influences to produce a way out of the *malaise* of the Greek Revival. From henceforward his work is to be a kind of Greek Mannerism.

Palladio, like Alberti before him, was preoccupied at the Villa Barbaro with the application of the antique temple front. Palladio's engaged order carrying a pediment and his richly adorned round-headed window are echoed by Cockerell though differently disposed. The rich spandrel sculpture of the Loggia del Capitaniato, its blocky corbels supporting balconies and the details of its attic, also seem to have influenced the Westminster Life Office. Cockerell's spandrel sculpture will remind one, too, of Jean Goujon in the mid-sixteenth century and more particularly of Sanmicheli's Palazzo Bevilacqua at Verona of the 1530's. Another feature of the rich texture of the Life Office which Cockerell may have derived from the Palazzo Bevilacqua is the prominent Greek key frieze which weaves its way round the building immediately below the windows. Finally, Cockerell's pedimented attic with its lunette window affords a definite hint of Wren's Sheldonian Theatre at Oxford.

One of the most memorable features of the building is the rusticated podium on which it stands. This is no mere plinth for there is a plinth above it. Perhaps Cockerell had in mind Alberti's belief in the need for public buildings to stand raised on a platform. The plinth, incidentally, was built of Bath stone as were the two raked cornices of the pediment. The steps and surrounds to the windows and door were of Portland stone and the horizontal cornice of Yorkshire stone. All this is specified in the contract drawing for the south front, dated 25 April 1831, and well exemplifies the immense care Cockerell gave to the choice of materials, even in a building that was largely faced with stucco.

Cockerell had at one blow produced a building whose subtle allusions made it unique for its date in Europe. If the equally independent Hanover Chapel of ten years before had first established his reputation, the Life Office opened the way for his career as an architect of commerce. Thus, the year after its completion he was appointed architect to the Bank of England in succession to Sir John Soane who had retired on 17 October 1833. Shortly after Cockerell's appointment, Soane, who was apparently unfamiliar with his work asked his old friend C. H. Tatham to give him his opinion of Cockerell's newly-built Westminster Life Office. Tatham, a ham-fisted though interesting architect, wrote unflatteringly of the Life Office in his letter of reply to Soane, 'L'exteriore cattivo! L'interiore peggio!'[3] At about this time Cockerell wrote to Soane asking for the loan of his drawings for the Bank of England. Goodchild records that Soane returned the message, 'You may tell Mr. Cockerell I'll not leave a scrap, not a bit of paper for him to go to the water closet with.' Goodchild contrasts this graceless response with Cockerell's generosity on retiring from the Bank in 1855 in leaving behind all his drawings for the benefit of his successors.

The richest plum of his connection with the Bank of England was the commission to design a series of branch banks in the mid-1840's. Though rather later in date than the Westminster Life Office, it is appropriate to discuss them here since they depend on it stylistically more than do his other commercial buildings of the 1830's.

In December 1833, Cockerell was inspecting the existing branch banks at Liverpool, Manchester and Leeds, and in the following year was considering alterations to those at Portsmouth, Birmingham and Gloucester. The decision was now taken to replace the Exeter branch with one at Plymouth. Cockerell accordingly built new premises at Plymouth in 1835 although he

---

3. Tatham's letter, dated 29 November 1833, is quoted in A. T. Bolton, *The Portrait of Sir John Soane*, 1927, p. 496.

replaced these in 1842 with the simple stuccoed building in Courtney Street which still survives.[4] In 1836 he made suggestions for a branch at Dean Street, Newcastle, which was designed by Grainger and was ready for occupation in June 1838. His remodelled premises at Portsmouth were ready by April 1839 and in 1842 he designed the sub-agent's house at Plymouth and carried out repairs at the Norwich branch.

There had been discussion since 1841 about the site for a new branch at Bristol; in 1843 a site was acquired for a new branch at Manchester; and on 5 June 1844, Cockerell was directed to provide plans for new branches at Manchester, Liverpool and Bristol. It is clear that the designs for these three main branches were being turned over in Cockerell's mind at the same time in 1844–45 – indeed, a ground-plan and elevation for Manchester were accepted as early as November 1844. The dates of the contract drawings are as follows: Manchester, April 1845; Bristol, January, 1846; Liverpool, September 1846 to June 1847, though the consoles of the entrance door were not designed until March 1849. Thus the accepted chronology for Cockerell's surviving banks must be revised.

The weakest of the three is undoubtedly Manchester (Pl. 129). The three central bays with their powerful applied order of unfluted Greek Doric columns make a striking impact, though this is lessened by the bays which are strung out rather weakly on either side. The isolated columns terminating these bays are particularly unfortunate in the way they needlessly stress that fact that the order has no structural significance. On the other hand, the massive arched windows contained within the four central columns correspond to the splendid banking-hall inside. Behind the middle window a tunnel vault runs back to a saucer dome on pendentives carried by four cast-iron columns. Here, as often in his bank interiors, his experience of Wren's City churches was a formative influence.

The contract price for the Manchester bank, constructed of Darley Dale stone, was £17,913. In the Broad Street branch at Bristol (Pl. 130), which cost less than £6,000, Cockerell was able to give on the much shorter frontage a more cogently compressed and brilliant expression to the theme he had developed rather uncertainly at Manchester. Designed thirteen years after the Westminster Life Office, this is still very much a variant on the same theme, though it lacks the sculptural adornment of the earlier building. Instead, the grid-like area behind the columns makes a bold linear pattern. As at the Life Office, we are presented with a Greek Doric temple-front with

4. The Plymouth architect George Wightwick (1802–1872) applied to design this building. Cockerell kindly arranged for his appointment as resident supervisor.

R

pediment and columns, though the pediment is, once again, daringly raised above a very Roman attic with three arched windows. The lateral terminations of the façade which break forward in the most subtle manner as though to protect it from its more plebian neighbours, are worthy of the closest possible attention. Masterly, too, is the contrivance of the side porches, capped exuberantly with embryo metal balconies which animate the austere rusticated planes from which they rise. The complex but powerful articulation of the façade and the grand, assured scale of the mouldings help to make this one of Cockerell's most characteristic and individual masterpieces, and one which makes no concession whatever to an uninformed public.

In 1912 the critic Heathcote Statham made the profound observation that Cockerell 'produced two or three façades for the branch Banks of England – one especially in Liverpool – the study of the details of which is a liberal education.'[5] Certainly, the most brilliant of Cockerell's branch banks was that on the corner of Castle Street and Cook Street in Liverpool (Pl. 131). The Villa Barbaro theme is re-stated here with a confidence and vigour which are exceptional in Cockerell's work. No one who has not seen the building in the flesh can appreciate the almost breathtaking impact made by its sheer largeness of scale, the bold articulation of all its members and particularly of the colossal bracketed cornice. Everything is larger than life with the intention, one somehow feels, of demonstrating the most elemental attributes of architecture: support and shelter. Thus the immense rusticated corner piers overpower us with a realization of depth, mass and solidity, whilst the brooding, shadowy depth of the eaves recalls the primeval urge for shelter. The quite extraordinary granite plinth on which the whole building is raised strikes the same note. The four great slabs beneath the entrance-front are separated in two places by apertures which, too narrow to suggest windows, seem to be rather the natural fissures of some primeval geological outcrop. These apertures somehow emphasize the repose of the great slabs which rest on the pavement supporting the weight above them. The whole building is the statement of a man who believes that the Orders, far from being an esoteric superfluous luxury, are ultimately the mainstay of the architecture of all known civilizations and are consequently in tune with man's deepest expectations and aspirations. He emphasizes the point in a different way by making the order of his building an unique blend of Greek and Roman Doric.

5. H. H. Statham, *A Short Critical History of Architecture*, 1912, p. 527.

The side elevation in Cook Street (Pl. 132), though a well-organized composition in its own right, is uneasy in its relation to the entrance-front in Castle Street. Two of the three Piranesian rusticated arches incorporate mezzanine windows but the central one is fully expressed as a complete window and connects with a tunnel vault running through the centre of the banking-hall itself.

The materials of the building were carefully selected by Cockerell to give the maximum monumental effect. After the tender of £23,135 from Messrs Holmes had been accepted on 24 September 1845, Cockerell persuaded the building committee to increase it by £880 so as to allow for the substitution of a hard Derbyshire grit-stone from the Darley Dale quarries in place of Glasgow stone, and for the incorporation of a grey Aberdeen granite in 'the plinth and surbase'. Hitchcock has pointed out[6] that the simply designed, continuous fascia of polished red Peterhead granite surrounding the principal entrance-door is one of the earliest and best uses of this favourite Victorian colour accent.

The Liverpool bank was completed in the summer of 1848 and in August that year, Cockerell submitted designs for offices to cost £10,000 at 3 Cook Street, immediately behind the bank itself. Known as Bank Chambers (Pl. 133), these offices were at first let to cotton and sugar brokers and were, alas, demolished in 1959. A tender for £13,565 from Messrs. Jones and Jump was accepted in January 1849; the contract drawings mostly date from February to June 1849; and the building was completed in 1850. Twelve bays long and three storeys high, plus basement and attic, this was a noble composition with scarcely any decorative detail. What there was, Cockerell confined to the two bays containing the entrances. The design of these is at once novel and unobtrusive: both the doorways and the second-floor windows are set in shallow concave reveals, while the first-floor windows are flanked by Mannerist rustication unexpectedly broken off so as to form quoins. Doubtless because of its avoidance of the orders, which is surprising in so large a building by an architect of Cockerell's convictions, Hitchcock regarded Bank Chambers as 'the finest commercial edifice of the 40's'.[7]

The work Cockerell carried out at the Bank of England itself, in Threadneedle Street, was slight compared with his work in the provinces. In view of his earlier criticism of the disagreeable chill of Soane's top-lit halls at the Bank, it is amusing that his first task in October 1833 on his appointment as Soane's successor was to provide adequate heating in the £5 Note and

---

6. H.-R. Hitchcock, *Early Victorian Architecture in Britain*, 2 vols, Yale & London, 1954, I, p. 359.
7. Ibid., p. 349.

Dividend Pay Offices and, in the following February, in the celebrated Stock Office where the atmosphere had become quite 'impregnated with sulphurous particles'.[8]

In April 1834 he presented a scheme[9] for completely remodelling Sir Robert Taylor's Dividend Pay and Warrant Offices and Accountants' Drawing Office in the south-west corner of the Bank of England (Pls. 134-5). He claimed that he had 'borne in mind that architectural character by which the buildings of the Bank of England have always been distinguished': and his designs justified this claim by retaining Taylor's five Venetian windows looking into the Garden Court on the north, and by incorporating six bas-reliefs carved by George Rennie (1802–1860), his wife's cousin, which depicted Mercury, Britannia, Ceres, The Thames, Industry and Calculation. This splendid room was divided longitudinally into three aisles by two rows of coupled Corinthian columns; the central aisle was considerably higher than the others and was lit by a skylight. Cockerell produced a lithograph of this interior in which he justly claimed that it resembled 'the Basilica of the Ancients'.[10]

However, in 1849 he was called upon to remodel the room once again. At a cost of £3,953 he removed his colonnade and upper storey and, by incorporating Taylor's rooms to the north-west, created a single large, L-shaped hall. His favourite diagonally coffered coving ran round the edge of the room supporting the flat central ceiling pierced with impressive sky-lights.

In 1848 he spent £5,000 in raising and reconstructing the attic storey of the entire bank so as to form a fortified parapet walk. The occasion for this was the alarm engendered by the Chartist rising of 1848 when it became clear that Soane's parapets were too low to form a breastwork for the guard. It might be considered that Cockerell made aesthetic gain out of practical necessity by strengthening Soane's mannered and uneven skyline. He substituted massive balustrades for Soane's line of acroteria. On the other hand, there is a sense in which he evidently threw himself into the task of designing as he imagined Soane himself might have done faced with the same commission. Thus he re-used Soane's anthemion blocks and vases as crowning

8. Bank of England, Building Committee Minutes, February 1834.

9. In fact he presented two schemes, one to cost £4,728 and the other £3,745.

10. Cockerell's lithograph is the only record of the appearance of this room after his first re-modelling. A photograph of it after his second remodelling in 1849 appears in A. E. Richardson, *Monumental Classic Architecture in Great Britain and Ireland*, 1914, pl. XX, but not, rather curiously, in the official record of the Bank (H. R. Steele & F. R. Yerbury, *The Old Bank of England, London*, 1930). The contractor for Cockerell's works at the Bank in 1848 and 1849 was William Cubitt.

features over the piers of his new balustrades and even, over the seven-bay frontispiece in Threadneedle Street, introduced a splendid row of eight Sonean urns.

The transference of his architectural office to the Bank of England in the late 1830's indicated clearly the extent to which Cockerell had accepted his role as an architect of commerce. His position as architect to the mother of all banks naturally led to further commissions. The first of these was for the London and Westminster Bank in 1837.[11] This bank had been founded in 1833 in the face of considerable opposition from the Bank of England. The growing tendency of the public to use the Bank of England as a depository of funds indicated the necessity of a new banking establishment, but the Bank of England, reluctant to lose its monopoly, refused a drawing account to the London and Westminster Bank until as late as 1842. The Bank of England's intransigent stand was aided by the uncertainty surrounding the government's attitude towards the setting up of joint stock banks of deposit in the metropolis.

Cockerell's relative by marriage, Matthew Boulton Rennie, was on the committee of the London and Westminster Bank from the start, and in June 1836 was appointed to the Building Committee. However, the architect William Tite (1798–1873) had a strong supporter on the committee, and in 1836 he was brought in to arrange for the purchase at £14,250 of new premises for the bank at 41 Lothbury. The committee also acquired the adjacent property for £9,500, thus providing a site for the proposed new building with a depth of ninety feet and a street frontage of nearly eighty. The City of London took advantage of the rebuilding to widen Lothbury by eight feet, the Directors of the Bank receiving £1,000 compensation.

The Building Committee, it seems, had now reached a position of deadlock over the choice of architect, support for Tite and Cockerell being exactly equal. However, a terse minute of 15 March 1837 records the decision 'that Mr. Cockerell and Mr. Tite be appointed jointly the Architects for building the new Bank.'[12] Tite subsequently claimed that this suggestion had originated with him. Matthew Rennie had refrained from voting, but in any case Cockerell's claims could hardly be challenged for he had recently completed substantial new offices in the Bank of England. Tite's *oeuvre* was less impressive and at two successive meetings of the Building Committee

11. See T. E. Gregory, *The Westminster Bank through a Century*, 2 vols, Oxford, 1936.
12. Information from the Committee Minute Book of the London and Westminster Bank. Miss J. M. R. Campbell, Archivist of the National Westminster Bank Limited, kindly supplied me with extracts of committee minutes from June 1836 to January 1838.

unsuccessful attempts were made to appoint Thomas Allason (1790–1852) in his place.

Goodchild tells us that the collaboration with Tite 'fell in with Mr. Cockerell's theory that there should be "the Art Architect to design, and the practical architect to carry out and superintend." ' Whether Tite saw his role in this light is not clear, but it is interesting to find Cockerell believing so strongly in such a division of labour. They set to work quickly and within three months had prepared plans to a contract price of £15,654. Tenders from twelve builders had been submitted by 12 July, the highest being £17,544 from the well-established contractor, George Baker, while the lowest – the one accepted – was £15,654 from Samuel Grimsdale. The sum of £1,400 was raised from the sale of materials from existing buildings on the site, so that the total cost of the new premises, including the purchase of the site, amounted to £37,000. The new buildings were opened on 26 December 1838.

The three storeys with attics and the seven-bay frontage with a central door was a disposition quickly settled (Pl. 136), though in one project the articulation of the façade with an applied stripped-Doric order is somewhat stilted. However, in the building as executed (Pl. 137) the order has been dissolved into a trabeated framework logically satisfying both to the eye and to the mind as a visual paraphrase of constructional method. The European master of this grid-like reduction of the classical language to its basic elements was Schinkel – though both Charles Barry and Cockerell's old master, Robert Smirke, had developed the theme in two buildings, both in Pall Mall: Barry's remarkable office building in 1833 (now demolished) at 16–17 Pall Mall, and the Oxford and Cambridge Club designed three years later by Robert and Sydney Smirke. Cockerell's contemporaries were quick to note the revolution he had effected at the London and Westminster Bank. In March 1840 *The Civil Engineer and Architect's Journal* welcomed a building that was 'no hundredth edition of an approved portico, but . . . [displayed] a perfect expression of purpose.' Even more remarkably, Cockerell had filled the interstices on the ground floor between his great rusticated piers with glass. Before he had ever designed a building in the City he had given thought to the problems of adequate light for offices. After a visit in 1824 to Wyatt's Masters of Chancery offices he noted in his diary: 'Light is the soul of offices and houses in the city. If I ever have anything to do there I will create an architecture expressly for this end.' This splendidly resourceful, independent and creative attitude at last bore fruit in the London and Westminster Bank.

Another remarkable feature was the division of the large ground-floor windows with slender cast-iron mullions and transoms, the mullions rising from elegant bases shaped, so contemporaries thought, like antique candelabra, and terminating in scrolls or consoles. The windows were fitted with Bunnett and Corpe's iron shutters. On the first floor, the windows were narrower and consequently gave space for carved panels on either side suggestive of the existence of a wall plane behind that of the rusticated piers. These panels which did not appear in the first or alternative project, contained carved fasces alternating with the caduceus, emblem of the God of traders, Mercury. There was more sculpture in front of the attic storey, though it was confined to two female figures surmounting the projecting end piers of the façade, representing London and Westminster. Cockerell not only designed these but modelled the figure of London, that of Westminster being executed by William Nicholl. The façade was of Portland stone, and the substantial plinth from the Bramley Fall quarries near Leeds. These provided a tough Millstone grit which resisted the effects of industrial atmosphere as well as, if not better than, Portland stone.

As an essay in subtle rustication, horizontal up to the first cornice, and both horizontal and vertical in the attic, the building has perhaps been equalled in London only by Lutyens' brilliant Midland Bank in Poultry of 1924. Cockerell's cessation of all rustication or ornament immediately above the attic windows creates a dramatic effect in so plastic a façade, as well as defining a zone which can be read as an architrave.

It was generally accepted at the time that while Cockerell was responsible for the exterior, Tite provided designs for the interior. It seems, however, both from Cockerell's early sketches and from his contract drawings (Pl. 138) that the whole internal disposition of the building was his and that Tite merely remodelled certain features of the principal banking-hall at the rear.

The banking-hall, square in plan, was surrounded by a Doric colonnade, and to Cockerell was certainly due the logical notion of linking this space with the long entrance vestibule by extending the Doric order into the latter. This use of an order to unite disparate interior spaces is one of the civilizing virtues of the classical language which Cockerell, unlike so many dabblers in classical architecture, understood to perfection.

From the entrance vestibule, thirty-eight feet long and flanked by five pairs of Doric columns, access was gained to the country bank on the right and to the main staircase which led, ultimately, to the resident manager's private apartments. The ground-floor rooms on the left were at first let to a firm of solicitors. The principal, or town, bank was the *tour de force* of the building and gave clear expression to the considerable status which the newly-founded bank had achieved. Thus, the only rivals to this room were to be found in Soane's Bank of England. However, it exceeded in height any of Soane's interiors. Flanked on two sides by aisles, the room rose from a ground-plan about thirty-seven feet square to a height of fifty-nine feet six inches – the full height of the building. Up to the gallery which rested on the arches of the ground-floor colonnade, the room as executed seems to have corresponded largely with Cockerell's surviving drawings. Above this level, however, Cockerell had intended a tall first floor with an order based on that of the Tower of the Winds in Athens though incorporating, rather surprisingly, a Doric frieze. This was to support in turn a large lantern carried on a deeply coved ceiling – a device to which he returned a year or so later in his project for the courtyard roof at the Royal Exchange. However, in the banking-hall as executed, his first floor was suppressed in favour of a large domed roof supported on pendentives. This impressive feature, almost certainly an improvement on Cockerell's design, may well represent the extent of Tite's contribution.

When, in 1851, the Bank found it necessary to take over the rooms previously let to solicitors, Tite made substantial alterations to the building without consulting Cockerell. In the course of the rebuilding, which cost as much as £5,984, Tite deprived the banking-hall of its dome. In 1866–67 the bank was considerably extended to the east, thereby destroying the delicate balance of Cockerell's composition in Lothbury although, as a remarkable tribute to Cockerell, the façade of the new wing was closely modelled on that of the original building. In 1924 this in turn was replaced by the present fine building by the firm of Mewès and Davis. They, too, had learnt much from Cockerell though their debt is more clearly stated in the shorter frontage to Angel Court than in the principal Lothbury elevation.

We have noted the admiration which Cockerell's contemporaries felt for his bank. In 1839 he came across an account of it which particularly amused him and wrote of it to a friend: 'the London & Westm[inste]r Bank is described in the Argus three Sundays ago. it comes out well & satisfies the Citie folk who call it Solomon's Temple ... the statues of London & Westm[inste]r are called Principle & Interest – they say it is a fine building & a bad concern – all sorts of jokes & jibes are rife while a nine days wonder lasts – but the Proprietors are greatly satisfied with the character & dignity the Bank acquires by it – & this is the main.'[13]

13. Letter from Cockerell to Sir Thomas Acland, Bart., of 21 January 1839 at the Devon County Record Office.

Despite the interest expressed in the bank, it had little or no influence on either the development of commercial architecture in general or on Cockerell's work in particular. However, shortly after its completion in 1838, he began work on another building in the City which was a programmatic monument in the history of the Victorian commercial *palazzo*. This was the premises on the corner of Bartholomew Lane and Threadneedle Street of two linked companies, the Sun Fire Office, founded in 1710, and the Sun Life Assurance Society, founded exactly a century later.[14] The latter, intended to be merely a supplement to the former, eventually outgrew it considerably – though as late as the 1840's the staff of the Life Office still numbered only three. Each company had the same board of managers amongst whom, from 1824 to 1847, was John Cockerell, C. R. Cockerell's brother. The family's life-long friend, W. R. Hamilton, was also a manager from 1809 to 1859 – so we need look no further to understand why Cockerell was approached in 1839 to prepare designs for the Company's new premises. The circumstances of his birth and family background assured him of commissions in a way which some of his struggling contemporaries must have found galling. However, in the course of the commission he ran into a number of technical problems which must have made him wish at times that he had taken a firmer stand with his father in 1817 over his choice of career. The remarkable speed and ease with which the London and Westminster Bank had been conceived, designed and executed were not to be taken as typical.

Until 1838 the Sun offices were in Exchange Buildings and adjacent premises in Cornhill. These were incorporated by Act of Parliament that year into the site for the proposed new Royal Exchange. In August, the Sun's managers selected a new site on the corner of Bartholomew Lane and Threadneedle Street, partly occupied by Wren's St. Bartholomew Exchange. This site was chosen on the understanding that the Bank of England would obtain statutory powers to pull down the church and other buildings in Threadneedle Street as far as Prescott's Bank. Cockerell began to prepare designs in 1839, but it was two years before the Sun's building committee was in a position to invite tenders for construction. The reason for the delay was that the Bishop of London insisted on being paid £6,500 compensation for the church and churchyard, even though it was rebuilt by Cockerell as St. Bartholomew, Moor Lane. The Sun also had to pay for the removal of the remains in the churchyard to a specially constructed mausoleum

14. See P. G. M. Dickson, *The Sun Insurance Office*, Oxford, 1960.

at the nearby Wren church of St. Margaret, Lothbury. A further £11,700 had to be paid for the freehold sites of nos. 63, 64, 67 and 68, Threadneedle Street which had formed part of the glebe of the church.

Eight tenders for construction were presented in March 1841, the highest being £21,980 from Cubitt and the lowest, £18,740 from Webb. The first brick was laid on 14 April 1841. However, a week before this the City authorities had informed the Bank of England that Threadneedle Street was to be widened to at least fifty feet. Since this would necessitate grave alterations to Cockerell's building the Sun's managers, having taken legal advice, instructed the builders to continue with their work. The City now brought in the ancient Commissioners of Sewers who had powers of compulsory purchase over houses projecting unnecessarily into the street. The Sun's managers accordingly filed a bill in Chancery to curb the Commissioner's greed and the Vice-Chancellor granted a decree in the Sun's favour. The Commissioners replied by appealing to the Lord Chancellor whose view was that the matter was of such complexity that if it could not be settled privately it would have to be tried at law. It was not until October 1841 that the Sun's managers and the Commissioners reached a compromise by which the Sun would surrender a strip of land four feet and half an inch wide at the corner of Threadneedle Street and Bartholomew Lane. They agreed to refer to arbitration the amount of compensation the Sun ought to receive for this. The arbitrators' decision which was not reached until June 1842, was to award the Sun £1,250. Thus the foundations of Cockerell's building had twice to be altered, the contractors claiming £1,100 compensation. The building was not ready for occupation until Lady Day 1843, the total cost, inclusive of site, building and fittings, amounting to £55,842.

We shall return shortly to the modifications Cockerell was obliged to make to his design as a result of the unfortunate decision of October 1841. His original design (Pl. 139) was quite different from that eventually executed. Dated 31 August 1840 it was approved by the building committee in October that year. It was a monument of high originality, a *palazzo* which, though it might have owed something to Soane's revival of this mode at the State Paper Office ten years earlier, displayed a subtlety of surface moulding which went beyond anything Soane ever dreamed of. Cockerell incorporates an engaged Corinthian order on the principal Threadneedle Street front, the entablature broken in the centre in the way he liked so as to allow for a magnificent arch crowded with Michelangelesque figure sculpture. The isolated corner column is an unforgettably eloquent feature, embedded in the wall surface in a way that recalls the similar antique fragments one sometimes sees in Rome, half buried in the walls of later buildings which have grown up around them. Cockerell's column also answers the adjacent Corinthian columns of Soane's screen wall at the Bank of England. That this effect is deliberate is clear from his otherwise unnecessary inclusion of the terminal column of the Threadneedle Street façade of the Bank in his perspective view of the Sun Fire Office. His extremely delicate handling of the rusticated corner pier which rises above the isolated column at the corner of the Sun Fire Office has an exquisite Mannerist charm – Mannerist because the whole pier is recessed, not advanced as the logic of the structure would suggest. This characteristically Mannerist sensation of compression echoes, of course, that already created by the embedded column beneath.

The modifications (Pl. 140) subsequently made to this design as a result of the battle with the Commissioners of Sewers were of a very substantial nature, since they sprang from the need to cut back the corner of the building diagonally at the junction of Threadneedle Street and Bartholomew Lane. The result is still a Mannerist composition, but it is Mannerist in a rather different way. Cockerell seems to have felt that the loss of the whole corner of his building, and thus of the splendid corner column, must necessarily involve the loss of the ground-floor order altogether. His solution was the surprising one of lifting the Corinthian order up to the second floor of the building. The height of the building had been restricted from the start to fifty-five feet, so that in order to give sufficient scale to the columns they are deprived of their pedestal course. Another result was the squeezing of the third-floor windows immediately under the soffit of the entablature. The Corinthian order unites this attic storey with the second storey below in a way that may owe something, like the extravagant bracketed *cornicione* above, to the upper storeys of Vignola's Villa Farnese at Caprarola. More complex than any source in Vignola is the articulation of the windows behind this columnar screen which seem to have an independent existence in a trabeated framework of their own. The whole building, having lost the central emphasis of the first design with its huge, arched entrance in Threadneedle Street, has acquired instead that scattered over-all richness of effect, that complex play with flickering wall-planes, that we associate with Italian Mannerism. Even the truncated corner (Pl. 141), destined to be so influential on Victorian architecture, can be seen as contributing to the Mannerist effect in that it tends to dissolve, or render ambiguous, the true perspective. Particularly Mannerist is the frustration of finding that what appears to be the grand entrance on the corner is just an elaborately disguised window, the real entrance being tucked away in Threadneedle Street. The false door on the corner is flanked by the Greek Doric columns of the order Cockerell used so often with fluting confined to the top and bottom of the shaft. These support an entablature with a rich pulvinated guilloche frieze – also a familiar Cockerell hall-mark – which continues at this level round the entire building. The window immediately over the Greek Doric columns is round arched – the only one anywhere in the building – and surrounded with carved festoons probably inspired by Wren. The order above is Greek Corinthian. Further Greek orders were used inside the building (Pl. 142): Ionic from Bassae and Corinthian from the Tower of the Winds in Athens.

Thus, the Sun Fire Office is an extreme example of what one can only call Cockerell's Grecian Mannerism. His contemporaries were quick to imitate the richness of effect though could scarcely emulate its idiosyncratic scholarship. There was evidently something about the richness and the ambiguities or uncertainties of Italian Mannerist architecture which fascinated the Victorians. It is typical of Victorian taste that James Fergusson should have found this building preferable to the branch Banks of England which are so much admired today. Following his criticism of the design of the branch Banks, he went on to argue that: '. . . of his commercial buildings the most successful is the Sun Fire Office . . . Nothing in the City is more elegant and appropriate than this. The upper range of columns gives lightness and variety just where it is wanted, and the cornice is well proportioned to the whole. The angles, too, are well accentuated; and it need hardly be added all the details most elegant.'[15] One motif of the Sun Fire Office which was repeated *ad nauseam* later in the century was the haunched segmental arches of the ground-floor windows. Cockerell's contemporaries doubtless noted also that, like the London and Westminster Bank, it was constructed of Portland stone.

When it was enlarged in the mid-1890's it was treated with the same remarkable tact and respect afforded slightly earlier to Cockerell's nearby London and Westminster Bank. The Sun's architect, F. W. Porter, inserted two additional storeys immediately above the first floor and faithfully rebuilt Cockerell's colonnaded top storeys above. His own preference would have been to add an attic storey above Cockerell's crowning cornice. Even so, the damage done to the composition was less than might appear from

15. J. Fergusson, *History of the Modern Styles of Architecture*, 2nd ed., 1873, p. 348.

this description and certainly insufficient to justify the recent demolition of the building.

It was a tribute to the building that its remodelling in the 1890's attracted considerable attention, particularly that of the young Scottish architect, J. J. Joass, who published a drawing of it in *The Builder* in 1896.[16] Joass was a pupil of Sir John Burnet, who had been trained at the Beaux-Arts, and subsequently became the partner of John Belcher. He was one of a group of enthusiasts for Cockerell and for what Sir Albert Richardson described as 'the neo-grec.' They never achieved the revolution in English taste they hoped for and Cockerell remained for them the unattainable ideal. He also represented an ideal for the popular classical painter, Sir Frederick Leighton. In 1890 Phené Spiers and the Baron de Geymüller came across Leighton gazing in rapt admiration at Cockerell's Sun Fire Office whereupon he explained to his surprised observers that, 'whenever he wanted to revivify himself with the sense of the beauty of Greek work he used to come down and look at Cockerell's works.'[17] The words sound somehow like those of a *poseur* or a charlatan, but nevertheless have a peculiar historical interest.

Closely related to Cockerell's Sun Fire Office design of 1840 is his design of fifteen years later for the Liverpool and London Insurance Company at Dale Street, Liverpool (Pl. 143).[18] The rich North Italian cinquecento hints of the London building have become more plastic and exuberant, while the composition is episodic, not to say turgid. The projects of 1844 for the Carlton Club (Pl. 148) in a Genoese *palazzo* style mark a half-way stage in this late development of his work.

Cockerell was invited to design new premises for the Liverpool company in May 1855.[19] Fire premiums with the company had risen to £54,306 in 1851 and had more than trebled by 1855, in which year they reached the figure of £186,272. The company now acquired a large isolated site, 170 feet by 85 feet, immediately north of Wyatt's Town Hall. In common with many contemporary and subsequent site developers, the company used scarcely more than a quarter of the new premises for its own offices, leasing the rest of the space to a variety of commercial concerns.

16. LXXI, 1896, p. 131. The interior had already been extensively remodelled in 1881.

17. Quoted in the *R.I.B.A. Journal*, 3rd series, VII, 1899–1900, p. 367.

18. During Cockerell's association with the firm it expanded and changed its name to the London and Liverpool and Globe Insurance Company.

19. I am grateful to Mr V. G. Lunt of the Royal Insurance Group for kindly supplying me with copies of the minutes of Committee Meetings of the London and Liverpool Insurance Company from May 1855 to January 1859.

S

Though the design of the building is usually attributed to a collaboration between Cockerell and his son, F. P. Cockerell, there is no doubt that his son's assistance was given only after the first designs had been drawn up. Further help was given at this stage by Christopher F. Hayward who had just completed his articles with Hardwick. The resident architect was Joseph Boult, brother to the secretary of the Liverpool and London Insurance Company. The minutes of the building committee have been preserved and from them it is clear that Cockerell's designs were prepared by December 1855. Construction was halted in May and June 1857 by a masons' strike but by November of that year thought was being given to the furnishing of the Board Room. It may be of interest to record what in the 1850's struck prosperous northern business men as an appropriate setting for their deliberations. The room was to contain 'an oval Board Table covered with green cloth, a Turkey carpet, 27 chairs, 3 window curtains, and 4 side tables, the aggregate cost being £335.' The chairs were to be copied from 'one used in the House of Commons' and, at Cockerell's suggestion, the room was to be lighted by a gas chandelier costing £16 and similar to one in the Grand Jury Room at St. George's Hall.

Characteristic Cockerell details on the exterior are the pulvinated guilloche frieze above the ground-floor windows, the vigorous iron-work balconies, and the complex surface moulding. The framing of the first-floor windows should be especially noticed. There is a tough, sculptural animation here which, as at the Ashmolean, can only be called Michelangelesque. It is Sansovino, however, who has inspired the general form of the composition. Its huge presence recalls the uncompromising mass of the Palazzo Corner della Ca' Grande at Venice, while the Library of St. Mark's provides a source both for the swagged frieze pierced by windows and treated as a mezzanine and also for the round-headed arches of the second floor recessed behind a bold columnar screen. Cockerell's method of turning the corner of this floor is worth observing in detail. A wholly unexpected feature is the way the staircases are expressed externally on the south façade (Pl. 145) in as ruthlessly 'functional' a manner as in any design by Pugin or Webb. We can see the diagonal lines of the treads set within great glass windows which rise in deeply recessed bays over the arched ground-floor doorways.

These two staircases are placed on either side of a great, central, glazed area (Pl. 144) which lights the inner suites of rooms. Such an area, which became common in subsequent office buildings, was something of an innovation at this time. Rather remarkably, its width increased as it ascended though its length was a constant ninety feet. Thus it was ten feet wide in the basement, fourteen in the ground floor, eighteen in the first floor and twenty-eight in the second. Another ingenious feature was the carrying up of the smoke flues inside the cast iron Doric columns on the ground and first floors so as to dispense with bulky brick walls and flues.

The building cost nearly £42,000 of which Cockerell's commission of five per cent plus travelling expenses came to £2,311.2.9. Another costly item was the stone carving by Cockerell's beloved William Nicholl whose bill amounted to £733. There is reason to suppose that Alfred Stevens helped Cockerell with the design of this sculpture.[20] Certainly there was much work for Nicholl on this richly modelled façade, in particular the monumental doorways with their French or Wren-inspired concave arches, their full fat swags and carved key-stones. Of the central Dale Street entrance, which is further complicated by the insertion of a pedimented Doric doorcase, Reilly remarked, 'There is no more original, and at the same time satisfying, public doorway in England.'[21] The doorway pushes up in front of the first-floor window suggesting somehow that it has been designed for a larger or a different building. Indeed we know that a quite different arrangement had originally been intended. The building committee had perversely insisted on an asymmetrical entrance in Dale Street. Cockerell had, therefore, concealed this by proposing two adjacent doors, one of which was false. Goodchild records what happened when Sir Charles Barry happened to see the drawings for this unhappy feature:

'C. Barry saw this and said, you cannot call it a sermon in stone but it is a *lie* in stone. so when we came back Mr. Cockerell said now we are in for it. we must not ignore such a criticism as that. sponge out that part of the plans. we must make a new elevation, we must not allow a little fancy for business arrangements to spoil the architecture.'

There could surely be no more apt quotation with which to conclude a chapter on Cockerell's relation to the architecture of commerce.

20. See S. McMorran, 'Alfred Stevens', *R.I.B.A. Journal*, LXXI, 1964, p. 437.
21. Quoted in J. Dyer Simpson, *1936 – Our Centenary Year*, privately printed for the Liverpool and London and Globe Insurance Company, 1936, p. 37.

CHAPTER XIV

A Late Flowering

IT IS impossible not to feel that Cockerell's later career must have been something of a disappointment to him. We have seen him losing the competitions for the London University, the National Gallery, the Houses of Parliament and, after appalling suspense, the Royal Exchange. In 1844 he lost the competition for the Carlton Club and within three years two brilliant young friends had died tragically, Basevi and Elmes. It is a measure both of Cockerell's generosity and of the poor state of his architectural practice that he agreed to complete the buildings on which these two architects were working at the time of their deaths, the Fitzwilliam Museum at Cambridge and St. George's Hall, Liverpool. Cockerell's interiors at Liverpool, designed and executed between 1851 and 1854, are amongst the finest of the century anywhere in Europe. Their 'inexplicable splendour of Ionian white and gold' constitutes the late flowering which this chapter has been written to honour.

Before looking at the project for the Carlton Club of 1844 it is appropriate to glance at the scheme with which he had lost the competition for the Reform Club in 1837. The façade (Pl. 146) is a chaste, columnar exercise though slightly marred by the trivial bay windows. Inside (Pl. 147), the centre of the club is occupied by a large top-lit hall containing an extraordinarily inventive staircase. A short central flight of only fifteen steps leads up to a large platform in mid-air. From here another similar flight leads in the same direction to an apsed landing from which one would sense that further ascent would be necessary though the position of the flights is carefully concealed. Two steps on either side of the apsed landing eventually lead one away to the final stages of the staircase. Should anyone find this dramatic, though teasing, experience too much for him there are four other staircases in different parts of the building. The Athenaeum and the Travellers' Club had been content with two staircases each, but to design a club with five suggests a mind disagreeably obsessed with the problem of ascent. Indeed, there are two ground-floor rooms in the north-east corner of the club which can only be entered from staircases to which there appears to be no access on the ground floor. Nor are the great public rooms of the club much happier in their arrangement; for example, the hundred-foot saloon along the south front can only be entered from doors in the sides of a shallow segmental recess which is asymmetrically placed rather less than half way down one side. A room with a much more peculiar rhythm is that placed in the north-west corner of the club. The disposition of windows and chimney-piece on the west wall, which eventually blossoms out into a asymmetrically-placed bow window in the corner, has to be seen to be believed.

The bow windows at the extremities of the façade turn up again in his project for the Carlton Club (Pls 148 & 149). In 1844 the Carlton decided to hold a limited competition for designs for new premises next door to the Reform Club in Pall Mall. Fourteen architects, including Cockerell, were invited to compete, but architects in the 1840's were, with good reason, growing impatient with the fiascos into which competitions always seemed to degenerate. Thus eight of these fourteen, including Cockerell, declined the invitation but agreed to send in projects for elevations, though not for plans. It was an odd compromise for an architect of Cockerell's calibre to adopt, particularly when, in his Royal Academy lectures at this time, he was urging students of architecture always to begin by considering the plan and not the elevation. Cockerell's finished drawing for the façade, dated May 1844, shows a richer composition than that of the Reform with evocations not only of Sansovino and Sanmicheli but also of the exuberant Genoese architect, Galeazzo Alessi. Immediately reminiscent of Alessi is the diamond-pointed rustication below the ground-floor windows.

Although Cockerell lost the Reform to Barry and the Carlton to Sydney Smirke, the new Carlton and the Army and Navy Club of 1848 by Parnell and Smith both owe much to Cockerell's fertile suggestions. They were modelled respectively on two buildings by Sansovino, St. Mark's Library and the Palazzo Corner. The grid-like treatment of the ground floor of the Army and Navy Club might possibly have owed something to Cockerell's London and Westminster bank of ten years earlier.

One of the happiest and most characteristic projects of Cockerell's later years was his rebuilding on a new site of the Wren church of St. Bartholomew Exchange. Initiated in 1840, it was a typically protracted undertaking, for the new church was not consecrated until ten years later. Cockerell's veneration for Wren[1] was demonstrated with peculiar force in his insistence

---

1. In 1843 Cockerell sent drawings to the R.I.B.A. of the foundations of St. Bartholomew Exchange, 'removed in 1841 under my direction', together with a descriptive letter (R.I.B.A. MS. SP. *Papers Read*, V, 'Construction', no. 9). He particularly applauded Wren's re-use of the foundations of the mediaeval church on the site.

not only in re-using fittings from the former church but in rebuilding the tower with many of the old stones and generally echoing the design of the west front. Such a procedure, rare enough in our own conservationist age, was so revolutionary in the 1840's as to evoke bitter, though not wholly unexpected opposition, in the pages of *The Ecclesiologist* where the church was described as 'disgraceful to the age and city in which it is built.'[2]

We have already touched on the circumstances in which Wren's church was demolished to make way, ironically, for offices designed by Cockerell himself. It must have been a particular pleasure for Cockerell, who had done so much to further the architecture of commerce in the city, to be able to follow, on this occasion, Wren's example in the provision of a house of God. The vestry had not wished originally to save even the organ of Wren's church but, possibly at Cockerell's instigation, this was incorporated in the new church together with its splendid case.[3] Cockerell also retained the elaborate reredos, pulpit and pews. The fittings that were not to be re-used were sold in January 1841 for £483.15s.[4] The new site near Bishopsgate was a long narrow plot bordered by Tenter Street, and New Union Street with a west front in Moor Lane. Cockerell's church, which contained sittings for a thousand people, was designed in 1847 and executed in 1849-50. The west front and tower were of stone as was the south front up to the sills of the windows. The rest was of red brick.

Cockerell's early sketches (Pls 150 & 151) show that he had originally hoped to provide a more elaborate exercise in the English Baroque than that eventually executed. Drawings at the Victoria and Albert Museum and the R.I.B.A. show towered compositions not a little reminiscent of Vanbrugh's Seaton Delaval. However, the Bishop of London, Dr Blomfield, was unimpressed. Goodchild records for us what transpired at his interview with Cockerell:

'The Bishop of London, said "Mr. Cockerell, I care but little about fine architecture. What I want is four walls and a roof to house my flock, and if those who come after me do not like the Churches I put up, if they can get the money they may spend it upon them." After this interview, Mr. Cockerell said, now then we are not to have our own way, we will just follow Sir Chr. Wren and reproduce the old church as near as we can in its architectural character.'

2. VIII, 1847, p. 54.
3. Guildhall Library, Vestry Minutes of Parish of St Bartholomew by the Exchange, MSS. 4384/8, 27 October 1840.
4. See *The Builder*, LXXVI, 1899, p. 363.

Thus, for the contract price of £5,993, all that Cockerell was able to achieve was a version of Wren's simple west front with a central arched window and a tower adjacent on the south. In the historically nonsensical opinion of *The Ecclesiologist*, the front 'suffers by the really superior character of "Gannaway's Noted Stout House" next door, from which the window is a plagiarism, debased in composition while exaggerated in size.' The tower, which Cockerell altered little in rebuilding, was a characteristically Wrenian fantasy with free-standing arches on the skyline which Cockerell had already echoed at his University Library, Cambridge. He raised the side wings of Wren's west front and added doorways leading into large vestibules at the ends of the aisles. The aisles were separated from the nave by four bays of round arches and were filled with cast-iron galleries which also extended round the west end. In a later remodelling these were removed, a rose window was inserted above the reredos whilst the west doorway reappeared in Romanesque disguise in an attempt to 'lend tone' to the existing fabric, to borrow the words with which Sir George Gilbert Scott justified another similar venture.

The Ecclesiologist attacked Cockerell for preserving Wren's 'ugly oak pues, the pulpit and organ, and the sprawling altar-piece, of the cabbage and cauliflower pattern.' It argued that ' "fittings" may rightly be designed to accomodate themselves to a given church, but to build a church in style and place only to harmonize with such "fittings" as Wren's brown pues, and fubsy cherubs, is a caricature of reverence. If it were felt to be irreverent to sell, (which it were,) or to burn (which it were not,) these precious "fittings", surely a little of this piety might have been expended upon an attempt to preserve the Church itself.'

A later age, however, was yet more iconoclastic. The amalgamation of the parish of St. Bartholomew, Moor Lane, with that of St. Giles, Cripplegate, in 1900 led to the closure of St. Bartholomew's in the same year and its demolition shortly after. The site was sold in 1902 for £20,400.[5]

It is one of the characteristic ironies of Cockerell's career that though he was attacked in *The Ecclesiologist* for designing a church in the Wren style, he had put up a Gothic church a few years before in Athens of all places! The little Anglican church of St. Andrew's, Athens (1840–43), is cruciform in plan and is constructed of Aberdeen granite in an austere Early English style. Osbert Lancaster, unaware of its architect, has described how the interior, 'with plain continuous mouldings round the Chancel Arch, is

5. See the *Daily Graphic*, 29 January 1897, and the *Builders Journal*, 18 January 1900, pp. 435–6.

entirely devoid of frills and seems to foreshadow with its marked emphasis on height the work of Comper.'[6]

In 1845 Basevi fell to his death from the tower at Ely Cathedral and Cockerell offered to carry on his work at the Fitzwilliam Museum, 'in the interest of Mrs. Basevi', as Goodchild put it. It was fortunate that the offer was accepted, for the styles of the two architects, particularly in the treatment of interiors and of decorative plasterwork, were virtually indistinguishable.

The museum had been designed in competition in 1834 and the first stone laid in 1837.[7] By 1845 the only major works that remained to be done were the library and staircase-hall. Cockerell's designs for the library with its oak shelves and panelling are dated 1846. Its large south-facing windows make it a light room but it is warm and dignified and has a particularly splendid chimney-piece (Pl. 152) flanked by large scrolled brackets and containing an original steel grate with applied brass enrichments.

In Basevi's original design for the entrance-hall the visitor was faced on entering with a central staircase descending through a tunnel-like archway to the libraries planned along the west front. He subsequently felt that this contradicted the logic of the ascent from the street and prepared a design in which the central staircase ascended to the first-floor galleries, while two side staircases descended to the libraries. However, he soon changed his mind again and in the course of construction prepared the walls and floors for a central descending staircase. By the time of his death, work on the staircase itself had not begun and Cockerell was thus enabled to revert to the second or alternative scheme. Another change from his original designs was Basevi's substitution of three small lanterns, described at the time as 'cucumber' lights, for the large glazed dome first projected. Goodchild tells us that both Basevi and his clerk of works came to regret their decision to change the design of the staircases and of the lantern. Although by the time of Basevi's death the roof had been prepared with cast iron beams resting on the columns, the lanterns themselves had not been executed. Cockerell, therefore, suppressed the side lanterns and created a central dome of as large a diameter as the beams would allow. The side lights of this were nearly vertical and were divided by caryatids.

An extraordinary feature of Cockerell's staircase was that 'every step was drawn to a slight curve so that from whatever point of the hall one went, the

6. *Classical Landscape with Figures*, 1947, p. 60.

7. See R. Willis and J. W. Clark, *Architectural History of the University of Cambridge*, 4 vols, Cambridge, III, pp. 215–17, and J. Cornforth, 'The Fitzwilliam Museum, Cambridge', *Country Life*, CXXXIII, 1962, pp. 1278–81 & 1340–43.

step presented itself to the tread.'[8] (Pls 153 and 154). This description is taken from Phené Spiers' recollections of how Matthew Digby Wyatt, out of respect for the subtlety of the staircase, refused to touch it when invited to remodel the staircase-hall in 1870. Something had to be done, however, for funds had run out late in 1847 and Cockerell's hall was still in an uncompleted state in the 1870's. Disappointed by Wyatt, the Syndics turned to E. M. Barry who returned in some measure to Basevi's original plan by substituting for Cockerell's staircase one with two side flights ascending to the galleries. Wisely he did not reinstate Basevi's central descending flight but instead provided a descending flight on each side of the hall on the sites of the former Keeper's and Attendant's offices. To increase light in his enlarged entrance-hall Barry not only heightened and enlarged Cockerell's dome but also altered the glazing of the six side lunettes.[9] Otherwise, the design of the three elaborately ornamented tunnel-vaults on each side of the dome and of the coving below the dome is undoubtedly Cockerell's (Pl. 156). When Digby Wyatt saw Cockerell's drawings for the ceiling he was struck by the fact that they contained scarcely one horizontal line. All had been set out with a delicate entasis derived from his observation of ancient Greek practice. Another of Cockerell's departures from Basevi's plan was his use of pink granite for the great first-floor columns of the hall rather than the scagliola round an iron core which Basevi had intended. Cockerell was insistent on this point and asked for £900 to cover the cost. In the midst of much agitation his request was granted – though by a majority of only one vote.

There are no drawings to confirm the point but there is little doubt that the magnificent ironwork along the front wall of the museum was designed by Cockerell (Pl. 155). Placed a foot above pavement level, it consists of a series of thirty-six huge and succulent scrolls linked by a continuous horizontal member which is bristling with spikes and terminated by gorgeous pineapples. It sounds odd, but in Cambridge we have come to know and love it and to marvel at its costly audacity.

Rich metalwork is also a feature of the major work of Cockerell's later years, the interiors of St. George's Hall at Liverpool. In 1839–40, Harvey Lonsdale Elmes had won two competitions for a new concert hall and for new Assize Courts at Liverpool. Subscriptions for the concert hall were fewer than had been expected so the city took over and decided to provide a

---

8. Quoted in the *R.I.B.A. Journal*, 3rd series, VII, 1899–1900, p. 366.
9. According to H. Stannus, *Alfred Stevens and his Work*, 1891, p. 8, Barry is also supposed to have removed from the entrance hall some panels carved by Stevens for Cockerell.

single large building for both functions. Elme's new designs for this, approved in 1841, resulted in the finest neo-classical public building in Europe.

After Elmes' death in 1847, caused by worry and ill-health, work was continued by Robert Rawlinson, Clerk of the Works, with some assistance from Cockerell. In 1848 Cockerell designed the terrace steps under the south portico and in 1851 began work on the decoration of the interior. Elmes had, in fact, already consulted Cockerell more than once. In 1843 Cockerell had exhibited at the Royal Academy a 'Sketch of an idea for the frontispiece of a Public Building.' This was a monumental sculptured pediment dominated by a figure of Britannia enthroned, protecting her agriculture and arts with a spear and offering an olive branch to the four quarters of the globe. Elmes was so impressed by it that he invited Cockerell to execute it on the south pediment of St. George's Hall. In 1849 Cockerell asked Alfred Stevens to make a drawing of the proposed pediment for publication. He did so from the as yet unfinished work in the studio of Cockerell's sculptor, William Nicholl. In the course of his work Stevens made a few alterations in the grouping of the figures which, at Cockerell's request, Nicholl subsequently carried into execution.[10] Compared with the stilted figures in the pediment of the Fitzwilliam Museum, designed in 1837 by Eastlake, the quality of Cockerell's work is immediately striking. It is a marvellous composition, full of movement and variety, but most unfortunately has been removed into storage on the grounds that its condition had become dangerous.

Elmes had also asked both Cockerell and Tite whether it would be possible to construct the enormous vaulted roof of the great hall in brick and solid materials instead of wood. They gave a favourable opinion and the vault was accordingly carried out after Elmes' death with hollow wedge-shaped bricks designed by Rawlinson.

With his own huge enthusiasm for the Baths of Ancient Rome, Cockerell must have been captivated by the extraordinary drama of Elmes' plan (Fig. 1) which, placing the Great Hall between the two Court Rooms from which it was separated only by columnar screens, created a vista of three hundred feet from one end of the building to the other. This disposition was inspired by the great vaulted Tepidarium of the Baths of Caracalla which Elmes knew from the publication of 1828 by G. Abel Blouet, *Restauration des Thermes d'Antonin Caracalla à Rome.* Unfortunately Elmes did not know much about music and when it was pointed out to him that

10. See K. R. Towndrow, *Alfred Stevens*, 1939, p. 88 and, for further discussion of the contributions of Cockerell, Stevens and Nicholl, see W. M. Conway, 'The Work of Alfred Stevens in Liverpool', *The Builder*, LIV, 1888, 223–4.

the organ must necessarily impede the vista he exclaimed, 'Do you think I have made my hall as a case for your organ?'[11] It was thus left to Cockerell to block the vista with an organ which, though of splendid curvaceous design, undoubtedly impairs the spatial unity.

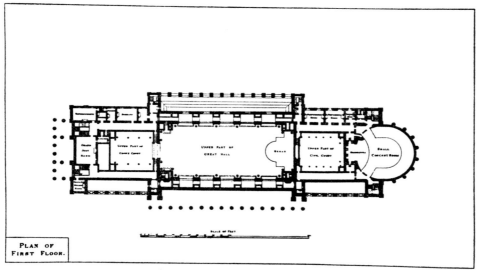

St. George's Hall, Liverpool. First-floor plan. 1841

Of the few changes which Cockerell made to the structure of the room, the most important concerned the galleries placed over the external corridors which fill the lateral bays on the ground floor (Pl. 157). In Elmes' drawing the balconies to these galleries are not continued in front of the massive piers or buttresses which divide the bays and support the weight of the vault. Undue emphasis is thus placed on the blank faces of these some-what ugly piers. Cockerell therefore screened them by extending the balconies in front of the piers so that they run right up to the columns. The complex layered impression thus created is typical of the richness with which Cockerell overlaid Elmes' neo-classical austerity. The design of the niched wall below the balconies is also due to Cockerell. Other changes concerned the design of the spandrels (Pl. 160) and of the coffering. Here Cockerell eliminated Elmes' rather fussy system of panelling round the arches and substituted huge spandrels filled with enormous winged figures as in the

11. Quoted in R.I.B.A. *Transactions*, new series, VI, 1890, p. 261.

Angel Choir at Lincoln of 1256–80. Cockerell's article on the Angel Choir, published in 1850, contained illustrations by Alfred Stevens and it is attractive to think of the two men discussing the daring notion of combining Gothic choirs and Roman baths. The splendid sculptures are symbolic of 'Fortitude', 'Prudence', 'Science', 'Art', 'Bacchus and Temperance', 'Justice', and so on. They are not, of course, Gothic in feeling. Indeed, their Roman triumphalism undoubtedly owes much to Raphael's female figures of 'Fortitude', 'Prudence' and 'Temperance' in the Stanza della Segnatura in the Vatican. The closest to a Raphael prototype is Cockerell's helmeted figure of 'Fortitude', holding an oak branch with one hand and stroking a lion with the other.

The coffering of the ceiling (Pls 158 & 159) is a less successful contribution to the room. Many of the motifs are similar to those he had employed much more successfully a few years earlier in the tunnel-vaults at the Fitzwilliam Museum, but in so monumental a space as St. George's Hall the numerous small panels and flat over-delicate decoration of Cockerell's ceiling simply do not tell. The brilliant design of the enormous tiled floor (Pl. 157) is far more sympathetic to the scale and sweep of the room.[12] Cockerell's huge circles of brown and blue Minton tiles move and swirl like water, an effect which is greatly aided by the fact that the whole floor is sunk two steps below the level of the surrounding outer border. The rich sub-aqueous colouring was taken up by the varied materials Cockerell chose for his balcony fronts between the piers: green Irish marble, blue Derbyshire spar, Irish black marble and white alabaster. Above, white and gold predominated until a richer scheme was adopted in the 1870's.

As unique as the design of the floor was that of the ten huge coronas which still light the hall. The upper tier of each corona terminates in a circle of projecting, beak-like forms which are inspired by the prows of Greek ships. Cockerell's grandson found that in connection with the design of these remarkable objects he had made 'a sheet of exquisite drawings of various forms of trireme copied from Greek coins.'[13] Further evidence of Cockerell's genius as a metal-work designer are the numerous sets of sumptuous, cast bronze gates both in the hall and elsewhere in the building (Pls 161 & 162). Despite their acanthus scrolls and Roman motifs, their rich and exuberant patterns show an imaginative understanding of the interlaced forms of

12. The mythical sea personages in the floor were designed for Cockerell by Alfred Stevens (Stannus, op. cit., p. 14 and pl. XXV).

13. R. P. Cockerell, 'The Life and Works of C. R. Cockerell, R.A.', *Architectural Review*, XII, 1902, p. 141.

Celtic art. Cockerell had given more than a foretaste of this in his library chimney-piece at the Taylorian Institution. The nine sheets of rapid, fertile sketches for these gates are amongst the most personal and attractive of the many drawings by Cockerell preserved at the Victoria and Albert Museum. There is more fine ironwork by Cockerell on the plateau before the East façade. Here, in 1854, he designed a series of bold dolphin lamp-standards which anticipate those set up in 1870 on the Victoria Embankment in London.

The Small Concert Hall (Pl. 163) on the first floor at the north end of the building is entirely the work of Cockerell, save for its basic elliptical shape. It is small, just seventy feet by seventy-seven, with a stage only twelve feet deep. Its general form is probably inspired by the circular Calidarium at the Baths of Caracalla where, in like manner, half the circle is embedded in the main building while the other half projects externally as an apse. It is acoustically excellent. Indeed, it was described in 1875 as being as good for its purpose as the great hall was bad. This must partly be due to the wooden panelling which, fixed free of the walls, acts as a sounding board.

Undoubtedly the finest interior of Cockerell's career, it is so much in a class of its own that it is difficult to compare it with any other interior of the century. Its luxurious decoration anticipates the Second Empire Style as displayed, for example, in Hector Lefuel's Salle des Spectacles at Fontaine-bleau, but there is a Grecian grace at Liverpool which gives the whole room an unmistakably Cockerellian flavour (Pl. 164). Thus the order of the Corinthian columns on the stage is derived from the Temple of Apollo at Bassae and the undulating balconies are supported by a remarkable ring of caryatids, fancifully echoing those on the north porch of the Erectheum (Pl. 165).

Cockerell's gifts as a designer of ornament never found fuller expression than in this room. Here all is ornamented from frieze to ventilator grill, from pilaster to balcony railing. Bold but filigree, ubiquitous but not domi-nant, this gay and lovely decoration, these lithe arabesques and fecund swags, flowed like music endlessly, effortlessly, from his pen. Stored with the fruits of a lifetime's observation of line and pattern, he blurs the distinctions between periods so that now we feel ourselves in ancient Greece, now in Quattrocento Italy, now in the splendours of Imperial Rome. The light soft colouring is all white and cream and honey. The highlights are all flecked with gold. Hitchcock, not normally appreciative of Cockerell's merits, is for once unstinting in his praise. He points out attractively how in an age supposedly dominated by the art of music, architecture was on this occasion more than capable of matching it. He also indicates the irony by which the room 'is above all a masterly exercise in the use of those "shams" the Camdenians most abominated.'[14] Certainly, so much use is made of synthetic or sham materials that one can only interpret the room as a gesture of defiance against the puritanical moralizing doctrines of Pugin and Ruskin. Thus, the richly decorated pilasters and friezes are of papier mâché; the wall panels are of deal,[15] grained and varnished in convincing simulation of ornamental woods; the ventilating grills and the pierced cresting round the edge of the stage are of cast-iron; the trellised balconies are also of cast-iron though they look like some kind of woven wicker-work; and, most remarkably, the caryatids, seemingly of stone or plaster, are hollow and cast from some synthetic material whose composition is as yet unidentified. Whether they really support the balconies or whether these are cantilevered out on iron joists is also a mystery, since few of Cockerell's drawings for St. George's Hall can be found and none for this room. By a final paradox, as Hitchcock points out, only the large mirrors between the columns on the stage are what they appear to be, and these, ironically, create a deliberately ambiguous spatial effect giving one some sense of the perspective vistas envisaged by Elmes.

14. H.-R. Hitchcock, *Early Victorian Architecture in Britain*, 2 vols, Yale and London, 1954, I, p. 336.
15. According to *The Builder*, XIII, 1855, p. 594. But Hitchcock (loc. cit.) calls them plaster.

EPILOGUE

SAVE for his office for the Liverpool and London and Globe Insurance Company, also in Liverpool, St. George's Hall was Cockerell's last work and he gave up his practice in 1859.

In any study of his career the biographical interest disappears early. His years of travelling and of intellectual exploration ended with his marriage in 1828. Thereafter he reaped the benefits of his first forty years' experience and settled down to being a father to his ten children and also, in a sense, to the architectural profession itself. In 1848 he was the first recipient of the Royal Gold Medal of the Royal Institute of British Architects and in 1860 became the Institute's first professional president. His first son, Charles Robert, was born in 1829 but died five years later. In 1831 came a second son, John Rennie, in 1832 a daughter and in 1833 Frederick Pepys who became an indifferent architect and who failed to write the book on his father which filial piety demanded and access to sources made possible. Out of respect for William of Wykeham, Frederick Pepys Cockerell was sent in 1845 to Winchester. In that year C. R. Cockerell noted in his diary: 'with my boys to the Academy Exhibition. Judgement & taste in Fred; more combativeness in Robert.'[1] His description of his son Robert was to prove sadly prophetic for in 1854 he was killed as a Lieutenant at the Battle of Alma, aged only twenty. Two more daughters followed and three more sons of whom the youngest, Samuel Pepys Cockerell (1844–1921), edited his father's travel diaries in 1903.

Cockerell moved on his marriage to a fashionable address in the newly-built Eaton Square but ten years later wrote to his friend Robert Willis: 'I mean to get rid of my Ho[use] after a time and live at Highgate – seeing & feeling the benefits of the air ... Highgate is the Montpelier of G[rea]t Brit[ai]n. I shall build a villa there, please God – a *model*.'[2] In fact he did not build a villa at Highgate but moved to Ivy House, North End, Hampstead. His views on this subject seem to have changed since writing to Willis, for on the completion of the drawings for the Fitzwilliam Museum in 1847, he gave Goodchild £100 towards the purchase of a house telling him that 'an architect should buy an old one not build a new one.'

---

1. Quoted in 'Frederick Pepys Cockerell, a Memorial Sketch', *R.I.B.A. Transactions*, 1879–80, p. 22.

2. In a letter dated Cambridge, 14 October 1838 (Cambridge University Library, Add. MS. 5031, f. 535). Cockerell enclosed notes and sketches on the use of iron clamps in the cella wall of the Parthenon, and also on modern techniques of supporting free-standing architraves with iron ties.

By the middle of the century his health began to fail and his practice, never very extensive, virtually ceased. At the end of the summer of 1851 he told Goodchild: 'my medical men tell me I must go away for two years to Madeira, or some warm climate; I shall go to a warmer climate than Hampstead but not to Madeira. I shall go to my sister's in Somersetshire, and so I must leave you to do the best you can with our remaining works . . . there must come a time of parting, and when it does come it will be something like the parting of *Father and Son*; I have often thought we seemed to go through our work together as if we were in love with it . . . It would often be, "I am sorry to spoil your nice drawing but suppose we try this" . . . I must see if I can wipe off some of the disgrace in the delay in publishing my Aegina and Phigaleia work.'[3]

However, in the autumn he returned from his sister, Anne Pollen, greatly improved in health and Goodchild remained with him for another eight years. In the meantime he overcame his earlier disapproval of Nash's Regent's Park terraces and moved from Hampstead to 13 Chester Terrace. Here, in a modest house despite the air of grandeur which Nash knew so well how to create, he died on 17 September 1863. Although his career had been studded with disappointments, he was by now laden with honours; he had always been ready to descend from Mount Olympus to don the mantle of the elder statesman – though the results rarely seemed to justify the effort. He had sat for years on the committees connected with the dreary and ineffectual Government Schools of Design;[4] in 1839 he had been consulted by Henry Cole over the design of a Post Office envelope to bear an embossed as opposed to an adhesive stamp.[5] The commission was given to William Mulready, R.A. but his envelope was not a success with the public for more than half its surface was covered with ornament and it was pilloried in a *Punch* cartoon by John Leech. In January 1850 Cockerell was appointed to the Building Committee of the Great Exhibition but ill health prevented him from attending its meetings. In 1852 his arrangements for the lying-in-state of the Duke of Wellington at Chelsea Hospital (Pl. 166) were described, not unfairly, by *The Ecclesiologist* as in 'the mixed style of classical upholstery.'[6]

---

3. Quoted from the Goodchild Album, Richardson-Houfe Collection.

4. Those wishing to pursue the Schools further may turn to the monograph devoted to them in 1963 by Professor Q. Bell.

5. See Sir Henry Cole, *Fifty Years of Public Work*, 2 vols, 1884, I, p. 63.

6. Vol. XIII, 1853, p. 412. The reviewer admitted that there was 'much good taste in the disposition and combination of the scenic effects', but added: 'The large mortuary tapers were duly lighted, and were almost the only religious accessory . . . It was very generally felt that there was something wanting here.'

In 1854 he prepared plans to set before the Prince Consort for the transformation of South Kensington into an uplifting area of museums; and in the following year he and his rival, Sir Charles Barry, were appointed to represent English architecture on the juries of the *Exposition universelle des produits de l'industrie* in Paris.[7] The Exhibition was memorable chiefly for its iron and glass building in the Champs-Elysées with a span over twice that of the Crystal Palace.

Perhaps Cockerell's most valuable contribution at this time was the part he played in securing for the sculptor Alfred Stevens the commission for the Wellington Monument in St. Paul's Cathedral. He had been appointed one of the judges of the competition in 1857 but, a lone voice to the last, dissociated himself from the decision of his fellow jurors who included Lord Lansdowne, Dean Milman and Mr Gladstone. Their selection of William Calder Marshall, R.A. outraged the feelings of a man who appreciated the genius of the design submitted by Alfred Stevens. As we have seen, Cockerell employed Stevens on a number of occasions and it is not hard to imagine how much the great triumphal arch of bronze and marble would have appealed to him. There can be no doubt that it was the weight of Cockerell's support that finally gained the commission for Stevens.[8]

Another battle Cockerell may be supposed, in some sense, to have won was that of the Foreign Office. In 1859 he was called upon to knock some sense into an unrepentant George Gilbert Scott whose Gothic designs for the Foreign Office had offended the Italianate tastes of Lord Palmerston. Scott had compromised by producing what he called a 'semi-Byzantine design to meet the opposing views half way.' He recalls in his *Recollections* how 'Professor Cockerell, being a pure classicist, had the greatest difficulty in swallowing my new style. He lectured me for hours together on the beauties of the true classic, going over book after book with me, and pouring forth ecstatic eulogies on his beloved style of art. I did not argue against his views which I respected, but rather took the line of advocating variety and individuality, and of each man being allowed to follow out his individual idiosyncrasies; but it was a bitter pill for him.'[9] In the end Scott was forced to swallow Cockerell's medicine and thus, with further help from Matthew Digby Wyatt, produced one of his best buildings.

7. See *Report on the Paris Universal Exhibition*, 1855, H.M.S.O., 1856.

8. See H. Stannus, *Alfred Stevens and his Work*, 1891, p. 19, and J. Physick, *The Wellington Monument*, Victoria and Albert Museum publications, 1970.

9. G. G. Scott, ed., *Personal and Professional Recollections by the late Sir George Gilbert Scott, R.A.*, 1879, p. 195.

T

In our close concentration on Cockerell we have laid stress, perhaps too much stress, on his isolation from contemporary trends. A minor architect whom he undoubtedly influenced is his pupil at the Royal Academy, John Clayton (c. 1820–1861). His project for remodelling the National Gallery (c. 1848) is a blend of Cockerell and Wren; his Hereford Market Hall (1861) of Wren and Gibbs. His monumental volume on Wren's city churches, published in 1848–49, is dedicated to Cockerell who had given him both the initial impetus for the work and much subsequent assistance. Moreover, if we take a broader glance at the nineteenth century, it is clear that the classical tradition survived, in a form of which Cockerell would probably have approved, for much longer in Scotland and the north of England than in the south. A building like David Bryce's British Linen Bank in Edinburgh of 1852 (Pl. 167) is consciously Cockerellian in its Imperial Roman way, as is Lanarkshire House, Glasgow, of 1875 by John Burnet senior, in its neo-Renaissance way. Burnet's brilliant son John, trained at the Ecole des Beaux-Arts in Paris, continued and developed this tradition into the twentieth century. His Fine Arts Institute at Glasgow of 1879 is pure French classicism, while his Glasgow Athenaeum of 1886 owes more to Cockerell. His monumental additions to the British Museum of 1905 brought this tradition to London. The powerful web of trabeation which defines the interior space of Burnet's North Library at the British Museum recalls the effect at which Cockerell was aiming in his early sketches for the Hanover Chapel. Cockerell's description of the interior of the Chapel as one in which the ceiling 'will at all times be the best index of the design' is equally applicable to Burnet's Library.

If Burnet and other nineteenth-century Scottish architects were merely developing a Cockerellian tradition which had never died in the north, it was necessary in the south of England to revive the tradition consciously. Thus W. R. Lethaby complained in 1911 of the contemporary 'endeavour to bring about a Renaissance of Professor Cockerell's Greek.'[10] The kind of building he must have had in mind is represented by the magnificent classical pile erected by the side of Euston Station for the London, Edinburgh and Glasgow Assurance Society in 1907 from designs by the eccentric Beresford Pite (Pl. 168). Its sculptural richness, its bracketed cornice and its Asiatic Ionic order, are the fruits of Pite's worship at the shrine of Cockerell. Like Lethaby, Pite was basically an Arts and Crafts experimentalist but, unlike Lethaby, he understood that the best of the Arts and Crafts ideals

10. W. R. Lethaby, *Architecture, an Introduction to the History and Theory of the Art of Building*, 1911, p. 238.

could be incorporated into the Classical tradition. Another fine Cockerellian work is the New Theatre at Manchester of 1912 by Richardson and Gill (Pl. 169). Richardson had studied not only Cockerell but also the classical tradition in France from 1840 to 1900, the style he called the Neo-Grec. If we wish to place Cockerell in a European context then it is to the French nineteenth-century tradition from Hittorff to Nénot that we must look. Though the robustness and the large scale of much French work of this period is distinctly Cockerellian, it must be realized that Cockerell anticipated, not followed, this style. Thus, the Palais de Justice at Rheims of 1841 by A.-N. Caristie (1783–1862), the archaeologist and friend of T. L. Donaldson, has a pedimented centrepiece on its west front which recalls two earlier works by Cockerell, the Hotwells church and the east front of the Cambridge University Library. Hittorff's church of St. Vincent-de-Paul in Paris with its twin Grecian towers was designed later than the Hanover Chapel. His grand Gare du Nord of 1861 and also Duc's Palais de Justice have all the strength and sculptural richness towards which Cockerell was working.[11]

It is not surprising, then, that the Continent, which had not succumbed to the Gothic Revival, should have showered Cockerell with dignities. France especially honoured him: he became Chevalier of the Legion of Honour, member of the Institute of France and one of the eight foreign associates of the Académie des Beaux-Arts de France. He also became a member of the Academy of St. Luke at Rome and of the Royal Academies of Belgium, Munich, Berne, Denmark, Genoa and Athens, and of the American Institute of Architects.

Beneath the weight of honours lay a man of strong views and strong emotions who had disciplined himself to conform to the standards of a society that was still Christian. R. P. Cockerell observed of him in 1902: 'he was loved as few are loved, both by his own folk and his friends. Meanness, coarseness, or wrong-doing were abhorrent to him, but he never indulged in railing.'[12] Aitchison had earlier remarked: 'In the roll of British architects few have brought so many titles to admiration – ripe scholarship, exquisite delineation, masterly composition, uprightness, integrity, genius and enthusiasm: and withall the dignified and refined manners of the high-bred

11. This Beaux-Arts style was carried at the end of the century to North America. It had been a dream of European architects from Palladio to Cockerell to recreate the baths of ancient Rome. Elmes and Cockerell came close to realising this dream at St. George's Hall, but McKim, Mead and White brought the theme to a triumphant conclusion at Pennsylvania Station, New York, 1906.

12. R. P. Cockerell, 'The Life and Works of C. R. Cockerell, R.A.', *Architectural Review*, XII, 1902, p. 146.

English gentleman.'[13] Goodchild makes the further point that he was not proud, 'but he had a good idea of all gentlemen being treated *as* gentlemen, and was especially jealous of any want of respect to his art. This was shown on one occasion when he was invited to attend a meeting at Cambridge in which he was to take a part. Knowing that all the University gentleman would appear in their Academical dresses, he put on his Institute of France hat and coat. On some not quite complimentary remarks by some gentlemen present, he replied, "You, gentlemen, do not seem to be aware that there is a world beyond your own tollgate where art is honoured. But there is, and this is an evidence of it." '

13. Quoted in R.I.B.A. *Transactions*, new series, VI, 1890, p. 261.

List of Architectural Designs by Cockerell

The location of architectural drawings is indicated in brackets at the end of each entry.

ABBREVIATIONS

BE   Bank of England Archives
RIBA   Drawings Collection, Royal Institute of British Architects
V & A   Print Room, Victoria and Albert Museum
GA   Goodchild Album

1816   Palace for the Duke of Wellington. Unexecuted. (The Duke of Wellington; Mr B. Weinreb; RIBA)

1816?   Design for a town-house for the Hon. Frederick North. Unexecuted. (RIBA).

1817   Project for a Greek University. Unexecuted. (RIBA).

Sevenoaks, Kent. Lady Boswell's Charity Schools. (RIBA).

1818   Harrow School, Middlesex. Additions.

1819   London House, St James's Square. Dr Howley, Bishop of London. In co-operation with S. P. Cockerell. (Mr B. Weinreb).

Oakly Park, Shropshire. The Hon. Robert Clive. Work in progress till 1836. (The Earl of Plymouth).

1820   Clubhouse for the Travellers' Club. Unexecuted. (RIBA).

Lough Crew, County Meath. Mr J. L. W. Naper. Work in progress till 1825. Demolished *c.* 1960. (Mrs B. J. Crichton; RIBA).

1821   Hanover Chapel, Regent Street. Demolished 1896. (V & A).

Travellers' Club, 49, Pall Mall. Remodelling of existing building. Demolished.

Gloucester House, Park Lane. Duke of Gloucester. Repairs costing £2,950. Demolished.

St Paul's Cathedral. Restoration completed in 1822 at a cost of £16,133 of which the new cross and ball accounted for about £700.

Albany Cottage, Regent's Park. Mr T. B. Lennard, M.P. In co-operation with the Burtons. In Cockerell's plan the back stairs were brought up through the centre of the main staircase, an arrangement he was afterwards pleased to find at Amesbury House, Wiltshire. Now known as North Villa, Albany Cottage still exists though greatly altered.

St David's College, Lampeter, Cardiganshire. Executed 1822–27. (Royal Library, Windsor; RIBA; St David's University College, Lampeter).

The Palace, Abergwili, Carmarthenshire. The Bishop of St David's. Repairs.

Literary and Philosophical Institution, Bristol. (RIBA).

Woolmers Park, Hertfordshire. Sir Gore Ouseley, Bart. Remodelling of existing house.

Bowood, Wiltshire. The Marquess of Lansdowne. Addition of chapel, library and breakfast-room. (V & A).

St Mary's church, Banbury, Oxon. West portico and tower developed from designs by S. P. Cockerell.

Gothic church at Belper, Derbyshire, for Mr Evans. Unexecuted.

Blaise Castle, Bristol. Lodge for Mr J. S. Harford.

Killerton, Devon. Cottage for Sir T. D. Acland, Bart.

Oldcastle, County Meath. School.

Castle Pollard, County Meath. Mr W. D. Pollard. Remodelling of existing house with new portico, staircase-hall and wing running the length of the garden front. Known today as Kinturk.

1822 East India House. In co-operation with S. P. Cockerell a substantial office wing added to the west of existing building. Extensive use was made of cast-iron beams. Subsidence occurred in 1824 leading to S. P. Cockerell's resignation as Surveyor to the Company. Demolished.

33 Brook Street, Grosvenor Square. Mr Henry Trail. Alterations completed in 1824 at a cost of £3384.7.11. Demolished.

1 Upper Grosvenor Street, Grosvenor Square. Cockerell carried out alterations for his brother John which were completed in April 1823. Demolished.

Scottish National Monument, Calton Hill, Edinburgh. Uncompleted.

Broomhall, Fife. Earl of Elgin. Unexecuted. (Earl of Elgin).

Birdsall, Yorkshire. Chapel for Lord Middleton. Cockerell's design, with its tetra-style Ionic portico, was rejected in favour of a Gothic design by Hodgson Fowler (executed in 1823). (V & A, where the drawing is wrongly catalogued as intended for Peper Harow).

'Lodge in the Florentine style of Architecture from ideas suggested by Sir Robt. Laurie Bart.' Unexecuted. (RIBA).

1823 Albion Club, 85 St James's Street. New window. Built in 1786 by S. P. Cockerell for Saunders's Chocolate House, this building became the Albion Club in 1811. Demolished.

Hurlingham House, Fulham. John Horsley Palmer, later Cockerell's brother-in-law. Lodge. Executed?

Greenmount, County Antrim. Mrs Anna Maria Thompson. Remodelling of existing house. A simple classical building now gutted and used as the Agricultural and Horticultural College of Northern Ireland.

Derry Ormond, Cardiganshire. Mr John Jones. Demolished c. 1950. (Mrs B. J. Crichton)

Walcot, Shropshire. Earl of Powis. 'Gaze tower' based on the Tower of the Winds in Athens. Unexecuted.

St James's church, Longborough, Gloucestershire. North transept, or Sezincote Chapel, designed for Cockerell's uncle Sir Charles Cockerell. Angel-corbels in Coade stone copied from those in Cirencester parish church. There are drawings at the RIBA by S. P. Cockerell for additions on the south side of the church (unexecuted).

Sezincote, Gloucestershire. Sir Charles Cockerell, Bart. Lodge on the Moreton-in-Marsh road.

Grange Park, Hampshire. Mr A. Baring. New wing (demolished 1972), and conservatory rebuilt c. 1880 save for the portico). (RIBA).

Gothic chapel for Sir Edmund Antrobus, Bart. Unexecuted?

Cottage for Mr Ker. Unexecuted?

Cottage near Lampeter, Cardiganshire, for Mr J. S. Harford.

'Rustic cottage for two families,' i.e. the Worcester Lodge, Sezincote. (RIBA).

1824 St Thomas's church, Regent Street. The formation of Regent Street enabled this eighteenth-century church in Kingly Street to have an entrance from the new street. Cockerell provided the new façade in Regent Street and Thomas Hardwick provided a vestibule behind leading into the church. Cockerell's and Hardwick's additions were remodelled in 1854 and demolished in 1903. The church was demolished in 1973.

7 Old Buildings, Lincoln's Inn. Minor alterations for Cockerell's brother, S. P. Cockerell.

Alms Houses, Poplar. Minor alterations to buildings erected for the East India Company in 1686.

Langton House, Dorset. Mr J. J. Farquharson. Work in progress till 1832. Demolished in 1947. (RIBA; model in possession of Mr A. Grogan).

Killerton, Devon. Sir T. D. Acland, Bart. Lodge. Completed in 1825.

Pentre, Boncath, Pembrokeshire. Mr Davies. Plans for minor alterations in 1824 and 1825. Executed?

1825 University College, London. Unexecuted. (V & A; RIBA).

Walcot, Shropshire. Earl of Powis. Window in picture gallery. Demolished.

Cwmcynfelin, near Aberystwyth, Cardiganshire. Mr J. Lloyd Williams. Stables. Now converted into dwellings.

Crossdrum, near Oldcastle, County Meath. Farmhouse for Mr. J. L. W. Naper to be inhabited by John Muldoone.

Designs for a church in Barbados. Executed?

1826 Connaught Chapel, Paddington (now St John the Divine, Southwick Crescent). Cockerell's classical designs were rejected in 1827 in favour of Gothic designs by Charles Fowler. (V & A; RIBA).

Lansdowne House, Richmond Hill, Surrey (demolished). The Marquess of Lansdowne. Picture gallery. Unexecuted.

House in Regent's Park. Sir John Leach. Unexecuted.

Hinchwick Farm, Condicote, Gloucestershire. Sir Charles Cockerell, Bart.

1827 90 Eaton Square. Mrs Belli, Cockerell's aunt.

94 Eaton Square. Captain W. A. Clifford, R.N. Designed to fit into Cubitt's scheme.

North Weald Basset, Essex. Rev. Henry Cockerell, brother to C. R. Cockerell. Parsonage in the Tudor style, costing £2060.

Middle Claydon, Buckinghamshire. Cockerell sent an estimate to Sir Harry Calvert Verney, Bart. for a school to cost £1,400.

Sezincote, Gloucestershire. Sir Charles Cockerell, Bart. Substantial office wing added to north of existing house.

Wynnstay, Denbighshire. Sir Watkin Williams-Wynn, Bart. New dining-room (demolished) and lodge. (RIBA).

Lynford Hall, Norfolk. Sir Richard Sutton, Bart. Extensive remodelling of early eighteenth-century house; addition of conservatory executed by Messrs Jones and Clark; designs in 1830 for bridge and fountain. Demolished c. 1856.

Langleys, Essex. Mr J. J. Tufnell. It seems from his diaries that it was Cockerell's idea to bring forward the three central bays of this fine early eighteenth-century house so as to form a new entrance hall. Characteristic of his tact was the re-use of the old doorway with its segmental pediment and of the curved window above.

Church for Ohio. Executed?

1828 3 Tilney Street, Park Lane. The Hon. Robert Clive. Minor alterations. Demolished.

21 Cavendish Square. Mr Edmund McDonnell. Minor alterations. Demolished. 36 South Street, Grosvenor Square. Sir John Leach. Minor alterations. Demolished.

Holy Trinity Church, Hotwells, Bristol. Consecrated 10 November 1830.

Holy Trinity church, St Philip's, Bristol. Cockerell's Grecian designs were rejected in favour of Gothic designs by Rickman and Hutchinson.

Cottage for Dr Miller. Cockerell sent an estimate for £2,100 including cast-iron windows at £3.10 each.

1829 Designs for the approaches to London Bridge, some dated 1831. Unexecuted. (RIBA).

University Library, Cambridge. The only wing executed was not designed until 1837. (V & A; Cambridge University Library; GA).

1831 Westminster Life and British Fire Office, Strand. Demolished 1907. (V & A; RIBA).

1832 Enstone Vicarage, Oxon. Tudor. Blaise Castle, Bristol. Mr J. S. Harford. Glazed octagonal picture gallery. Attributed by Goodchild to 1839.

Falkland, Fife. House for Mr Bruce. Further plans made December 1833. Unexecuted. (RIBA; GA).

Duke of York's Column. Unexecuted.

1833 National Gallery, Trafalgar Square. Unexecuted.

1834 Seckford Almshouses, Woodbridge, Suffolk. Tudor. (GA)

Bank of England. New Dividend, Warrant and Cheque Offices and Accountant's Drawing Office. Demolished. (GA).

1835 New Palace of Westminster. Unexecuted. (V & A; Royal Academy; RIBA; GA).
Branch Bank of England, Plymouth, Devon. Demolished. (BE).

1837 Reform Club, Pall Mall. Unexecuted. (V & A; RIBA).

London and Westminster Bank, Lothbury. With W. Tite. Demolished 1924. (V & A; RIBA; GA).

1838 Harrow School, Middlesex. Chapel in Tudor style. Demolished 1853. (GA).

Killerton, Devon. Sir T. D. Acland, Bart. Chapel in Transitional style. Executed 1840–41. (RIBA; Devon County Record Office).

1839 Taylorian Institute and University Galleries, Oxford. (V & A; RIBA; Oxford University Archives; GA).

Royal Exchange. Unexecuted. (RIBA; GA).

Sun Fire Office, Threadneedle Street. Design altered 1841. Remodelled 1895; demolished 1971. (V & A; RIBA).

Stoke Park, near Bristol. Mr A. G. Harford-Battersby. Conservatory to be executed by Messrs Jones and Clark. Unexecuted (though the same firm provided one in 1841). (GA).

Basildon Park, Berkshire. Mr James Morrison. Stables. Unexecuted. (RIBA).

1840 St Bartholomew, Moor Lane. Rebuilding of Wren's St Bartholomew Exchange. Final designs prepared 1847; executed 1849–50; demolished 1902. (V & A; RIBA).

Protestant church, Athens. Gothic. Executed in modified form.

1842 Branch Bank of England, Plymouth, Devon. (BE).

Caversfield House, Oxon. The Rev. R. B. Marsham. (GA).

Burton Hill House, Malmesbury, Wiltshire. For Cockerell's brother John Cockerell. Burnt in 1846 but replaced in the same year by the present house in Tudor Gothic style and presumably also by C. R. Cockerell.

1843 Peper Harow, Surrey. Lord Midleton. Addition of porch and of balustrade in front of the attics. (GA).

Queen's College, Oxford. Conversion into library of cloister under Upper Library.

Design for pedimental sculpture subsequently used at St George's Hall, Liverpool. (RIBA; Liverpool University Library).

1844 Carlton Club, Pall Mall. Elevation only. Unexecuted. (RIBA; London Museum; GA).

Branch Bank of England, Manchester, Lancashire. Completed 1845. (BE; RIBA).

Branch Bank of England, Bristol. Completed 1846. (BE; RIBA).

Branch Bank of England, Liverpool, Lancashire. Completed 1847. (V & A; BE).

1845 Fitzwilliam Museum, Cambridge. Staircase hall (stairs replaced 1860–75), and library. (V & A; Fitzwilliam Museum).

1846 National Debt Redemption Office, Old Jewry. Extension. Demolished.

1848 Bank of England. Remodelling of attic storey. (BE; GA).

Bank Chambers, Cook Street, Liverpool. Demolished 1959. (BE; GA).

1849 Bank of England. Remodelling of Dividend, Warrant and Cheque Offices and Accountant's Drawing Office. Demolished.

University College, London. Arrangement, with T. L. Donaldson, of the Flaxman Gallery to receive the plaster models given to the college in 1848. Work was not finished till 1857.

1851 St George's Hall, Liverpool. Completion of interiors and of southern terrace. Work finished in 1854. (RIBA; GA; Liverpool University Library).

1852 Grange Park, Hampshire. Lord Ashburton. Addition of attic storey to his south wing of 1823. According to Goodchild, F. P. Cockerell assisted with the construction but not the design of this work.

1854 Block plan of the South Kensington estate laid out as an area of museums. Made for Prince Albert. Unexecuted. (V & A).

1855 Liverpool and London Insurance Company, Dale Street, Liverpool. Attic storey added later. (GA; Liverpool University Library).

1856 Liverpool Free Library and Museum. With F. P. Cockerell. This large domed structure was rejected, like all the other entries in the abortive competition, on grounds of cost. (V & A; Liverpool University Library).

List of Designs for Monuments and Plate by Cockerell

1818 Funerary Monument for Princess Charlotte. Unexecuted.

1819 Admiral Lord Collingwood, Newcastle Cathedral. Executed by Rossi.

1821 Plate and Vase presented to General Alava by the staff of the Duke of Wellington. Made by Rundell and Bridge. Cockerell was told not to exceed price limit of 1,000 guineas.
John Jones and his wife, Derry Ormond church. Attributed.
John Deverell. Executed by Rossi. Gunnis claims that this is at Hampton, Middlesex. The diaries confirm that it was made, but it is not to be found at St Mary's church, Hampton.

1822 Casket presented to the Prince of Denmark. Designs completed in 1824.

1823 Mrs H. Battersby, St Mary's church, Henbury, Bristol. Executed by Rossi.
Mrs B. Harford. Executed by Rossi. Wherabouts unknown.

1824 'Silver mirror in the antique mode', for Mr Naper of Lough Crew.

1827 Wine coaster for Sir Richard Sutton, Bart., of Lynford Hall. Made by Sharpe's, of Dean Street.

1834 John Bridge, All Saints' church, Piddletrenthide, Dorset. Gothic. Carved by W. G. Nicholl.

1842 Granite pedestal for the copy of the Warwick Vase given to the University of Cambridge. Unexecuted.

1849 Lady Pulteney, Kensal Green Cemetery. Illustrated in A. W. Hakewill, *Modern Tombs Gleaned from the Public Cemeteries of London*, 1851, pl. 23.
Granite obelisk in commemoration of the Victory of Chillianwallah erected in the grounds of the Royal Hospital, Chelsea.

1852 Catafalque for the lying-in-state of the Duke of Wellington in the Hall of the Royal Hospital, Chelsea.

1853 Design for a Monument to the Duke of Wellington, Guildhall, London. Unexecuted.

1854 Design for a medal. Unexecuted.

1856 Henry James Prescott, Governor of the Bank of England, 1847–1851. Brighton Cemetery.

1858 Monument to the officers and men killed in the Indian Mutiny, Chapel of the Royal Hospital, Chelsea.

Bibliography

Place of publication is London unless otherwise stated

1. WRITINGS BY COCKERELL (excluding correspondence)

(a) *Unpublished*

1821–1832 *Diaries* (Coll. Mrs B. J. Crichton).

1841–1856 *Royal Academy Lecture Notes* (Library of the Royal Academy of Arts; R.I.B.A. Drawings Collection; Library of Trinity College, Cambridge).

(b) *Published*

1810–17 *Travels in Southern Europe and the Levant, 1810–1817, the Journal of C. R. Cockerell, R.A.*, S. P. Cockerell, ed., 1903.

1816 *Progetto di collocazione delle statue antiche esistenti nella Galleria di Firenze che rappresentano la favola di Niobe*, Firenze. Plate and text, large fol.

1818 *Le Statue della Favola di Niobe dell' Imp. e R. Galleria di Firenze situate nella primitiva loro disposizione da C. R. Cockerell*, Firenze. Plate, 8vo.

1819 'On the Aegina Marbles', *Journal of Science and the Arts*, VI, 327–31, 3 folding plates and addendum.

1820 'On the Labyrinth of Crete', in *Travels in Various Countries*, Robert Walpole, 2 vols, 1817 and 1820, vol. II, 402–9, 4to.
Description of the Bassae frieze, 28 pls, as part IV of *A Description of the Collection of Ancient Marbles in the British Museum*, 10 pts, 1812–1845.

1828 'An Account of Hanover Chapel, in Regent Street', in *The Public Buildings of London*, J. Britton & A. C. Pugin, 2 vols, 1825–28, vol. II, 276–82.

1830 *The Temple of Jupiter Olympius at Agrigentum*, pls fol.
Antiquities of Athens and Other Places of Greece, Sicily, etc. supplementary to *The Antiquities of Athens* by J. Stuart and N. Revett, illustrated by C. R. Cockerell. 5 parts, fol. German translation fol. Leipzig and Darmstadt, 8vo, 1829 etc.
The Pediment Sculptures of the Parthenon, 24 pls, as part VI of *A Description of the Collection of Ancient Marbles in the British Museum*, 10 pts, 1812–1845.

1835 *Plan and Section of the New (Bank of England) Dividend, Pay, and Warrant Offices, and Accountant's Drawing Office above; together with six allegorical subjects forming the decoration of the lower offices*, 4 pls, oblong fol.

1846 'The Architectural Works of William of Wykeham', *Proceedings of the Archaeological Institute at Winchester*, 1845, 46 pp.

1848 *Ancient Sculptures in Lincoln Cathedral*, 12 pls, 8vo. Reprinted in *Proceedings of the Archaeological Institute*, 1850, 215–40.

1851 *Iconography of the West Front of Wells Cathedral, with an Appendix on the Sculptures of other Mediaeval Churches in England*, Oxford and London. Imperial 8vo.

1857 *Illustrations, Architectural and Pictorial of the genius of M. A. Buonarroti with descriptions of the plates by C. R. Cockerell, Canina, &c.* fol.
'Statement by Mr. Cockerell, R.A. on the Wellington Monument Competition', *The Builder*, XV, 1857, p. 472.

1859 *Address*, Royal Institute of British Architects, Session, 1859–60, 111–13.
'On the Painting of the Ancients', paper read at the Architectural Museum, published in *The Civil Engineer and Architect's Journal*, XXII, pp. 42–44 & 88–91.

1860 *Presidential Address*, Royal Institute of British Architects, Session, 1861–2, 1–16.
The Temples of Jupiter Panhellenius at Ægina, and of Apollo Epicurius at Bassae, fol.

1861 'Architectural Accessories of Monumental Sculpture', paper read at the R.I.B.A., published in *The Civil Engineer and Architect's Journal*, XXIV, pp. 333–6.

1862 *A Descriptive Account of the Sculptures of the West Front of Wells Cathedral photographed for the Architectural Photographic Association*, 4to.

2. WRITINGS ON COCKERELL

Aitchison, G. 'C. R. Cockerell', *R.I.B.A. Transactions*, n.s., VI, 1890, 255–61.
Arkell, W. J. *Oxford Stone*, 1947.
Boase, T. S. R. *English Art, 1800–1870*, Oxford, 1959.
Brydon, J. M. 'The Work of Professor Cockerell, R.A.', *R.I.B.A. Journal*, 3rd ser. VII, 1899–1900, 349–68.
The Builder. Obituary of C. R. Cockerell, 1863, XXI, 683–5.
    Obituary of W. G. Nicholl, 1871, XXIX, 1002.
'Frederick Pepys Cockerell, a Memorial Sketch', *R.I.B.A. Transactions*, 1879–80, 21–36.
Cockerell, R. P. 'The Life and Works of C. R. Cockerell, R.A.', *Architectural Review*, XII, 1902, 43–7, 129–46.
Colvin, H. M. *A Biographical Dictionary of English Architects, 1660–1840*, 1954.
Cornforth, J. 'The Fitzwilliam Museum, Cambridge', *Country Life*, CXXXIII, 1962, 1278–81, 1340–43.
    'Bowood, Wiltshire, Revisited', *Country Life*, CLI, 1972, 1448–51, 1546–50, 1610–13.
Crook, J. M. 'Grange Park Transformed', *The Country Seat*, H. Colvin and J. Harris, eds., 1970, pp. 220–8.
    The Greek Revival, Neo-Classical Attitudes in British Architecture, 1760–1870, 1972.
Dictionary of National Biography, XI, 1887.
Dodd, E. M. 'Charles Robert Cockerell', in *Victorian Architecture*, P. Ferriday, ed., 1963, 103–22. (This article is over imaginative in its use of sources).

Goodchild, J. E. *Reminiscences of my Twenty-six Years association with C. R. Cockerell Esq.* (MS. scrapbook in Richardson-Houfe Collection).

Harris, J. 'C. R. Cockerell's "Ichnographica Domestica"', *Journal of the Society of Architectural Historians of Great Britain*, 14, 1971, 5–29.

Hitchcock, H.-R. *Early Victorian Architecture in Britain*, 2 vols, New Haven and London, 1954.

Howell, P. 'Wynnstay', *Country Life*, CLI, 1972, 853.

Hussey, C. 'Stratfield Saye', *Country Life*, CIV, 1948, 1107.

'Oakly Park', *Country Life*, CXIX, 1956, 380–3, 426–9.

Hutton, C. A. 'A Collection of Sketches by C. R. Cockerell, R.A.', *Journal of Hellenic Studies*, XXIX, 1909, 53–9.

Johnson, Lee. 'Géricault and Delacroix seen by Cockerell', *Burlington Magazine*, CXIII, 1971, 547–51.

Laborde, E. D. *Harrow School, Yesterday and Today*, 1948.

Naef, H. 'Griechenlandfahrer im Atelier von Ingres zu den Bildnissen von Charles Robert Cockerell, Otto Magnus von Stackelberg und einer Unbekannten', *Archaeologischer Anzeiger*, 3, 1970, Berlin, 1971, 428–40.

Oswald, A. 'The Old University Library, Cambridge', *Country Life*, LXXVI, 1934, 416–21.

Pevsner, N. *Some Architectural Writers of the Nineteenth Century*, Oxford, 1972.

Prestwich, E. 'The Life and Work of Professor Cockerell, R.A.', *R.I.B.A. Journal*, XVIII, 1911, 669–85.

Richardson, A. E. *Monumental Classic Architecture in Great Britain and Ireland*, 1914.

'Design for Ionic Capital by Professor Cockerell', *R.I.B.A. Journal*, 3rd series, XXV, 1918, pp. 229–30.

'Charles Robert Cockerell, R.A.', *Architecture*, IV, 1925, pp. 30–2.

'Some Early Drawings by Professor C. R. Cockerell', *R.I.B.A. Journal*, XXXVII, 1930, pp. 725–7.

Royal Commission on Historical Monuments, *City of Cambridge*, 2 vols, 1959.

Royal Institute of British Architects, *Catalogue of Drawings, C–F*, 1972.

St. Clair, W. *Lord Elgin and the Marbles*, Oxford, 1967.

Smirke, S. 'Some Account of the Professional Life and Character of the Late Professor C. R. Cockerell', *R.I.B.A. Transactions*, 1863–6, 17–28.

Spiers, R. P. 'Cockerell's Restorations of Ancient Rome', *Architectural Review*, XXIX, 1911, 123–8.

Steele, H. R. & Yerbury, F. R. *The Old Bank of England*, London, 1930.

Summerson, J. *Georgian London*, 1st ed. 1945.

Waterhouse, P. 'Hanover Chapel', *R.I.B.A. Journal*, 3rd ser. IV, 1897, 111–14.

Watkin, D. J. 'The Country Houses of C. R. Cockerell (1788–1863)', *Atti del convegno internazionale promesso dal Comité International d'Histoire de l'Art*, 1971, Neoclassicismo, Genoa, 1973, pp. 118–22.

Willis, R. & Clarke, J. W. *Architectural History of the University of Cambridge*, 4 vols, 1886–7.

'The Making of The Ashmolean', *Country Life*, CLV, 1974, 242–5.

Worthington, J. H. 'Drawings by C. R. Cockerell, R.A.', *R.I.B.A. Journal*, XXXIX, 1932, 268–71.

THE PLATES

I. J. A. D. Ingres. C. R. Cockerell. 1817.

2. John Philip. Podium of the Albert Memorial, London. 1864. Pugin, Cockerell and Barry.

3. Temple of Apollo Epicurius at Bassae (from *The Temples of Jupiter Panhellenius at Aegina, and of Apollo Epicurius at Bassae*).

4. Temple of Apollo Epicurius at Bassae (from *The Temples of Jupiter Panhellenius at Aegina, and of Apollo Epicurius at Bassae*).

5. Ali Pasha's Kiosk at Janina. 1814.

6. Palace for the Duke of Wellington. 1816. Elevation.

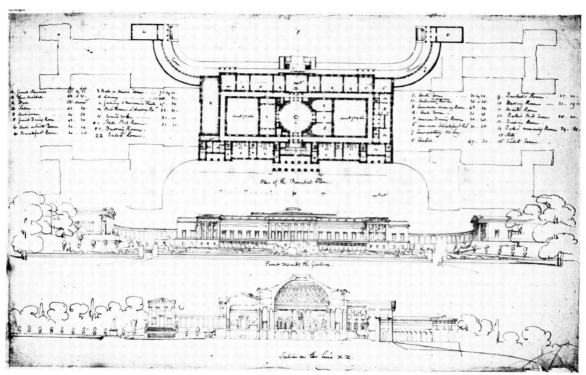

7. Palace for the Duke of Wellington. 1816. Plan, section and elevation.

8. Reconstruction of Athens in the time of the Antonines. 1824.

9. *A Tribute to the Memory of Sir Christopher Wren, 1838.*

10. J. J. Chalon, R.A. C. R. Cockerell.

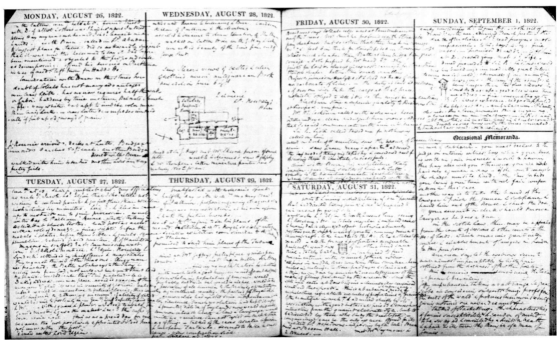

11. A double page from the diary, 1822, with a plan of Dalmeny.

12. Sculpture at Wells Cathedral (from
Iconography of the West Front *of Wells*
Cathedral).

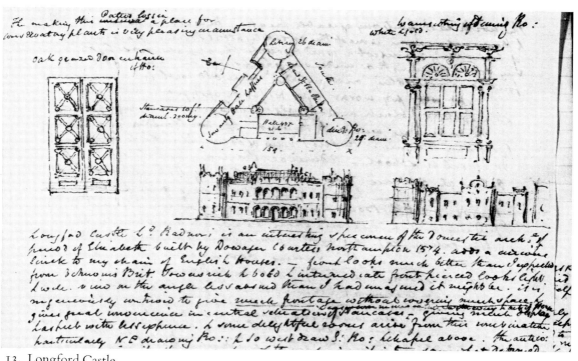

13. Longford Castle.

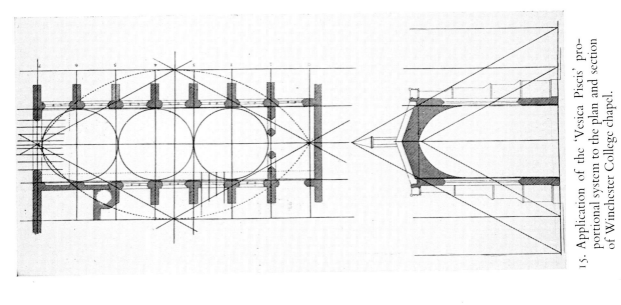

15. Application of the 'Vesica Piscis' proportional system to the plan and section of Winchester College chapel.

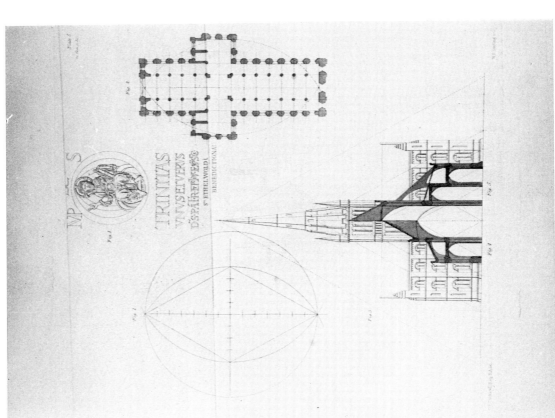

14. Application of the 'Vesica Piscis' proportional system to the plan and section of an ideal cathedral.

16. *The Professor's Dream*, 1848.

17. Harrow School. The Old Schools. 1818 (from *The Builder*).

18. Harrow School. Words-
worth's Chapel. 1838 (from a
lithograph by C. J. Hull-
mandel).

19. Monument to Admiral Lord Collingwood. Newcastle Cathedral. 1819.

20. Design for Monument to Princess Charlotte. 1818.

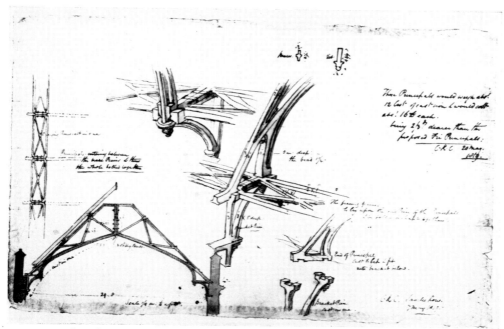

21. Design for a hammer-beam roof in cast-iron. 1819.

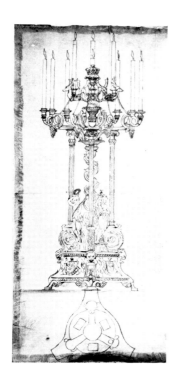

22. Design for a candelabrum. 1820.

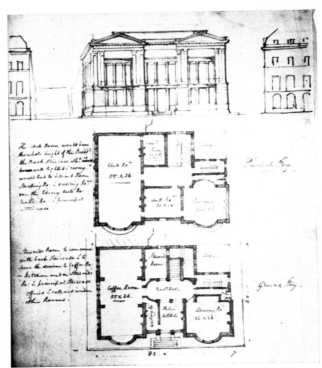

23. Design for a club-house for the Travellers' Club. 1820.

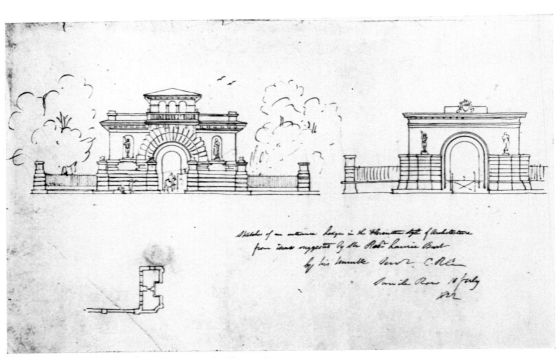

24. Design for a lodge for Sir R. Laurie, Bart. 1822.

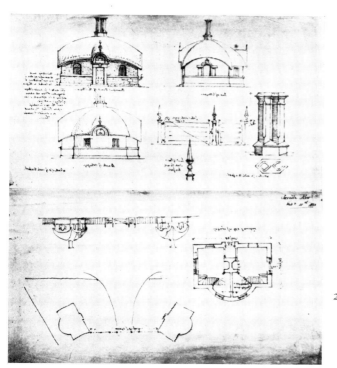

25. Design for the Worcester Lodge, Sezincote. 1823.

26. St Thomas's church, Regent Street, London. 1824 (redrawn by Gavin Stamp from Tallis' *London Street Views*).

27. Hanover Chapel, London. 1821. Entrance front.

28. Hanover Chapel, London. 1821. Elevation.

29. Hanover Chapel, London. 1821. Perspective sketch.

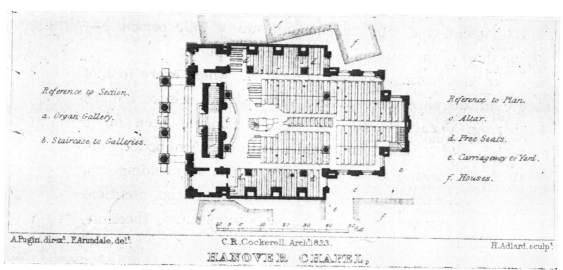

Reference to Section.

a. Organ Gallery.

b. Staircase to Galleries.

Reference to Plan.

c. Altar.

d. Free Seats.

e. Carriageway to Yard.

f. Houses.

A.Pugin. direx*. F.Arundale, del*.   C.R.Cockerell. Arch*.1823.   H.Adlard. sculp*.

HANOVER CHAPEL.

30. Hanover Chapel, London. 1821. Ground-floor plan (from *The Public Buildings of London*).

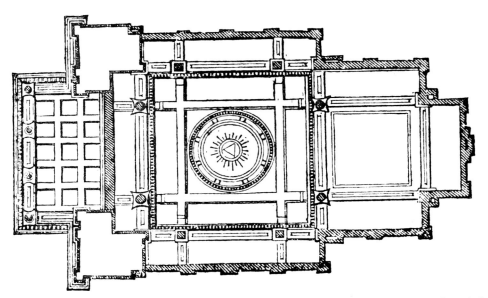

31. Hanover Chapel, London. 1821. Plan of ceiling (from *The Public Buildings of London*)

32. Hanover Chapel, London. 1821. Sketch for interior.

33. Hanover Chapel, London. 1821. Section.

34. Hanover Chapel, London. 1821. Interior.

36. Holy Trinity, Hotwells, Bristol. 1828. Exterior.

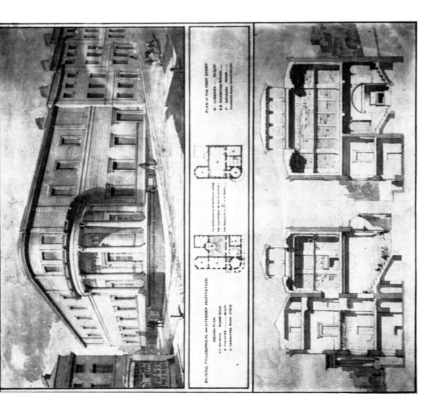

35. Literary and Philosophical Institution, Bristol. 1821. Plan, elevation and sections.

38. St. Mary's church, Banbury. West front. 1821.

37. Holy Trinity, Hotwells, Bristol. 1828. Interior.

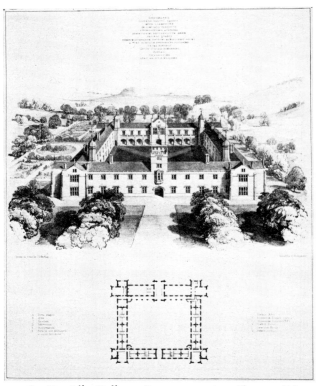

39. St. David's College, Lampeter. 1821 (from a lithograph of 1823).

40. Scottish National Monument, Edinburgh. 1822.

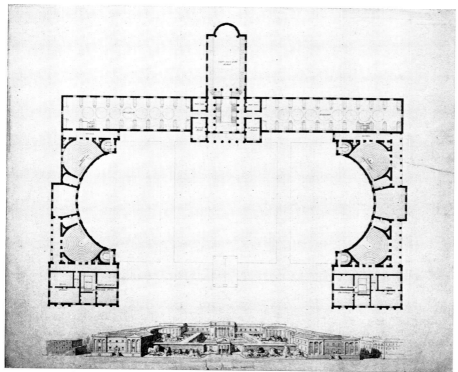

41. Design for University College, London. 1825.

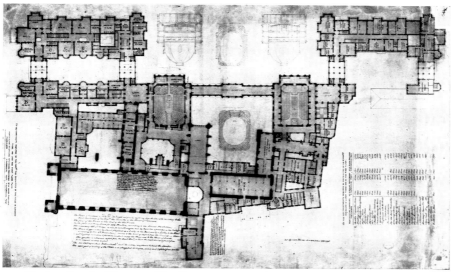

42. Design for the Houses of Parliament. 1835. Plan.

43. Design for the Houses of Parliament. 1835. Elevation.

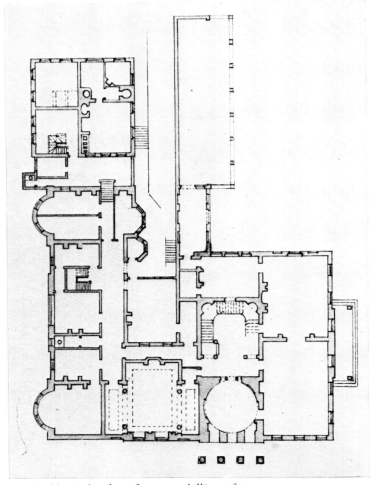

44. Oakly Park. Plan after remodelling of 1819-21.

45. Oakly Park. West and south fronts in 1821.

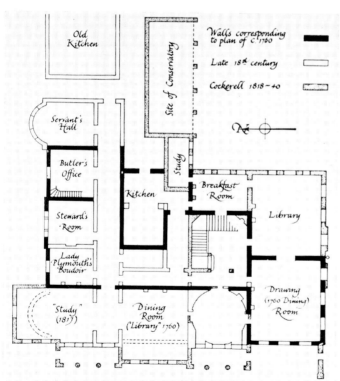

Old
Kitchen

Walls corresponding
to plan of c. 1760

Late 18ᵗʰ century

Cockerell 1818–40

Servant's
Hall

Site of Conservatory

Butler's
Office

Study

Kitchen

Breakfast
Room

Steward's
Room

Library

Lady
Plymouth's
Boudoir

"Study"
(1817)

Dining
Room
("Library" 1760)

Drawing
(1760 Dining)
Room

46. Oakly Park. Plan showing alterations of 1836.

47. Oakly Park. Staircase hall. 1823.

48. Oakly Park. West front as remodelled in 1836.

49. Castletown. Staircase.

50. Oakly Park. Library. 1821.

51. Oakly Park. Bromfield Lodge. 1826.

52. Wynnstay. Lodge. 1827.

53. Bowood. Chapel. 1821.

54. Bowood. Library. 1821.

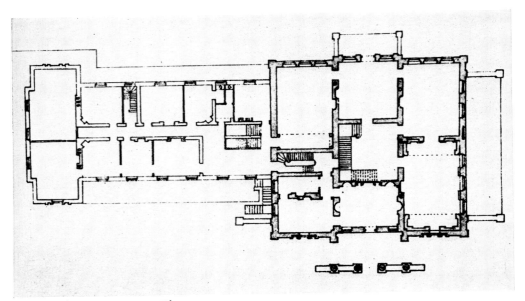

55. Lough Crew. 1820–22. Plan.

56. Lough Crew. 1820–22. Portico.

57. Lough Crew. 1820–22. Garden front.

58. Lough Crew. Lodge. 1825.

59. Oldcastle. School. 1821 (drawn by Gavin Stamp).

60. Castle Pollard. 1821.

61. Woolmers Park. 1821.

62. Grange Park. Dining room. 1823.

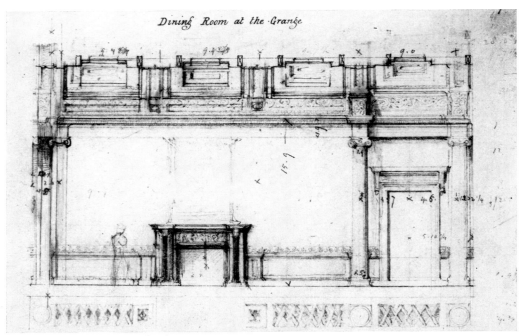

63. Grange Park. Design for dining room. 1823.

64. Grange Park. Chimney-piece in dining room. 1823-4.

65. Grange Park. Entrance to conservatory. 1823.

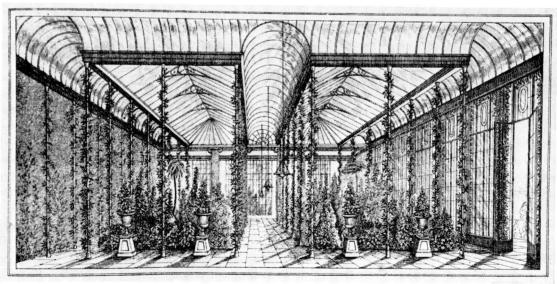

66. Grange Park. Interior of conservatory. 1823.

67. Derry Ormond. West front. 1823.

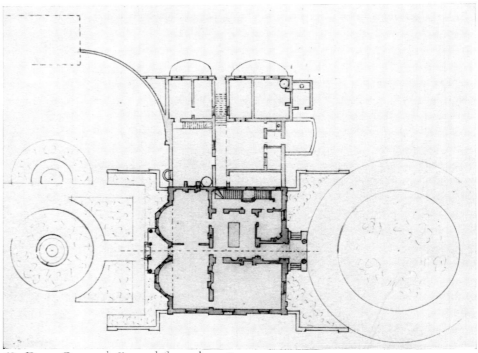

68. Derry Ormond. Ground-floor plan. 1823.

69. Derry Ormond. South and east fronts. 1823.

70. Caversfield House. 1842.

71. Langton House. Design for entrance front. 1824.

72. Langton House. 1824 onwards. Entrance front.

73. Langton House. Design for garden front. 1824.

74. Langton House. 1824 onwards. South east front.

75. Langton House. 1824 onwards. Drawing room.

76. Langton House. 1824 onwards. Staircase.

77. Langton House. 1824 onwards. Entrance to stables.

78. Langton House. 1824 onwards. Stable yard.

79. Hinchwick Manor. 1826.

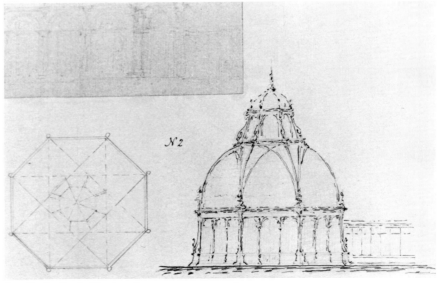

80. Stoke Park. Design for conservatory. 1839.

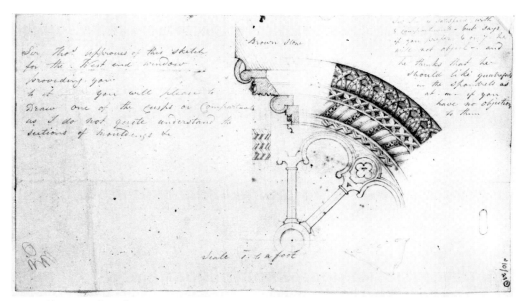

81. Killerton. Chapel. 1838.

82. Killerton. Chapel. 1838. West front.

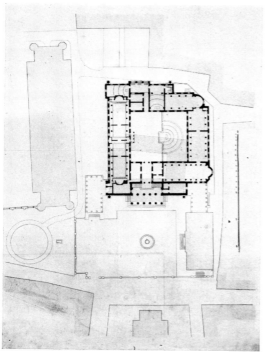

83. Cambridge University Library.
Ground-floor plan. 1830.

84. Cambridge University Library. Detail
of east front. 1835.

85. Cambridge University Library. Design for east front. 1830.

86. Cambridge University Library. Design with circular vestibule. 1830.

87. Cambridge University Library. Design for Divinity School. 1830.

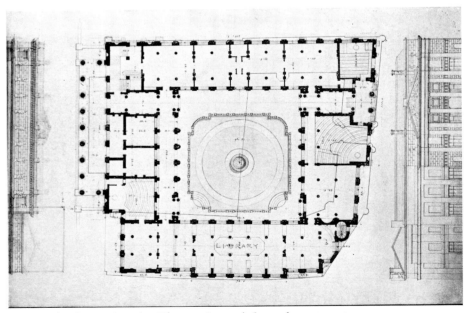

88. Cambridge University Library. Ground-floor plan. 1835-6.

89. Cambridge University Library. Design for north range of courtyard. 1835-6.

90. Cambridge University Library. Design for west range of courtyard. 1835-6.

91. Cambridge University Library. Design for west front of west range. 1835-6.

92. Roman temple at Bordeaux. From Perrault's edition of Vitruvius.

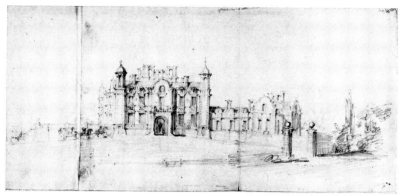

93. Design for a house at Falkland, Fife. 1832.

94. Cambridge University Library. Design for Tribune Library. 1836.

96. Former Cambridge University Library. North front. 1836-7.

95. Former Cambridge University Library. East front. 1836-7.

97. Former Cambridge University Library. East and north fronts. 1836-7.

98. Cambridge University Library under construction, from *Cambridge University Almanac*, 1839.

99. 'The New Public Library, as it will appear when completed', from Le Keux's *Memorials of Cambridge*.

100. Alberti. San Sebastiano, Mantua. 1460.

101. Hawksmoor. Christchurch, Spitalfields, London. 1723.

102. Former Cambridge University Library. South front. 1836-7.

103. Former Cambridge University
Library. Interior. 1836-7.

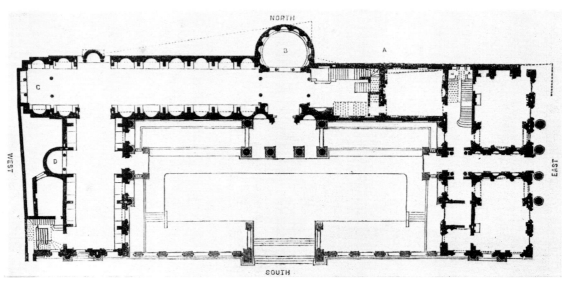

104. Ashmolean Museum and Taylorian Institute. 1839-40. Ground-floor plan.

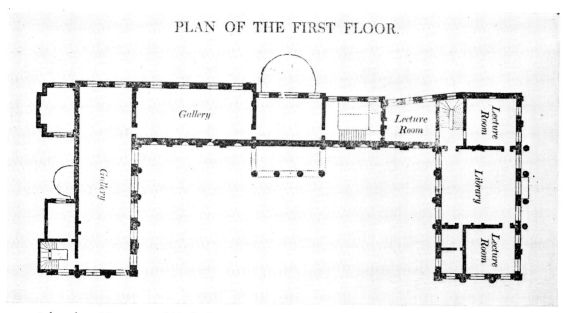

105. Ashmolean Museum and Taylorian Institute. 1839-40. First-floor plan.

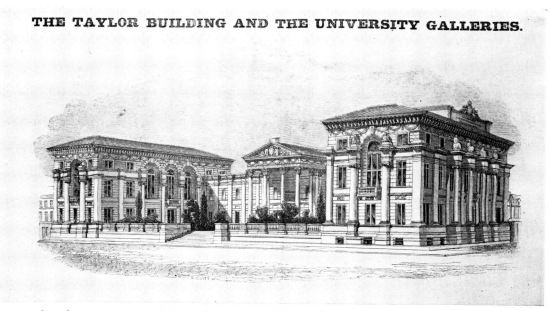

THE TAYLOR BUILDING AND THE UNIVERSITY GALLERIES.

106. Ashmolean Museum and Taylorian Institute. First project. 1839. From an engraving by Orlando Jewitt.

107. Ashmolean Museum and Taylorian Institute. 1839-40. From the south-east.

108. Ashmolean Museum and Taylorian Institute. 1839-40. From the south-west.

109. Ashmolean Museum. 1839-40. Detail of the west pavilion.

110. Taylorian Institute. 1839-40. Design for St Giles's front.

111. Taylorian Institute. 1839-40. View through archway.

112. Taylorian Institute. 1839-40. St Giles's front.

113. Ashmolean Museum. Design for pediment. 1843.

114. Ashmolean Museum. Pediment. 1843.

115. Ashmolean Museum. 1839-40. Staircase.

116. Ashmolean Museum. 1839-40. Sculpture gallery.

118. Taylorian Institute. 1839-40. Chimney-piece in library.

117. Taylorian Institute. 1839-40. Library.

119. Royal Exchange, London. Design for entrance front. 1839.

120. Royal Exchange, London. Design for entrance front. 1839.

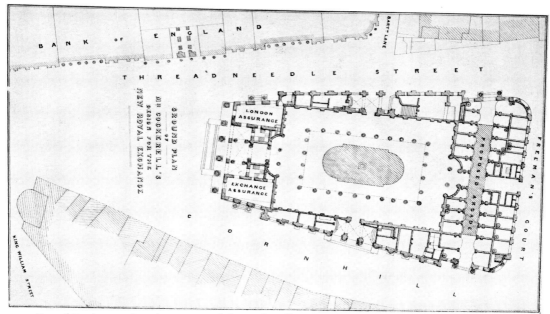

121. Royal Exchange, London. Ground-floor plan (from a lithograph of 1840).

122. Palladio, Loggia del Capitaniato, Vicenza. 1571.

M.ᴿ COCKERELL'S DESIGN FOR THE ROYAL EXCHANGE. 1840.

123. Royal Exchange, London. Entrance front (from a lithograph of 1840).

124. Royal Exchange, London. Interior (from a lithograph of 1840).

125. Royal Exchange, London. Sketch for interior. 1839.

126. Palladio. Villa Barbaro, Maser. *c.* 1555-9.

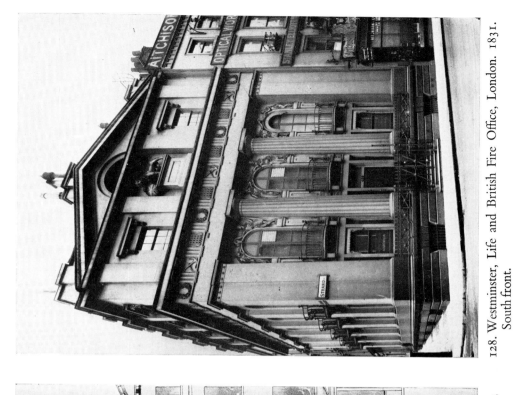

128. Westminster, Life and British Fire Office, London. 1831.
South front.

127. Westminster, Life and British Fire Office, London. Design
for south front. 1831.

129. Branch Bank of England, Manchester, 1844.

130. Branch Bank of England, Bristol. 1845.

131. Branch Bank of England, Liverpool.
1845.

132. Branch Bank of England, Liverpool.
1845. Cook Street elevation.

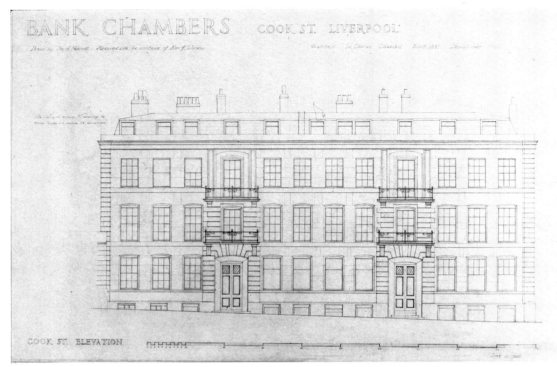

133. Bank Chambers, Cook Street, Liverpool. 1848.

134. Bank of England, London. Dividend Pay Office. 1834. Design for decoration of cove.

135. Bank of England, London. Dividend Pay Office. 1834.

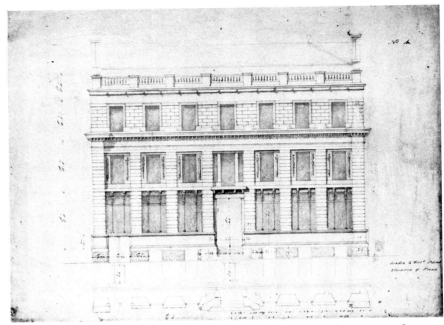

136. London and Westminster Bank, London. 1837. Design for entrance front.

137. London and Westminster Bank, London. 1837. Entrance front.

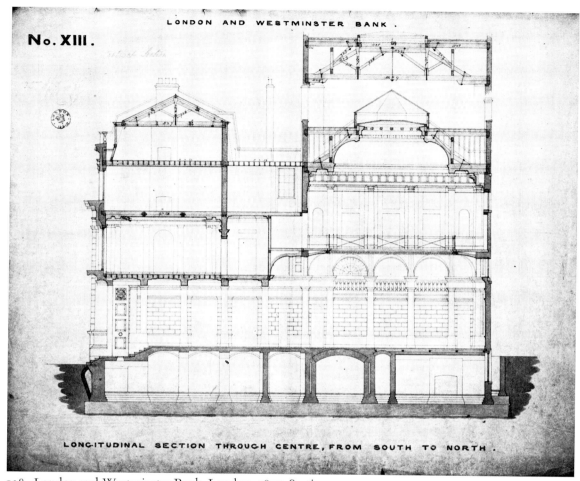

No. XIII.

LONGITUDINAL SECTION THROUGH CENTRE, FROM SOUTH TO NORTH.

138. London and Westminster Bank, London. 1837. Section.

139. Sun Fire Office, London. First project. 1840.

140. Sun Fire Office as executed. 1841.

141. Sun Fire Office. Detail of angle. 1841.

142. Sun Fire Office. Staircase. 1841.

143. Liverpool and London Insurance Office, Liverpool. 1855.

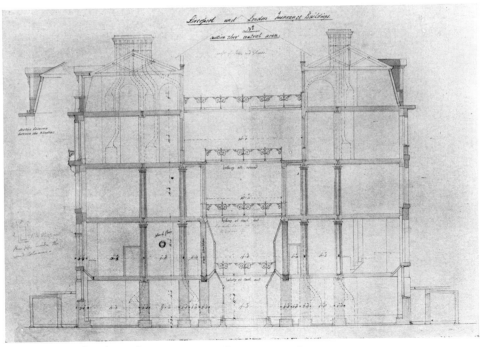

144. Liverpool and London Insurance Office, Liverpool. 1855. Section.

145. Liverpool and London Insurance Office, Liverpool. 1855. Detail.

146. Reform Club, London. 1837. Design for elevation.

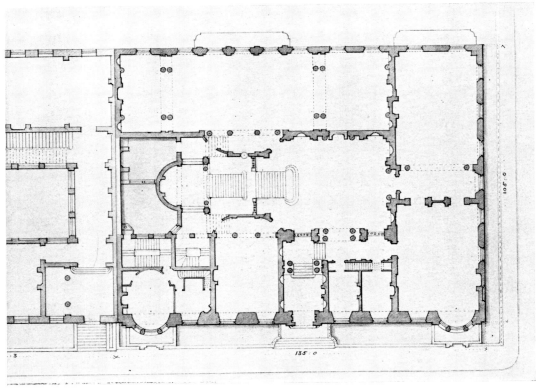

147. Reform Club, London. 1837. Plan.

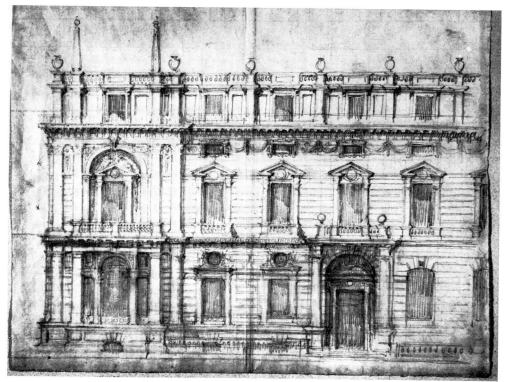

148. Carlton Club, London. 1844. Design for elevation.

149. Carlton Club, London. 1844. Elevation.

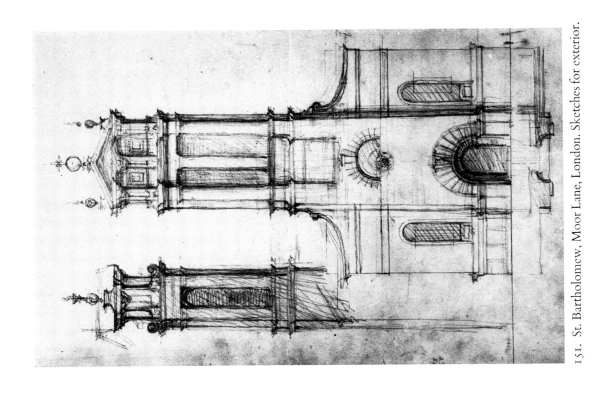

151. St. Bartholomew, Moor Lane, London. Sketches for exterior.

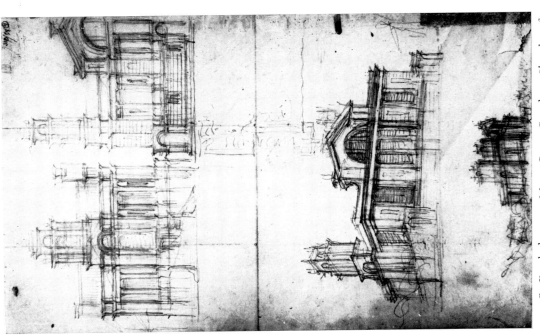

150. St. Bartholomew, Moor Lane, London. Sketches for exterior.

152. Fitzwilliam Museum, Cambridge. Chimney-piece in
library. 1846.

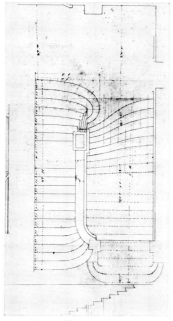

153. Fitzwilliam Museum,
Cambridge. Sketch for
staircase. 1846.

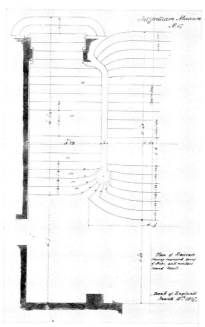

154. Fitzwilliam Museum, Cambridge. Sketch for staircase.
1846.

155. Fitzwilliam Museum, Cambridge. Railings.

156. Fitzwilliam Museum, Cambridge. Entrance hall.

157. St George's Hall, Liverpool. 1841-54. Interior of Great Hall (from *The Builder*).

158. St George's Hall, Liverpool. Vault of Great Hall. 1851.

159. St George's Hall, Liverpool. Detail of vault of Great Hall. 1851.

160. St George's Hall, Liverpool. Spandrel in Great Hall. 1851.

161. St George's Hall, Liverpool. Bronze gates in Great Hall. 1851-4.

162. St George's Hall, Liverpool. Vestibule beneath organ in Great Hall. 1851-4.

163. St George's Hall, Liverpool. Concert Hall. 1851-4.

164. St George's Hall, Liverpool. Stage in Concert Hall. 1851-4.

165. St George's Hall, Liverpool. Caryatid in Concert Hall. 1851-4.

166. Lying-in-State of the Duke of Wellington at the Royal Hospital, Chelsea (from a lithograph of 1852).

167. David Bryce. British Linen Bank, Edinburgh. 1852.

168. Beresford Pite. London, Edinburgh and Glasgow Assurance Society, London. 1907.

169. Richardson and Gill. New Theatre, Manchester. 1912.

170. Sir William Boxall, R.A. Professor C. R. Cockerell, R.A.

INDEX

INDEX